The Age of Reason

The Age of Reason
(1700–1789)

Harold Nicolson

With a new foreword by
Adam Nicolson

Axios Press
P.O. Box 118
Mount Jackson, VA 22842
888.542.9467   info@axiospress.com

Distributed by NATIONAL BOOK NETWORK.

Library of Congress Cataloging-in-Publication Data

Nicolson, Harold, 1886–1968.
       The age of reason: (1700–1789) / Harold Nicolson; with a new foreword by Adam Nicolson.
              p. cm.
       Originally published: London : Constable, 1960.
       Includes bibliographical references and index.
       ISBN 978-1-60419-011-3 (pbk.)
       1. Civilization, Modern—18th century. 2. Intellectual life—History—18th century.
   3. Eighteenth century. 4. Enlightenment. I.
       Title.
       CB411.N5 2009
       909.8–dc22

                                                    2009004431

Contents

List of Illustrations
& Photographs

Foreword

by Adam Nicolson

WHEN IN 1958, Doubleday's, the New York publishers, first suggested to Harold Nicolson that he should write the volume on the 18th Century for a wide-ranging series they were planning on world history, "portraits of epochs" as they called them, he said no. He was 72, had already suffered two mild strokes, was haunted by the idea that he was past his best and threatened with a sense of his own impending death. But the next morning he thought about it in bed and decided that he liked the 18th century and might as well agree. It was to be 150,000 words long, due on January 1, 1960. "I shall be dead by then," he wrote to his wife, the novelist and poet Vita Sackville-West, "but it will keep me happy and busy for the remainder of my life and they will pay me £3,000 in installments to keep me going."

It is a book which has both the benefits and drawbacks of coming at the end of a long, extraordinarily wide-ranging, deeply curious and active life. Nicolson was born in 1886, the third son of a family, as he described it, of "impecunious high civil servants." He inherited from them a high-minded belief in the central role public service should play in a man's life. Honor, propriety, dignity, honesty, and moral courage remained his touchstones. In that way he was a Victorian all his life. He became first a diplomat, then a politician and for a time was a junior minister in Churchill's wartime government. But many other colors and tissues were laid over that foundation. He was a literary critic, biographer, and autobiographer; a garden designer of genius; a brilliantly witty and delighted describer of the world around him; multi-lingual, passionately internationalist, in love with the civilizations of Greece and France; and above all filled with curiosity for anything which life might bring him. "Only one man in a thousand is a bore," he told my father and my father quoted repeatedly to me, "and he is interesting because he is one man in a thousand."

But against this sparkling multiplicity was a constant fear that although he had lived and loved as widely and fully as anyone he knew (through a long and loving marriage he nevertheless maintained an unassuageable appetite for beautiful and clever young men), there was always the erosive feeling that what he had done had never added up to enough. He had written many brilliant sentences but never a great book; he had loved the House of Commons but never succeeded as a politician; Churchill had always liked but never admired him; he lacked steel; his life had been an alpine meadow, spotted with pretty flowers but none of them very tall or long-lived.

By the time this book was finished in May 1960, a few months late, Harold was not well. He felt "relieved but not elated," as he wrote in his diary. "Poor old Hadji [his name within the family]. Decline and fall, that's what it is." He had been mocked in a contemporary London journal (along with his friends the critics Cyril Connolly and Raymond Mortimer) as "a superannuated apostle of gracious living, a Francophile, a dilettante, [and] an upper-class snob with no social conscience."

The background against which it was written had been difficult. Vita had been chronically ill with the undiagnosed cancer from which she would die in 1962. Their younger son Nigel's political career was on the slide, accused by his own Conservative party in his Bournemouth constituency of being "a traitor to his country" when he had questioned the behavior and honesty of the Prime Minister Anthony

Eden over the Suez crisis. Harold was short of money, besieged by tax bills, his own friends were dying, and his elder son's marriage was on the point of collapse.

Much of *The Age of Reason* was written on board a series of liners, during cruises which he and Vita took in the winters of the late 1950s: to the Far East, down the east coast of Africa, to the Caribbean and South America. The first words were typed off the coast of Crete, the last off the coast of Peru. And that too is a curiosity: the focus of the book remains rigidly European throughout. There is a gesture here and there towards America (but not enough) but otherwise the 18th century is seen to happen on an axis that runs almost exclusively between London and Paris, now and then taking in Berlin and St. Petersburg. The dynamo of the globalizing 18th-century imperialist economy, let alone the vast shaping presence of the slave trade, scarcely gets a look-in. This is history as seen from the salon and the coffeehouse, blind to anything beyond its upholstered and paneled boundaries. The world he saw when the ships docked in Manila or Macao never appears. In his letters and diaries written at the same time, that unregulated, even irrational un-European world does appear but seen through a gauze of disdain and apprehension. "The Philippinos have the most wonderful skin I have ever seen, torsos the color of apricots. But . . . then . . . grinning teeth encrusted with gold." Japan is "the ugliest country I have ever visited, strewn with ramshackle industrial suburbs. . . ." In many countries, he could scarcely be persuaded to disembark. Sometimes *The Age of Reason*, written in the cabin where the fan turned, reads like a denial of that busy, hot, half-comprehensible world outside on the docks. Instead, it enshrines a treasured, elegant, brilliant, indoor place which had come to exist only in memories and books. As such, it is a book which seems colored with loneliness and regret, written by an old man who knows that the world has left him behind.

But no one reads a book out of pity and this sequence of portraits and mentalities is afloat on all the virtues Nicolson had marshaled throughout his writing life. He is constantly amused by, curious about and sympathetic with the varieties of human nature that stroll or mince on to his stage. Individuals are never boxed into a pre-deter-mined frame. They are allowed their individuality. Lytton Strachey, who was Nicolson's master in terms of style and historical approach, had long ago written, in a gauntlet thrown down to the Marxists, that "Human beings are too important to be treated as mere symptoms of the past. They have a value which is independent of any temporal pro-cesses" and this book is a long demonstration of that fact. Individual-ity, the quirk and the wrinkle, is all. No one, seen for what they are, is a type. Typology, when it comes to people, is intellectual laziness.

As a result, if you pick this book up anywhere, it is sure to be enter-taining, an encounter with a person, much as you might encounter him or her in life. Not only is the salon or the coffeehouse the focus of this history, it is also, in a sense, its method. The reader swims through these crowds in the wake of the author, introduced by him to the most interesting individuals he can find in the room. He seems to have known everyone all their lives. There are old friends but he doesn't like all of them—the portrait of Dr. Johnson bristles with hos-tility ("his attitude toward contemporary politics was as unintelligent as that of a resident of Bournemouth") and he treats Rousseau like something the cat has brought in. He often makes a beeline for those many others might fear or despise. The picture of Horace Walpole, so often considered pure human poison, is filled with affection and sympathy. And although this was written in the 1950s, there is still a Stracheyesque air of putting the Victorians in their place. Macau-lay had dismissed Horace Walpole as an "unhealthy and disorganized mind." Not at all, says Harold. "He should be studied and admired as one of the most gifted, lovable, typical, prophetic, outspoken, and original of eighteenth-century characters."

There is a rough theory at work here. The 18th century consisted of three ages: the escape from the fanaticism and mutual destruction of the century before; a polishing of that cult of placidity and normality into a heightened Augustan perfection; and finally a movement away from that highly refined condition into one where feeling could be liberated from the tyranny of good taste, the ante-chamber for the age of Romance which was to follow. There is nothing either surprising or original about this scheme and it is not the point of the book. Instead it should be read as an enviably fluent and friendly primer on the subtleties and nuances of an age often seen through the gauze of cliché. Was early 18th-century England smug? Yes, but not really. Rationalist, yes, but not completely. Believing in the growing freedom of the individual, yes but also alarmed by the subversion of order which that suggested. In awe of the state, yes, but doing everything it could to limit its power. Radical, yes, but only intermittently. Violent, yes, but also increasingly sentimental. It is a book dedicated not to the statement but to its qualification, to the more unlikely aspects of human nature. It is less interesting that Frederick the Great dominated Europe than that his love-letters to Voltaire are quite so embarrassing or that he played his flute to calm down after battles.

It is not an "important" book and it doesn't overturn any accepted view. It is the accumulation of a highly literate man's life and, for all its limitations, is immensely enjoyable for that. It is also a portrait of the author. It doesn't like power but it admires fortitude; it doesn't like fanaticism, but it admires conviction; it loves reason but also understands the limits of reasonability. It is entranced by the brilliant remark but values honesty, understanding, precision and integrity. It stakes a claim for civilization as a form of goodness.

When he had finished, Doubleday was delighted and Harold signed a contract for a sequel, *The Age of Romance*. But in June 1962, Vita died, Harold's world collapsed, and he never wrote the book. He died in 1968.

September, 2008

Author's Note

I shall, I well know, be abused for not having provided references to the numerous quotations that I have introduced into this book. The omission was deliberate, since this study is not intended to be a work of historical research or reference, but to contain portraits of individuals and an account of changing states of mind.

H. N.

Sissinghurst, May 1960

Introduction

IT WOULD BE unwise to give precise dates for the Age of Reason, although conventionally it is identified with the eighteenth century. The origins must certainly be traced back to the publication of Isaac Newton's *Principia* in 1687 and to John Locke's *Essay on the Human Understanding* in 1690. Horace Walpole, in his *Memoirs of the Reign of George II* goes even further back, and claims that the Age of Reason began in 1657: "A century had now passed," he wrote of 1757, "since Reason had begun to attain that ascendant in the affairs of the world, to conduct which it had been granted to man six thousand years ago. If religions and governments were still domineered by prejudices, if creeds that contradict logic, or tyrannies that enslave multitudes to the caprice of one, were not yet exploded, novel absurdities at least were not broached, or, if propagated, produced neither prosecutors nor martyrs."

This is not an accurate or comprehensive statement. Yet it would not be denied that Newton first taught men that existing myths were not in accord with scientific fact; or that Locke taught men that ideas were not innate but derived from experience, that rationalism should convince us that government must be based on consent, that property is the reward of labor, and that toleration in politics and religion is the glory of civilized man. Montesquieu, who visited England between 1729 and 1731, preached the doctrine of the separation of powers and the rule of law. And the *Encyclopédistes* and Voltaire denounced all superstition and intolerance as "Infamous." "They rendered," wrote Dr..Fisher in his *History of Europe*, "the incomparable service of attacking all that was cruel, all that was superstitious, all that was obsolete, unequal or unjust, in the constitution of European society and in the fabric of its religious and social beliefs. . . ."

I should suggest that the climax of the Age of Reason was reached with the publication, between 1751 and 1776, of the French Encyclopédie.

They had their faults, the philosophes, as well as their virtues. They appealed to intellectuals only, and their influence was thus restricted to the educated classes. "This minority," wrote Mr. F. L. Lucas, "was too small, the problem too difficult, the strain too great." Being essentially a clique of intellectuals and aristocrats, they tended to become arrogant and optimistic. They really did believe that they were the prophets of the new enlightenment and the legislators of the world to be. Being segregated from the common man, they failed to realize that their doctrines, if pushed to logical conclusions, would create among the masses bewilderment and even worse. By attacking so successfully all the myths of revealed religion, they created a vacuum which was filled by irrational gullibility, a defect skillfully exploited by charlatans such as Casanova and Cagliostro. They had little trust in democracy and therefore looked for the accomplishment of their desires to despots whom they believed to be benevolent, such as Frederick the Great and Catherine II. Their influence was destructive rather than constructive. "People mean nowadays by a philosopher," wrote Rivarol in 1772, "not the man who has mastered the fine art of controlling his passions and extending his insight, but the man who has cast off prejudices without acquiring virtue." Their passion for criticism and dissection rendered their philosophy essentially unproductive. They generated light without warmth and, since man cannot live happily in a frigid intellectual climate, they created a reaction which, by insisting that the irrational was a surer guide than the rational, that the heart was more important than the head, brought much unhappiness to mankind. They were bad psychologists and failed entirely to see that even men of intelligence need some "feeling" in their lives. They were curiously optimistic, believing that reason was common to all men, that "Nature" was an evidence of conformity, and that Deism, as Swift sneered, was a faith that "contained nothing which cannot be presently comprehended by the weakest noodle." The confusion into which they fell between "the law of Nature" and the condition of primitive man led to these most reasonable beings becoming utterly unreasonable. They really did confide in:

> Great Nature's law, the law within the breast:
> Formed by no art and to no sect confined
> But stamped by heaven upon the unlettered mind.

Even the most skeptical of the eighteenth-century intellectuals had a pathetic faith in what Professor Lovejoy has called "the plans of common sensibility and average understanding." They were anything but egalitarians, but they did, even in their worst moments of doubt, have the illusion that common sense was a gift shared even by the commonest man.

Yet, if the intellectuals of the eighteenth century cherished their illusions, even if their teaching was sterile, negative, and heartless, they certainly did contribute much to the mental and moral habits of mankind. In the first place they created an ideal of sincerity, both towards oneself and towards one's fellow human beings. They certainly did inspire a passion for good sense, balance, moderation, order, taste, intellectual truthfulness, and tolerance. They believed in cosmopolitanism and regarded nationalism, whether political or intellectual, as uncivilized. They believed in the rule of law, although they did not see how it could be applied by elected chambers, and felt it could only be imposed by such enlightened autocrats as Voltaire's Frederick, Grimm's Catherine, or Mirabeau's Charles William Ferdinand of Brunswick. The only autocrat who sincerely strove to remold his Empire on "philosophic" principles was Joseph II, who failed nobly. Frederick and Catherine, while writing at length on the

Chapter 1

Courtly Standards

(Saint Simon, 1675–1755)

————— •◆• —————

The duc d'Anjou, grandson of Louis XIV, is on November 16, 1700, designated as King of Spain—The consequences of this action—The prestige and glory of the Great Monarch—The persecution of the Jansenists and the Revocation of the Edict of Nantes—Saint Simon as the recorder of his age—His perplexing personality—His value as a historian diminished by his passion for rank and precedence—Origins of Saint Simon's family and his early career—He earns the disfavor of Louis XIV—He attaches himself to the Orléans faction—He has an old-fashioned view of the autocracy of Louis XIV and feels that the separation of powers could best be restored by giving more power to the feudal nobility—His Memoirs—His failure in public life—His retirement to his country estate—His merits—He represents the transition between the seventeenth and eighteenth centuries.

One

In his diary for Tuesday, November 16, 1700, the duc de Saint Simon made the following entry:

> On quitting his levée, the King summoned the Spanish Ambassador to his private study. The duc d'Anjou had already reached the room by the back staircase. The King

pointed to the duc d'Anjou and informed the Ambassador that he could now do homage to the boy as King of Spain. The Ambassador, according to the Spanish custom, flung himself on his knees and delivered a complimentary address in the Spanish language. The King explained that the duc d'Anjou did not yet know that language and that he would himself reply on his grandson's behalf. Thereafter the King, against all precedent, ordered that the double doors of his study should be thrown wide open and invited the courtiers to enter.

Majestically his eyes wandered over the assembled company. "Gentlemen," he said to them indicating the duc d'Anjou, "I present to you the King of Spain. He has by his birth been called to that throne; the late King of Spain has in his will designated him as successor; the Spanish nation desires him to become their sovereign and have begged me to agree. I regard it as the command of Heaven. It is with pleasure that I have given my assent."

Then turning to his grandson he said: "You must prove a good Spaniard, that is now your first duty. But never forget you were born a Frenchman in order to foster the union between the two nations; by that means you will satisfy both France and Spain and preserve the peace of Europe."

This prophecy was but half fulfilled. The little duc d'Anjou, on becoming King Philip V of Spain, did in fact show himself a good Spaniard and eventually won the loyalty, and even the affection, of his subjects. But the War of the Spanish Succession which had thus been provoked proved one of the most stubborn wars in history. The French armies suffered successive defeats at Blenheim in 1704, at Ramillies in 1706, and at Oudenarde in 1708. The prestige of Louis XIV which had till then proved unsurpassed and seemed unassailable, was shattered forever. In the sixty-second year of his age and the fifty-seventh year of his reign he had allowed his thirst for glory to entice him into a decision which united against him the armies of Austria, England, and the Netherlands. By 1709 France was on the verge of collapse. Had it not been for Queen Anne's weakness in succumbing to the wiles of Abigail Masham and the intrigues of Harley and the peace party, Louis XIV might have been forced to accept inglorious surrender.

It should be remembered that throughout the eighteenth century Europe was almost constantly at war. In the 127 years between 1688 and 1815 Great Britain was engaged in seven major wars with France which lasted sixty years. The fact that this study deals mainly with the development of ideas should not blind the reader to the fact that the Age of Reason was also an Age of Violence.

The War of the Spanish Succession continued for thirteen years and when peace was eventually concluded at Utrecht, France found herself diminished, her finances in disorder, and her social and economic conditions so chaotic that they remained precarious throughout the ensuing century, and her position as the dominant Power in Europe seriously compromised. The concluding fifteen years of the Great Monarch's life were darkened by humiliation and remorse. The glitter of his gigantic palace of Versailles, which for a generation had dazzled the eyes of the whole world, sunk into sad solemnity. Louis XIV himself, who by the astounding force of his personality had raised the conception of absolute monarchy to a pinnacle of grandeur, saw all his sunlit glory shrouded into fog around him. With his morganatic wife, Madame de Maintenon, he sought solace in religious devotion and in practical austerity.

Hour after hour they would sit there facing each other in two armchairs beside the fireplace, while she hemmed nightdresses for her seminarists at Saint Cyr, and he brooded over the dispatches which informed him of defeats by sea and land; of the continued triumphs of the Grand Alliance forged by his enemies; of the military exploits of Prince Eugene and the Duke of Marlborough; of seething internal discontent; and of national penury and starvation. The courtiers, whom in his days of supremacy he had forced to assemble round him, and to minister to his greatness, lolled in the galleries under the dimmed lights of chandeliers, perishing from boredom and a sense of wastage. Such was the nemesis brought upon his people by a ruler, who possessed a genius for display, an almost mesmeric gift of personal dominance, but who for all his gifts had deficient insight into reality; and who lacked moderation.

The scene which took place in Louis XIV's study at Versailles on November 16, 1700, was the first link in a chain of historic consequences. It marked, though few realized it at the time, the end of the seventeenth century and the beginning of a new century so dynamic as to change the shape of history and the minds of men. The three dominant Powers of the past—Spain, France and Austria—declined in magnitude. Three new Powers—Russia, Prussia and eventually the United States—started on a course of forceful expansion which within two hundred and fifty years was to alter the proportions of world power. The minds of men, abandoning the old disciplines and contentions of theology, turned to what they called "natural philosophy," namely the faith in individual reason rather than in divine revelation; they welcomed the excitement offered by the ever widening opportunities for discovery and commerce; and by the prospect of immeasurable progress owing to the inventions of science and technology and the spread of education.

If we are to understand the significance of the disastrous ceremony that took place at Versailles on that November day in 1700, some explanation of causes, circumstances, and illusions is required.

Louis XIV succeeded his father in May 1643 when he was but five years of age. His childhood was darkened by the feline vigilance of his mother's favorite, Cardinal Mazarin, and by the rebellions of the nobles and the parliament, known as the Fronde. On two successive occasions the Cardinal, the Queen Mother, and the infant King were forced to escape from Paris. Even when the city had been recaptured from the rebels, the Parisians, having been told that the young King was dead or had at least been smuggled out of the country, insisted on obtaining access to the royal person. A deputation of citizens was admitted to his bedroom. Propped on his pillows the child watched them file past him, gazing at them in fear and scorn. It is to this humiliating episode that is attributed his dislike of the capital and his horror of the Parisian mob.

Mazarin died in 1660 and thenceforward Louis XIV exercised undisputed authority. He was for long assisted by two ministers of great ability, by Colbert who placed the economics and the finances of the realm on a sound basis, and by Louvois who reformed and reequipped the armed forces. In the swamps that surrounded his father's little hunting lodge at Versailles, he constructed a palace of unprecedented splendor. This cost the State some sixty-six million livres and caused the sickness and death of many thousand workmen. In this vast and glittering concentration camp he gathered together the leading nobles of France, determined by constant vigilance to prevent any conspiracy and to avert another Fronde. By inventing the most elaborate ceremonial he managed to hypnotize them into the belief that they were fulfilling some useful function, and by grants of money or purely decorative posts he allayed their greed and their ambition. He gave encouragement to art and science and it was during the great days of Versailles that Racine, Molière, Lulli, Despreâux, Quinault, Mansard, and Le Nôtre produced their masterpieces. He had many mistresses, of whom the most outstanding, who bore him several bastards, were the gay and loving Louise de la Vallière and the witty if unscrupulous Madame de Montespan. He adopted the emblem of the sunburst, designed for him by the interior decorator Douvrier, and was flattered to be acclaimed by his courtiers as "le roi soleil." The rays of this sun dazzled the eyes of his generation and its beams illumined all Europe. He became the idol and example of continental dynasties and even the smallest German princeling sought to emulate his autocracy and the glories of Versailles.

His prestige was much enhanced during the seventeenth century by three wars of aggression. In the war, known as "The War of Devolution," which lasted only from 1667 to 1668, his great general, Marshal Turenne, won victory after victory and by the ensuing Peace of Aix-la Chapelle, France obtained Flanders and its fortresses, which were thereafter rendered impregnable, by the technical skill of Vauban. In the Dutch War of 1672–1678, having by the Treaty of Dover bribed Charles II to promise the neutrality of England, he rapidly with his

age that he painted with such brilliance, and when we detect a note of irony, almost a note of hatred and contempt, twanging like a brass wire through the minuets of his court gossip. With Boswell also there come moments when we are astonished at his insensitiveness to reality and at his apparent inability to realize how intrusive, objectionable, and tactless he really was. But Boswell always kept his pictures in focus, and always directed his lens towards the center of the composition, that is towards himself and the person whom he was describing. What is so disconcerting about Saint Simon is that the clarity of his portrayal will suddenly become distorted by his obsessions and that we find ourselves pondering whether this intelligent annalist could discriminate between the significant and the trivial, between what was serious and what was not. Although he describes the genesis and the development of world-shattering events, although he provides us with vivid portraits of the figures of his time, we still, when we have finished the fascinating volumes of his memoirs, ask ourselves whether the man was a genius or a fool.

His judgment was warped by an almost maniac concern with rank and precedence, by what Madame St. René Taillandier has well called "his ducal apoplexy." He was himself not unaware of this obsession. "The most cherished and the liveliest passion," he confessed, "that I experience, is that for my dignity and rank. I care far less about my personal fortune, and it would be in a transport of delight that I would sacrifice the present and the future, if only I could enhance my dignity." Thus although occasionally he would pretend to have some sympathy for the submerged classes, he in fact possessed little interest in, or understanding of, the social and economic dangers with which France was threatened. Even in his moments of illumination (and he was not wholly without vision) he refused to accept the theory that all men are born equal. He ardently looked forward to the day when, as he expressed it in his own crotchety manner, "these frivolous French will be cured of the leprosy of egalitarianism." The focus of his attention remained fixed on the Court of Versailles and his incessant preoccupation was the rise or fall in royal favor of the various men and women who dawdled in those decorated saloons seeking to catch the eye of their tribal god, *Le roi Soleil*. Never could he quite forgive Louis XIV for his prudent habit of entrusting the affairs of the realm to men who had risen from the professional classes by their proven ability, rather than to those who were descended from the great feudal families of France. Never could he forgive the furtive marriage of the mighty monarch to the widow of a scurrilous middle class scribbler; never, above all, could he reconcile himself to the fact that the King with the approval of the parliament accorded to his bastards a rank just below the princes of the blood and above the hereditary peers. His ecstasy when, after the King's death, the Regent deprived the bastards of their semi-royal rank rose almost to frenzy. His loathing of the duc du Maine in particular amounted to an obsession and when this particular bastard was compromised by the conspiracy of Cellamare, he used all his influence with the Regent to have him tried and executed. "This little twirp," writes d'Argenson in his memoirs, "wanted them to prosecute the duc du Maine and to cut off his head. This reveals the odious, unfair and cannibal instincts of this stupid little bigot."

His monomania regarding the status due to him as a hereditary duke and peer of France is all the more inexplicable since in fact the de Rouvroy family were not of feudal origin. His father had been page of the stables to Louis XIII and had attracted that monarch's attention by his ability to sound the hunting horn loudly without the accumulation of saliva and by inventing a method by which the King could change horses while hunting without being obliged to dismount. According to the marshal de Bassompière he was not, as were most of the favorites of that reign, a young man of physical attraction: the marshal in fact tells us that he was "as meager in body as in intellect." Yet the King accorded him a dukedom and permitted him to invent the legend that his family, obscure though it might appear to be, was in fact descended through the Counts of Vermandois from Charlemagne himself.

Saint Simon's father was sixty-two years of age when his son and heir was born on January 16, 1675. The old man died in 1692 and his son, then a lad of seventeen who had already manifested a passion for genealogies, succeeded to the dukedom, to the moated castle of La Ferté-Vidame, to the house in the Avenue de St. Cloud at Versailles, and to the family mansion in the Rue Dominique in Paris, with its dark library enlivened by straight-backed chairs of red velvet fringed with gold. The young duke had been educated by Jesuit tutors and was by then an ensign in the grey musketeers. He served for ten years in the army, was present at the battle of Namur, acquitted himself gallantly at the siege of Nerwinden, and was well on the way to make a promising military career, when his crotchety disposition induced him suddenly to resign his commission. He had been incensed by the reforms being introduced by Louvois under which officers were to be promoted with at least some regard for merit and less exclusively according to their aristocratic precedence. He was particularly enraged when a man not of ducal family was promoted brigadier above his head.

The King, on hearing of his resignation, remarked crossly, "Another one of them to desert!" It may well have been his abrupt refusal to continue his army career that first earned him the dislike, even the contempt, with which Louis XIV continued to regard him. "It is strange," His Majesty was heard to remark, "that since leaving the army M. de Saint Simon has thought of nothing but the relations between the different ranks of the nobility." But it was worse than that. Louis XIV, with his insistence on uniformity, or what he called "symmetry," suspected that Saint Simon was in some way "different" from the other courtiers. He did not enjoy hunting; he neither danced, nor drank, nor gambled. It was rumored even that he remained unswervingly faithful to his wife. He was known to be constantly scribbling notes in notebooks and that he took an interest in works on philosophy, geography, and history. "I see no point," Louis XIV remarked irritably, "in reading." Moreover the King complained that Saint Simon was always grumbling about something, that he talked far too much, that he was often indiscreet, that he "found fault," and that he had too many "personal ideas." Madame de Maintenon shared and perhaps encouraged this repugnance. Although she only spoke directly to Saint Simon on one single occasion, she suspected him of latent hostility, and accused him of being "conceited, ambitious, critical, and full of odd ideas" (*glorieux, frondeur, et plein de vues*). They may have suspected even that his attachment, first to the duc de Bourgogue, and on the latter's death to Philippe d' Orléans, the eventual Regent, savored of heresy, even of opposition. Thus, although in 1710 the duchesse de Saint Simon was given the post of lady in waiting to the duchesse de Berri, and although this carried with it the privilege of lodging in the palace itself, the rooms accorded to them were of inferior distinction. Situated on the first floor of the north wing of the Palace of Versailles, they comprised three rooms only, the study allotted to the duke being windowless and deprived both of light and air. "My little black hole" he called it, yet, such was the attraction which the Great King exercised upon his courtiers, that his sense of the honor done to his wife and himself far outweighed the necessity of exchanging his fine house in the Avenue de Saint Cloud for this moldy little apartment in the palace itself. Moreover his constant attendance at court gave him unlimited chances of gathering gossip, and observing human nature at its worst.

Conscious of latent disapproval, Saint Simon became more and more attached to the Orléans faction. It is necessary therefore to discount his comments on Louis XIV and on Madame de Maintenon. Much as he worshipped the principle of monarchy, much as he was dazzled by the personal grandeur and authority of Louis XIV, there were moments when he allowed himself to hint criticism of the established system. He even went so far as to suggest that Louis XIV was essentially selfish, that he "lacked heart," and that he possessed but "a second-rate intelligence." His repeated suggestions that the King was entirely in the hands of his ministers, are demonstrably superficial and untrue. He is definitely unfair to Madame de Maintenon. He contends that she dominated her husband, whereas in fact she slavishly pampered his every whim. He contends that her sole desire was to have her clandestine marriage publicly recognized and to assume the status of Queen. He even goes so far as to assert that the dismissal

LOUIS XIV

Oil on canvas, 1701 by Hyacinthe Rigaud

of Louvain and the disgrace of Fénélon are to be attributed to their opposition to Madame de Maintenon's elevation to the throne. Yet in fact she had but little influence in such matters and had no desire whatsoever to share the splendor and burdens of majesty. Unless we remain constantly aware of his wry prejudices, we may attribute to his historical judgments more importance than they merit. Saint Simon's record of great events must always be read with caution. Yet his *Memoirs* are essential to any study of the gradations by which the seventeenth century slid slowly into the Age of Reason.

Three

Saint Simon is thus a useful exhibit for this study of the eighteenth century since, although a man of acute observation, he possessed an essentially seventeenth-century cast of mind. He was always thinking back to the great days of Louis XIII and Richelieu, to the days before the Fronde, when the aristocracy really was the aristocracy and before bastards and bourgeois had acquired prominence and pretensions. He remained utterly indifferent to the new ideas that were already changing the mental habits of his generation: to him the disturbing suggestion of Newton and Locke savored of heresy and as such were of interest only to the bourgeois intellectuals, he never worried, as so many of his contemporaries worried, about the conflict between the philosophic conception of a Social Contract and the ancient theory of the Divine Right of Kings; he never succeeded even in spelling the name of Voltaire correctly.

We are apt to look back upon the system of highly centralized autocracy established under Louis XIV as a curious survival from the past; Saint Simon regards it as a dazzling if dangerous innovation. We are apt to assume that the principles of liberalism and egalitarianism which, during the eighteenth century, transformed the thoughts and feelings of mankind were a natural reaction against the rigidity, incompetence, and oppression of an outworn theory of governance. Saint Simon had his own almost mediaeval plan for the proper distribution his carriage when he drove through the streets. Yet when other courtiers and clients turned their backs upon him, Saint Simon displayed courageous loyalty, and would walk up and down the terrace with him, under the very windows of the King.

For this act of moral courage, the duc d'Orléans was grateful and when he became Regent in September 1715, Saint Simon was, for a short time at least, regarded as a power behind the throne. He failed entirely to grasp this opportunity.

Although at the outset he was offered the key position of controller to the infant Louis XV, Lord Privy Seal, and chairman of the Finance Council, he refused, from dread of taking any responsibility, to accept any of these appointments. He did succeed however in persuading the Regent to abolish the system of Louis XIV whereby affairs were conducted by professional Ministers, chosen for their experience or ability, and to substitute for them a number of Councils, whose members were mainly drawn from the aristocracy. He himself was appointed to the Council of Regency, which was at first regarded as the most important of all. Yet the Regent soon recognized that his friend, being passionate in regard to detail and indecisive when it came to principle, did not possess any of the qualities of an administrator. Thus although Saint Simon was opposed to the policy of the English alliance and regarded the financial speculations of John Law with the gravest suspicion, he was unable to deter the Regent from either of these two pet projects. Before long it was seen that the system of Councils was not proving effective and Saint Simon's influence rapidly declined. "Of all men," he wrote, "I am the one who has least influence with His Royal Highness." He was thus dispatched on a diplomatic mission to the Court of Spain, which was devoid of any serious political intention or result. Yet Saint Simon was entranced by the honors paid to him as the Ambassador of a friendly Monarch and reveled in the complicated mysteries of Spanish etiquette. As René Doumic has observed, the six months that he spent at Madrid represented the only period in his life when he was supremely satisfied. On his return to Versailles he realized that his influence had utterly waned and on December 2,

1723, fell the final blow. On that day his patron the debauched and red-faced Regent died suddenly of apoplexy and Saint Simon was left without a friend. Fleury, the new power in the land, let him know that his presence at the court was no longer required. He left Versailles immediately and retired to his castle at La Ferté-Vidame, where he remained almost without interruption until his death thirty-two years later at the age of eighty. His two puny sons having predeceased him, the dukedom which he had loved so passionately became extinct.

Four

It would be a mistake to dismiss Saint Simon as a lightweight, or as a laughable little snob interested only in points of etiquette and in court gossip. His sharp eyes, his constantly alert ear, enabled him to see and hear things which by others were taken as no more than part of the daily routine. We have only to compare his *Memoirs* with the contemporary diary kept by Dangeau (which Saint Simon himself described as "so dull as to make one sick") to realize the skill with which, by the accumulation of detail after detail, he was able to paint a massive landscape of the age and to people it with living figures of bewigged and powdered men and women, waiting for hours in the Gallery of Mirrors for the quick passage of their sovereign from his bedroom to the chapel, or strolling in groups amid the statues and fountains of the vast terrace, reduced by the expanse of sky above them to the size of crawling ants. The fact that he was both fascinated and repelled by the artificiality of the whole apparatus renders his record neutral, almost objective, and helps us to appreciate the strength of personality that enabled Louis XIV to impose his legend upon his courtiers, whom he confined and pampered as five thousand macaws bickering and making love in one enormous gilded cage.

Nor, as Madame de Maintenon noticed, was the little duke devoid of individual ideas. He differed from the ordinary courtiers in his refusal to share either their vices or their amusements, in his personal integrity and asceticism, and in his lifelong respect for the domestic

Chapter 2

Rationalism

(Pierre Bayle, 1647–1706)

———•◆•———

The transition between the uncritical acceptance of the established order and the growth of individual analysis and doubt—The four generations of the Ségur family as an example in this change in the climate of thought and feeling—Philippe de Ségur typical of the intellectual aristocrat of the eighteenth century—His service in the United States—His mission to Russia and his relations with Catherine II—Pierre Bayle as the precursor of the *Encyclopédistes*—His immense contemporary influence—His *Historical and Critical Dictionary*—His attack upon the theologians and upon arbitrary government—Bayle as a mighty prophet of freedom of thought—Fontenelle the epicurean—His early failure and eventual success—His avoidance of all passion—His *Dialogues des Morts* and his *Histoire des Oracles*—His compelling influence on the literary salons of Paris—As representing the transition between synthetic and analytical habits of thought.

One

EW PERIODS OF history can show so complete a transformation in the thoughts and feelings of both the educated and the uneducated classes as that between 1650 and 1789. Until the middle of the seventeenth century the vast majority of Europeans, whether Protestant or Catholic, accepted without question the

The American Revolution dawned for these young men as a release for their pent up passion for Liberty, as a practical expression of their idealism, and as an opportunity for glory and self-sacrifice.

"In those days," writes Ségur, "we used to call the Americans 'the Bostonians'; their audacity electrified our souls, aroused universal admiration, especially among young people enamored of novelty and longing for glory. I was astonished to see so unanimous an outburst in favor of the revolt of a people against its king. The American rising became the fashion; the English game, whist, was succeeded in every drawing room by an equally difficult card game which they called *le boston*. This change, trivial though it may seem, was a notable presage of the vast convulsions by which the whole world was before long to be overwhelmed, and I was by no means the only young man whose heart palpitated at the thought of this dawn of Liberty freeing itself from the yoke of arbitrary power. Those who have since blamed us for our excitement should remember that at the time they shared our enthusiasm."

Thus fevered and inspired, the young Ségur persuaded his father to allow him to sail for the United States. He was unable to leave France, however, until May 1782, more than six months after the surrender of Yorktown and when the fighting was almost over. His journey was not, however, without its adventures. The ship in which he traveled carried a large quantity of specie, a generous gift from the impoverished French government to the equally impoverished Treasury of the United States. They were chased by a British frigate and only succeeded in escaping by dashing into the Delaware River where they landed on a sandbank. The money was transshipped, the English evaded, and Ségur managed to reach Philadelphia unscathed, rejoicing to find himself in "the home of reason, order and liberty." Having presented his dispatches and his commission to Rochambeau, he joined the Soissonnais regiment, of which he had been appointed second in command. He went to pay his respects to General Washington and was deeply impressed by the "simplicity, majesty, dignity, calm, kindness and strength" of his deportment and expression. Ségur went up the Hudson River and visited West Point. Writing his memoirs in 1824 he records that "the wild and sinister landscape inspired me with melancholy and deep feelings, or what would today be called 'romantic sentiments.'"

He then embarked again, hoping to take part in the capture of Jamaica, but the French fleet was dispersed by storms and his own ship was captured by an English frigate, under the command of "a young captain of the name of Nelson who in later years became only too famous as the man who destroyed our naval forces in Egypt." He records that on that occasion Nelson treated his French prisoners with the utmost courtesy and let them go free.

On his return to France the comte de Ségur, in spite of the fact that he was only just thirty years of age, was appointed Ambassador to Russia where he spent the next five years. He succeeded in gaining the confidence of Catherine II and Potemkin and in concluding with them a treaty of commerce admitting French merchant ships into the ports of the Gulf of Finland and the Black Sea. He was invited, together with the British and Austrian ambassadors, to accompany the Empress on her amazing visit to her newly acquired territories in the Crimea. They were joined on their journey by the Emperor Joseph II of Austria, by the King of Poland, and by the Prince de Ligne, with whom Ségur established relations of intimacy. He also admired the qualities of his rival, the British Ambassador, Sir Alleyn Fitzherbert, later Lord Saint Helens, to whom Ségur in his memoirs, and with pardonably false association, calls "Lord Saint Helena."

He much admired Catherine II, although he deplored her impulsiveness and the variability of her temperament. During the many hours they spent together in the course of their long journeys, by sledge, by carriage and in richly decorated barges, they discussed philosophy, the art of government, the nature of happiness, and the merits of aristocracy. He even tried to teach her poetry, an art to which her great intelligence was not attuned. "I therefore abandoned my lessons on poetry, informing my august pupil that it was inevitable that henceforward she must make her laws and her conquests in prose." He was fascinated by Potemkin but regretted that he should be so unreliable and was distressed by "his inconceivable blend of greatness that their own minds are nimble, fashionable, and up to date. Thus in the eighteenth century the Paris intellectual acquired the habit of questioning, not the supernatural only, not only existing institutions, but anything that had been believed in, or reverenced by, their fathers and mothers. And since Paris in those days was the crucible of ideas, what was felt and thought in Paris rapidly spread throughout the civilized world.

Although it was Voltaire, Diderot, and the *Encyclopédistes* who rendered skepticism the fashion, they were not in fact the pioneers of the movement. They had their predecessors and their precursors. No study of the Age of Reason can omit some mention at least of the skepticism of Bayle and the epicureanism of Fontenelle.

Pierre Bayle (1647–1706) was the true originator of skepticism. Sainte-Beuve describes him as "the great precursor" of Voltaire, and Voltaire himself hailed him as "one of the greatest men that France has produced," as "more learned than Plato or Epicurus." Voltaire described Bayle's writings as "the library of Nations." "He was," he wrote, "the greatest dialectician that has ever written: he taught doubt." Gibbon praised him: Hume followed him: Leibnitz, although he did not agree with his conclusions, admired the force of "the marvelous Dictionary": Frederick the Great considered the Dictionary as "the breviary of good sense": Bayle influenced Lessing, and through Lessing the whole German Aufklärung: his impact on Shaftesbury was sharp and lasting: Lecky considered that he "did more than any previous writer to break the spell which Saint Augustine had so long cast over theology" and asserted that Bayle's *Historical and Critical Dictionary* was the true foundation of rationalism. Yet today it is very seldom read or consulted.

Pierre Bayle was born in the village of Carlat, near Foix, in the lower Pyrenees. His father was the local Huguenot pastor, but he was sent to a Jesuit college, which accounts, not only for his momentary conversion to Catholicism, but also for the excellence of his prose style. On rejoining the Protestant Church, he took refuge for a while at Geneva and then was employed as a tutor in Rouen and Paris. He was before long appointed to the chair of Philosophy at the Protestant College at Sedan and when that Academy was liquidated he migrated to Rotterdam, where he obtained a professorship. He first attracted attention in 1680 when he wrote a pamphlet on the great comet of that year, arguing that comets were not intended to be supernatural portents, but were perfectly natural, explicable, and indeed foreseeable, events. In that pamphlet he allowed himself the audacious statement that "it is only a common prejudice that induces us to believe that atheism is a most fearful state." The revocation of the Edict of Nantes exposed his family at Carlat to direct persecution and as a result he published a pamphlet contending that constraint in religious matters was "criminal and contrary both to Reason and to Scripture." In the same year he published his *Philosophical Commentary* and started editing at Rotterdam the *News of the Republic of Letters* which had a wide circulation and brought him international repute.

His former friend and colleague Professor Jurieu, who regarded himself as the champion of Protestant orthodoxy, detected in the *Philosophical Commentary* a degree of tolerance, so dangerous as to excuse even the Socinians, who denied the divine nature of Christ and the miracle of the Sacrament. To Jurieu tolerance amounted to indifference, even to atheism. He was under the impression that before many years had passed the Huguenot cause would be everywhere triumphant. He identified the Church of Rome with the beast of the Revelations and, by juggling with figures, forecast that the Papacy would be abolished in France and Spain in the year 1689. When this event did not occur, he contended that God had sent William III into the world as a modern Joshua. In 1691 Professor Jurieu attacked Bayle as an atheist, a pacifist, and a traitor, and managed to enlist the support of the Calvinist Church elders in Rotterdam on the ground that, like Socrates, he was "corrupting the youth." Bayle was therefore deprived of his professorship but this did not distress him unduly, since the salary was small, he could support his modest needs by what he gained by his books and his newsletter, and he was relieved to have the leisure to devote himself exclusively to his Dictionary. The first volume of this great work appeared in August 1697, and immediately became, as Faguet states, "the bible of the eighteenth century." He remained on unpersecuted at Rotterdam until his death.

Bayle's *Historical and Critical Dictionary* is cast in the form of a biographical dictionary. The biographical data were followed by comments on the character of the individual described and it was in these character sketches that Bayle expounded his philosophical views. The dictionary is of no value as a work of reference, since the composition is eccentric, people of no importance being included and no mention being made of significant figures such as Cicero and Montaigne. For instance Abraham gets only three pages, whereas his wife Sarah, who was surely a less compelling figure, is accorded seven. His contemporaries do not appear to have resented these disordered proportions; what fascinated them was that the dictionary was rich in incisive attacks upon superstition and dogmatism.

He starts from the axiom that all written history is unreliable, being composed from a subjective point of view and influenced, in the pernicious form of flattery or satire, by personal affections or prejudices. He attacks superstition in all its many varieties. He points out that every sect has its own favorite miracles and denies the validity of those miracles which are believed in by other sects. Superstition, he argues, is a purely subjective emotion. He suggests that the bones of a dog would prove as efficacious as the relics of a martyr, provided that the worshipper were subjectively convinced of their magic. He attacked priest craft and the *odium theologicum*, and even allowed himself to be ironical about Saint Augustine. He contended that, whatever the Church might teach, there did exist such a person as the good pagan, and the good unbeliever, taking Atticus as an example as well as Spinoza. He advocated "natural religion," by which he meant the "ethics of a man of reason." His moral was that "every action committed against the light of conscience is essentially evil."

What shocked his contemporaries more even than his tolerance was that, while pretending to be a Protestant, he attacked the very basis of Protestantism, namely the Bible. He was too conscientious

VOLTAIRE

a historian not to analyze and criticize the chronology of the Old Testament. He points out that it is a delicate problem to determine whether Eve really lived to nine hundred and forty years of age, or whether Sarah really conceived Isaac at the age of ninety. Such a phenomenon, he remarks slyly, must have been due to "a peculiar blessing of God." He did not hesitate to record that Abraham often indulged in falsehood or that David was in fact too disreputable to have really been "a man after God's heart." "We cannot say," he adds maliciously, "that, with regard to the pleasures of love, David took much trouble to mortify the flesh."

"The best way," he writes insidiously, "to extricate ourselves from the difficulties that confound our reason is to implore the direction of the Holy Spirit. Yet I do not really see how this method can compose differences, since each sect will argue that it alone has been granted divine guidance." "Those," he writes again, "who rely on the dogmas of the theologians are relying upon weathercocks that turn with every wind and use the word of God as a nose of wax to the great scandal of good and pious souls."

His attitude towards skepticism, or "Pyrrhonism" as it was then called, was equally subversive. He admitted that skepticism was dangerous to religion which must be based on certainty. Yet the Grace of God and the fortunate fact that the majority of mankind were stupid and gullible brought it about that active skepticism was confined to a small minority. To most people "the ends of religion are better found in incomprehensible things."

Contemporary divines were much shocked also by his treatment of the doctrine of original sin. Warburton, Bishop of Gloucester, attacked his treatment of the origin of evil, calling Bayle "the foster-father of infidelity." Bayle contended that it seemed to him inconceivable that a man who revered God could believe that evil was of divine creation. Those who argued that God permitted the existence of evil in order to manifest his divine wisdom appeared to Bayle to degrade God to the level of a father "who should suffer his children to break their legs in order to manifest to the whole city his skill in mending broken bones." I am not surprised that Bishop Warburton should have been shocked. Bayle, assuredly, was a disturbing prophet of freedom of thought.

Three

A curious link between the seventeenth and the eighteenth century was Bernard de Fontenelle, who lived for exactly one hundred years from 1657 to 1757. He was not so much a skeptic as an epicurean, who believed that the sole aim of life was happiness and that this could only be achieved by detaching oneself from all passion and all worldly ambition and by reaching a condition of almost complete ataraxy. In a way he succeeded in this ambition. His contention was that the gift of happiness was born in an individual character, even as a sound constitution and healthy organs are inherited. Man is granted but a limited ration of happiness upon this earth and must preserve and expend his ration with care and forethought. His precept was "do not by your imagination create for yourself imaginary ills, since we are not perfect enough to be continually miserable." When misfortunes do occur, it is a wise practice to look forward to the time when one will have forgotten all about them and thus to project oneself into a calm future. He pities those "agitated persons" who despise tranquility. Nothing is so fragile as the state of happiness and we should do everything to avoid giving it shocks. Ambition, for instance, is a most dangerous emotion, since even when it is successful it increases a man's bulk and thus enlarges his area of vulnerability. One should strive to be "on good terms with oneself," *être bien avec soi*, since when misfortunes occur one is inevitably thrown back upon oneself and it is thus very important to render oneself "an agreeable place into which to retreat."

He thus avoided all emotion, all passion, all unattainable desires, anything that might ruffle his equanimity. As Madame Geoffrin recorded, he never laughed; like Lord Chesterfield, he only smiled. He never wept; he never lost his temper; he never "broke into a run." He never allowed himself any feelings, other than those that might profit his felicity. As his biographer, Le Cat, remarked, he was like a bee who sucked nectar from every pleasure but never allowed himself to be pricked by a thorn. He avoided all romantic attachments and busied himself, as Stendhal said, "by addressing subtle remarks to young women." When Diderot commented upon this insensibility, he replied, "It is now eighty years since I relegated emotion to my eclogues."

His attitude towards women, as Madame de Tençin observed, was "purely mechanical." He liked pretty women, but never allowed their charm to trouble his repose. D'Argenson remarked that his attitude towards women was that of Madame Geoffrin towards her cat. He rejected any idea of marriage, despised money, and refused all honors and emoluments. All he ever accepted was a flat lent him by the Regent in the Palais Royal. In the same way he never permitted ideas to disturb his equanimity. He hated arguments, even discussions. "Everything is possible," he would say, "and everybody is right." When people sought to provoke him into argument he would relapse into silence saying that he had a bad throat or a weak chest. He was not in the least jealous of his literary rivals; he disliked Racine and Rousseau but never bothered to attack either of them. He was immensely affable, although people were well aware that his universal good manners arose from indifference and a basic contempt for his fellow mortals.

He believed in a very vague way in the loveliness of virtue. "I have never," he said, "in the course of a long life made fun of even the tiniest virtue." He always noticed the merits of his friends rather than their faults. "Faults," he said, "are often disagreeable and it is to our *interest* not to emphasize the disagreeable." Yet he was not without a certain moral courage. When the Academy wished to expel the Abbé de Saint-Pierre in order to please the Court he refused to be a party to "a measure of such hypocritical servility" and was the only academician to vote against the proposal. When the Regent once remarked to him that he "did not believe in virtue," he replied, "But, Your Royal Highness, there are many decent people in this world. It is merely that they are not of your company."

Often he was criticized for his impassivity. "I could," remarked Lord Hyde, "live through the whole of Fontenelle's hundred years in the space of a quarter of an hour." "Fontenelle," said Madame de Tençin, "has two brains. One is in his head and the other where his heart ought to be." Yet he enjoyed praise. "I should like to praise you," an admirer once said to him, "but in order to do so I should require your own gift of expression." "Don't worry about that," replied Fontenelle, "go on praising just the same."

Yet Fontenelle was something more than a selfish centenarian. He did much to render superstition unfashionable. His literary work is by no means despicable.

Four

As a young man, in any case, he was not in the least devoid of ambition. He wanted to be an academician and he wanted to shine in society. It was only when he had achieved each of these ambitions that he relapsed into apathy.

He was born in Rouen, where his father was a lawyer of established practice. His mother was Martha Corneille, the sister of Pierre and Thomas Corneille. He was educated in a Jesuit college and, although he always remained on excellent terms with his teachers, he refused to enter the Church. At the age of seventeen he came to Paris with his uncle Thomas and soon found journalistic employment on the *Mercure Galant*. He wrote the words for two of Lulli's operas *Psyché* and *Bellerophon* which, owing to the genius of the composer, were performed with success. He then tried his hand at a tragedy called *Aspar*. It was more than a flop: it was a fiasco. Fontenelle returned to Rouen conscious that his ambition to conquer Paris had proved a humiliating defeat. His discomfiture was celebrated in some cruel verses, which, without any documentary evidence, have been attributed to Racine. The author of *Phèdre* might not have been inclined to view with any great indulgence the nephew of Corneille, but it seems improbable that a man of such high genius should have devoted his talents to ridiculing a boy of seventeen.

But the verses show in any case that Fontenelle while still a boy had attracted the attention of the literary world of Paris:

> *Adieu ville peu courteoise*
> *Où je crus être adoré.*
> *Aspar est désespéré.*
> *Le poullaillier de Pontoise*
> *Me doit ramener demain*
> *Voir ma famille bourgeoise;*
> *Me doit ramener demain*
> *Un bâton blanc à la main.*
> *Mon aventure est étrange:*
> *On m'adorait à Rouen*
> *Dans le Mercure Galant*
> *J'avais plus d'esprit qu'un ange.*
> *Cependent je pars demain*
> *Sans argent et sans louange;*
> *Cependent je pars demain,*
> *Un bâton blanc à la main.*

> Farewell, discourteous town,
> Where I expected to be adored.
> Aspar is in despair;
> The chicken cart of Pontoise
> Will tomorrow take me
> To revisit my bourgeois family;
> Will take me back tomorrow,
> Carrying a "failed to pass" in my hand.
> My adventure is strange.
> They loved me at Rouen;
> In the *Mercure Gallant*
> I was wittier than an angel.
> Yet I am leaving tomorrow
> Without money or esteem.
> Yet I am leaving tomorrow
> Carrying my "failed to pass" in my hand.

On his return to Rouen, Fontenelle wrote his *Dialogues des Morts* which ran into several editions and was translated into English and Italian. He also published anonymously his *Lettres Galantes*, a feeble packet of pornography. He was working hard at practical science and especially at what he called "atrocious geometry." He served his salon apprenticeship in the society of the local gentry and it was for the marquise de Mésangère that he composed his *Entretiens sur la pluralité des mondes*. He then discovered that his true gift was to expound the mysteries of science in language which would be understood by ladies of society. It was at Rouen that he wrote his *Histoire des Oracles* which at last brought him the fame for which he yearned. This work, which purported to be a perfectly objective criticism of certain pagan superstitions, was immediately recognized by the Jesuits as concealing the "venom of infidelity." The père Le Tellier endeavored to obtain a *lettre de cachet* against Fontenelle and to have him interned in the Bastille; he was rescued by the minister d'Argenson, who always did his enlightened best to protect intellectuals in trouble. Fontenelle, who was not the stuff that martyrs are made of, resolved that he would be much more cautious in future.

He returned to Paris, determined that by some means he would achieve literary success and be elected to the Academy. For an Academy competition he composed an essay *Sur La Patience*, which dripped with the unction of piety. In order to follow a prevailing fashion he also composed his *Eclogues* which enjoyed a certain boudoir success. Fontenelle was never an inspired poet and there was no real affinity between him and a shepherd's pipe. He hated natural beauty and his only sympathy for the pastoral was his taste for tranquil ease and his envy of shepherds who spent the whole hot day piping under the shade of beech trees. With the aid of his two distinguished uncles he then began his assault on the Academy. Four times was he rejected, but the fifth time, when Racine was absent with the King besieging Mons, he passed the ordeal. Having attained his ambition of becoming an academician he flung himself seriously into the study of the sciences and worked really hard at mathematics, astronomy, anatomy, and botany. He became permanent secretary of the Académie des Sciences and inaugurated the *Histoire de l'Académie* which he continued to edit for years and which brought him esteem far beyond the frontiers of France. At the same time he plunged into the social life of the capital and became the ornament of all the salons:

> *Depuis trente ans un vieux berger normand*
> *Aux beaux esprits s'est donné pour modèle;*
> *Il leur enseigne à traiter galamment*
> *Les grands sujets en style de ruelle.*

> For the last thirty years an old Normandy shepherd
> Set up as an example to the clever set.
> He taught them to treat serious subjects
> With a bedside manner.

He became a brilliant social success, thus satisfying the second of his only two ambitions. D'Argenson recorded that he managed to reproduce the tone of the Hotel Rambouillet in modernized form. "He has the gift of speech," wrote Madame de Lambert, "and persuasive lips." Unlike Diderot however, he did not impose himself on the conversation, but was able to pose as a modest listener:

> *Plus modeste qu'un écolier*
> *Et plus galant qu'un chevalier*
> *Où diable trouver son semblable?*

> More modest than a schoolboy
> And more enterprising than a young spark—
> Where shall we find his equal?

He was always gay; always amusing; but never controversial, coarse or malicious. As an old man he abounded in anecdotes of the past. "I remember," he would begin, "one evening when I was calling on Madame La Fayette, Madame de Sévigné was announced. . . ." And then would follow a vivid description: the young people present would lean forward to catch his bronchial tones.

He managed until he was a hundred years old to avoid the worries and chores of this difficult world. He always lived in other people's houses and was therefore spared domestic complications. He was a greedy man who was able to appreciate the excellence of Madame Geoffrin's suppers and had a passion for fat asparagus cooked in the best Italian oil. Until he reached the age of ninety-four he could still read even the smallest print without glasses. At eighty-eight he became slightly deaf and had to use a speaking trumpet which diminished his social amenity. On January 8, 1757, he died of a stroke, as gently as he had lived, and at the age of one hundred years.

Five

Fontenelle is of interest as the perfect specimen of the drawing room man of letters. His best and most serious work, the *Entretiens sur la Pluralité des Mondes*, composed at Rouen when he was twenty-nine, was written for the purpose of expounding to a local marquise the mysteries of astronomy. It is simple, informative, and entertaining. The immense success of the *Dialogues des Morts* is difficult to account for, since it is in truth a silly work. I entirely agree with Voltaire's comment that "it is disgraceful that so frivolous a book, full of false thinking, should have captivated the public." The various characters that he introduces into his dialogues are not various at all, since they are all different facets of Fontenelle's own personality and ideas. The composition is almost childish in its immaturity and the conversations that take place between the illustrious dead (as for instance the discussion on grammar between Berenice and Cosimo di Medici) are often boring in the extreme. Although Fontenelle, even at the age of twenty-six when he composed the *Dialogues*, was a well-read man, the *Dialogues* give the impression of almost schoolboy ignorance and presumption. It is probable that the success of the book was due to his talent for discussing in a light manner subjects which had hitherto been dealt with solemnly and pedantically. It is possible also that discerning people saw that the *Dialogues* represented a transition between the synthetic or didactic manner of the seventeenth century and the analytical manner of the eighteenth. If there exists any thread of continuity, stringing together these disparate fragments and these occasionally snappy epigrams, it is the thread of skepticism and pessimism. He destroys accepted legends. Thus in the dialogue between the courtesan Phryne and Alexander the Great they agree that she may have over done the business of love even as he had exaggerated the profession of conquest. Yet they also agree that if he had rested content with minor conquests, the world would never have heard of him, and if she had been less lavish of her favors she would never have accumulated enough money to rebuild the walls of Thebes out of her savings. Each comes to the conclusion that those who practice moderation in life seldom achieve fame and fortune.

Fontenelle, in the mouths of his characters, reveals his skeptical view of human nature and his disbelief in the great legends of human nobility. Thus Socrates and Montaigne agree together that the majority of mankind are or were as stupid in fifth-century Athens as they were in the valley of the Dordogne. "Men are like birds, constantly being trapped by the same nets and the fools born in any century always have outnumbered the wise." The legend of Cato's magnificent suicide at Utica is dismissed as due to inordinate vanity and a sullen temper. The glory of Charles V is ascribed, in a discussion between him and Erasmus, as wholly due to luck, owing to the chance that his great uncle happened to be impotent. The duc d'Alençon is represented as reproaching Queen Elizabeth for vaunting too much about her virginity. "You gave the name of Virginia," he complains, "to the continent of America in memory of the most doubtful of your many qualities." It is certain that an oaf like Alençon would never have dared to make so insolent a remark. Nor is Elizabeth's reply any more in character. She is represented as saying, "Pleasures are not solid enough to enable us to go deeper; one should only skip across them; they resemble those marshy lands over which one has to trip lightly without pausing for one moment." This flat sentiment was certainly a true expression of Fontenelle's own flat thought; but Queen

Elizabeth would assuredly have replied to her little frog friend with shorter, sharper, more incisive words. Nor would Mary Queen of Scots have remarked to Riccio, "One ceases to be happy the moment one becomes conscious of the effort made to become so. Happiness, like health, must be unconscious." That certainly is pure Fontenelle. It is not even diluted Mary Queen of Scots. The fact is that Fontenelle lacked not imagination only, but literary integrity and taste.

The *Histoire des Oracles* is a more attractive book. It is in fact an adaptation of a work on the same subject recently published by the Dutchman van Dale. "The rough diamond of van Dale," wrote Voltaire correctly, "glittered infinitely more brilliantly when cut by Fontenelle." Its main theme is that the supernatural derives from a subjective state of mind. He examines and exposes the Thamus legend and contends that the Delphic oracles, so numinous in seeming, were but the product of hashish and the exhalation of intoxicating gas. Moreover, every oracle can if examined be shown to be the product of ingenious charlatanism on the part of priests. It was not reasonable to contend, as the theologians contended, that oracles were the product of demons and that the great oracles, such as those of Delphi or Dodona, ceased to function from the date of the birth of Christ. If oracles were really a device of demons, then God would never have permitted even favorable oracles, even the Thamus legend, to be believed by good Christians such as Eusebius. "It is just possible," writes Fontenelle slyly, "that God may on rare occasions have given permission to some demons to animate idols. If that happened, then God had his reasons and they must be treated with profound respect." Nor is it true to say that the great oracles of antiquity ceased to operate once Christ appeared. There are many instances of oracles having been consulted and believed as late as CE 400.

Fontenelle concludes that oracles were not due to any supernatural agency but either to chance or to the wily stratagems of the temple staff. If the ancients themselves had taken oracles seriously, then Cicero would not have been allowed to throw doubts upon the divine revelation conveyed to man through the condition of calves' livers, the flight of birds or the eating habits of sacred hens. How came it that Augustus obtained so favorable an oracular answer when he desired to marry Livia? Was it not that the pythoness on that occasion "*savait faire sa cour*"? And was the great answer given to Alexander by the priests of Ammon due only to the fact that the Egyptian priests at Siwa could not pronounce Greek distinctly? "I like," writes Fontenelle, "to discover small chance origins for important events. It seems natural to me and worthy of the play of fortune."

The power of great conversationalists, as the genius of great actors, is not transmissible to future generations. Fontenelle was certainly a frivolous and superficial philosopher, but his skepticism had a lasting effect on the intellectuals of French society. It may be that he had no conception of the sublime and that he preferred the pretty to the beautiful, the sensational to the profound. "An author," he wrote, "whose works are agreeable is to be classed above an author whose works are admirable." That is a mean literary precept and one that might have done harm to French literature had not Voltaire arrived at the right moment to adjust the relative values of brilliance and seriousness. Yet the fact remains that Fontenelle for more than seventy years became the arbiter of literary elegance and, by destroying the pragmatic manner of the seventeenth century, did much to prepare the path for the *Encyclopédistes* and the Age of Reason.

Chapter 3

Setting Sun

(Louis XIV, 1700–1715)

———— • ◆ • ————

Europe as the center of the universe and France as the center of Europe—The glitter of Versailles—Louis XIV's misconceptions—The victories of Marlborough and Prince Eugene—The famine of 1709—France on verge of collapse—The tide of fortune then turns—The Tories hope by exploiting war-weariness to oust the Whigs—Abigail Hill succeeds in setting Queen Anne against the Marlboroughs—Godolphin dismissed and succeeded by Harley and Bolingbroke—Marlborough fights his last campaign and captures Bouchain—Negotiations for a separate peace are opened in Paris—Marlborough is dismissed—We abandon our allies and Eugene, on being deserted by the English, is defeated at Denain—The Treaty of Utrecht—Death of Queen Anne and accession of the Elector of Hanover as George I—Death of Louis XIV's son and grandsons—On death of the King the duc d'Orléans seizes the Regency—The virtues and defects of Louis XIV—His massive selfishness—Madame de Maintenon retires to Saint Cyr—Peter the Great's visit.

One

IT MAY SEEM irrelevant that at the outset of a study of the Age of Reason I should have devoted a whole chapter to Saint Simon, who, although a masterly diarist may appear to unsympathetic minds to have been an insignificant and silly little man. Yet I have learnt more about the period of Louis XIV from Saint Simon's querulous gossip and astringent analysis than from the official histories or the balanced eulogy of Voltaire. Europe, during the first half at least of the eighteenth century was accepted without question as the center of the universe; France, at least from 1660 to 1709, was the dominant Power in Europe; and Louis XIV in his sumptuous palace at Versailles was both feared and reverenced as the autocrat and symbol of France. Never since the days of the Roman Emperors had the rule of a single man been accepted with such acquiescence; never had the principle of monarchy and the Divine Right of Kings commanded such wide assent; and never again was any sovereign to create around his person a legend of equal awe, majesty, and splendor.

Night after night, the flicker of ten thousand candles would be reflected in the mirrors of saloons and galleries, throwing a radiance on tapestried or marbled walls, on painted ceilings, upon crowds of silk and velvet courtiers, upon the rubies and diamonds looped in their high headdresses, upon blue liveries and white wigs. From the garden terraces outside would come the sound of violins mingling with the splash of fountains and cascades. The King was about to enter. The courtiers, with only apparent casualness, would range themselves down each side of the gallery, still laughing and chattering among themselves. Suddenly the halberds of the guards would crash sharply upon the parquet of the anteroom and a hush would descend. The doors would be flung open and Louis XIV, followed at a carefully prescribed distance by the reigning mistress, the bastards, and the great officers of State would pass rapidly down the aisle, acknowledging the bows and curtsies with a slight but majestic inclination of the head—undeviating, formidable and superb.

The magic, until he was well over sixty years of age, never failed to work. It has often been asserted that the decline began when, on that disastrous November day of 1700, he accepted on behalf of his grandson the legacy of Spain and her undivided Empire. Admittedly, by so doing, he violated the treaties into which he had entered with

Austria, England, and the Dutch, and ran the risk of uniting against him the three Powers by whom France was encircled. But was not the risk worth taking in order to win so rich a prize? After all, the population of France at that date was twenty million, that of England no more than six million, and that of Holland but two million five hundred thousand. His army, he believed, was invincible; his marshals a match for any that the stupid English or the democratic Dutch or the decadent Austrians could hope to produce; and he was assisted by such able administrators and diplomatists as Torcy, Chammilard, and Beauvilliers, and such distinguished marshals as Boufflers and Villars. It might be true that the financial stability of France had been shaken by his Dutch wars and by the King's passion for building mighty palaces and sumptuous gardens, but financial stringency could be remedied. Had not Colbert within but a few years transformed the whole economic system and rendered France a prosperous commercial country, rapidly expanding overseas? What strength, what riches would accrue to him by acquiring as a satellite both Spain, the Indies and the two Sicilies! Certainly the risk was worth taking and prospects good.

Louis XIV possessed but little respect for finance and he constantly underestimated the strategic importance of sea power and the combined naval strength of England and Holland. In spite of what old Colbert had taught him, he failed to realize that the insular position and the ever-increasing wealth of England would, in spite of her comparatively small population, render her an obstinate antagonist. After all, Charles II had been his paid satellite and the House of Stuart, the legitimate reigning family, remained his subservient pensioners. Moreover England had but recently suffered a revolution, had even adopted a form of democratic constitution. She must therefore, in any conflict with a centralized monarchy, prove weak, hesitant, and disunited. How easy it would be to bribe the English politicians and to exploit the rivalry of their conflicting cabals for his own purposes! It was absurd to suppose that England would remain resolute and pugnacious under an illegitimate sovereign and exposed to the debilitating influence of democratic institutions. It was his duty to man and

God to crush these heretics and to render France, united with Spain, the unchallenged mistress of Europe and the world. How could these Protestants with their many sects and corrupt politicians, prevail against the monolithic Throne and Church of France? The House of Stuart and the Catholic religion could be reimposed on England and that tiresome little island again reduced to the position of a subsidized satellite.

The Great King in so believing may have been suffering from illusions: but as the event proved they were not entirely baseless illusions. He could scarcely have foreseen the military and diplomatic genius of Marlborough and Eugene. He certainly did not expect such catastrophes as Blenheim, Ramillies, Oudenarde and Turin or the fierce famine of 1709. Was he so foolish in expecting that sooner or later one of the political Cabals would exploit the war-weariness of the English public and be prepared to accept a peace of compromise?

Two

This book is not a political, still less a military, history: it is a gallery of portraits and a study of conflicting characters and successive states of mind. Those who wish to learn about the campaigns of Marlborough and Eugene can study Winston Churchill's tremendous biography of his ancestor. Suffice it to say that as a result of Blenheim, Louis XIV lost his best army, the whole of Bavaria, and the Rhineland. Turin lost him Italy. Ramillies deprived him of the Flanders fortresses. Oudenarde cost him Lille and opened the road to Paris.

To the French, these defeats seemed almost incredible. Nobody had the courage to tell Louis XIV of the Blenheim disaster and it fell to Madame de Maintenon, as Voltaire writes, to break the news to him "that he was no longer invincible." The name of Marlborough, whom Voltaire describes as "a man who did more damage to France than any man for centuries" became a name of fear. Even Voltaire, who was not addicted to praising Englishmen who did not happen to be Quakers, economists or philosophers, admits, in a quaint phrase, that Marlborough possessed astounding serenity of spirit "and what the English call *a cold head.*" Then in 1709 frost and famine descended upon France and the realm came to the very edge of bankruptcy and starvation. The King was obliged to sell his gold plate and the silver tables, mirrors and orange tubs that lined the great Gallery of Mirrors at Versailles. "We must," wrote Madame de Maintenon to her friend the Princesse des Ursins "regard all these happenings as the will of God. Our King was too triumphant; God humiliates him in order to save him." Madame de Maintenon, it must be remarked, was a pessimistic woman and as such something of a defeatist. "You think," she wrote to the Princesse des Ursins again, on April 29, 1709, "that we should perish rather than surrender. I think we should bow to superior force, accept the chastisement of God (who is obviously against us) and that the King owes more to his people than he does to himself. But it will not be *my* advice that will settle the issue between peace and war."

Louis XIV had by then realized that the French people were willing to make great sacrifices if only they could obtain a reasonable peace. He opened secret negotiations with the Dutch, proposing substantial concessions in return for a separate armistice or even peace. But the Dutch, elated by victory, asked for too much. At the same time an enormous bribe was offered to Marlborough if he would consent at least to suspend operations, and the Tories in London, who were already scheming to oust the Whigs, were sounded as to the terms on which they would agree to abandon the Grand Alliance. Both sides were, however, bound by previous pronouncements and assurances which they found it difficult to recant. English statesmen of both parties had frequently pledged themselves not to conclude peace so long as Philip V remained on the throne of Spain. To their surprise they discovered that the obstinate Spaniards actually preferred a Bourbon monarch to an Austrian Archduke and that an arduous peninsular campaign would be necessary if the Archduke were to be imposed by force upon the Spanish nation. They suggested that as a condition of peace Louis XIV should himself repudiate Philip V and even help to turn him out of Spain by force. Louis XIV as might have been foreseen rejected this suggestion with scorn. "If the war is to be continued," he protested, "I prefer to fight my enemies rather than my grandchildren." He also, in a mood of defiance, or of what Voltaire called "dangerous magnanimity," had placed himself in an awkward position from which it was difficult to retreat without loss of honor. On the death of James II at Saint Germain, he had publicly recognized the Old Pretender as "James III." His ministers had been opposed to this unnecessary challenge to English opinion. But his confessor, the Jesuit Le Tellier, and Madame de Maintenon, not realizing the granite strength of Protestant prejudices in England, thought that it would be possible to induce Queen Anne to designate her Catholic nephew as her successor and thereby to impose the true faith upon the English heretics. The peace feelers of 1709 thus proved abortive; thereafter the tide began to turn in favor of stricken France.

In Spain Marshal Vendôme drove the allies across the Tagus, surrounded and captured Lord Stanhope's army, and soundly defeated the Austrian Staremberg at Villa-Viciosa. The Austrian Emperor died in April 1711 and the Archduke on succeeding as Charles III became less intent on acquiring the throne of Spain. And, what was more important, Marlborough and his powerful supporter, the great Whig Minister Godolphin, lost the favor of Queen Anne, on whose support they had relied through all those years of glory.

Three

It all began when the Queen's devotion to the Duchess of Marlborough was undermined by the ingenious intrigues of the Tory Robert Harley assisted by one of the ladies of the bedchamber, Abigail Hill, Mrs. Masham. "Abigail," writes Winston Churchill, "was probably the smallest person who ever consciously attempted to decide, and in fact decided, the history of Europe." Queen Anne, who was then forty-five years of age and had eighteen times been deprived of an heir either by miscarriage or death, was in an ailing and nervous condition. It was not difficult for Abigail to persuade her that the time had come to free herself from the Duchess of Marlborough's fuss, bullying domination, and Whig ideas. The climax arrived when the Queen attended the public service of thanksgiving on the victory of Oudenarde. The Duchess, as mistress of the robes, had laid out the jewels appropriate for such an occasion: Mrs. Masham suggested that it was impertinent of the Duchess to dictate what Her Majesty should wear: the Queen entered her state coach in a foul temper and devoid of jewels. The Duchess, in view of her official status, was obliged to sit beside Her Majesty. It cannot have been an agreeable drive from Whitehall to the City. On mounting the steps of St. Paul's, the Queen said something harsh to the Duchess, who, being addicted to violent outbursts of temper, replied, in the hearing of the court and cathedral authorities, "Be quiet—not here." This incident, to Abigail's delight, transformed the ailing Queen's long affection into hatred. She turned away from the Marlboroughs and the Whigs and fell increasingly under the influence of the peace party led by Abigail, Harley, and the Tories.

At this stage, feeling that his influence was waning, the Duke of Marlborough committed one of the few errors of his career. In the autumn of 1709 he sought to buttress his position against the Tory cabal by obtaining the post of Captain General for life. The Queen refused this unprecedented appointment and the Tories profited by the incident to spread the rumor that the Duke was aiming at a military dictatorship, that he intended to force Queen Anne to abdicate, and that he was prolonging the war for purposes of his own greed and ambition. The Whigs, at this dangerous point in their fortunes, made the capital error of prosecuting a certain clergyman, a Dr. Sacheverell who on November 5, 1709, had preached a sermon in which he had attacked Godolphin as "that wily Volpone." Public opinion rallied to the foolish prelate's side and the Whigs for the first time became fully aware of their increasing unpopularity. Marlborough also got into trouble by refusing to promote Colonel Hill, the brother of Abigail. The attacks against him, directed by Harley, Swift and other pamphleteers, increased in violence and his known parsimony and avarice were exaggerated by the pamphleteers to suggest that he had been guilty of peculation. He wrote to the Queen regretting that his devoted service and their long friendship had not sufficed "to protect me against the malice of a bedchamber woman." But Abigail's intrigues had done their work.

On June 14, 1710, Marlborough's son-in-law, Lord Sunderland, was dismissed from office. On August 7 Godolphin himself was obliged to hand over the seals to Harley. At the General Election that followed in October the Whigs lost 270 seats and the Marlborough-Godolphin combination, which in the course of eight years had raised the country to the peak of glory, was destroyed. Harley became first minister and Henry St. John, later to become infamous as Lord Bolingbroke, became Secretary of State. For a while Marlborough was retained as Commander in Chief "to struggle on, like a weary baited bear, chained to his post." The Tories continued to defame him and to blacken his repute. Henry St. John in particular did everything he could to deny him supplies and to deprive him of any further successes. Winston Churchill has described his conduct as "exceeding in malice and meanness anything which is known—and it is a wide field—in the relations between a British Government and a British General." Meanwhile in Flanders the French had remained on the defensive awaiting Marlborough's expected dismissal from his command. But the mighty general, although defamed at home and obstructed at every turn by his government, was not so readily disposed of. In this tenth and last campaign (which many military historians have acclaimed as the most brilliant of his whole career) he deceived Marshal Villars by a feint to the west of Arras, then swung thirty-six miles to the east, broke the defensive line which the French had so laboriously constructed, and captured the key fortress of Bouchain.

Harley and St. John, leaders of the Tory party, which, as they so repeatedly affirmed represented "the gentlemen of England," had already decided to make a separate peace behind the backs of their allies. Mathew Prior was sent on a mission to Paris, possessed of full powers, signed by Queen Anne herself, to negotiate this perfidy.

Four

On the last day of 1711 the Queen wrote to Marlborough relieving him of his command. "This," remarked Louis XIV, "will do for us all that we desire." Eugene was chosen as Commander in Chief of the allied forces, the English army being under the command of the Duke of Ormonde with secret orders not to fight. Eugene captured Quesnoy and was about to advance on Paris when Ormonde had to inform him that the English had already concluded a secret armistice with the French and were unable to cooperate any further. Twelve thousand English troops were, to their shame, withdrawn from the front. Thus abandoned, Eugene was defeated at Denain and Marshal Villars was able to recapture Douai and Bouchain. "Nothing," writes Winston Churchill, "in the history of civilized people has surpassed this black treachery."

On January 29, 1712, the French, English, Austrian, and Dutch plenipotentiaries met in conference at Utrecht. The Treaty of Utrecht, between France, England, Holland, Portugal, Prussia, and Savoy was signed on April 11, 1713. Austria held out for a few months longer but in March following, having been abandoned by all her allies, was obliged also to negotiate and sign a peace at Rastadt. The Dutch were accorded their barrier fortresses. The Austrian Emperor was eventually compensated for losing his claim to the throne of Spain and the Indies, by the cession of Lombardy, Sardinia, and Naples. England received Gibraltar, Port Mahon, Newfoundland, Nova Scotia, the right, known as the "Asiento," to conduct the slave trade with the Spanish colonies; and the abandonment by Louis XIV of his recognition of the Old Pretender as the legitimate King of England and of his support of the House of Stuart. But the British public regarded these as but minor rewards for all Marlborough's tremendous victories.

The Marlboroughs, fearing that Harley and the Tories might carry their revenge to the point of impeachment, exiled themselves from England and for a while settled at Frankfurt and Antwerp. On August 1, 1714, Queen Anne died. The Elector of Hanover, under the title of King George I, was brought to England on September 18. He was not destined to win the affections of his new subjects. He loathed England and, perhaps with some justification, despised English politicians. He was, in the words of Winston Churchill, "a narrow, vindictive, humdrum German martinet, with dull brains, coarse tastes, crude appetites, a commonplace and ungenerous ruler and a sluggish and incompetent commander in the field." He could not speak English and was unable to understand the schoolboy Latin in which his new ministers sought to communicate with him. But at least he was a Protestant, and that, to the English people, was a cause of comfort.

A new Parliament was elected and the Whigs were returned to power, retaining their dominance for the next forty years. Marlborough was exonerated from the charges that had been brought against him and returned to his great palace at Blenheim, which was then nearing completion. Harley, who had by Queen Anne been created Earl of Oxford, was sent to the Tower of London. Bolingbroke bolted to France where for a while he took service under the Old Pretender. On May 28, 1716, the Duke of Marlborough had a stroke from which he never completely recovered. He died on June 16, 1722, at the age of seventy-two. His duchess survived him for twenty-two years.

The turn of fortune which had enabled France to recover from the disasters of 1709 may have rescued her from complete catastrophe, but did not enable her to recover her dominance of Europe. Even Madame de Maintenon, that grim pessimist, had recovered something of her confidence. "What glory," she had written to the Princesse des Ursins, on November 30, 1711, "for our King to have sustained war for ten years against all Europe, undergone every misfortune that could be inflicted, experienced a famine and a sort of plague that carried off millions of souls, and to see it all finish in a peace which keeps the Spanish monarchy in the family and reestablishes a Catholic King upon his throne." She was mistaken in supposing that Queen Anne or the British people would ever consent to the restoration of the Catholic Stuarts, and they, to do them credit, refused, when secretly approached, to gain a Crown at the price of abjuring their faith.

Yet destiny, which had been so lavish to Louis XIV during the first sixty-six years of his reign, had further cruel blows in reserve. In April 1711 his son the Dauphin died. On February 18, 1712, his grandson, the new Dauphin also died, as did his brother the duc de Bretagne. This left as sole heir in the direct Bourbon line of succession a sickly little boy of two, who eventually reigned as Louis XV. After him would come Philippe d' Orléans, Louis XIV's nephew, descended from Gaston d' Orléans, brother of Louis XIII. The court and public regarded this rapid sequence of mysterious deaths as so inexplicable that they became convinced that they had all been poisoned by Philippe d' Orléans in his ambition to secure the throne in his own branch of the family. This was certainly an unjust suspicion, but it was believed by Madame de Maintenon and perhaps even by the King himself. He therefore decided to legitimize his two bastards by Madame de Montespan, the duc du Maine and the comte de Toulouse, and by his will he provided that his infant successor should be placed under a Council of Regency, of which the duc d'Orléans as the eldest surviving male of the family, should be chairman but watched and assisted by the two bastards. In a codicil to that will, moreover, he appointed the duc du Maine as Governor of the infant King. On the death of Louis XIV Philippe d' Orléans induced the parliament of Paris to declare the will invalid, deprived the bastards (much to the almost fiendish delight of Saint Simon) of their legitimacy and their semi-royal status, and assumed the undivided powers of Regent for himself.

Louis XIV died at Versailles on September 1, 1715, from gangrene of the leg. He was in his seventy-seventh year and had reigned for seventy-two years.

Five

The death of Louis XIV, perhaps the most acceptable autocrat that ever lived, marked the end of the unquestioning assumption that the best form of human governance is the rule of a single man. For almost seventy years he had mesmerized the world by his grandeur. As the clouds gathered round his sunset, the beams of his glory failed to illumine or to warm. As his coffin rumbled on its way from Versailles to St. Denis, the young François Arouet, son of Maî-tre Arouet, the worthy solicitor of Ninon de l'Enclos and of the Saint Simon family, at that time a young man of twenty, watched with a cynical smile its passage through the Paris suburbs. The more enter-prising hucksters, foreseeing that such a pageant would attract a large concourse, had erected tents and booths along the route, in which they provided sausages, melons, brioches, and cups of chocolate and wine. The crowd giggled and danced as Louis XIV, preceded and fol-lowed by rows of gilded coaches, by squadrons of musketeers and cav-alry, by the courtiers and ministers in their velvet carriages, by cardi-nals and bishops, bumped along. François Arouet, who had not by then adopted the name of Voltaire, was much amused.

He was too intelligent not to realize that Louis XIV was a remark-able man or that during his long reign France had achieved, if not the conquest of the Old and New World, then at least the supremacy of Europe in the graces and the arts of life. Much as he disliked the sys-tem, and the power it accorded to arbitrary impulse in the place of known and accepted law, or to the dogmatic tyranny of the Church and the Jesuits, he never denied that it possessed unexampled mag-nificence. He was enraged only when despotism fell into the hands of less intelligent men.

Voltaire admitted that, in his way, Louis XIV was a man of genius. He may, as the King himself confessed when on his deathbed, have allowed his subjects to starve when spending millions on his palaces and his favorites: he may, for the sake of glory, have embarked on unnecessary and finally on one disastrous, war. But the majesty with which he maintained his own legend appeared to Voltaire (who liked grandeur and who worshipped success) as something phenomenal. As indeed it was.

The Whig interpretation of history, by which we have all been molded, has taught us to regard the monocracy of Louis XIV as some-thing as childish in theory as the tale of Cinderella, and in practice as iniquitous as the tyranny of Tiberius or the ravages of Tamerlane. We are apt to forget that under the enlightened and not wholly rigid rule of this great man, invention and taste expanded as never before, since the distant days of fifth-century Athens. It was his encouragement of art and science which to this day has rendered Paris the most beautiful city on this earth and the intellectual capital of the whole world. It is unintelligent to dismiss Louis XIV as an anachronism arrayed in velvet and ermine, subduing lesser mortals by the glance of his terrifying eyes and the resolute sulkiness of jaw and lip, or as an extravagant hedonist surrendering to the strong physical lusts, by which all the Bourbons, with the exception of Louis XVI and Louis XVIII (poor impotents), were afflicted, and driven only by a passion for display. He was much more than that.

Saint Simon, who disliked him personally, could not but admire the unsurpassed skill with which he fulfilled his function. "Never," he writes, "has any Prince possessed to so high a degree the art of reigning." He admired his unwavering dignity and that "terrifying majesty of bearing which came so naturally to him." He admired his capacity for regular hard work and the extreme punctuality with which he carried out his many duties. He admired what he called "the mechanism" that he had invented for his courtiers, providing them with intricate ceremonial functions and thus diverting their attention from politics or the affairs of state. The pattern of servitude that he imposed may appear to our minds degrading. Yet when we were schoolboys we took it as quite natural that those who excelled in games or became prefects or monitors should be granted privileges, which although utterly trivial in practice, were esteemed and sought for as symbols of distinction. It was at Versailles regarded as a high honor to be permitted to hand the King his shirt in the morning or to hold the candle for him when he retired to bed. Elderly ladies of the court would protest venomously if anybody not possessing the right to sit on a footstool was granted a footstool by royal favor. Endless quarrels arose over the right, when in church, to kneel on a square of cloth laid on the marble pavement; on the right to have both panels of a double door opened for one by the lackeys; on whether one was privileged to attend the King's smaller levees or only to enter with the others when the doors were opened to the crowd. Perhaps the most absurd of all these distinctions and badges was what they used to call "*le pour.*" When the King went to Marly, only the most favored of his courtiers were asked to accompany him and it became a matter of intense preoccupation to know whether on arrival one had, or had not, been granted "*le pour.*" What did this so desired distinction amount to? It was regarded as infinitely more glorious if the master of the household had written in chalk upon one's bedroom door "*Pour M. le duc de Soubise,*" or merely "*Le duc de Soubise.*" By such tiny points of differentiation did the King impose upon his courtiers the illusion that they were in fact playing an honorable and useful part in public life.

Saint Simon again was constantly impressed by the immense politeness of Louis XIV, who was only very rarely ruffled by ill temper, and who could mark the slightest gradations of favor or disfavor, of approval or resentment, by the raising of an eyebrow or by a passing look. He expressly records that the King would never pass a woman, not even a housemaid at Marly, without making a slight bow or raising his hat. He had an astonishing memory for faces, knowing by sight every single member of his court, and noticing immediately if they committed the crime of absenting themselves without good cause, or the even graver crime of stopping a night or two in Paris. "I do not see him," he would remark of such an absentee and this comment was regarded as no less fatal than being dismissed from a regiment or asked to resign from a club. Saint Simon, with his finicky, fussy, mind, was naturally delighted by the intricacy of this fairy tale. But his reverence for the mesmeric genius of Louis XIV did not in the least blind him to his defects. Foremost among these he placed his overwhelming egoism. Not only did the King take it for granted that his slightest whim was law, but he took an embarrassingly contemptuous view of lesser mortals. Having himself been denied by Mazarin and his mother any serious education, he disapproved of culture, and was angered by those whom he felt to be either morally or intellectually superior to himself. So precise was he in all his arrangements that he would never agree to alter his timetable for the convenience of others. However ill a courtier might feel, whatever might be the sufferings of his mistresses and their attendant ladies, they were obliged to be present when wanted and in full court dress. Saint Simon describes in acid detail the occasion when his granddaughter, the duchesse de Bourgogne—one of the few people of whom he was really fond—had a miscarriage owing to his having forced her, when in an advanced state of pregnancy, to accompany the court from Versailles to Marly and then on to Fontainebleau. The doctors had warned him that she was not in a fit state to travel but he had petulantly silenced their advice. Soon after their arrival at Fontainebleau (and journeys in those days, even in the *carosses du Roi*, were anything but smooth) the duchesse was taken ill. The King at the time was on the terrace teasing the ancient carp which to this day slumber in the depths of the central pond. The duchesse de Lude was seen hurrying from the castle and the King advanced to meet her. She whispered something to him and he turned and rejoined the courtiers who were still grouped around the central pond. "The duchesse de Bourgogne," he informed them sulkily, "has had a miscarriage." Since this meant the loss of a possible heir to the throne, the courtiers expressed dismay and horror. The King, realizing that his selfishness had been perhaps responsible for the catastrophe, lost his temper. "Good gracious," he exclaimed. "She had a miscarriage because it was fated that she should. And I refuse to have my journeys, or anything I want to do, upset by what doctors or old women may say." "This outburst," narrates Saint Simon, "was followed by a silence in which one could have heard an ant walking; we cast down our eyes and scarcely dared to breathe. Everyone was dumbfounded, even the gardeners standing there and the workmen by the pool. The silence lasted more than a quarter of an hour. The King broke it eventually, leaning on the balustrade of the pool. He began to speak about a carp." This incident convinced Saint Simon that he had been correct in assuming that Louis XIV never thought of anybody else but himself and that "his only ultimate object was his personal convenience." It was this gigantic egoism that persuaded him that his people existed only in so far as they could minister to his own glory and blinded him to the fact that he himself was but the first servant of the State. For all his sense of duty he had little sense of service and, strong and gifted though he was, he scarcely deserves the epithet of great. Even during that last ghastly fortnight, when he lay in his gigantic bed while the gangrene spread through his entire frame, he does not seem to have had even a glimpse of reality. He admitted in his last hours that he had been too fond of war during his life and too fond of architecture. It did not seem to dawn on him that he had also been too fond of himself.

Six

And what about Madame de Maintenon? When the King lapsed into a coma, she ordered her carriage and drove away from the great palace to Saint Cyr. The King recovered consciousness for a space and asked for her. She was hastily summoned to return. Yet when he again lapsed into unconsciousness she again made off to Saint Cyr and she was there when he died, "There is," wrote Saint Simon gleefully, "no more to fear from that old fairy now almost eighty years of age; her powerful and pernicious wand is broken; she has reverted to her former position as the widow Scarron."

Madame de Maintenon did not deserve such slander. She was, as Madame de Sévigné described her, "straightness itself." To the King in his declining years she was a rock of support: "Your Solidity" he would call her affectionately. She provided him with the one pleasure that he had never experienced in his life, the pleasure of domestic affection. Yet all her life she had lived in false situations. She had started as the wife at the age of sixteen of the cripple Scarron, a writer of scurrilous verse. It was only gradually that she crept into society through visiting the Anet circle. It was there that she met Madame de Montespan who had her appointed governess to the bastard boys she had borne to Louis XIV, the duc du Maine and the comte de Toulouse. She adored these children and particularly the duc du Maine who was ailing and a cripple. Eventually she married the King when she was fortyeight and he was forty-five, but the marriage was always kept a secret. Her first marriage to Scarron was never consummated; the children to whom she devoted the best years of her life were the bastards of another woman; and although she married the Great King, she was never openly accorded the dignities of that position. Nor were her relations with Louis XIV always easy. She was bored by his passion for punctuality and timetables. "We shall all," she remarked to her niece, "have to die symmetrically." She hated drafts whereas he was a fresh air fiend; on entering her apartments he would have all the windows flung wide open. She shivered in subservient silence. She claimed, and perhaps rightly, that she did not interfere in politics, although her enemies have accused her of influencing the King in such matters as the persecution of the Protestants and the Jansenists and in the disgrace of Fénélon. She certainly believed that she had been entrusted by Providence with the mission of bringing the King to repentance and inducing him to lead a life of virtue. It was not an easy task. "You have no idea," she wrote to her niece, "how difficult it is to amuse a man who is not amusable." Their domestic life was grim.

Her real passion and success in life was Saint Cyr, which she built and founded as a seminary in which two hundred and fifty young ladies of good family should receive an excellent education and a dowry on marriage. Being a schoolteacher by nature and predilection, she adored Saint Cyr and would when at Versailles spend most of her days there, supervising the classes, and instructing the pupils in their duties towards God and marriage. It was at Saint Cyr that she spent her final years of widowhood. She dismissed her establishment at Versailles, presented the furniture of her apartments to her maids and footmen, discarded all her finery, and severed herself completely from the court and the politicians. She burnt all the King's letters to her in the fireplace of her room. Surrounded by the nuns of Saint Cyr she died peacefully on April 16, 1719, at the age of eighty-four. She was buried in the chapel of Saint Cyr. In 1794, her coffin was broken open, her body stripped naked, a rope put round her neck, and her corpse dragged out into the garden and thrown into a ditch. Her remains were later reburied in the Chapel where she now rests.

Before she died she had received a curious visit, which must have convinced her that the fame of her strange destiny had spread far beyond the confines of France. On June 11, 1717, she was visited by the Tsar of Russia. On learning that he was anxious to see her she retired to bed, not desiring to face the fatigue of any more ceremonial receptions.

"The Tsar," she wrote to her niece Madame de Caylus, "came here at seven. He made the interpreter ask me whether I was ill. I said I was. He then asked me what was the nature of my illness. I answered 'Extreme old age and a not very robust constitution.' He did not know what to say to that and his interpreter did not seem to hear me very well. His visit was very short. He is still somewhere about the building but I am not sure where. I forgot to say that the Tsar got them to draw the curtains of my bed so that he could look at me. You can well believe he must have enjoyed the sight."

A strange picture assuredly of the old woman flat in her little convent bed and the giant Peter staring at her silently, holding apart the curtains with his vast möujïk hands. The picture of a fading past, confronted with a colossal symbol of the future.

Chapter 4

The Emergence of Muscovy
(Peter the Great, 1672–1725)

——•◆•——

The Duke of Muscovy—His birth and childhood—His half-sister Sophia seizes power—He escapes to Preobrajenskoe—His marriage to Eudoxia Lapouhine and her unhappy end—Sophia is ousted and he is proclaimed Tsar—His visit to Archangel and passion for building ships—First Turkish War and capture of Azov—His visit to Europe—He returns to Moscow and suppresses the Streltzy or jannissaries—He meets Augustus II of Poland and they plot the partition of Sweden—He is defeated by Charles XII at Narva in humiliating circumstances—He reconstitutes his army and utterly defeats Charles XII at Poltava—Russia thereby gains mastery of the Baltic—The Second Turkish War—He is surrounded and barely escapes capture on the Pruth—His economic and administrative reforms—His cronies Menchikov and Romodanovski—He founds St. Petersburg—His visit to France in 1717—The Treaty of Nystadt with Sweden—Was he insane?—His wild visions and mystifications—His drunkenness—His sadism—His wife the Empress Catherine—His legacy to Russia and the world.

One

WALKING IN THE royal park at Brussels the enquiring traveler, if he diverge but a few yards from the graveled alleys of pleached lime, will come across a hollow among the shrubberies which is now used as a midden in which the gathered leaves are rotted down for leaf mold. In this declivity there is a small stone bearing a Latin inscription. It tells the enquiring traveler that on this spot, the Duke of Muscovy, having drunk heavily, was violently sick. What is interesting about this memorial is that the Belgians at that date should have regarded the public vomiting of a reigning, even if barbarous, prince as so odd as to merit being recorded for posterity. It is strange also that, even after Poltava, they should have styled him Duke of Muscovy and not given him his correct title of Tsar of All the Russias.

Indeed, until the second half of the eighteenth century, most Europeans had scarcely heard of Russia, regarding the Duke of Muscovy as some remote Tartar chieftain, as some semi-mongolian Khan. In the eight volumes of Louis XIV's dispatches for the year 1697, the year in which the young Tsar first visited Europe, Peter is only mentioned once, and then wholly incidentally. Those merchants who had penetrated as far as Moscow would tell stories in the London coffee houses or in the cafés of the Palais Royal, about Ivan the Terrible and his massacres, about wolves and bears, or describe the Kremlin with its fantastic churches, its bulbous cupolas, and its high Chinese walls. Even to this day the older buildings in the Kremlin suggest the palace of some minor oriental potentate. The small and ill-lit chambers are connected with each other by low passages which twist and turn in order to delude the assassin or to impede the access of armed bands. The sheen of mosaics, the occasional flicker of candles upon the gold and jewels of blackened ikons, give to these huddled habitations a byzantine, an ecclesiastical, semblance. We seem to hear priests and monks intoning in adjoining chapels; their litanies are pierced by sudden screams or ululations; in our nostrils linger the smell of incense and the smell of blood.

It was in such an atmosphere that Peter the Great was born and nurtured. His father, Alexis Mihailovitch, married a Miloslavski as his first wife. She bore him five sons and eight daughters. Three of the sons died in infancy and the remaining two, Feodor and Ivan, were mentally deficient. On the death of his first wife, Alexis decided to marry again. Since no European ruler would at that date consider allowing his daughter to marry a Muscovite, it had become the custom for one hundred girls of suitable age to be collected in the terem, or harem, of the Kremlin where the Tsar, accompanied by a doctor, would examine their naked bodies in every detail and select the healthiest. Peter's mother, it seems, was not subjected to this unromantic scrutiny. Alexis had already set his eyes on Natalia Narishkine, the ward of his favorite, Artamon Matvieev, who had married a Miss Hamilton and whose home was conducted in a comparatively European way. The marriage took place on January 22, 1671, and Peter was born on May 30, 1672. The place of his birth has never been known and, owing to the fact that he was physically and mentally so utterly different from his half-brothers and half-sisters, the legend arose that he was not in fact the child of Alexis, but some substitute or bastard. He himself, when in his cups, would occasionally proclaim that he had never known the identity of his real father.

Alexis died in 1674 when Peter was but two years old. A struggle for power, which lasted for thirteen years, then arose between the family of Alexis' first wife, the Miloslavskis, and the family of Peter's mother, the Narishkines. Feodor, the rightful heir of Alexis by his first marriage, died in 1682. His brother Ivan was blind and mad. The Narishkine party thereupon proclaimed Peter, then a lad of ten, as the legitimate successor to his father. For a few weeks he was recognized by the majority of the nobles or boyars; he was surrounded by his mother's family and treated with ceremonial respect; on the rare occasions when he was allowed to leave the Kremlin he was escorted by dwarfs holding high screens around him, so that he should neither see, nor be seen by, the outer world. Meanwhile his half-sister Sophia, then a clever buxom woman of twenty-eight, was determined to rid herself of the Narishkine clan. With the assistance of her lover, Vasili Galitzine, she persuaded the Miloslavskis and their supporters to declare the election of Peter null and void and to proclaim herself as Regent for her brother, Ivan. She at the same time suborned the Streltzy, who were the jannissaries or praetorian guard of Muscovy. Arrayed in their blue, and green and red caftans, with their yellow boots and embroidered fur hats, they burst into the Kremlin and cut the throats of all the Narishkines to be found in the corridors and rooms. Peter and his mother managed to escape from the Kremlin to the Sloboda or foreign quarter of Moscow, then inhabited by Scottish, German and Huguenot merchants and artisans. They were then exiled to Preobrajenskoe and remained there for the seven years that the Regency of Sophia endured.

Peter at that date was eleven years of age and could neither read nor write. He was a nervous and even timid boy and throughout his life his memory was haunted by the screams of his Narishkine uncles and cousins when their throats were being cut by the Streltzy in the Kremlin passages. This experience left him with a dislike of Moscow, a horror of the Kremlin, and the resolve one day to exact revenge upon the Streltzy for these murders. He was subject to fits and to the day of his death he was tortured by night fears. He always refused to sleep alone and, if no wife or mistress were available, he would take an orderly to bed with him, pillowing his head upon the man's stomach and clinging to him throughout the night with his hands. If the orderly moved, snored, or gave way to internal regurgitations, he was soundly flogged when morning dawned.

At Preobrajenskoe his mother managed to obtain for him the services of a Dutch tutor, Franz Timmermann, who taught him how to read and write and do simple arithmetic. He developed very slowly. His passion was never for intellectual studies or reflection but for manual industry. He became an efficient carpenter and even studied the elements of dentistry, a science which made a strong appeal to his sadistic tastes. At Preobrajenskoe he found the wreck of an English hulk, and with the help of two Dutch seamen, Brandt and Kort, he repaired the boat and launched it on the lake at Pereiaslav. His companions were almost exclusively of humble origin, the sons of cooks and grooms and sailors. They became his favorites and eventually his Ministers of State. He would group them into companies and amuse himself by organizing mock battles between the land contingents and the frigate that he had built for himself out of the old English hulk. He had by then grown into a gigantic adolescent with wild eyes and powerful limbs.

On January 27, 1682, his mother forced him to marry Eudoxia Lapouhine, the daughter of a noble. She became the mother of the ill-fated Tsarevitch Alexis. Peter quickly became tired of her and when in England he wrote ordering her to enter a convent. He refused (since he was very mean in money matters) to allow her any subsistence allowance. She remained incarcerated in this convent for twenty years. At one time during her imprisonment she fell in love with a Major Glebov, who was convalescing from illness in the convent's precincts. He was arrested, tortured, and impaled; he endured twenty-eight hours of atrocious agony before at last he died. She was sent off to a monastery on Lake Ladoga where she was whipped regularly by the monks. On the death of Peter she was removed by the Empress Catherine, her successor, and cast into a dungeon full of rats. She was released on the accession of her grandson Peter II and even attended his coronation. But she had lost all grip on life and thereafter voluntarily retired to another convent, where she died. It was not a happy marriage.

Meanwhile in Moscow Sophia and Galitzine had been ruling, not inefficiently, with the support of the Streltzy. By 1689, however, the latter were showing signs of disaffection. The opposition boyars then started a pro-Peter movement under the slogan, "Down with Galitzine!" Sophia and her lover became alarmed and retired to a monastery outside Moscow. From there they managed for a space to regain control and to execute some of the leaders of the Streltzy mutiny. Sophia thereupon proclaimed herself, no longer Regent for her sick brother, but Autocrat of Russia in her own right.

On August 7, 1689, news was brought to Peter at Preobrajenskoe that Sophia had sent men to murder him and that they were already on the way. Dressed only in his nightgown he escaped from his hut and hid in the woods. His friends joined him the next morning, bringing food and clothes. They urged him that his only hope was to depose Sophia, execute Galitzine, and himself assume the crown. He was undecided and frightened; but his supporters persuaded him to place himself openly at the head of the anti-Galitzine movement. Sophia realized her danger and appealed to the Streltzy for their support; they only agreed to assist her if she would hand over to them her second favorite Chaklovityi. This wretched man revealed, under torture, the sinister plots of Galitzine and Sophia against the jannissaries and the army. Galitzine was exiled, his accomplices put to death, and Sophia interned in a convent. Peter returned to Moscow and was proclaimed joint Tsar with his idiot half-brother. At first he refused to take charge of the government, leaving everything to the patriarch Joachim and to those of the Narishkine family who had managed to survive the holocaust.

He was, as has been said, a slow-growing plant. It was not until he was twenty-four that he suddenly developed the daemonic energy which rendered his autocracy the most dynamic, as well as the most despotic tyranny that since the days of Alexander the Great the world had seen. For the seven years that followed the coup d'état of 1689 he spent his days and nights with his chosen cronies and in the elaboration and enjoyment of his curious hobbies and games. His two most constant companions were Patrick Gordon, a Scotsman from Aberdeen, and Francois Lefort, the son of a Geneva apothecary and a man of unbridled licentiousness and considerable cunning. Lefort built for himself a house outside Moscow where he would sumptuously entertain members of the Sloboda, or foreign colony. Peter was not attracted by polite society; what he enjoyed were orgies. All his life he preferred living in log cabins and during those years he spent most of his time in his old hut at Preobrajenskoe, sailing boats upon the lake, and organizing his cronies into battalions to fight sham battles and to conduct sham sieges. Fireworks, for which he had a lasting love, played a great part in these games, which did not pass without casualties. The most lasting result of this schoolboy jousting was the creation of the two regiments of guards, the Preobrajenskis and Seminovoski.

In 1693 he obtained his mother's permission to visit Archangel and it was there that he first saw the sea and gazed at the great vessels tied up along the wharves. It was there also that he acquired his passion for seafaring people and for naval construction. He dressed as a Dutch sailor and spent most of his nights drinking with bargees in the quayside taverns. His love of mystification and make-believe induced him, once he had acquired a boat or two at Archangel, to appoint his friends admirals and vice admirals, himself choosing the subordinate title of captain.

In 1694 his mother died and Peter decided that the time had come for him to abandon his charades and to take some direct part in public life. He thought it would be an excellent idea to make war upon the Turks and to capture from them the harbor of Azov on the Gulf of Taganrog. He collected a few boats and a rabble army of 31,000 men which he placed under the command of Golovine, Gordon, and Lefort. He himself took the rank of captain in a grenadier regiment. This first campaign was a humiliating fiasco. Peter, to whom nothing ever seemed impossible, was galvanized into activity. He was possessed to a superhuman degree of the Slav qualities of resilience and ruthlessness, and was determined to redeem this disgrace. By 1697 he had managed by working at the boats himself and by a liberal application of the knout to those of his fellow workers who flagged or muddled, to launch upon the Don a fleet of twenty-three galleys. The Turks, not unnaturally, were taken by surprise by this galvanic achievement. The fortress of Azov surrendered on July 17.

Peter now felt himself free to embark upon a project which Lefort had for long been urging upon him. He decided to complete his education by visiting Europe. It was the strangest tour that any Prince had ever undertaken outside the pages of the *Arabian Nights*.

Two

The Muscovites in those days were sufficiently old-fashioned to consider that to abandon the soil of Holy Russia was both dangerous and disloyal. Moreover, once it was generally known that the young Tsar had left the country, troubles might well break out among the Streltzy or the boyars might start plotting again. Thus Peter, who in any case delighted in disguises and stratagems, announced that an Embassy was being dispatched to Europe under Lefort as Ambassador in Chief with the task of securing the assistance of the Great Powers against the Turks. Lefort was accompanied by a large personal staff, including eleven attachés, seven pages, fifteen valets, two goldsmiths, six musicians, and four dwarfs. Attached to this retinue was a non-commissioned officer of the Preobrajenskoe regiment, styling himself Peter Mihailoff, who was in reality the Tsar. With his usual inconsequence he did not maintain this disguise with any consistency. At one moment he would appear as Duke of Muscovy, as Tsar of all the Russias: at the next he would retreat into the anonymity of a sergeant in the guards. Much confusion and some resentment was thereby caused.

The mission met with a chilly reception at Riga, which was then in Swedish territory, but were welcomed with amusement and some courtesy at Mittau. Peter decided to abandon his diplomatic companions and took a boat alone to Königsberg. He passed through Berlin without tarrying, but at the castle of Koppenbrügge, in the province of Nassau, he stayed with the Electress of Brandenburg, the future Queen Sophia Charlotte of Prussia. She had spent two years at the Court of Versailles, having once been intended as a bride for the duc de Bourgogne and had an alert, vivid and enquiring mind. She was the first European to recognize that, under the appearance of an unkempt bear, Peter possessed a streak of the extraordinary; it might be insanity, but it might also be genius. He was shy in the presence of these elegant women. When addressed, he covered his face with his hands and muttered, "I have not the gift of speaking." When asked politely whether he enjoyed hunting, he raised his huge carpenter hands aloft and exclaimed, "I am a workman. I have no time for sport." The attachés whom Lefort had brought with him were invited to dance with the ladies of the Court. They were so perplexed by the feel of whalebone stays, which they had never before encountered, that they concluded that German women possessed an entirely distinct type of ossature, their ribs being outside the flesh and arranged in an unfamiliar order. The table manners of the Muscovite diplomatists were so atrocious that most Europeans came to regard them as little more than animals. Nor were they in the very least house trained.

From Germany, Peter traveled to Holland, settling for a few days at Zaandam, from which village had come some of his old sailor friends of Preobrajenskoe and Archangel days. He then moved to Amsterdam, where he worked in the shipbuilding yards of the East Indies Company. He dressed as a Dutch boatman and the hut in which he lived is still preserved. Lefort and the Embassy staff lodged separately and in grander style. Occasionally Peter would have a day off from the building yards and take his compatriots with him to see the sights. He had no interest whatsoever in art or literature or history. What fascinated him always were technical inventions, appliances, or skills. He continued the practice of dentistry, learnt the art of engraving, and inspected hospitals and even schools. On one occasion, when visiting Dr. Boerjaave's academy of anatomy, some members of his staff expressed disgust at an exposed cadaver. Resenting such delicacy, Peter forced them to bite the thighs of the corpse. This was typical of his lack of consideration for his dependants and ministers. It must indeed have been an ordeal to serve Peter. It entailed constant beatings and submission to those ghastly practical jokes, in which autocrats have always delighted to indulge. Yet if his servitors succeeded in avoiding imprisonment, torture, and execution, they were able to amass vast fortunes and to found princely families. For men of tough ambition, the penalties and humiliations were matched by rich rewards.

In January 1698 Peter crossed to England, where he spent three months. He was received by William III at Kensington Palace and lodged for some weeks at Sayes' Court, the house of John Evelyn, from where, dressed in workman's clothes, he labored daily in the dockyard at Deptford. To someone as fussy as John Evelyn regarding his possessions and gardens this was by no means an agreeable tenancy. One of his servants wrote to him that the house "was full of people and right nasty." The Russians were not cleanly, did damage to the furniture and paneling, and amused themselves by trundling their master in a wheelbarrow through the holly hedges which Evelyn had planted with such symmetry. "I went to Deptford," Evelyn noted in his diary for June 9, 1689, "to view how miserably the Tzar of Muscovy had left my house after three months making it his Court." Sir Christopher Wren and George London, the King's gardener, were sent down to make an estimate of the destruction caused. Evelyn was accorded £107.7.0 for damages to the house and £55 for damages to the garden.

In April 1698 Peter was again in Holland on his way to Vienna, having failed to be taken seriously by any of the European Courts or to persuade any ministers to consider his scheme for a crusade against the Turks. On reaching Vienna he was granted an audience with the Emperor, who avoided all mention of the Turkish crusade and merely talked about the weather and the condition of the roads. Peter was never a linguist nor did he ever speak or understand any foreign language, with the exception of a few words of bargee Dutch. The prim, pompous, conventional Court of Vienna was even more shocked by his eccentricity than had been the citizens of Amsterdam or the dockers of Deptford. They were outraged when, at an official dinner offered to the Ambassador Lefort, Peter insisted on standing behind his friend's chair in the livery of a footman. The Austrians concluded that the Duke of Muscovy must be mad and that in any case his behavior was too rough and violent to be endured. His diplomatic experiment, for these and other reasons, was not in any way a success. His utter ignorance on all matters other than carpentry, shipbuilding, and dentistry prevented them from taking him with any seriousness. Yet he had profited much from this his first journey to Europe. Not only had he acquired practical experience of industry and science, but he had all the time been recruiting experts in technical crafts and engaging them at high salaries to come to Russia and to teach the Russians the elements of engineering, naval construction, mining, building, and the manufacture of munitions. He desired before everything to create for himself an army and navy sufficiently trained and equipped, not merely to crush the Cossacks and Tartars who threatened his eastern frontiers, but also to stand up to the assaults of modern European armies.

From Vienna he had intended to continue his journey as far as Venice. After all, he reflected, the Turks and the Venetians had for centuries been at loggerheads and the Adriatic Republic, whatever the western Powers might say, would certainly join in his crusade. Yet before he could test the reality of this dream, news reached him that the Streltzy had mutinied. He hurried home to deal with this revolt.

Three

On arrival in Moscow Peter found that the early reports of a revolution, presumed to have been engineered by his half-sister Sophia with the help of the Streltzy, was exaggerated. It is true that the reactionary elements were already grumbling about Peter's adoption of foreign clothes, cronies, and habits and that his tour of foreign countries was regarded as presaging some unwelcome change. But no evidence was discovered of any widespread rebellion, or of any attempt on the part of Sophia to organize an opposition among the reactionary boyars against Peter's supposedly European predilections. A single detachment of the Streltzy had in fact mutinied and had threatened to march on Moscow. But while Peter was still at Vienna the mutineers had been intercepted by a regiment of the regular army and disarmed. When Peter therefore reached his capital, the episode was over and the danger passed. Yet Peter, who had for long realized that the Streltzy were of no military value but constituted a constant menace to internal order, determined to seize this opportunity to dispose of them forever.

Fourteen separate torture chambers were constructed at Preobrajenskoe and officers and men of the Streltzy were subjected to atrocious questioning in the hope of discovering some plot on the part of Sophia, her sister, and the reactionary boyars and clergy. Even Sophia herself was interrogated under torture, but nothing was revealed. Peter then decided to decimate the Streltzy by summary executions. He cut off many heads himself and sought to persuade his favorites to do likewise. Lefort refused to take any part in this butchery, but Menchikov (the new first favorite) and Romodanovski proved themselves excellent headsmen. Nearly a thousand Streltzy were decapitated in the Red Square at Moscow, being led out in batches of fifty and their necks aligned along a huge tree trunk which served as a communal block. Another two hundred were hanged outside Sophia's window and she herself and her sister were transported to an even more distant convent, where they were kept in close confinement, and where they died six and seven years later. Those of the Streltzy who were not summarily executed were packed off to Siberia where they perished of exposure and starvation. The way now lay open to the Tsar to form a professional army on modern lines.

Professor Waliszewski, in the massive study of Peter the Great which he published in 1896, contends that he was in no sense the reforming genius that he has sometimes been represented, but essentially an aggressive imperialist, who realized that he could not hope to annex the territories of his neighbors unless he possessed a modernized army and navy and unless at least the nucleus of an efficient administration were created. His foreign policy, and the wars that it provoked, were the cause rather than the result of his reforms.

At Rawa in October 1698 he had stayed with Augustus II, King of Poland, who shared his taste for carousal and debauch. A Swedish renegade of the name of Johann Reinhold Patkul suggested to the two monarchs that the accession of the young and inexperienced Charles XII to the throne of Sweden presented a favorable opportunity for a smash and grab raid on the Swedish provinces south of the Baltic. The plan was that Poland, Russia, Denmark, and Brandenburg should make a simultaneous attach on Sweden and share the spoils. Peter stipulated, however, that before he could move his armies to the north he must first conclude peace with the Turks and during the delay that ensued Charles XII, to the surprise of Europe, soundly defeated both the Poles and the Danes. It was not until August 8, 1700, that peace was concluded with Turkey and Peter was able to turn his armies against Sweden. He had undertaken that his first objective would be the fortress of Pskov, but instead of this he marched straight on Narva, the port of Livonia. He had expected that Charles XII would be too fully occupied in repelling a Danish invasion to afford time or troops to defend his more distant provinces and that Narva could be captured almost without a blow. Yet on the very day that the Russian armies crossed the Livonian frontier, the Danes signed with the Swedes the separate peace of Travendal. On reaching Narva, therefore, Peter was horrified to find it in a state of defense. It was reported that Charles XII would himself be in Narva and assume command within the space of a few hours. This information threw Peter into one of his not infrequent panics. Abandoning his armies to their fate he bolted off into the woods. Charles XII, on reaching Narva, defeated the Russian forces within the space of a few hours. Fortunately for Peter, however, the victorious Swede, instead of pursuing and destroying the beaten Russians, turned aside into Poland. Peter was afforded a respite in which to reconstitute his forces and to recover his shattered nerves. He arranged a meeting with the King of Poland at the castle of Birzé and it was agreed that they should join forces in an attack on Riga. Again they were defeated by Charles XII whose military prowess had by then inspired awe and admiration throughout central Europe.

Meanwhile, the fiasco of Narva and the fantastically untruthful communiqué that Peter issued in the hope of representing as a victory what had indeed been a resounding defeat, had given him a bad international repute. Although, as the Northern War continued, the Russian General Chermetiev won some minor victories, capturing Marienburg in 1702 and at the end of that year the fortress of Schlüsselburg at the mouth of the Neva, and finally taking Narva in 1704, Peter's attempts to obtain help from Austria and Holland were rejected with derisive scorn. As a culminating blow, Augustus of Poland made a separate treaty with Charles XII by which, among other concessions, he agreed to surrender the person of the renegade Patkul who was handed over to the Swedes and by them broken on the wheel. Peter was left to face the formidable Charles XII alone.

The victorious Swedish army advanced on Grodno, and an alliance was concluded between Charles XII and Ivan Mazepa, the Hetman of the Cossacks. Peter immediately evacuated Poland and withdrew into Russia, adopting a scorched earth policy and leaving nothing but waste behind him. This policy was effective and within a few months the Swedish army was decimated by famine and sickness. Charles XII was himself wounded on patrol and was forced, as the only means of extracting himself from a perilous situation, to make a desperate attack on Poltava. On June 27, 1709, the Swedes were utterly defeated. Charles XII and Mazepa had to flee for their lives, eventually reaching Bender and taking refuge with the Turks. The Russians were so elated by their victory that they forgot to follow up the Swedes. But Poltava had in fact been decisive. From then onwards Russia became the dominant Power in the north and was henceforward in a position to oblige the Courts of Europe to treat her with more respect.

Meanwhile Charles XII, having been treated by the Turks, first as a distinguished refugee, then as a potential ally, and finally as a highly inconvenient prisoner of war, managed to escape from Bender and at midnight on November 11, 1714, after an absence of fourteen years, suddenly arrived back in Sweden attended by a single adjutant. He collected another army and in 1717 declared war on Norway. On December 11 of the following year, while reconnoitering the fortress of Fredriksten, he looked over the parapet of the entrenchment and was shot by a chance bullet through the head:

> His fall was destined to a barren strand,
> A petty fortress, and a dubious hand;
> He left the name at which the world grew pale,
> To point a moral or adorn a tale.

Had Peter been content to consolidate the territories that he now occupied, he might indeed have established his Empire of the Baltic. Yet once again he allowed his sense of the practical to become distorted by dreams. He conceived the idea of gaining the whole of Poland and even part of Mecklenburg. While his attention was distracted by these visions the Turks, encouraged by the refugee Charles XII, suddenly declared war. Peter, with reckless impetuosity, advanced to the Pruth where, on July 18, 1711, he and his army were completely surrounded by the Turks. The Tsar, supposing there was no alternative to capitulation and captivity was stricken by a complete nervous collapse. The situation was saved by the slutton Tsaritsa who, by offering an enormous bribe to the Turkish commander, and by agreeing to the surrender of Azov, procured their release.

Four

It was Peter the Great who, within a quarter of a century, transformed Russia from a barbaric Asiatic principality into a centralized monarchy, capable of playing its part in the European balance of power. Yet his reforms, although they startled the world by the speed and ruthlessness with which they were imposed, did not derive from any wish to further the prosperity or happiness of his people. They were dictated by the ambition to extend and strengthen his own power. He realized, although not with any consistent clarity, that power implied military and naval strength; that in order to create a modernized army and navy he would have to improve the finances of his duchy; and that this would entail economic and administrative reform.

When he took charge of affairs the main source of Russian wealth was timber and fur; there was no industrial production, little agriculture, and the rich black soil of the steppes remained untilled. He first concentrated on establishing iron foundries and transported twenty-five thousand serfs to work in the Ural mines, establishing there eleven foundries under the direction of Antoufief, a workman from Toula, who made a vast fortune and assumed the name of Demidoff. In order to adjust the trade balance, he placed an almost prohibitive duty on imported luxuries, set up as many as fifteen textile factories in Moscow, dispatched trade commissioners, or consuls, to Europe, and sought to improve the almost nonexistent communications system by cutting a canal from the Neva to the Volga. He thus increased Russian exports to 4,300,000 roubles a year, while imports were reduced to 2,100,000. Even then he had difficulty in financing his armament. In 1701, he confiscated the revenues of the Church, created State monopolies in salt and tobacco, and imposed taxes on individual wealth, even taxing such items as beards, baths, and windows. By such measures he more than doubled his revenue in fifteen years.

But it was not money only that he needed for his armies and navy; he also needed men. The population of Russia in 1725 was slightly over fourteen million, of whom 90 percent were peasants. He proceeded with the violent russification of the Ukraine, southern Finland, and the Bashkirs of the Urals. In order to build up an officer and administrative class, he insisted that the primary duty of the boyars or nobles was service to himself. His methods were drastic and ingenious. As an outward symbol of the new order which he was ferociously resolved to impose, he forced his fur-clad boyars to adopt the suits of the Amsterdam burghers and to cut off their shaggy beards. He himself presided at their shaving, wielding a razor in his enormous hands. The nobles were then classified according to their "tchin," or degree of service, and a system of entail and primogeniture was introduced for the purpose of creating a pool of younger sons who would be obliged by penury to enter the public service. These young cadets were ordered to go to school between the ages of ten and fifteen; if they failed in their leaving examination they were conscripted into the army or navy, the term of service for all ranks being for life.

His administrative reforms were also devised to strengthen his own autocracy and to provide further manpower for the military forces. In 1721, he proclaimed himself Tsar and Autocrat of All the Russias and thereafter ceased, except by pamphleteers, to be called the Duke of Muscovy. He suppressed the Patriarchate, replacing it by the Holy Synod under a Procurator appointed by himself, and drastically disciplined the monasteries, which had proved too facile a sanctuary for young men desiring to evade military service. He created a "Senate" of nine members, whose discussions were supervised by a commissar responsible to himself alone. He introduced a few minor penal reforms, but the practice of torture was maintained and "confessions" were thereby extracted from the accused.

In general he administered his Empire with the assistance of favorites, responsible to himself alone. Foremost among these were Menchikov and Romodanovski. The former, who had started life as a baker's boy, was unable to read or write. As a soldier, according to Lord Whitworth, he was "without experience, knowledge, or courage." Peter adored him, writing to him as "my heart's brother" and lavishing decorations, riches and even whole provinces upon him with a reckless hand. His rapacity was so overt that he fell into disgrace. He redeemed himself by appearing at court dressed in his old habit as a baker's boy and crying his wares in a shrill voice. Peter, who was always bewitched by farce, forgave him for the moment, although his situation remained precarious. When Peter was succeeded by his wife the Empress Catherine, who had started her career as Menchikov's mistress, he returned to favor. But once again his rapacity proved his undoing and he ended his days in poverty and exile.

Romodanovski, who came from the provincial nobility, was a man of comparative honesty, who fulfilled his function as chief of the Secret Police with cruelty and effect. In the early days Peter had devised an elaborate farce, which he maintained for several years, according to which Romodanovski was called "Prince Caesar" and accorded in that disguise all manner of fantastic honors. People were obliged to grovel in his presence; when he went hunting he was escorted by a suite of five hundred grooms and squires; and those who attended his receptions were forced on entry to gulp down a beaker of brandy seasoned with pepper and handed to them by a bear who had been trained for that purpose. The Tsar assisted at their charades under the pseudonym of Peter Mihailoff.

Apart from old cronies and a few educated men, such as Golvine and Apraxine, Peter relied on foreign experts, notably the Norwegian Cruys for naval affairs, the Scotsman Ogilvy for military matters, James Bruce, who was in charge of the artillery, and Ostermann, an educated German from Westphalia. He always carried a heavy cane, or "doubina" with which he would thrash these ministers or civil servants who did not agree with him. The methods by which he maintained his supremacy were those of despotic terrorism. He employed an elaborate spy system; delation was rampant and none of his courtiers ever knew when they were to be subjected to the knout, or the strappado, to torture or decapitation. "To be close to the Tsar," ran a contemporary proverb, "is to be close to death."

An enduring example, both of his wild fancy and his ruthless resolve, was the creation of St. Petersburg in the Ingrian swamp. There is no satisfactory explanation why he did not select a healthier and less ice bound port such as Riga, Reval, or Libau. On May 16, 1703, with his own hands he cut the first sod of what was to become his capital and one of the most majestic cities in Europe. He began by building a wooden citadel on the site where today the Fortress of St. Peter and St. Paul raises its slim gilt spire into the dark skies. The word "Neve" in the Finnish language means "mud" and the construction of the city cost the lives of 200,000 conscripted workmen. The nobles, on the threat of beating or exile, were commanded to build palaces in this marsh. For himself Peter constructed a log cabin similar in design to the hovel of a Dutch fisherman. Amid all the architectural splendors of Leningrad this dark little hut has been preserved, almost as a place of pilgrimage. Even at the time, this fantasy was regarded as absurd, even as insane. Yet, such was the Tsar's superhuman force of will, that within ten years he had rendered his new capital a port of international commerce. In 1714, only sixteen foreign vessels visited the harbor; in 1715 there were forty-three: by 1724 the number had risen to one hundred and eighty. For all its immense cost in money and human lives, the capital with its rushing river, its constant canals, and its superb public and private buildings, remains one of the wonders of the world.

Peter's second visit to Europe took place in 1717. He had conceived many new schemes of aggression and spoliation and hoped to obtain French support. He contemplated another war with Turkey, Franco-Russian invasion of England on behalf of the Pretender, a campaign to capture Delhi and grasp the riches of the Great Moghul, and the seizure of Madagascar as a convenient base for his Indian conquests. He had some idea also of marrying his daughter Elizabeth to Louis XV, or failing him, to the duc de Chartres. He was not an ingratiating diplomatist. The marquis de Mailly-Nesle, who was sent to meet him at Dunkirk, was turned out of the carriage and given a sound thrashing with the doubina. "Usually," the horrified marquis reported to Paris, "men are inclined to accept reasonable suggestions; but these men, if indeed one can apply the word 'man' to what is a subhuman species—do not understand what reasonableness means." On arrival in Paris the Tsar behaved abominably. Dining at Fontainebleau he drank immoderately and was sick in the coach; on visiting Marly he locked himself up in Madame de Maintenon's former bedroom with a girl whom he had picked up in the streets of Paris. He was violently offensive to the elegant women whom he met. Instead therefore of obtaining French support for his matrimonial and military plans, he was regarded with shocked curiosity, as if he were a gorilla trained to wear the clothes of a Dutch bargee, to make fierce gestures with his cane, and to utter articulate if incomprehensible grunts and cries. Yet he did succeed in inducing Cardinal Dubois, that astute diplomatist, to mediate between Russia and Sweden, a negotiation from which resulted the profitable Treaty of Nystadt. The treaty was signed on September 3, 1721, and Peter secured from an exhausted Sweden the cession of Livonia, Esthonia, Ingria, and the southern half of Finland. In spite of Poltava, which most experts regarded as a chance victory, Peter never acquired among his contemporaries (with the exception of Maurice de Saxe) the reputation of a military leader. His grasp of detail may have been Napoleonic; but his conception of strategy was that of a boy of fifteen.

Not unnaturally, the French regarded him as an abominable monster and demonstrably insane.

Five

W as Peter the Great insane? He was certainly an epileptic; his face twitched continually and he was subject to fits. His constant buffooneries, his ghastly practical jokes, his taste for elaborate mystifications and masquerades, certainly implied a lack of proportion and an unbalanced invention. When drunk (and he was usually drunk) he would kill his servants; on one occasion, when visiting a uniat monastery at Polock, he murdered six of the monks with his own hands, because their superior had been tactless enough to assert that they were schismatics. Even when sober, he would succumb to bouts of uncontrolled sadism; he enjoyed watching operations, or extracting teeth, or flogging his courtiers and attendants. When he suspected one of his mistresses of being unfaithful to him, he executed her himself and then examined the severed head sarcastically, explaining to his friends the function of the arteries, and then kissing the dead lips. His wife Catherine, who as servant to the Lutheran pastor Gluck had escaped into the Russian lines at Marienburg and become the camp strumpet, was the only person who was able to control him. He married her in 1711 and had her declared Empress in 1721. She cooked his meals, washed his linen (which was the only object about which he was in any way fastidious), and was generally as drunk as he was; there was a peasant jollity in their love. She was dumpy, slatternly, superstitious, warm hearted and lewd: she hung herself with amulets, barbaric jewelry and charms which, as she waddled from the kitchen to the living room, jangled like gongs. When in 1724 he discovered that she had a lover of the name of William Mons, he had the man decapitated, plunged his head in a glass jar of alcohol and forced Catherine to keep this relic in the window of her bedroom. Although the circumstances of the murder of his son Alexis are still a mystery, it was widely believed at the time that he had been knouted to death in his father's presence. Assuredly Peter was capable of every atrocity.

We who have been educated in the tradition of law, logic and charity, are inclined to ascribe to mental aberration the Slav aptitude for mingling the practical with the visionary. Peter possessed all the faults of the Russian temperament; he was febrile, violent, impulsive, and utterly averse from reason; he had no regard for human life or death. Yet by the superhuman force of his will, he rendered his country a Great Power. There are those who contend that his very ruthlessness left an abiding legacy of nihilism to his people.

"This great reformer," writes Waliszewski, "was also one of the greatest demoralizers of the human race. Russia of today owes to him both her grandeur and most of her vices."

The "Testament of Peter the Great" from which Napoleon extracted such propaganda value as indicating that the Slavs aimed at subjugating the world, was probably a forgery devised by the ingenious Chevalier d'Eon. But would Peter the Great, or his varied successors, have described it as a travesty of their ambition?

Chapter 5
Skepticism
(Voltaire, 1694–1778)

————•◆•————

Voltaire is the supreme intellectual influence of the eighteenth century—His apotheosis in 1790—His genius destructive rather than constructive—But he revered established order and was not a revolutionary—Nor was he an atheist—The shock given to his optimistic deism by the Lisbon earthquake—It inspired his best poem and his fable *Candide*—His birth and early adventures—He becomes a literary and social success—His large fortune—He is flogged by the footmen of the chevalier de Rohan and imprisoned in the Bastille—On release he spends three years in England—His *Letters on the English*—He retired with Madame du Châtelet to Cirey—His life at Cirey—On the death of Madame du Châtelet he takes his niece, Madame Denis, to live with him—His *Princesse de Navarre* obliges him to go to Versailles—His hatred of the Court and his hurried departure—He visits Frederick the Great—Ferney—His lasting legacy to mankind—*Écrasez l'Infâme*—His defense of the defenseless—Calas, Sirven, La Barre, Lally—One of the wittiest men of all time and the undaunted champion of the oppressed.

One

THE SUPREME INTELLECTUAL, as distinct from emotional, influence of the eighteenth century was that exercised by Voltaire. He was born in 1694 and died in 1778 at the age of eighty-four. It was he who taught three generations that superstition was ridiculous, sentiment absurd, fanaticism unintelligent, and oppression infamous. He was a brilliant satirist rather than a constructive or even logical philosopher. His plays, his epic and his occasional verse, were much admired by his contemporaries; his historical writings remain perfect models of French prose; his short stories, although not fully appreciated at the time, had a lasting influence; his conversation was witty and his vast correspondence a monument of lucidity and almost of candor; his open quarrels with the eminent became the talk of Europe; and, although his literary taste was questionable, his political and philosophic apophthegms changed the thinking habits of the civilized world.

He was the inventor of that critical habit of thought which sapped faith in the established system, which deprived the upper class of its self-confidence, and which became one of the causes of the French Revolution. Thus when in 1791 the Revolution had triumphed, the National Assembly decreed that his coffin should be removed from the distant village in which he had been buried and transported in state to the Pantheon in Paris. Escorted by the National Guard it rumbled through the streets of Paris in a hearse designed by the painter David and bearing the inscription "He taught us to be free." The funeral procession was followed by a hundred thousand mourners and the windows, the balconies and the sidewalks were packed with further thousands gathered to acclaim its passage. The hearse halted outside the opera, outside the Palace of the Tuileries, and stopped at the house on the Quai de Théatins (thenceforward and to this day to be known as the Quai Voltaire) where he had died. It was there that the two daughters of Calas, whom he had defended against oppression, stepped forward and kissed the coffin. The crowds cheered and sobbed. Then on to the Comédie Française where a huge placard carried the words "He wrote *Oedipe* at seventeen," to the Theatre Français where another placard proclaimed "He wrote *Irène* at eighty-four." At last the vast procession reached the Pantheon and the coffin was carried to its vault.

Twenty-three years later, when the Bourbons were restored to the throne, the reactionaries had his bones, together with those of Jean Jacques Rousseau, exhumed from the Pantheon and cast into a pit outside the city where they were consumed by quicklime. This posthumous revenge was not discovered until 1864 when the coffin, on being opened, was found to be empty. It at least proved that the adherents of the old regime regarded him and Rousseau as their bitterest enemies.

He was not, as has been said, a profound thinker. He taught men to question every legend, every conventional idea transmitted to them by their parents, and to believe nothing that could not be confirmed by the evidence of the senses. He exposed shams. Since the whole structure of society at the outset of the eighteenth century was founded on make-believe, the blast of his irony, the flame of his sarcasm, had a withering effect. He was one of the most potent destructive writers that have ever lived: but he was not constructive.

Although it is correct to acclaim him as a great champion of the freedom of thought and expression; although he was assuredly the unflagging and unflinching opponent of oppression, whether political or religious; it would be an error to describe him as a revolutionary. He was not a political scientist, and if he had any ideal of human government, it was the Platonic ideal of the Philosopher King, assisted by an élite of cultivated nobles. He did not believe that all men were created equal, nor did he possess any real conception of liberty as a balance of rights and duties guaranteed by an impartial and known system of laws. He was an absolutist, even as Rousseau was an absolutist: but whereas Rousseau desired the dictatorship of the proletariat, Voltaire desired the dictatorship of Kings.

Thus, whereas he was constantly extolling freedom of thought and expression as secured in England, he felt that the central Government had every right to prosecute those who openly attacked them. He refused to accept, or even to recognize, Montesquieu's distinction between despotism and constitutional monarchy. The very idea of a limited central authority was to him abhorrent. "No government," he wrote, "can be in any manner effective unless it possesses absolute power." He had no sympathy whatsoever for the common man. "Once the populace begins to reason," he wrote to Frederick the Great, "then everything is lost. I abominate the idea of government by the masses." One of his most frequent mottoes was a line from Racine: "*Que Rome soit toujours libre et César tout puissant*»—"Let Rome be ever free and Caesar all powerful."

That it never occurred to him that this was in itself an untenable paradox shows that his political thought was immature and muddled. He looked to his benevolent and all-powerful monarch, his Philosopher King, to introduce practical reforms. He was not blind to the fact that the whole theory and system of the ancient régime was out of date. He was in favor of the most drastic administrative reforms, such as more equitable taxation, the abolition of arbitrary arrest and secret trials, the suppression of the feudal privileges of the aristocracy, the elimination of all internal customs barriers, and the promulgation of a new penal code by which both torture and the death penalty should be abolished. There were times even when he dimly realized that true liberty meant the absolute equality of all citizens under the law. "To be free," he wrote, "implies being subject to law alone. The English love their law in the same way as a father loves his children, because they created it themselves, or are at least under the impression that they created it."

He regarded nationalism, even patriotism, as emotions unworthy of the rational man. Whereas Montesquieu was tenderly patriotic and Rousseau, when it suited him, could sob aloud when he thought of his native Geneva, Voltaire had no special feelings for France. He thought it most "unreasonable" for nationalists, such as the patriots of Poland or the American plantations, to rebel against the established government. He would have agreed with Goethe that nationalism is the sign of a low standard of culture. He would have regarded himself, not so much as a French subject, but as a good European, even as a citizen of the world. And we must admit that patriotism, for all its inspiration and splendor, is an emotional rather than an intellectual concept.

Two

A similar lack of logic can be observed in his attitude towards religion. He had learnt from the Englishman, Lord Bolingbroke, that any man of intelligence should feel nothing but contempt for ideas based on ecclesiastical injunctions or doctrinal superstition. This was the fashionable point of view adopted by the intellectuals of his day; but whereas they restricted themselves to sneering at popular religion in private, Voltaire was the first man to deliver a frontal public attack. He certainly detested any form of religious fanaticism or what he called "enthusiasm." It was not merely that he denied the claims of the Pope to be spiritual and even temporal arbiter of the universe, and that he assailed all persecution on the part of the ecclesiastical or state authorities of those who differed from them in their form of belief; it was also that he detested any form of religious intolerance, whether Catholic, Protestant or Presbyterian. He did not mind the Jesuits so much, since they were subtle, cultured, and believed to some extent in the Divine Right of Kings. What he loathed were the Jansenists, "the Calvinists of Catholicism," who taught the doctrine of original sin, of salvation through Grace, and who believed, as did the Puritans of New England, that only the "elect" would be saved, whereas the rest of humanity was destined for eternal damnation. He suspected the Jansenists of being at heart "sour republicans" and in his shocking but widely read lampoon on Joan of Arc he describes a typical Jansenist as "the slave of destiny, the lost child of Grace."

He certainly admitted the social value of some organized religion and remarked sarcastically that if the most violent atheist "had five or six hundred peasants to manage he would certainly inculcate into them the doctrine of a God dispensing punishments and rewards." On his estate at Ferney he pulled down the village church, since it obstructed his view, but he obtained permission from the Bishop to build a new one in its place and inscribed over the portal the words "*Deo er exit Voltaire.*» "Voltaire built this Church for God." He even on Easter Sunday attended mass in this church and insisted on preaching a sermon from the pulpit. On his deathbed he agreed to receive the Sacraments and was buried according to the rites of the Church.

Such inconsistencies render it hard for us to determine whether Voltaire was merely anti-clerical, or whether he denied the fundamental truths of revealed religion. He would have described himself as a Deist. He contended that the facts that some men are possessed of better minds than others, and that the firmament moves in circles with intricate regularity, implies that there must exist a "supreme geometrician" who ordains and orders such things. It is absurd to assert that there is no such thing as "superior intelligence" or that all men are born with equal capacities. "Certainly," he writes, "there exists a difference between the ideas of Newton and the droppings of a mule." He does not pretend to define the nature or location of his "supreme geometrician." "All I can do," he asserts, "is to worship him." The assumption is that the geometrician is all-powerful and benevolent. "From an all perfect being," says Voltaire, "evil cannot result." Thus to him "atheism is the vice of clever people, even as superstition is the vice of fools." Such vague deism was denounced by John Morley as little more than "a doctrine of self-complacent individualism," or as "the gratitude towards destiny experienced by those who have had a successful life." Morley rightly draws attention to the fact that Voltaire possessed no conception of the meaning of "holiness," that most reverent of all mysteries. "He had no ear," writes Morley, "for the finer vibrations of the spiritual voice . . . He never rises from the ground into the region of the higher facts of religion."

It is probable that Voltaire would all his life have maintained this comfortable balance between conformity, deism, and a hatred of intolerance and persecution, had it not been for the shock given to his conscience by the Lisbon earthquake of November 1, 1755. The report, as it first reached him, was that fifteen thousand men, women, and children had, within the space of six minutes, been crushed beneath the bells and towers of Lisbon's churches, which were packed for divine service on All Saints day. The disaster of Lisbon produced on the minds of that generation an effect as morally and mentally disturbing as the destruction of Hiroshima has produced on ours. How can God, they questioned, really be an all powerful and benevolent deity if he can murder thousands of innocent humans, at the moment that they are gathered together to do him worship?

Several different answers were returned to this distressing question. It was not denied that, out of a population of 275,000 some 10,000 to 15,000 lost their lives; that damage to the extent of twelve million pounds had been caused to the city; that thirty churches had been destroyed either by the earthquake itself or by the ensuing fire and tidal wave; and that valuable libraries and monuments had perished, including pictures by Titian, Correggio and Rubens. How was this ferocious act of God to be explained? The Portuguese themselves were convinced that the disaster was an act of divine vengeance upon a sinful world. But if so, then why should so many priests and nuns, as well as so many sacred images, have been obliterated by the catastrophe and so many heretics, evil persons, and objects of idolatry have been spared? The Jesuits also contended that the earthquake was not due as some unbelievers had the audacity to aver, to natural causes, but was an overt demonstration of the wrath of God. The Jansenist, Laurent Etienne Rondet, wrote a whole book to prove that the disaster was a divine comment on the iniquity of the Inquisition and the Jesuits. The Protestants of London argued that it must be ascribed to God's disapproval of the Portuguese in general, and Lisbon in particular, for their addiction to abominable papal practices and their avowed worship of the Mother of God. It was even suggested that the Saints had begged God to choose their own particular festival as the date for his demonstration.

Voltaire was shaken by the event out of his facile optimism, his confidence in the doctrine that all is best in the best possible of worlds, his adherence to the theodicy of Leibnitz, his egoistic complacency. His poem on *The Disaster of Lisbon* is one of the most sincere that he ever wrote. How can we believe that this frightful holocaust was planned and desired by a benevolent God?

> Quel crime, quelle faute, ont commis ces enfants
> Sur le sein maternel écrasés et sanglants?

"Of what crime could these children have been guilty when they were crushed little bleeding objects against their mother's breasts?" If God had in fact desired to inflict punishment on the Portuguese, could he not have chosen a less atrocious method? Only He can explain His actions, but He refuses to do so, leaving his children as "bewildered atoms in a mass of mud." It was then that Voltaire first conceived the idea of his excellent story *Candide* which is in effect a satire on the whole optimistic school. Candide, who had been taught by the philosopher Pangloss to believe in the loving-kindness of God and the perfectibility of man, is exposed to a series of frightful misfortunes and finds that throughout the world, with the solitary exception of the legendary country of Eldorado, man is cruel, greedy, and inconceivably stupid. He is at Lisbon at the time of the earthquake and exclaims in agony, "If this be indeed the best of all possible worlds, then what must the other worlds be like?" He meets the philosopher Martin who takes a more realistic view of this world and the next. Candide asks him whether men have always been as wicked, cruel, hypocritical, perfidious, greedy, and stupid as they seem today. The following dialogue ensues:

> "Do you believe," said Martin, "that hawks have always wanted to devour pigeons?" "Certainly," answered Candide. "Well," replied Martin, "if hawks have always had the same character, how do you expect man to alter theirs?" "Oh," explained Candide, "there is a great difference between hawks and men, since the latter possess free will. . . ." Arguing in this manner they reached Bordeaux.

The Lisbon earthquake taught Candide to reject the theories of his old teacher Pangloss, and to adopt the agnostic stoicism of Martin. "You should work," says the latter, "and not waste time in speculation: this is the only way to render life endurable." Candide sighs deeply and accepts this doctrine. The story ends with the famous words *"mais il faut cultiver notre jardin."*

After the Lisbon earthquake Voltaire ceased to be so certain about his deism, so confident in the great Geometrician, and lapsed into a vague form of agnosticism arguing that, since we could never expect in this world to understand the purposes of Providence, we must avoid abstract speculation, content ourselves with our daily tasks, and cling to hope. "Why do we exist?" he wrote, "why is anything anything?"

If we are to understand the movement of thought in the eighteenth century it is thus necessary to be aware of the deep and wide repercussions produced by the Lisbon earthquake throughout Europe and beyond. Goethe, who was but six years old at the time, remembered how "the demon of fright" then spread across the world. Everybody explained this Act of God as a justification of their own prejudices. Rousseau took it as a warning to mankind that it was highly dangerous to live in crowded cities. Warburton, in his Fast-Day sermon, argued that the earthquake was a benevolent warning to all mankind and "displayed God's glory in its fairest colors." John Wesley, who can have known nothing of what had really occurred in those Lisbon churches and along the harbor wharves, asserted that God's warning had been directed, "not to the small vulgar, but to the great and learned, the rich and honorable heathens commonly called Christians." If Wesley were correct in this deduction, then why was it the "small vulgar" among the Portuguese people who had suffered the greatest casualties? Certainly the news of the earthquake aroused a mood of self-examination and repentance throughout the world. "Between the French and the Earthquake," wrote Horace Walpole to Henry Conway, "you have no notion how good we are grown. Nobody makes a suit now but of sackcloth turned up with ashes."

And it is a fact that masquerades, which until then had been the rage of London, were abandoned forever.

Three

The life and character of Voltaire is a fascinating study and one which amply repays the labor involved. The strange thing is that for all his literary activity (he would rise at dawn and start dictating to a secretary in the very act of clambering out of bed) he found time to amass a huge personal fortune. He was himself reticent about his moneymaking methods and in *Candide* he asserts that the art of making money consists in "having been born lucky." It seems however that as a young man he speculated on army contracts and thereafter prospered as a moneylender, providing cash advances to impoverished nobles at a high rate of interest. He was stingy in small ways, being mean about tips and candles. Until he purchased the estate of Ferney, he lived most of the time at the expense of other people, accumulating a fortune meanwhile which rendered him, by modern standards, a multimillionaire. No wonder that Rousseau in his hermitage or Diderot in his attic should have looked on Voltaire as different from themselves.

He was born in Paris on November 21, 1694, the son of Maître Arouet who was highly respected in legal circles and acted as solicitor to the Saint Simon family as well as to the ageless courtesan Ninon de L'Enclos. He was educated at Louis Le Grand, but refused, much to his father's fury, to study for the bar. At the age of nineteen, he was attached to the staff of the marquis de Châteauneuf, Ambassador to the States General. At The Hague he had a passionate love affair with Olympe Dunoyer, which caused such scandal that he was sent back to Paris in disgrace and for a short period sought to allay his father's displeasure by entering a lawyer's office. At the age of twenty he attracted the attention of the marquis de Saint-Ange who invited him to stay at the Château de Saint-Ange and instructed him in the manners of the court while telling much about the grandeur and pettiness of Versailles in the time of the Roi Soleil. He was always a brilliant talker, and his malicious sallies and epigrams gave him a welcome in the salons of Paris. He was even admitted into the charmed circle of the duchesse du Maine at Sceaux. His facility for composing monkeyish little lampoons upon the great soon earned him the repute of being a dangerous young man. On May 16, 1717, at the age of twenty-two, he was suddenly sent, under a *lettre de cachet*, or administrative order, to prison at the Bastille. He was charged with being the author of an epigram which had in fact been written by someone else. The injustice of this sentence filled him with a lasting hatred of arbitrary arrest and instilled into him the principle that nobody should be convicted without open trial and on the ground that he had broken some known and published law. So disgusted was he by this episode that he decided to change his name. In the first half of the eighteenth century the word "Roi" was not pronounced in the best of circles as rhyming with "Loi," but was pronounced "Rouet." This assonance between his own name and that of the monarch irritated him and he therefore invented for himself the anagram of "Voltaire" under which, after the successful performance of his tragedy *Oedipe*, he became immediately famous. His literary position was confirmed by the publication in 1723 of the *Henriade*, his epic on Henri IV. To our minds, both his plays and his epic are dreary reading, being composed of platitudes and wearisome versification, but to his contemporaries they seemed models of correct drama and poetry. They were unaware of the fact that Voltaire, as a writer, lacked both ear and passion and that his facile verses were both stilted and unmelodious. Already before he reached thirty he was acclaimed as a literary genius; the whole of Parisian Society lay at his feet.

It is not surprising that his early literary and social success should have turned the head of young Voltaire. He was always sensitive to flattery as he was hypersensitive to criticism. It may have been that he often allowed his conversational powers to run away with him and that his verbal and even his written epigrams caused offence. On one occasion, when supping with the duc de Sully, he showed off vauntingly and the chevalier de Rohan, who resented his uppishness, exclaimed, "Who is that young man who talks so loud?" Voltaire replied that he was a man of letters and as such the equal even of the mighty family of Rohan. The chevalier, incensed by this impertinence, ordered his footmen to seize Voltaire in the street and to give him a sound beating. The chevalier watched this drubbing from his coach, peeping through silk curtains with a leer. Voltaire sent a challenge to the chevalier, which was regarded as a further act of impertinence, since nobles, especially Rohans, did not fight duels with people so far below them in rank. A further *lettre de cachet* was obtained and for the second time Voltaire was cast into the Bastille for a period of six months. On his release, he was ordered to leave Paris. He decided to visit England then reputed to be the asylum of the persecuted and the island of the free. He landed at Greenwich in May 1726 and remained in England until March 1729.

John Morley contends, with pious patriotism, that this English exile marked a turning point in Voltaire's life. He goes so far as to state that he "left France a poet and returned to it a sage." This is an exaggerated statement, but it is clear that Voltaire did in fact gain many new ideas from his sojourn in London.

In the first place he was fascinated by the aloofness of the English and by their calm pride. In *La Pucelle* he has two comments on the English character:

> *Les Saints anglais ont dans leur caractère*
> *Je ne sais quoi de dur et insulaire.*

> The English Saints possess
> Something hard and insular in their characters.

Or again:

> *Parfait anglais, voyageant sans dessein,*
> *Achetant cher des modernes antiques;*
> *Regardant tout avec un air hautain*
> *Et méprisant les Saints et leurs reliques.*

> The perfect Englishman, traveling aimlessly,
> Buying faked antiques at exorbitant prices;
> Gazing at everything with a disdainful expression
> And despising the Saints and their relics.

He spent much of his time with his friend Everard Fawkener, a leading cotton merchant, and subsequently ambassador to Turkey, at his house in the London suburb of Wandsworth. He met Bolingbroke, Peterborough, and Swift. He studied Newton, Hobbes, and Locke. He was impressed by the comparative liberty enjoyed by writers in London, where men of letters could not be clapped in to the Tower by a *lettre de cachet* owing to the whim of the King, his mistress, his courtiers, or his ministers. He was impressed by the fact that successful businessmen, such as Everard Fawkener, were treated with as much respect as scions of even the noblest or most ancient families. He certainly was deeply influenced by Locke and his theory that there was no such thing as innate ideas and that principles should be based, not upon conventional or deductive assumptions, but on the inductive results of actual experience. He derived and preserved throughout his life an admiration for the English Constitution. "We can well believe," he wrote subsequently, "that a constitution that has established the rights of the Crown, the aristocracy and the people, in which each section finds its own safety, will last as long as human institutions can last." He appreciated the religious toleration which, as compared to France, was so widespread and generally accepted in England. He acquired a respect for Presbyterians, a respect which might well have been mitigated had he known of the theological tyranny imposed by the Puritans of New England. He had a special affection for the Quakers, attending their meetings and stating that, had it not been for his dread of seasickness, he would cross the ocean and settle in Pennsylvania.

His appreciation of our national literature was less discerning. He compared the English genius to a forest tree, different in its strength and naturalness from the clipped avenues of Marly. He regarded Addison as the most "correct" among English writers, but he also admired Pope. Of Shakespeare he wrote: "He had a genius both powerful and fecund, but without a spark of good taste. He had no conception at all of the rules of drama." He described *Hamlet* as a "rude and barbarous piece" composed by "a drunken savage." He disliked our love of imagery. "The stilts of metaphorical language," he wrote, "on which the English language is perched gives to it a walk which is sometimes elevated but always irregular."

On his return he wrote, although he did not yet dare to publish, his *Letters Concerning the English* in which he had the audacity to suggest that the democratic institutions of England were preferable in practice and likely to last longer than the monolithic autocracy of

France. When in 1734 a pirated edition of these Letters was issued in Paris, it was publicly burnt by order of the parliament. Voltaire was so alarmed by the outcry that it provoked that he fled with Madame du Châtelet to her château at Cirey-sur-Blaise which, being close to the Lorraine frontier, offered a convenient escape route should prosecution threaten.

Four

Émilie de Breteuil had been forced by her family when aged nineteen to marry the marquis du Châtelet, a professional soldier of amiable and accommodating disposition and small interest in intellectuals pursuits. She herself was a mathematician and astonished French society by translating Newton's *Principia* and by writing several treatises on natural philosophy and sums. It was regarded as admirable but eccentric that a woman of such excellent family, who could have qualified for posts of the utmost distinction at Versailles, should have been content to exile herself to this bleak northeastern corner of France, to pay but slight attention to fashion or personal cleanliness, and be content to remain the avowed and faithful mistress of the commoner Voltaire for fourteen years. The manner of their domestic life at Cirey, the rigid timetable that they imposed upon themselves, the studies that occupied their days and nights, have been recorded by Madame de Graffigny, who stayed at Cirey for three months as an observant if unwelcome guest, and excellently described by Miss Nancy Mitford in a gay and scintillating book. When staying at the court of King Stanislas at Lunéville, they met the comte de Saint Lambert, a man who combined unusual charm and enterprise with a predilection for women who were past their first youth. It was he who had robbed Rousseau of Madame d'Houtetot and who now robbed Voltaire of Madame du Châtelet. The latter was well over forty and had lost her figure and her looks, having all her life devoted far more attention to the laws of gravity than to the preservation of her charms. One evening in October 1748 Voltaire strolled casually into her sitting room and found her locked in the embraces of Saint Lambert. After two or three hours of intense rage and mortification, the philosopher felt it wiser to accept the position. Madame du Châtelet was already pregnant and in 1749 she died in childbirth. Voltaire was deeply afflicted by the loss of his old friend, but he was consoled by the friendly and tactful condolences of Saint Lambert, and by the fact that since 1745 he had been having an affair with his own niece, Madame Denis.

Louise Mignot, the daughter of Voltaire's sister, had in 1738 married Monsieur Denis of the Commissariat Department who died in 1744. Her uncle on the occasion of her marriage had presented her with a dowry of 30,000 francs. On the death of Madame du Châtelet, his niece became his mistress and constant companion; they lived together until the day of his death. His friends were perplexed by this infatuation. Madame Denis was ugly, unintelligent, a bad housekeeper, snobbish and intellectually pretentious. It seemed strange indeed that Voltaire, who was so fastidious and tidy in his habits, could have loved, or even tolerated, this dull and slatternly woman. What was even worse, she had extravagant tastes and Voltaire, who was careful about money, much resented her gift for ostentation and the lavish expenditure which she indulged in when hostess at Ferney. She had no taste for country life and was not reticent in expressing her longing for Paris. In fact in 1768 Voltaire gave her leave of absence for eighteen months, and profited by the interlude to cut down expenditure and to give to Ferney a thorough spring-cleaning. On her uncle's death she became his residuary legatee. She immediately disposed of Ferney and sold his library to Catherine the Great. Being now an heiress she married a young man of the name of du Vivier: she died unlamented in 1790.

Voltaire himself was happy in the comparative seclusion of Ferney. Being only three and a half miles from Geneva, it offered an easy escape in the event of danger. He acquired the property in 1758 and lived there magnificently for the next twenty years. He built a private theatre, became interested in agriculture and gardening, started a watch factory for the relief of unemployment, had an excellent cook, kept sixty servants, and entertained lavishly. He would sometimes argue that it was in order to please Madame Denis that he had turned himself into "the innkeeper of Europe." In fact he was delighted that his home should become a place of pilgrimage for international intellectuals. La Harpe came and stayed for a year: the great actress Mademoiselle Clairon came, and d'Alembert, and Condorcet and Dr. Burney: Charles James Fox came and charmed Voltaire as he charmed everybody: Boswell came and fired such insistent questions at Voltaire that he pretended to have a fainting fit in order to rid himself of so bumptious an interviewer; the Emperor of Austria, Joseph II, actually drove past the gates of Ferney without calling. Voltaire regarded this as "a disgrace."

It was during the Madame du Châtelet period that Voltaire spent some uneasy months at the court of Versailles. In 1744, the duc de Richelieu had suggested to him that it might be useful if he wrote a play to celebrate the marriage of the Dauphin with the Infanta of Spain. He therefore composed *The Princesse de Navarre* and in order to adjust his verses to the music specially composed for the occasion by Rameau, and to supervise the production and the scenery, he was accorded a tiny little room in the palace, adjoining the latrines of the Swiss Guard. Madame du Châtelet, being by birth a Breteuil, was more comfortably housed. He took some pains to win the favor of Louis XV and Madame de Pompadour and even went so far as to write adulatory verses to the Pope. He was appointed Historiographer Royal, and a Gentleman of the Chamber. Having by these means rendered himself a respectable member of Society, he was elected a Member of the French Academy in 1745 when fifty-two years of age. He was unhappy at Versailles. He wrote to Madame Denis complaining that he was bored to death by court society and the conversation of the great. "I have," he wrote, "to deal with twenty actors, the opera the ballet, the decorations. And for what purpose? To get a passing nod from the Dauphine." He ended by referring to Versailles as "the place that I abhor."

The climax was reached when they were all at Fontainebleau playing cards in one of the saloons. Madame du Châtelet enjoyed gambling, but chess was the only game in which Voltaire indulged. Nor did he relish late hours and overheated rooms. Madame du Châtelet was seated at the card table of the duc de Richelieu with other courtiers. Voltaire took a chair and sat behind her, hoping that the game would soon be over. When she had lost 80,000 livres his patience snapped. "Why," he hissed at her, "must you persist in playing with a gang of cheats?" Realizing that his remark had been overheard and that the outraged courtiers would obtain a *lettre de cachet* against him, entailing a third period of incarceration in the Bastille, he and Madame du Châtelet left the card table, hurried to their rooms where they gathered a few things together, and escaped that very night to Sceaux, where they were hidden, until the storm subsided, by the duchesse du Maine. In vain did Voltaire strive to avert vengeance by writing adulatory verses to Madame de Pompadour. The Queen was incensed by this tribute to her rival and the King, feeling that his private affairs were not fit subject for public poems, was also annoyed. On January 13, 1748, having recovered from his panic, Voltaire summoned up courage again to appear at Court. The courtiers turned their backs upon him and he realized that the disfavor into which he had fallen was bound to lead to punishment. He therefore drove with Madame du Châtelet to Cirey and eventually crossed the frontier into Lorraine and took refuge with King Stanislas at Lunéville. It was there that they met Saint Lambert and that the final tragedy (or was it a liberation?) occurred.

Thereafter, in July 1750, Voltaire paid his visit to Frederick the Great at Potsdam. This fantastic but revealing episode will be described in a later chapter when I consider the two autocrats who sought to represent themselves as the champions and protectors of enlightenment and as the examples of Philosopher Kings. Frederick the Great and Catherine of Russia were assuredly despots of genius: but nothing illustrates so forcibly the capacity for self-deception possessed by the European champions of the Age of Reason than the contrast between their pose of enlightened liberalism and the flagrant immorality of their public and private lives.

Five

The satire which Voltaire directed against the shams and follies of his age, contrasting with his almost subservient conformity in regard to the established order, has exposed him to the charge of insincerity. He was, it is true, capable of stratagems and evasions as tortuous as those of Pope himself. His sallies and epigrams were often cruel and he took pleasure in shocking the feelings of the ordinary man. *La Pucelle* has often been condemned, even by John Morley himself, as an outrageous lampoon, and we must agree that Joan of Arc is not a fit subject for salacious ridicule. He was a pugnacious and litigious man and his quarrels with Jean Jacques Rousseau and Frederick the Great were attended by a degree of publicity which, it must regretfully be admitted, was not wholly unwelcome to him. We must remember that by his French contemporaries he was regarded as a mighty poet and as their greatest dramatist since Racine; to this day French critics deplore that so serious a writer should have descended to the trivial, the mean, or the jocose. Yet, however monkey-like may have been his gestures, jokes and impulses, his deep and wide influence was founded on a passionate hatred of stupidity and injustice. His lifelong motto, his signature tune if one may use such an expression, was *Écrasez l'Infâme*, by which he meant a battle to the death with every form of intellectual, doctrinal, or social intolerance: "To Voltaire," writes John Morley, "an irrational prejudice was not the object of a polite coldness, but a real evil to be combated and overthrown at every hazard. . . . Cruelty was not to him a disagreeable dream of the imagination, but a vivid flame burning into his thoughts and destroying peace. Wrongdoing and injustice were not simple words on his lips; they were as knives in the heart."

It was not personal oppression only that enraged him: all his life he fought against any form of obscurantism which "might extinguish a single ray from the great sun of knowledge." To him "reason and humanity were but a single word and love of truth and passion for justice but one emotion." Under his influence men of letters began to question all established institutions and conventions. He was pioneer and patron of a mighty intellectual rebellion. He marks an epoch in himself.

Consider, above all, the dangerous but unremitting battle that he waged on behalf of the victims of intolerance. In 1724, he had intervened to save the Abbé Desfontaines who had been accused of homosexuality, the penalty for which was to be burnt alive. The Abbé never forgave Voltaire for having rescued him from the faggots and in later years became one of his most vindictive enemies. But Voltaire was not deterred by such ingratitude. When Admiral Byng was sentenced to be shot on his own quarterdeck in order to assuage a burst of popular indignation, Voltaire persuaded his successful antagonist, the duc de Richelieu, to write an open letter in the Admiral's defense. In 1762, in the fanatical city of Toulouse, the Huguenot Jean Calas was accused of having murdered his own son, although everybody knew that the boy was a manic-depressive who had committed suicide. The whole family were cast into a dungeon and kept in irons for five months. The father, then sixty-three years old, was tortured and finally had all his limbs broken with iron bars. The younger daughters were interned in convents. The youngest son, Donat, then a lad of fifteen, managed to escape into Switzerland where he appealed to Voltaire to clear his father's name. With tremendous vigor Voltaire started the great Calas campaign. He wrote letters to everybody; he published pamphlets; he started a public subscription extracting contributions from such diverse figures as the Empress of Russia, the King of Poland and even George III of England. He enlisted the sympathy of Madame de Pompadour, the duc de Richelieu, and the duc de Choiseul. After conducting his campaign for three years (during which, as he asserted, he never allowed himself to smile) the innocence of the late Calas was vindicated by the Council of Paris and M. David de Beaudrigue, who as chief magistrate of Toulouse had been responsible for this atrocity, was dismissed from his post and committed suicide. Calas' two daughters were restored to their mother and the fame of Voltaire as the champion of justice was blazoned throughout Europe.

A similar case had also occurred at Castres, when the Sirven family were accused by the Toulouse magistrates of having murdered their daughter, who was in fact demented and had drowned herself in the well. Voltaire engaged the services of Elie de Beaumont, who had been so efficient in the Calas case, and after seven years the Sirven family were also exonerated. In 1765, he denounced an even more flagrant case of intolerance when the young chevalier de La Barre was accused at Abbeville of irreverence in failing to uncover and kneel at the passage of a religious procession. He was tortured, his tongue was torn out, his head cut off, and his body committed to the flames. With him was burnt the Philosophical Dictionary of Voltaire, which they said had been the cause of his irreverence. Voltaire was both enraged and alarmed by this incident and for a few weeks escaped into Switzerland and took refuge at Rolle in the Canton of Vaud. From there he wrote and published one of the most blistering of all his pamphlets, denouncing the execution of La Barre under the title *The Cry of Innocent Blood*.

His final battle was on behalf of Lally-Tollendal who begged him clear the memory of his father, General Lally, who had been defeated by Clive in India, had been accused on his return to Paris of having sold Pondicherry to the English, had been thrown into the Bastille and thereafter beheaded on the Place de Grève. Here again, by agitation and pamphlets, Voltaire succeeded in obtaining posthumous justice. On May 26, 1778, Louis XV pronounced that Lally had been unjustly condemned. That was the last of Voltaire's victories. He was already on his deathbed when Lally-Tollendal came to tell him that the reputation of his father had been cleared.

Voltaire was satisfied that in his own century he had witnessed the triumph of the Age of Reason. "It is certain," he wrote, "that the knowledge of nature, the skeptical attitude towards old fables dignified by the name of history, a healthy metaphysic freed from the absurdities of the schools, are the fruits of that century when reason was perfected."

It is as the champion of the oppressed that I like to think of Voltaire, rather than as the sneering philosopher of the Houdon statue, or as the mischievous monkey of Potsdam. I like to think of the cheering crowds who on July 10, 1790, watched his coffin being drawn to the Pantheon, and I share the enthusiasm of those who cheered the inscription on his catafalque: "He taught us to be free."

Chapter 6

Philosopher King
(Frederick the Great, 1712–1786)

———•◆•———

Patriotism and nationalism—Frederick the Great a cosmopolitan rather than a nationalist—He is hailed by the Paris intellectuals as a Philosopher King—His birth and childhood—His brutal father—He plots to run away—His friend Katte is beheaded—He surrenders contritely to his father—His marriage and retirement at Rheinsberg—His valet Fredersdorf—He succeeds to the throne—His invasion of Silesia—The defeat and victory at Mollwitz—His duplicity and courage—The Seven Years War—He is saved from disaster by the death of the Empress Elizabeth of Russia—In spite of his crimes, he is still regarded as the champion of enlightenment—His relations with Voltaire—The visit to Potsdam—The Hirsch scandal and the Maupertuis quarrel—The scene at Frankfurt—Friendship resumed.

One

NATIONALISM, WHICH IN the nineteenth and twentieth centuries has proved so disruptive a ferment, was born with the American Revolution. Until 1775 the emotion of patriotism—although often, as Dr. Johnson observed, exploited for unworthy motives—was associated with pride, glory and honor, and closely identified with the conceptions of loyalty and obedience. It was only in the last two decades of the century that patriotism became blurred by nationalism and acquired for itself such novel ideas as liberty, equality, emancipation, and even rebellion.

During the first two-thirds of the eighteenth century, culture was more international or cosmopolitan than it had ever been since the Middle Ages. Writers, artists, and thinkers did not regard themselves as natives of any particular country: they looked upon themselves as citizens of what they called "The Republic of Letters," and we must remember that in those days the word "Republic" was no commonplace term. Educated Englishmen, such as Lord Chesterfield or Horace Walpole, felt themselves equally at home in the salons of Paris as they did in the drawing rooms of Mayfair. Although it was as true then as now that very few French people thought it necessary or interesting to learn English, no European could claim to be a man of the world unless he possessed a thorough knowledge of the language, literature and art of France. The eighteenth century, it must again and again be emphasized, was intellectually dominated by French culture, even as French culture was in itself dominated, guided, and disciplined by Paris. Newton may well have been lauded as a god and Locke and Hume venerated as major prophets; but it was by the *philosophes* and *Encyclopédistes* that the thought and taste of the civilized world was formed; the whole of Europe thought in French. It must be repeated that the term "philosophy" during the eighteenth century was employed to designate, not merely the study of abstract ideas, but also scientific knowledge and technology. Benjamin Franklin was hailed as a typical "philosopher," not because of his ideas on ethics and metaphysics, but because of his experiments in electricity. We should thus bear in mind, when using the term "philosopher," or *philosophe*, that in the eighteenth century they were applied to describe such aptitudes or professions as would today be divided under such names as "scientist," "biologist," "economist," "inventor," or even "research worker." "Philosophy" was used as an equivalent for "advanced knowledge."

Frederick the Great furnishes the classic example of a man who, although he regarded himself as a passionate patriot, had no conception even of the meaning of nationalism. He is rightly lauded by the

Germans as the genius who rendered Prussia a Great Power and as the architect from whose designs the mighty German Empire eventually arose. But in fact Frederick had little or no conception of a German nation: his unflinching ambition was to widen and fortify the dominions of the House of Brandenburg, to enhance the glory of the Hohenzollerns, and to enlarge what he regarded as his family estate. With this in mind he ran inconceivable risks and displayed superhuman endurance and prowess: but the conception of a greater Germany hardly entered his mind.

Intellectually he was wholly French. French was his natural language; he wrote in French, he spoke in French, he thought in French. His knowledge of the German language was rudimentary; he spoke it, when obliged to do so, "like a coachman"; he could not spell it at all. He regarded his native tongue as some savage teutonic dialect, so crude and rough, that it could never give birth to any literature at all. And this at a date when Lessing had already published his *Laokoon*, and when the whole of Europe was shedding tears over the sorrows of Werther. To the young Goethe, Frederick the Great was a national hero; he forgave him his preference for the French language and French literature and even, in his delightful autobiography, *Dichtung und Wahrheit*, argues that Frederick's contempt acted as a stimulus to German letters, impelling the younger generation to storm the bastions of the Republic of Letters.

Frederick was hailed by Voltaire and the *Encyclopédistes* as the Philosopher King whose coming had been dreamt of by Plato and who was now incarnated in the person of the autocrat of Prussia. Yet, his conduct was not either philosophical or progressive. In the most rapacious manner he plunged Europe into a sequence of terrible wars. He tore up the treaties which he had signed, violated the pledges that he had given, destroyed such elements as then existed of the Law of Nations, committed the signal crime of partitioning Poland, and proved to the world that the only principle that he respected was the principle of force. Seldom has there existed a monarch whose ambition was so cynical and egoistic: he possessed no principles and few ideas beyond those of self-aggrandizement and *Realpolitik*. Compared to him Napoleon was cautious and highly principled. He found Prussia a feudal state and, in spite of his loudly proclaimed liberalism, he left it even more feudal than it had been before. His gospel of "success through strength" did permanent damage to the character of his countrymen. He was an utterly unscrupulous man, who may have gained great benefits for the Hohenzollerns, but who imposed much suffering upon his own country, upon Germany, and upon the world.

The extraordinary thing about Frederick the Great is that he was not a complete hypocrite. There were moments when he believed sincerely in the lofty ideals in which he rhetorically indulged. He really did believe that he was nothing but the "first servant (*domestique*) of his people" and he did really strive in many cases to see that justice was done. Even more extraordinary is the fact that, even after the Silesian and the Seven Years Wars, even after the Partition of Poland, the *philosophes* of Paris continued to regard him as a benevolent despot, as the champion of enlightenment. One of the two most startling aberrations in which the Age of Reason indulged was to take as its hero and heroine two tyrants who, to our minds, violated all the principles by which reason should be judged and applauded. If we are to grasp how utterly unreasonable the Age of Reason really was, it is useful to examine what was felt at the time about their strange heroines and heroes. It is merely curious that they should have been taken in by such obvious charlatans as Saint Germain, Cagliostro, and Casanova. What is to our minds almost incredible is that they should have continued to admire and applaud a feckless courtesan such as Madame de Pompadour, a murderess and adulteress such as Catherine II, and a bloodstained aggressor such as Frederick the Great.

Two

He was born in Berlin on January 24, 1712. His mother, Princess Sophia Dorothea of Hanover, was a kindly and intelligent woman but neither tactful nor discreet. She was far too terrified of her brutal husband to protect her children against his violent assaults. His early childhood was not unhappy. He had a devoted governess, Madame de Roucoull, who was as maternal as a pigeon. He had a clever tutor, M. Duhan, who gave him instruction in French literature and history and inspired him with a lifelong worship of Racine. His father would not allow him to learn Greek or Latin, regarding such studies as too esoteric to befit a Prussian officer. With the surreptitious help of M. Duhan he mastered the elements of Latin and of classical mythology on the sly. He read Plutarch in a French translation and decided that he also, when he came to the throne, would become a hero of great deeds.

His father, Frederick William I, had the mentality and physique of a drill sergeant. He bullied his fourteen children mercilessly, even striking his daughters on the forehead in the presence of the courtiers. He spent his days drilling regiments on the barrack square and his passion in life, which amounted to a monomania, was to collect and drill a regiment of giants. The sovereigns of Europe came to know that the King of Prussia could be persuaded to do anything if they could provide him with a recruit of over six foot seven. The King would stride through the corridors of his palaces, yelling in fury and laying about him to right and left with the stick that he always carried. His sole relaxation was his *Bierabends*, when he would gather some of his old regimental cronies around him, smoke pipe after pipe until the room became thick with tobacco fog, indulge in what Carlyle has called his "Brobdingnagian waggeries," and tell barrack room stories, laughing grossly.

It was not until Frederick was approaching the age of puberty that his father came to suspect that the heir to the throne showed unmistakable symptoms of being an intellectual. When the father thundered, the son twittered and twitched. It was reported even that he would read books privately and that, when alone in his attic, he would play the flute. Such habits were unworthy of a soldier and King William jumped immediately to the conclusion that his heir was, not a weakling only, but effeminate, decadent, and conceited. He must be toughened and humbled. The treatment to which he was thereafter subjected was worse than normal bullying: once his father realized that there existed in Frederick a filament of independence, even of resistance, he conceived for him a passion of hatred which was almost paranoiac. When his son hesitated to answer satisfactorily the questions that were bellowed at him, he would lose all self-control, strike the boy repeatedly in the face, knock him down with his fists, and drag him by the hair in the mud. The courtiers would observe these scenes with pity and terror. Frederick derived the impression (and he may have been correct), that his father by cruelty and humiliation hoped to drive him to suicide. He decided that his only hope of survival was to escape abroad.

One summer night in 1729 when driving from Berlin to Potsdam, Frederick heard the sound of a flute amid the conifers. He descended to investigate and found that the sylvan soloist was Jean-Hermann von Katte, a sympathetic lieutenant, the son of a general and the grandson of a field marshal, whose brown face was disfigured by the scars of smallpox. If we are to believe Frederick's sister, Wilhelmina Margravine of Bayreuth, Katte was a freethinker and a libertine, combining extreme ambition with utter recklessness of conduct. They became intimate and Katte introduced the Crown Prince to his friends Keith, Ingersleben, and von Spaen. Between them they devised a plan whereby, when accompanying the King on a tour of his western dominions, they would escape across the frontier and take refuge in England. The conspiracy was discovered. Keith managed to cross the frontier in time; but Katte, the Crown Prince, and the two other confederates were arrested, courtmartialed, and imprisoned in the fortress of Cüstrin. Frederick was cashiered as a deserter, deprived of his rank as Crown Prince, and placed in solitary confinement behind bars. Ingersleben and von Spaen were sentenced to long terms of imprisonment and Katte was condemned to death. On the morning of November 5, 1730, he was led under the barred windows of Frederick's cell and two officers were instructed to hold the Crown Prince's head pressed against the window so that he would be obliged to witness the ceremony. "Pardon! Pardon!" he shouted to Katte as he passed below the window and the condemned man answered that he was happy to die in the service of so beloved a prince. Frederick was still held by force to the window as the axe descended and his friend's head fell upon the sand that had been heaped round the block. He fainted and for a while he was taken down from the window and given restoratives. When he had recovered consciousness he was again held to the window that looked down on the scaffold. The body of his friend had by then been covered by a black cloth and the head removed. But the heap of scarlet sand remained and Frederick begged and begged them hysterically to have it cleared away.

For a while it seemed that this atrocious ordeal had in fact broken his spirit. He signed a deed of capitulation, promising in future to be obedient to all his father's wishes. The clergyman who was sent to interview him in prison reported to Frederick William that the young man had in fact experienced a change of heart. He was released from solitary confinement and permitted to work under supervision as a clerk in the local administrative office, the Kriegs und Domänen Kammer, at Cüstrin. In November 1730, he was visited there by his father and made humble homage. In November 1731, he was given permission again to wear uniform and in the next year he was appointed to command a regiment at Ruppin. He devoted himself with such assiduity to the training and discipline of this regiment that his father rejoiced at the thought that the spirit of his mutinous son had in fact been broken and that henceforward he would develop a military character and prove himself a worthy Hohenzollern.

In 1733, although his distaste for women was by then notorious, he was forced to marry Princess Elizabeth of Brunswick, a plain but dutiful girl whom he regarded with repugnance. The young married couple were accorded the estate of Rheinsberg, near Neuruppin, where the architect Knobelsdorff constructed a small château in the French style decorated with panels, looking glasses, chandeliers, and pictures by Watteau, Fragonard, and Lancret. The seven years he spent at Rheinsberg, surrounded by cultivated friends, reading philosophy and studying music, were the happiest of his life. The nightmare of Cüstrin slowly faded from his consciousness. He had learnt by subservience to evade the typhoons of his father's wrath. He started his correspondence with Voltaire and embarked on original compositions; his *Considérations* on the present state of Europe and his more famous *Anti-Machiavel*. As his friend and secretary, he had Charles Etienne Jordan, a French émigré and a man of character and culture. There was also Baron Dietrich von Keyserlingk, a gay companion, to whom Frederick gave the affectionate nickname of "Cesarion." And, there was his factotum, Fredersdorf, who was probably closer to him than anybody else.

Fredersdorf had been his footman at Cüstrin and Ruppin and was thereafter promoted to be successively valet, butler, and finally "private chamberlain." Voltaire described him as Frederick's "factotum." He looked after his household, conducted his accounts, sometimes directed his secret service, accompanied him on the flute, supervised the opera and ballet artists, managed his greyhounds and his "Leibpagen" or pages of the wardrobe, and even succeeded in interesting his master in his own experiments in alchemy. In him Frederick—who, as most of those who have been ill treated by their fathers, tended to be morbidly suspicious—placed unquestioning confidence. He addressed him by the intimate "du" and wrote him endless letters manifesting concern at Fredersdorf's poor health. "Wohr Dihr," he wrote for instance in November 1753, "das uriniren des Nacts Stärker quelet, so lasse Dirh nuhr erweichende milch-bäder machen, die aber beliebe nicht so Warm sind." Frederick's letters to Fredersdorf can only be understood if read phonetically, since he had no conception at all of the grammar or spelling of the German language. Many of the letters are concerned with the pranks of the young page Carl Friedrich Pirch, or "Carol," of whom both the King and Fredersdorf were very fond and who was killed in battle at the age of seventeen. There are letters authorizing Fredersdorf to buy fresh velvet for the liveries of "Sidau, Canegiser und Dinep" whose real names were von Sydow, Kennegiesser, and von Donop. And there are repeated references to the greyhounds and their love affairs and illnesses. Frederick's correspondence with Fredersdorf, although difficult to interpret because of their extraordinary "Kutscher" language, show him at his most human.

His wife, the Crown Princess, during the Rheinsberg years continued to inhabit the same house as her husband. He was quite polite to her in public, but would never admit her into private intimacy. Not long after succeeding to the throne he informed her that henceforward they must live separately and relegated her to a palace of her own. They only met thereafter on official occasions when he would treat her with glacial ceremony. Yet, was consideration always observed? "It is a melancholy sight," wrote Sir Charles Hanbury Williams to Fox in October 1750, "to see the Queen. She is a good woman and must have been extremely handsome. It is impossible to hate her; and though his unnatural tastes won't let him live with her, common humanity ought to teach him to permit her to enjoy her separate state in comfort. Instead of which, he never misses an opportunity of mortifying this inoffensive, oppressed Queen, and the Queen Mother assists her dearly beloved son in this to the utmost of her power by never showing her common civility or hardly ever speaking to her."

The misfortune was that Elizabeth of Brunswick loved her eccentric husband and was unable to conceal her affection. Frederick possessed what Professor Gaxotte has called "the terrible need to humiliate those who loved him." The psychologist may suggest that this must be ascribed to the humiliations from which he had himself suffered in his youth. This may furnish an explanation of his conduct; but no excuse.

Three

On May 31, 1740, Frederick William I died and the Crown Prince at the age of twenty-eight succeeded as King of Prussia. During the closing years of his life Frederick William had realized that his heir possessed exceptional qualities of character and mind. He may have been impressed even by the furtive obstinacy with which his son resisted complete subjection by his bullying father. In 1736, on an occasion when Frederick William imagined that he had been betrayed by Austria, he pointed to the Crown Prince with his cane and shouted "There stands one who will avenge me." In the last years of his life, when suffering much from dropsy, he exclaimed to those around him. "When I am dead, you will say 'Well that's the end of the old bully'—but believe me he who is to succeed me will tell you all to go to hell." Certainly the old brute acquired some conception of Frederick's adamant character before he died.

During his seven years at Rheinsberg Frederick had devoted deep study to the history of the House of Brandenburg and to the geography and resources of Prussia's scattered dominions. Although on paper the Kingdom of Prussia covered 12,000 square kilometers and contained 2,200,000 inhabitants, it consisted in fact of diverse scraps and pieces, held under varying forms of tenure and differing in resources and tradition. Frederick was as much convinced as his father had ever been that the only means of providing unity for so scattered a realm was a highly centralized autocracy. He may have proclaimed that the King was no more than the first servant of his people, but in practice he was, and remained, rigidly convinced that all power must be concentrated in the royal hands and that in no circumstances could that power be delegated or transferred. He was also convinced that of all the German States, Prussia, separated as it was from Brandenburg, could not possibly be preserved against absorption by Russia; and the Saxon frontier was only thirty miles from Berlin. It was essential, therefore, if Prussia were to survive, that her territory should be rendered more compact and her frontiers more defensible, even if that entailed seizing the possessions of other countries by force. Frederick was also fired by a Plutarchian ambition for glory and, what was more important, had inherited from his father a highly disciplined army and a war chest of over a million pounds.

The death of the Emperor Charles VI on October 20, 1740, provided him with an opportunity for a smash and grab raid. The Emperor before his death had promulgated what is known as "The

Pragmatic Sanction," proclaiming his daughter Maria Theresa as sole heiress to his vast dominions. By 1740 all the European Powers, with the exception of Bavaria and the Palatinate, had accepted the Sanction and pledged themselves to recognize Maria Theresa as the lawful heiress. Frederick, the moment he heard of the Emperor's death, decided to violate this pledge. Contending that Prussia possessed some inherited rights over the Silesian districts of Brieg, Leibnitz, Wohlau and Jagersdorf, he, without a declaration of war, invaded Silesia, taking the Austrians entirely by surprise and occupying the whole province, as he contended, at the cost of only twenty men and two officers. He did not himself set store by legal claims. "The question of right," he wrote to Podewils, his more cautious Foreign Secretary, "is for you to elaborate; work it out secretly since the orders to the army have already been issued." This flagrant violation of the Law of Nations shocked the conscience of Europe. In the noble bosom of Maria Theresa it kindled the flame of revenge. Carlyle in his worship of *Realpolitik* and the superman seeks to defend this aggression. Macaulay on the other hand contends that it was "the selfish rapacity of the King of Prussia" that set the whole of Europe on fire, and that owing to him the flames spread across the world. It was Frederick, writes Macaulay, in a flamboyant passage, who was responsible for the fact that "black men fought on the coast of Coramandel and red men scalped each other by the Great Lakes of North America." It must be admitted that Frederick's seizure of Silesia started a chain reaction which continued, with rare intermissions, until 1763. His adventure almost resulted in the extinction of his own country and earned him the reputation of reckless unscrupulousness, superhuman tenacity, outstanding military genius, and complete cynicism. The miracle of his success did permanent damage to the Law of Nations and to the political thinking of his own countrymen.

It is beyond the scope of this study to deal with wars, or to estimate whether it was the Napoleonic genius of Frederick or the discipline of his infantry that saved Prussia from extinction. He certainly shattered the old seventeenth-century conception that war was a matter of slow mass maneuver and the possession of strategic fortresses. He introduced the idea that the best form of defensive was rapid offensive, and the amazing mobility that he imposed on his army, as during the weeks between Rossbach and Leuthen, caused the pundits of the established school of strategy to gasp with amazement.

His military career was not one of uninterrupted victory. At Mollwitz, on April 10, 1741, the Prussians were at the outset defeated by the Austrian cavalry and the aged general, count Schwerin, told Frederick that if he wished to avoid capture he must leave the field. Accompanied by a solitary aide-de-camp the King galloped through the night and did not pause until he reached the safety of Löwen. He there learnt that, owing to the stubborn resistance of the Prussian infantry, defeat had been transformed into victory. He never recovered from the shock of realizing that he had absented himself from this unexpected triumph. In future, fearing that he might be suspected of cowardice, he exposed his person in battle with such recklessness as to fill his generals and soldiers with admiration and alarm. Yet he never wholly mastered his neurotic temperament and there were moments during his campaigns when he surrendered to despondency and even contemplated suicide. During these intervals of self-distrust he would fortify himself by playing the flute and writing execrable poems in the French language. What compels our admiration is that a man of so nervous a temperament could have displayed, amid dangers and disasters which would have affrighted the most stubborn soul, so fine a resilience and such stolid willpower. His Silesian campaigns ended in the Peace of Dresden under which Maria Theresa ceded to him the province of Silesia, although resolved to recapture it as soon as an opportunity offered. Frederick, although by his conduct of the campaigns he had achieved high repute as a military commander, had, owing to his tricky conduct towards his associates and allies, lost all diplomatic credit. His cynical disregard of all treaties and pledges earned him the reputation of the most unreliable of European monarchs. He was never trusted again. He was himself well aware of the suspicion he had aroused. "Henceforth," he wrote, "I would not attack a cat except in self-defense. We have drawn upon ourselves the envy of Europe by seizing Silesia and our action has put all our neighbors on the alert; there is not one who does not distrust us."

Although Frederick saw himself as one of the most deft of European statesmen, he failed to grasp the essential principle that diplomacy is the art of inspiring confidence and that cunning in international relations invariably defeats its own ends. In spite, moreover, of his intensive studies of the several European "systems," he committed the frightful blunder of assuming that even Kaunitz would be unable to reverse the historical rivalry between France and Austria and that whatever might happen there would never exist the danger of an alliance between Vienna and Versailles. It was with equal blindness that the German statesmen of the early twentieth century took it for granted that England would never be able to compose her differences with Russia and were thus taken completely aback by the Anglo-Russian Convention of 1907.

When the Seven Years War broke out in 1756, Frederick found himself faced with a coalition consisting of France, Austria, Russia, Saxony and Sweden, whereas his only friend in Europe was Great Britain, whose energies were concentrated on conquering an Empire overseas and who could do little to help Frederick beyond providing financial subsidies. Thus on June 11, 1756, Frederick was severely defeated at Kolin by the Austrians under Daun and only recovered himself next year by the resounding and totally unexpected victories of Rossbach and Leuthen. By the autumn of 1757, nonetheless, it seemed as if Frederick were doomed: the extinction of Prussia and the House of Brandenburg was universally regarded as inevitable. By then the Austrians had driven the Prussians out of Bohemia; the Russians had advanced into East Prussia; the French had crossed the Weser and were advancing into West Germany; and the Swedes were established in Pomerania. In August 1759, the Prussians were badly beaten by the Russians at Kunersdorf and Frederick, who by then had lost some 75,000 men of his army and who was entirely dependent on British subsidies for his finance, was reduced to a mood of nervous prostration. He was convinced that it would no longer be possible for little Prussia to continue the struggle upon four fronts. In January 1762, however, the miracle occurred. The Empress Elizabeth of Russia, who had never been very cautious in regard to her health, had a stroke on leaving church. Her successor, the demented Peter III, who had a passionate admiration for Frederick, withdrew the invading Russian armies; the Swedes followed his example; Prussia, on the very verge of catastrophe, was saved. In February of the next year Frederick managed to conclude a peace, which left him in possession of Silesia and enabled him to devote the rest of his life to repairing the damage that the Seven Years War had caused. He died at Potsdam on August 17, 1786. He had wished to be buried on the terrace of Sans Souci among his greyhounds. His successor ignored these wishes and had his coffin placed in the Garnison Kirche at Potsdam. When in the spring of 1945 the Russian armies were advancing on Berlin, the coffin of Frederick the Great was removed from Potsdam and hidden, together with the coffins of Marshal von Hindenburg and Frau von Hindenburg, in the castle of Marburg, where it was found by the advancing Americans. It was thereafter transferred to the Hohenzollern vault at Hechingen.

Four

When we consider that Frederick the Great was universally regarded as one of the most unscrupulous aggressors in history and as the most Machiavellian of diplomatists, we are left wondering how it came that the intellectuals of Paris persisted in praising him as the champion of enlightenment. They had faith in the equality of human beings and in their "natural rights": he contended that the ordinary man possessed no natural rights at all. They believed in Free Trade, whereas he imposed a most rigid system of protection and tariffs. They believed in the perfectibility of man, whereas he regarded human beings as "that accursed race" and one that was utterly incapable of improvement. The only ideas they shared in common was a vague deism, a faith in the "Universal Artificer" and a contempt for superstition and intolerance. Frederick was at heart a fatalist, who regarded religion merely as a convenient opium for the masses. But he was certainly sincere in his dislike of theological dogma and ecclesiastical tyranny and it was this liberal attitude that caused him to be hailed by the *Encyclopédistes* as a Philosopher King.

Yet, although he was continually prating about liberal reforms his own internal reforms were few indeed. He did abolish torture and took immense pains to see that justice was administered with expedition and without corruption. But he had no sympathy with the common man, regarding his subjects merely as taxpayers and cannon fodder. "The Prussian Monarchy," wrote the British Ambassador, Hugh Elliot, "reminds me of a vast prison, in the center of which appears a great keeper, occupied in the care of his captives." Lessing denounced Prussia as "the most slavish country in Europe." Sir Charles Hanbury Williams, another English observer, described Frederick as "the completest tyrant God ever made, for the scourge of an offending people. I had rather be a post horse than his first Minister, or his brother, or his wife. He hates in general to see people happy. For his sway is founded on vexation; and on oppression is his throne established." Even Thomas Carlyle, with his reverence for the superman, admits that Frederick was "a questionable hero," but contends that he justified himself by being "a Reality" and by not surrendering to hypocrisy. Yet, it was Frederick's cynical insistence that the interests of the State were above the rules of private morals that established in German hearts and minds the doctrine of *Realpolitik*—a doctrine which has brought much misery to mankind.

Of all the events of Frederick's life the most interesting, for any study of the Age of Reason, is the mutual infatuation that flamed between him and Voltaire. From the psychological aspect it furnishes a perfect case history of the manner in which adulation can be degraded into subservience and subservience lead to venomous hatred. It also demonstrates the fundamental contempt for the pure intellectual that, under the friction of personal contact, is aroused in the man of action. Conversely, it shows us how supreme and universal

Voltaire dictating

had by the middle of the eighteenth century become the prestige of the Paris intellectuals and how Voltaire in particular had come to be regarded as the dictator of the Republic of Letters. Dr. Johnson went so far as to describe Frederick as "Voltaire's foot-boy." Even if we admit that the literary vanity of soldiers passes human comprehension, we must agree that Frederick's reverence for Voltaire as his master and proofreader was a perfectly sincere emotion: Alexander the Great displayed less awe in the presence of Aristotle. It is a strange story, and one that does not increase our esteem for Frederick, for Voltaire or for human nature in general.

Frederick's correspondence with Voltaire, which contains 654 items and covers a period of forty-two years, began in August 1736 during the Rheinsberg period, when Frederick was twenty-four years of age and Voltaire forty-two. Frederick wrote to acclaim Voltaire as the greatest poet and thinker of the age. Voltaire in reply expressed his delight at discovering "a philosopher prince who will make men happy, a prince who would restore the golden age." Frederick compared Voltaire to the great legislators of history, to Solon and Lycurgus. "My future actions," he wrote, "will prove the fruit of your teaching." "You think like Trajan," Voltaire replied in January 1737, "you write like Pliny, your French is that of our best classical authors. . . . Under your auspices Berlin will become the Athens of Germany, perhaps even of Europe." He accompanied this letter with a poem in which Frederick is represented as possessing "the talents of Virgil and the virtues of Augustus." He begged the Crown Prince to continue in his mission of enlightenment. "Continue," he writes, "and you will destroy the monsters of superstition and fanaticism, these enemies of the Divinity of Reason. Be the King of philosophers, while other princes are no more than the King of men." Frederick responds by sending him the manuscript of *Anti-Machiavel*. "Monseigneur," replies Voltaire, "the welfare of the world demands the publication of this book."

On learning of the death of Frederick William, Voltaire composed for his royal pupil an Accession Ode:

Enfin voiçi le jour le plus beau de ma vie
Que le monde attendait et que vous seul craignez,
Le grand jour où la terre est par vous embellie,
Le jour où vous régnez.

Quelle est du Dieu vivant le véritable image?
Vous, des talents, des arts et des vertus l'appui,
Vous, Salomon du Nord, plus savant et plus sage,
Et moins faible que lui.

At last has come the finest day of my life;
A day the world has waited for which you were the only
    man to dread;
That great day when the world is to be embellished by
    your accession;
The day that you reign.

Who is the true image of the living God?
You—the support of talent, of art, of virtue,
You, the Solomon of the North, but more learned and
    wiser than Solomon,
And less weak than he was.

To which Frederick replied in clumsy doggerel:

Désormais ce peuple que j'aime
Est l'unique Dieu que je sers.
Adieu mes vers et mes concerts,
Tous les plaisirs, Voltaire même,
Mon devoir est mon dieu suprême.

Henceforward the People whom I love
Will be the only God that I serve.
Farewell my verses and my concerts.
Farewell all my pleasures, even Voltaire himself.
My duty is my supreme God.

After four years of this ecstatic correspondence they met near
Cleves in September 1740. Frederick was suffering from fever at the

time but much enjoyed Voltaire's conversation which, he asserted "combined the eloquence of Cicero, the gentleness of Pliny and the wisdom of Agrippa." They met again for a week in November of that year. This second visit was less successful. Frederick was irritated that Voltaire should have charged him so much for his traveling expenses and made so many corrections in the style and grammar of the *Anti-Machiavel*. Then came the unprovoked attack on Austria and Voltaire, who was by temperament pacific, was shocked. He wrote to Frederick urging him "To stabilize Europe now that you have shattered it. . . . You are the hero of Germany and the arbiter of Europe. May you also become their peacemaker." He at the same time, and with his usual penetration, urged Frederick to be a little less suspicious of others. This warning went unheeded. Frederick remained convinced that "deceit and duplicity are the dominant traits of most of those at the top who ought to set an example." But he continued, even from camp, to address to Voltaire his idiotic poems:

> *De vos œuvres je suis jaloux;*
> *Cher Voltaire—donnez-les-nous.*
> *Par cœur je voudrais vous apprendre;*
> *Il n'est pas salut sans vous.*

> I am jealous of your works,
> Dear Voltaire, give them to us.
> I should like to learn them by heart;
> You are my sole salvation.

By that time Voltaire had ceased to address his correspondent as "Your Majesty" and addressed him as "Your Humanity." This compliment was subtle but wholly undeserved.

The French Government by this time were completely bewildered regarding the motives and aims of Frederick's policy. They conceived the idea that it might be possible for Voltaire to find out more than an official ambassador. Yet if he were to visit Potsdam as a secret agent he must be provided with "cover." He had been rejected for the Academy, and the Court, with his knowledge and assent, proceeded to ban his play *La Mort de César* a few days before it was due to be performed. Thus outraged, Voltaire could appear at the Prussian Court in the guise of an ill-treated refugee, seeking patronage and comfort. It was whispered that Madame du Châtelet, Voltaire's formidable mistress, was strongly opposed to the visit. "Madame cannot stop me," he wrote to Frederick. "It is you, Sire, that are now my grande passion." Voltaire arrived in Berlin on August 30, 1743, and left it on October 12. Frederick had not for one moment been taken in by Louis XV's stratagem and realized that Voltaire had been sent to Prussia in order to ascertain his future intentions. "I am not," he informed Voltaire, "inclined to talk politics with you, which would be like offering a glass of medicine to a mistress. I think we shall do better to talk poetry." As a matter of fact Frederick had already decided by then to enter into an alliance with France, but preferred to conduct the negotiations through official channels. Voltaire, unable to furnish his government with any secret information, felt that he had been exposed to ridicule. A chill resulted. Between 1744 and 1748 the letters and love poems diminish in ecstasy and in number. Madame du Châtelet died in 1749.

Five

On hearing that Voltaire was free of all encumbrances (although in fact he had already before the death of Madame du Châtelet started his long liaison with his niece Madame Denis) Frederick felt that it was now the moment to secure him as a member of his household. He wrote to Voltaire, offering him the post of Chamberlain, the Order of Merit, free lodging, and a salary of £850 a year, if he would come to Potsdam. This disastrous visit lasted from June 1750 to March 1753.

For a while all went well. Frederick enjoyed entertaining Voltaire at his elegant suppers at Sans Souci and Voltaire was by no means indifferent to the homage which the monarch accorded him. It was Voltaire's inveterate cupidity that caused the first breach between them. Through the intermediary of a Berlin Jew of the name of

Hirsch, Voltaire indulged in a complicated plot to smuggle currency in from Saxony. As security for the stratagem Hirsch deposited some jewels with Voltaire and claimed afterwards that he had taken out the good stones and replaced them by fakes. Lessing, who by a strange coincidence was employed to translate some of the documents, recorded afterwards that it was impossible to decide the rights and the wrongs of the case since both parties to the dispute were rogues. Voltaire managed to win the case that Hirsch brought against him, but great scandal was aroused in Berlin and Europe. Frederick was enraged that a member of his household should have been publicly proved to be engaged in a smuggling operation. "It is a great pity," he wrote, "that a celebrity in the Republic of Letters should be so contemptible in character." Voltaire wrote groveling letters of apology and contrition. "If the Queen of Sheba," he wrote, "had fallen into disgrace with Solomon she could not have suffered more." Frederick was not appeased.

The Potsdam courtiers were not slow to stir the troubled waters. To Voltaire La Mettrie repeated Frederick's remark that "one squeezes an orange and then discards the rind." To Frederick Maupertuis repeated Voltaire's complaint that the King was "always sending him his dirty linen to wash," thereby casting reflections on the King's verse and prose. On returning to Potsdam after a short absence, Voltaire found that his apartments at Sans Souci had been repainted in yellow (the color of disfavor) and that monkeys and foxes had been depicted on the walls and embroidered on the sofa covers. Voltaire in his turn became suspicious. For Frederick's sake he had abandoned home, friends and country and yet the King did nothing to protect him against his enemies. Then came the Maupertuis scandal. Maupertuis, a French mathematician of eminence, had been appointed by Frederick president of The Prussian Academy of Art and Science. He and Voltaire were not well attuned and regarded each other with jealousy and suspicion. Maupertuis became involved in a controversy with König as to whether a letter from Leibnitz was authentic or not. Voltaire wrote a pamphlet taking the side of König: Frederick wrote a pamphlet taking the side of Maupertuis. It was then that Voltaire lost his head. Using the printing license which he had already obtained for a pamphlet *In Defense of Lord Bolingbroke* he published instead his *Diatribe on Doctor Akakia*, in which Maupertuis was ridiculed with skill and vigor. Frederick gave orders that this Diatribe should be burnt by the public hangman and the ashes sent in as a propitiatory gesture to Maupertuis. Voltaire wrote the King a cringing letter begging him to spare "an old man crushed by sickness and grief." Frederick replied: "Your effrontery astonished me.... If your works deserve statues, your conduct merits chains." He asks Voltaire to return to him both the Order of Merit and the Chamberlain's Key. Voltaire obeyed, but accompanied the key and the medal with these verses:

> *Je les reçus avec tendresse;*
> *Je vous les rends avec douleur;*
> *C'est ainsi qu'un amant dans son extrême ardeur*
> *Rend le portrait de sa maitresse.*

> I accepted them with tenderness;
> I return them in sorrow.
> Thus will a lover in his passion
> Send back the portrait of his mistress.

Frederick on this sent Fredersdorf to Voltaire to return him the two emblems. Voltaire left Berlin in March 1753 on the excuse of wishing to take the waters at Plombières. He had with him in his luggage a privately printed edition of Frederick's unpublished poems. The King, not without reason, foresaw that on arrival in France Voltaire would revenge himself by publishing and ridiculing these doggerel verses. He thus told Fredersdorf that he must see to it that the book was recovered at any cost. Fredersdorf, knowing that Voltaire would be stopping a few days at Frankfurt, where he was to be joined by Madame Denis, sent what may well have been muddled instructions to the Prussian Resident at Frankfurt, a typical civil servant of the name of Freytag. This ardent official placed Voltaire on arrival under domiciliary arrest and, when he tried to escape, had both him and Madame

Denis marched through the town under guard and interned in their hotel. Frederick, to do him justice, was unaware of such ill-treatment and once he heard of it sent immediate instructions that Voltaire should be released. Thereafter for a while the King only replied to Voltaire's whining and indignant letters through the hand of his secretary, the Abbé de Prades. But the fascination of Voltaire in the end proved too strong for him. He resumed his habit of sending his verses to Voltaire who was expected to correct and polish them. "The King," wrote Voltaire, "sends me more verses than he has battalions or squadrons. He tries hard to recapture me. He is an exceptional man—very attractive at a distance." Frederick forgave him his trickery and his lies. "After all," he wrote, "you have given me more pleasure than you have done me harm." He refused, however, to receive any more hysterical complaints about the treatment accorded by Herr Freytag to Madame Denis. "Understand," he wrote, "that I refuse to hear anything more about this niece of yours, who bores me." But on the whole the correspondence between the "Hermit of Sans Souci" and the "Patriarch of Ferney" resumed its old friendly tone. "The two most conspicuous figures," writes Dr. Gooch, "in the life of Europe parted in peace."

Chapter 7

Semiramis

(Catherine the Great, 1729–1796)

————•◆•————

The four Empresses—Elizabeth designates her nephew Peter of Holstein as her successor and wishes to find him a bride—Sophie of Anhalt-Zerbst is chosen—She comes to Russia with her mother, adopts the name of Catherine, is betrothed and married—Peter is impotent and alcoholic—The young couple are isolated and kept under surveillance—Catherine's patience, pride and courage—Her affair with Saltikov—Her son Paul is born—Poniatowski arrives—Gregory Orlov—Death of the Empress—Peter forced to abdicate and Catherine thereafter rules Russia as autocrat for thirty-four years—Her achievement—Her prudence—The Nakaz of 1767—Orlov succeeded by Vassiltchikov and then by Potemkin—Character of Potemkin as drawn by Prince de Ligne—He organizes the Crimean journey and provides Catherine with a succession of carefully selected lovers—Death of Potemkin—Platon Zubov—Catherine and the *Encyclopédistes*—Voltaire and Diderot—The decline of her glory and powers—Her sudden death—Her epitaph.

One

INHERITANCE, IN THE House of Romanov, was always precarious. Peter the Great had contended that it was the Tsar alone who, as autocrat, had the right to designate his successor. Having murdered his own eldest son, Alexis, he ignored the rights of his grandson, the Grand Duke Peter, and by an ukase of 1722 proclaimed that on his death the throne must descend to his widow Catherine. On May 7, 1724, she was solemnly crowned as Empress-Consort in the Uspensky Cathedral at Moscow. On this occasion the slatternly charwoman of Pastor Glück, the former camp callet, wore a crown enriched by as many as 2,564 precious stones, including a central ruby as large as an egg. After her coronation she risked her liberty and life by entering into an affair with one of the court ushers, Wilhelm Mons. Peter the Great, as I have already recounted, who seems to have regarded her as some magic mascot, moderated his revenge; he was satisfied by forcing her to keep on her dressing table the severed head of Wilhelm Mons, preserved in a large bottle of spirits of wine. Thus when Peter died on January 28, 1725, Catherine was proclaimed sovereign by Prince Menshikov and Count Tolstoy with the support of the palace guards. She could neither read nor write; she was a confirmed alcoholic; but she was a shrewd and strong-willed woman, who had learnt much from her late husband, and who ruled with firmness, and not without wisdom, during the two years that remained to her of life. She was succeeded by the rightful heir, Peter II, the son of the murdered Alexis, who however died of smallpox three years after his accession, on January 30, 1730. The throne then passed to the Grand Duchess Anne, daughter of Ivan V, the lunatic brother of Peter the Great. She ruled for ten years with the assistance of her hated lover, Ernst Johann Bühren. By her will she appointed Bühren regent for her great-nephew, the infant Ivan VI. On the night of December 6–7, 1741, the Grand Duchess Elizabeth, daughter of Peter the Great by Martha Skavronskaya, suborned the Preobrajensky regiment, marched on the Winter Palace, arrested Ivan VI and his mother, and proclaimed herself sovereign. She reigned with strength and cunning for the next twenty years. Her eventual successor was Catherine II, rightly called "Catherine the Great."

The great Peter, as I have said, had some idea that a monarchy ought to be elective rather than hereditary. He certainly condemned the system of primogeniture as illogical and "dangerous." He may even have wished to revert to the old tribal system, under which, on the death of a chief, his successor was chosen from among the sturdiest and most competent surviving males of the family. Yet the males of the Romanov family, throughout the course of the eighteenth century, proved neither competent nor sturdy. Four of them were mentally unbalanced and four of them were murdered owing to a palace or a praetorian revolution. Russia, from 1725 to 1796, was ruled by four unusual Empresses, Catherine I, Anne, Elizabeth, and Catherine II. Each of these was assisted, but not controlled, by favorites. Catherine I relied on Menshikov and Tolstoy; Anne on the egregious Bühren; Elizabeth's constant adviser was the sagacious Bestuzhev-Ryumin; and Catherine II had the support of the Orlov family and thereafter of the vast Potemkin. These four women consolidated the vast but unstable heritage that the great Peter bequeathed. Of the four of them, Catherine the Great was by far the most gifted and the most interesting. In that, in her eccentric way, she was representative of the flux and reflux of educated opinion in the eighteenth century, her life and character deserve to be studied in some detail. Compared to her contemporaries—the virtuous but flustered Maria Theresa of Austria, the frivolous Pompadour, the well-meaning but tactless Marie Antoinette—she can rank with Elizabeth I of England as one of the most masculine, as well as one of the most feminine, rulers that the world has ever seen.

Two

The Empress Elizabeth decided that the throne should after her death descend to her nephew Peter, son of her sister Anne, who had married the Duke of Schleswig Holstein. He was summoned from Germany to Russia, produced as hereditary Grand Duke, and instructed in the traditions and requirements of the Empire by his formidable aunt. He was a sullen boy, and proved recalcitrant to this education. His heart remained in Germany; he hated anything Russian and did not conceal his antipathy; he preferred German soldiers to Russian soldiers and the Lutheran to the Orthodox Church. He possessed a childish character, an incurable taste for low company, marked aversion from any form of study, and a violent temper. If not a certifiable lunatic, he was certainly a clinical specimen of arrested development. The Empress, who was a shrewd if uncultivated woman, realized her mistake. She decided that the only hope for this heir, whom she had selected perhaps impulsively and had entirely failed to train, was to secure for him an intelligent and very healthy wife. The Russian envoys in Europe received instructions to look about for desirable candidates among the many German princesses of marriageable age. Frederick the Great was himself consulted and put forward the name of the daughter of a very minor German royalty, Sophia Augusta Frederica, daughter of Prince Christian of Anhalt-Zerbst, a general in the Prussian army and at the time governor of the port and fortress of Stettin.

We know little of Catherine's Pomeranian childhood. She was educated by governesses and tutors and, as was the fashion in eighteenth century Europe, she acquired French as her main language. The governor's house at Stettin still exists in grim ugliness. The Anhalts were not a wealthy family and it is probable that Prince Christian had little income beyond his army pay. From time to time they would leave their dark Baltic harbor and pay visits to relations in Saxony and Thüringia. Catherine was devoted to her father, who was a serious, studious, and conscientious man. "I believe," she wrote in her *Memoirs*, "that it was his sincerity that caused him to be so attached to the republican ideas which I have inherited from him. This may seem almost unbelievable considering my position and the ambitions I have always fostered." There have, it is true, lived many stauncher republicans than Catherine II; but it would be an error to ascribe to hypocrisy, or to her outstanding gift for self-advertisement, the liberal and progressive sentiments that she so frequently, so widely and so loudly proclaimed. At least until 1790 Catherine remained a liberal at heart.

On January 1, 1744, to the astonishment of the governor and his wife, an official invitation was received from the Empress Elizabeth inviting them to pay a visit to St. Petersburg and to bring their young daughter with them. Her father was inclined to refuse the invitation, having no wish that either he or his family should become involved in high politics. Her mother, in spite of her vanity, was thoroughly alarmed. It was Catherine herself, then but a schoolgirl of fifteen, who insisted that they should accept. "It was I," she confesses in her *Memoirs*, "who finally made my parents take this decision." Frederick the Great can have had small conception of how formidable the child-candidate whom he had recommended was destined to prove.

On February 9, 1774, having bid a tearful farewell to her father, whom she never saw again, Catherine, and her tiresome mother arrived at St. Petersburg. They were lodged in the Annenhof Palace. The Empress Elizabeth realized immediately that this dim little German princess possessed the very qualities that she had hoped for in her nephew's wife. She was so wholesome that vitality was manifest in every curve of her buxom body; she possessed fine eyes and a skin that remained smooth and translucent until her death; she was remarkably intelligent, but seemed at the same time to be of a submissive nature. She was everything that the Empress had desired. Almost immediately the engagement was announced. The bride-elect was admitted to the Orthodox Church and changed her name from Sophia to Catherine. She started at once to learn Russian. "The Grand Duke," she records, "loved me passionately. My respect and gratitude to the Empress was extreme." Without delay this gifted and resolute German schoolgirl settled down to fulfill what were to be the three main objects of her early married life, namely "to please the Grand Duke, to please the Empress, to please the nation." She never managed to achieve the first two of these objectives; the third objective she mastered with remarkable subtlety and resolve. She decided that she must become more Russian than the Russians and thus acquire the popularity which her husband, with his undisguised preference for everything German, had flung away. She became intensely patriotic and devout. "God is my witness," she wrote, "that the glory of this country is my glory." Never did she visit a provincial capital, or even a village, without immediately entering the church and groveling in an ecstasy of worship in front of the local ikons. "I advise," she noted in her aphorisms, "avoiding consultation with Germans of either sex." "I may be too young," she wrote with characteristic shrewdness, "to become a favorite sovereign, but I must behave as if I believed myself to be one." "If I may venture to be frank," she wrote again, "I would say about myself that I am every inch a gentleman with a mind much more male than female. But together with this I was anything but masculine and combined with the mind and temperament of a man the attractions of a lovable woman."

The "passionate love" which, as she recorded, the Grand Duke manifested for her at their first meeting, rapidly cooled into indifference and later turned into aversion mingled with fear. He was almost certainly impotent and Catherine herself, until the age of sixteen, was ignorant of the facts of life. She believed that there was no difference between the sexes, except that men, for some odd reason, were expected to shave. In later life she did much to repair this gap in her experience.

She must soon have realized that the Grand Duke was incapable of consummating their marriage and that to her own company he preferred the society of his footmen and grooms and the childish games in which he indulged. He was forever playing with toy soldiers and when Catherine and he retired for the night he would lock the bedroom door and she, poor girl, would pretend to enjoy playing with the dolls that he spread, giggling with delight, upon the counterpane. It was only gradually that she realized that her boy husband was mentally as well as physically deficient. When drunk (and he was generally drunk) he would indulge in orgies of sadistic rage. He would scourge his attendants and on one occasion she came upon him flogging a dachshund who was suspended by a rope from the ceiling while its hind legs were held firmly by one of the kennel men. On that occasion she was terrified by the glint of insanity in his eyes.

He was sixteen years old when he married, small and infantile, but "quite good looking until he caught the smallpox." "To tell the truth," she admits in her *Memoirs*, "I believe that the Crown of Russia attracted me more than his person. Hope for a Crown, not of a celestial order, but very much of this earth, sustained my spirit and courage." It was not ambition alone that sustained her. She was possessed of unconquerable pride. "I did not like being pitied," she wrote in her *Memoirs*, "nor did I like to complain. I was too proud to grumble and the very idea of being miserable was repulsive to me."

She needed all the pride and courage that she could muster. Soon after her marriage on August 21, 1745, her mother who had remained on at St. Petersburg fell into disgrace. Intoxicated by the extravagance she saw around her, she contracted huge debts and refused to pay the jewelers and dressmakers who dunned her with their bills. The Empress Elizabeth was angered by this foolishness and ordered her to leave Russia. Princess Anhalt-Zerbst returned to Germany with tears of anger and already pregnant from a love affair in which she had engaged with Count Betsky. This incident did not increase Catherine's prestige at Court.

The Empress was difficult to please. She possessed a violent temper, and when her courtiers observed "the twitch in the corner of her eye," they would scatter rapidly, well knowing that the twitch was the portent of an approaching storm, when screams would echo and heavy blows be dealt right and left. Like all uneducated people, the Empress Elizabeth was intensely suspicious. She was jealous of women younger or more intelligent than herself. She was indolent and self-indulgent with coarse tastes. She loathed the suspected superiority of others and would forbid the very mention of subjects that she disliked, such as illness, death, Voltaire, French culture, scientific matters, Frederick the Great, or women more beautiful than herself. It says much for Catherine's superhuman patience and intellectual suppleness that she managed to avoid the extreme wrath of the Empress for eighteen years. Certainly she earned the glory and the pleasures which she eventually enjoyed.

Surrounded by spies on every side, the subject of constant court intrigues, Catherine had to watch her every step with wariness. "For eighteen years," she recorded in her *Memoirs*, "I lived a life that would have rendered ten other women mad, and twenty others in my place would have died of a broken heart." The life of the Court was to her intolerable. "There was no conversation, everybody cordially hated everybody else, slander took the place of wit, and any mention of politics was reported as *lèse-majesté*. Intricate intrigues were mistaken for shrewdness. Science and art were never touched upon as everyone was ignorant of such subjects. One could lay a wager that half the Court could hardly read and I would be surprised if more than a third could write." The Empress would give masked balls at which she insisted that her courtiers should appear, the men dressed as women and the women as men. Catherine was unable to conceal her hatred of such travesties. Gradually "the Young Court" as it was called came under suspicion. One by one the ladies and gentlemen, the dressers and footmen, who were reported to have gained the confidence of the Grand Duke or his wife, were sent into exile. Three watchdogs were attached to them, the Choglokov couple, and Frau Krause, who reported their every movement and conversation. It is symptomatic of Catherine's strength and charm that in the end she tamed these three watchdogs until they crouched at her feet and licked her hand.

The Grand Duke at one moment was so foolish as to allow his kennel men to introduce him to a Lieutenant Baturine of the Butirski regiment who was suspected of being involved in a plot to depose the Empress and to enthrone Peter in her place. Baturine was arrested, tortured, and condemned to imprisonment for life in the fortress of Schlüsselburg. The kennel men were sent back to Germany. The "young Court" were thereafter subjected to a discipline more rigorous even than before; they were not allowed to leave their apartments without the Empress' consent; Catherine was forbidden to write letters, even to her mother. If Catherine wished to communicate with the outside world she was obliged to drop little notes into the trombone of an Italian member of the palace orchestra, who at great risk had agreed to forward them. But still, with admirable submissiveness, she endured what she calls "the rigor of the political imprisonment to which we were subjected." Only on one occasion did she attempt to commit suicide, when she was saved at the last moment by one of her ladies in waiting. She bided her time.

One result of the isolation to which they were condemned was that the Grand Duke, having been deprived of the footmen and grooms who had hitherto been his confidants, came to rely for a time upon his virgin wife for comfort and protection. She gave him such advice as he was capable of comprehending, but he was generally too drunk to listen. He would spend his days scraping atrociously on a violin, or torturing his pets. "A strong mind," she wrote in the Aphorisms discovered among her papers after her death, "is not suited for advising a weak one, for it is incapable of following the thoughts of the latter." "Never," she wrote in her memoirs, "did two minds resemble each other less than ours. We had nothing in common in our tastes, nor in our ways of thinking. Our opinions were so different that we could never have agreed on anything, had I not often given in to him so as not to affront him too noticeably."

Three

During those eighteen years of isolation, Catherine had been so unfortunate as to rouse the animosity and suspicion of the Empress' successive lovers, Rasumovski, Shuvalov, Beketov, and the chorister Kachenewski. They persuaded the Empress that the failure of the Grand Duke and his spouse to produce an heir was due, not to the impotence of Peter, but to the fact that Catherine insisted on riding every morning. Madame Choglokov, who by then had become devoted to Catherine, was a better judge of the situation and endeavored to effect a consummation by attaching to the Grand Duke an expert mistress in the person of Frau Groot, the errant wife of a painter. The failure of this experiment induced Madame Choglokov to resort to more dangerous if more agreeable methods. She introduced Catherine to Count Saltikov who in his turn brought Catherine into friendly relations with the Grand Chancellor, Alexis Besthuzev-Ryumin. Catherine, who had spent the years of isolation reading Bayle's Dictionary and the works of Voltaire, was by then running short of her amazing store of patience and prepared to welcome activity and love.

The Chancellor and Madame Choglokov kept on implying that it was her "duty to Russia" to produce a child. She found Saltikov, as she confesses in her *Memoirs* with her accustomed frankness, "beautiful as the dawn." A son, the future Emperor Paul, was born on September 1755.

The Memoirs of Catherine II, which cover the first thirty years of her life, break off suddenly in the middle of an account of one of her final audiences with the Empress Elizabeth. On his accession in 1825 her grandson, the Emperor Nicholas I, ordered the destruction of the manuscript, fearing that her account of the Saltikov episode might throw doubts on the legitimacy of his father Paul. Copies of the manuscript had however been surreptitiously taken, and in 1859 Alexander Herzen published in London what must be regarded as an authentic edition. But the problem of Paul's legitimacy still remains. The Grand Duke was probably impotent; but on the other hand Paul, in physique and temperament, reproduced all the defects of Peter and none of the beauty and gentleness of the Saltikov family.

The moment the baby was born the Empress snatched it away from Catherine's bosom and removed it to her own apartments. Catherine, on recovering from her confinement, had to obtain special permission before she was allowed even to see the infant. Saltikov was sent off to Sweden on a diplomatic mission. Catherine was left to face her enemies alone. Her one consolation was that, on the birth of an heir, the Empress had presented her with a gift of money. This was most welcome, since, as she recorded, "I had not a kopek to my name and was crippled by debts." In order to curry favor with the Grand Duke, who might at any moment become Tsar, the Schouvalovs encouraged him to bring to St. Petersburg a detachment of his Holstein troops. This was much resented by the officers of the Russian Guards regiments and was the first of Peter's numerous mistakes. Catherine, who was always careful to cultivate Russian public opinion, disapproved of this action, describing it as "a highly dangerous, childish, prank." She no longer made any attempt to conceal her contempt and hatred of the Schouvalovs. "I drew myself up," she writes, "with head erect, and adopted the attitude of one bearing State responsibilities rather than of an oppressed and humiliated individual." The Empress, however suspicious she might be of "the young Court," always retained for Catherine a certain respect, even a certain affection.

In 1755, a few months after the birth of Paul, Sir Charles Hanbury Williams arrived as British Ambassador to the Court of Russia. Among the members of his staff was a young Polish nobleman, Stanislaus Poniatowski, who was not handsome only but who had been trained by Madame Geoffrin in all the arts and graces of her Paris salon. The Chancellor Besthuzev, who was descended from a Scottish adventurer of the name of "Best," had for some time been hoping to break the Franco-Austrian coalition against Prussia and to align Russia on the side of England and Prussia. He and the British Ambassador conceived the idea that it would be a good move to introduce Poniatowski into Catherine's immediate entourage; by that time her affection for Saltikov had begun to cool: it was with passion that she flung herself into the embraces of the beautiful Pole. It has since been suggested that, in order to mitigate her encumbered finances, Catherine consented to receive subsidies from the English Government and even conveyed to them, and through them to Frederick the Great, secret information through the agency of her jeweler Bernhardi. What is undoubted is that Besthuzev wished with the help of England to put an end to the Seven Years War. He also realized that the health of the Empress was declining and he dreaded the accession of the witless and debauched Peter. In any case the plot, if there ever was a plot, was discovered. The Chancellor was arrested, deprived of his offices, and condemned to death. The jeweler Bernhardi was also arrested. Catherine found herself in a dangerous situation. She knew that the Schouvalovs hated and feared her; she knew that her husband the Grand Duke, who was anxious to marry his mistress, or his confederate, Elizabeth Woronzov, would be delighted if she were exiled or confined in a convent. She could not tell what Bernhardi, when submitted to torture, might not reveal. She thus sought an audience of the Empress and asked that she might be allowed to rejoin her mother in Germany. The Empress refused this permission.

GREGORY POTEMKIN

Portrait of Prince G. A. Potyomkin-Tavrichesky
by Johann-Baptist Lampi, circa 1790

The death sentence on Besthuzev was commuted to one of banishment to his estate at Gorstovo where he remained until the accession of Catherine.

The Grand Duke, when Catherine became pregnant by Poniatowski, openly boasted of the fact that he could not pretend to be the father of this child. A little girl was born, again snatched from its mother by the Empress, and christened Anne: she died in infancy. When in 1761, Poniatowski was replaced as Catherine's lover by Gregory Orlov, there was no longer any pretence that the child born of this third liaison was anything but illegitimate. The boy was given the name of Count Bobrinski. Catherine disliked babies: it was upon the guards officers whom, in rapid succession, she chose as her paramours that she expended such maternal instincts as she possessed.

On January 5, 1762, the Empress Elizabeth died and was succeeded by her nephew as Tsar Peter III. He was by general consent utterly unfit to rule. His first act was to withdraw his victorious armies from Germany, to conclude a separate peace with Prussia, thus rescuing Frederick the Great from what had become a desperate situation. The Russian troops and generals were indignant at thus being deprived of the fruits of their victories. He made further blunders. He sought to impose German uniforms upon his troops, an imposition that caused bitter resentment. He exempted the nobility from military service and he proceeded to secularize the property of the Orthodox Church. He went so far as to give orders for Catherine's arrest. It was obvious that her life was at stake. With the aid of the four Orlov brothers, who were all officers in the Preobrajenski regiment, she organized a military coup d'état. Peter, who had withdrawn to Oranienbaum, was told that he must abdicate, an ultimatum which he accepted as Frederick the Great remarked, "with the docility of a child being sent to bed." Catherine was acclaimed as Empress by the St. Petersburg garrison. Peter was bundled into a coach and driven with the blinds lowered to Ropsha, a country house some twenty miles outside St. Petersburg. From there he wrote groveling letters to Catherine hailing her as his Empress and begging to be allowed to have with him his dog, his mistress, his Negro servant and his violin. On July 8, it was announced that he had died as the result of hemorrhage induced by a violent attack of colic. He had in fact been strangled by his gaoler, Alexei Orlov. Catherine's only surviving rival was the idiot Ivan VI, who for the last twenty years had been languishing in the dungeon of the Fortress of Schlüsselburg under the designation of "Prisoner No. I." When in the summer of 1764 a plot was discovered, or invented, to restore him to the throne he was quietly murdered by his guards. For the next thirty-four years Catherine ruled as undisputed Autocrat of All the Russias.

Four

She conferred immense benefit upon her adopted country. She did not, it is true, achieve her lifelong ambition of liberating the whole Balkan peninsula from Turkish rule and of establishing her grandson Constantine as ruler of an Eastern Empire with Constantinople as its capital. But even as Peter the Great had by force of willpower obtained an outlet for Russia on the Baltic, so also did Catherine by her two Turkish wars gain the Crimea, the Kuban, and command of the Black Sea. By her three partitions of Poland and her annexation of Courland she acquired vast territories in the west and brought the Russian frontier to the borders of Germany. She thereby rendered Russia a potent factor in the European Balance of Power.

Her ambition, although limitless, was restrained by caution. No despot has ever been more subtly aware that politics are the art of the possible and that everything can be lost if a statesman goes too fast or too far. She well knew (as is shown by her abandonment of her eastern ambitions and her modification of her early revolutionary schemes of internal reform) when it was advisable to retreat. Seldom has excess been so perfectly blended with moderation. Suppleness was the political quality that she most admired. "Often," she wrote, "it is better to inspire a reform than to enforce it." "The philosopher knows," she recorded in her aphorisms, "that there are prejudices of the nation which should be respected, prejudices of education that must be considered, prejudices of religion that should be encouraged."

Her original scheme of internal reform, as embodied in the famous "Instruction" or "Nakaz" of 1767, was so liberal that the French government considered it necessary to forbid its publication or circulation in France. Admittedly its principles were founded on Montesquieu and on Beccaria's *Dei Delitti e delle Pene*. But at least they were from the Russian point of view, startlingly original. She announced that the fundamental principle of Russian internal administration must be the rule of law. The liberty and equality of the individual could only be guaranteed and enjoyed by obedience to an equal law. The law should forbid nothing that was not prejudicial to the health of the individual or to that of the community as a whole. "It is moderation," wrote the Tsaritsa, "that rules a people, not excess of severity." Punishment should never be exercised for revenge or retribution but always with reform in mind. "The employment of torture is contrary to the dictates of Nature and Reason." Free trade should be established, agriculture encouraged, and laws enacted to secure that no landlord could ill-treat his serfs. Since universal education was impossible in so vast a country, the education of children must in the main be entrusted to the parents, who should nurture them in the love of God and their country and should teach them that "lying is the most pernicious of all vices." Children should be instructed in the virtues of industry, compassion, thrift, and cleanliness. The nobility should have regard for their own responsibilities and those of them who behaved without virtue or honor should be expelled from their order. Minority religions should be accorded "prudent toleration." Such were the lessons that this despot had learnt from the *Encyclopédistes*.

In order to give effect to this progressive manifesto, Catherine summoned to Moscow a congress of 564 deputies which sat for seventeen months. The Church and the Landowners were bitterly opposed to the suggested reforms and her chief Minister, Nikita Panine, warned her that they were calculated to destroy the very foundations of the State. Catherine did not insist; she in fact postponed her schemes of reform until 1775, when, with the assistance of a gifted German Civil Servant, J. Sievers, she introduced her "Statute of the Provinces" by which she created decentralized units of administration and corporations of the local gentry, which became the foundation of provincial and municipal self-government and one of the few solid institutions of the future Russia. It was these moderate but profitable reforms, as well as the advanced Liberal principles enunciated in the original *Nakaz*, that earned her in Europe the reputation of a Philosopher Queen. She was hailed as the "Semiramis of the North" by the intellectuals of Paris, who doubtless forgot that this Assyrian Queen had also risen to power as a result of the "suicide" of her husband.

Catherine was afraid of the Orlov brothers who had made one praetorian revolution and might easily make another. She loaded them with riches and honors. Her young lover, Gregory Orlov, was a simple soul, who believed that he would eventually marry the Empress and produce a son more sturdy and stable than the weakling Paul. He imagined that his aim would be more acceptable to public opinion if it could be proved that the Empress Elizabeth herself had married her lover Rasumovski, who was still living an old age of repentance upon his estates. Count Voronzov was sent down to interview him and to obtain the documents proving that he had in fact been the Empress' husband. The old widower opened the case in which his marriage certificate was preserved, tottered to the stove, and thrust the documents into the flames. "It shall never be said," he mumbled, "that I was ever anything more than the humble slave of Her Imperial Majesty." Count Voronzov returned to St. Petersburg with his mission unfulfilled.

Nikita Panine was strongly opposed to any idea of marriage between Orlov and Catherine. "The Empress," he said, "can do what she likes, but Mrs. Orlov will never be Empress of Russia." Catherine was impressed by this epigram and had in any case realized that Gregory Orlov was too stupid and indolent to make a reliable husband or even a lasting lover. He was sent off to Moscow, where an outbreak of plague had led to rioting, and where he restored health and order with efficiency and courage. On his return to St. Petersburg he was greeted as a conquering hero; a triumphal arch was erected in his honor at Tsarskoe Selo where it still stands lonely; and the Marble Palace on the Neva Quay was assigned to him as a residence. But he had already been turned out of the flat reserved for the official paramour and the young and even more beautiful Vassiltchikov had been installed in his place. Catherine, although she refused to see him and thought it prudent to have new locks affixed to Vassiltchikov's apartments, continued to write him affectionate letters and to send him orders and miniatures encrusted in diamonds. Whatever hopes Orlov may have cherished of regaining his influence, whatever ambitions Vassiltchikov may have had of becoming a lasting lover, were at this stage dashed by the advent of power of the mighty and devoted Potemkin. Orlov and his brothers were rewarded with military and administrative appointments. Vassiltchikov was given money and dismissed on a grand tour of Europe. Diderot, who happened to meet him in Paris, described him as "a saucepan always on the boil and never cooking anything." The way was open for Gregory Potemkin who ruled Catherine and Russia for seventeen years.

Five

He was born in the steam bath of the village of Tchisovo, in the government of Smolensk on September 13, 1739. His father was a retired colonel; he was expelled from the university for "laziness and truancy," but obtained a commission in the guards. He took part in the garrison revolution against Peter and is said to have been at Ropsha when the Tsar was murdered. He first attracted the attention of Catherine when he was an ugly young ensign and she was reviewing the guards on the very day of her accession. He was appointed a Court usher, or Kammerjunker, and in 1768 promoted to be a Court Chamberlain. In 1774, when Catherine was forty-four and he was ten years younger, he became her official lover and received the two posts traditionally associated with the office, namely that of Adjutant General and Colonel of the Preobrajenski regiment.

He also succeeded Vassiltchikov in the apartment in the Winter Palace which, by a secret staircase, gave him access to the Empress' private rooms. They became infatuated with each other. He felt for her an admiration and loyalty which never faltered. She saw in him, not merely a powerful bastion against the Orlov family, but also a passionate lover who satisfied her ardent physical desires. She would call him "my falcon" "my little father," "my Gregory-pops," "my Cossack" or "my little pigeon." He had lost an eye and was exceptionally ugly and unkempt. He would bite his nails to the quick, and indulge in long bouts of indolence or religious melancholy. He was a creature of impulses and contradictions. Phases of feverish activity would be succeeded by long periods of apathy and inattention; at one moment he would appear arrayed in lavish uniforms with eagle plumes and diamond buttons, and at the next would shamble into an audience naked except for a dirty old padded dressing gown; at times he would surround himself with the splendor of an oriental satrap: when at Bender his court (what Catherine would call "*la basse cour*") comprised 600 servants, 200 musicians, a corps de ballet, a troupe of mimes, 100 embroiderers, and 20 jewelers; at other times he would surrender to long dark days of religious melancholia. "Calmness," Catherine once wrote to him, "is for you a condition that your soul cannot bear." He was coarse and lustful, but loved music and poetry; he seldom read a book but never forgot anything that anybody told him; he was insanely jealous, but never revengeful; he was a marvelous impresario, a gifted mimic, and could be a charming host. No more brilliant portrait of Potemkin has ever been composed than that contained in a letter to the comte de Ségur from the Prince de Ligne, who was attached by his master the Austrian Emperor to Potemkin's headquarters outside Otchakov. His description deserves to be quoted:

> I here behold a Commander in Chief who looks idle and is always busy; who has no other desk than his knees, no other Comb than his fingers, constantly reclined on his couch, yet sleeping neither at night nor in the daytime.

His zeal for the Empress he adores keeps him incessantly awake and uneasy; and a cannon shot to which he himself is not exposed disturbs him with the idea that it costs the life of his soldiers. Trembling for others, brave himself, stopping under the hottest fire of a battery to give his orders, yet more an Ulysses than an Achilles; alarmed at the approach of danger, frolicsome when it arrives; bored in the midst of pleasure; unhappy in being too fortunate, surfeited with everything; easily disgusted, morose, inconstant, a profound philosopher, an able minister, a sublime politician, or a child of ten years old; not revengeful, asking pardon for any pain he may have inflicted, quick to repair an injustice; imagining he loves God, whereas he merely fears the Devil, whom he believes to be even greater than himself; waving one hand to the houris that please him and with the other making the sign of the cross; embracing the feet of a statue of the Virgin and at the next moment the neck of his mistress; receiving countless presents from his sovereign and passing them on immediately to others; alienating and repurchasing immense tracts of land in order to build a colonnade or to lay out an English garden; gambling from morn to night, or not at all; preferring prodigality in giving to regularity in paying; prodigiously rich and yet not worth a farthing; abandoning himself to distrust or confidence to jealousy or to gratitude, to ill-humor or to pleasantry; easily prejudiced in favor of, or against, a thing and as easily cured of a prejudice; talking theology to his generals and tactics to his bishops; never reading, but pumping everyone with whom he converses and contradicting them in order to elicit further information; uncommonly affable or extremely savage; affecting the most attractive or the most repulsive manners; appearing by turns the proudest satrap of the Orient or the most amiable courtier of the Court of Louis XIV; concealing under the appearance of harshness the greatest kindness of heart; whimsical in matters of time, meals, and inclination; wanting to have everything as a child, or as a great man knowing how to do without anything; sober although seemingly a glutton, gnawing his fingers, or it may be apples, or it may be turnips; scolding or laughing, mimicking or swearing; engaged in wantonness or in prayers; singing or meditating; sending for twenty aides-de-camp and saying nothing to any of them; withstanding heat better than any man, while he seems to think of nothing but the most voluptuous baths; not caring for cold, though he seems unable to exist without furs; always in a shirt without pants or in rich regimentals embroidered at all the seams; barefoot or in slippers embroidered with spangles; wearing neither hat nor cap; it is thus I saw him once in the middle of a musket fire; sometimes in a nightgown, sometimes in a splendid tunic with his three stars, his orders, and diamonds as large as a thumb round the portrait of the Empress; they seemed placed there to attract the musket balls; crooked and almost bent double when he is at home; and tall, erect, proud, handsome, noble, majestic or fascinating when he shows himself to his army, like Agamemnon in the midst of the monarchs of Greece. What then is his magic? Genius, natural abilities, an excellent memory, much elevation of soul, malice without the design of injuring, artifice without craft, a happy mixture of caprices, the art of conquering every heart in his good moments; much generosity, graciousness and justice in his rewards, a refined and correct taste, the talent of guessing what he is ignorant of, and a consummate knowledge of mankind.

Catherine regarded Potemkin as a warrior and statesman in whose devotion she could place unlimited trust. It is probable, although not proved, that she married him secretly. It was he who, with his huge biceps and his hold over the guards and the army would protect her against any conspiracy which the Orlovs might contrive. She would be fascinated by his fantasy and would roar with laughter when he mimicked her German accent when speaking Russian. She appreciated his miraculous gift of showmanship. It was he who organized her dramatic journey to the Crimea, the palaces which with their tapestries and chandeliers were constructed for her reception, the wooden house drawn by thirty horses that was her sledge in winter, the luxurious barges in which, like Cleopatra, she sailed down the Dnieper to the Black Sea. One evening, when she was dining in the mansion prepared for her at Inkermann, the curtains at the west end of the banqueting hall were suddenly drawn aside, revealing in the distance the new harbor of Sebastopol with the Black Sea Fleet thundering a salute. The dreams of Potemkin may to his contemporaries have appeared as the hallucinations of a maniac: but they all came true. The final banquet that he offered his mistress in the Taurida palace was compared to the feast of Sardanapalus. He then returned to the front. His health declined and he told his staff to take him to Nicolaiev to die. On the way there he had an attack of breathlessness, and insisted upon being taken out of his coach into the open air. On October 5, 1791, the grand Potemkin died gasping in a field beside the road that leads from Jassy to Nikolaiev.

One of the most astonishing of Potemkin's feats was the zest with which, when he noticed after 1776 that the physical attraction that he exercised over the Empress was ceasing to be compulsive, he chose the young men of strength and beauty to act as his successors. Catherine had never concealed her lust. "Despite," she wrote in her *Memoirs*:

> Despite the inculcation of moral principles, directly the senses begin to speak one is carried further than one imagines and I know not how they can be kept in check. Flight may perhaps help, but how can one flee in the midst of a Court? That would cause tongues to wag. If, therefore, one does not flee, nothing in my opinion is more difficult to resist than what gives one pleasure. All arguments to the contrary are prudery.

Potemkin was fully aware of Catherine's amorous disposition and himself selected with care the young ensigns in the Guards or other regiments, who, while able to assuage the Empress' lust, would be counted on not to interfere in politics or administration. None of the "temporary lovers" (*vremenshchki*) whom he chose for her caused any trouble. Catherine herself was not reckless in such matters. The prospective lover was first "tested" by one of her ladies in waiting, nicknamed the "*éprouveuse*," whose business it was to guarantee his cleanliness and attractions. It was only after Potemkin's death, when she was over sixty, that she fell under the spell of a truly atrocious cad, a young officer of twenty-two called Platon Zubov. Within seven years Zubov had managed to amass all the riches and the offices that it had taken Potemkin a lifetime to acquire. He was rude and arrogant and became so unpopular that he might have caused a palace revolution had not Catherine died. He thereafter became one of her son's murderers and left a vast fortune to his heirs.

That interesting historian, K. Waliszewski, is unable as a patriot Pole, to forgive Catherine her three partitions of Poland. Thus, while admiring her character, he is unwilling to pay unreserved tribute to her statesmanship. He questions the sincerity of her liberalism, ascribing it to her unequalled gift for self-advertisement. I do not agree with this critical attitude, believing that, at least until the French Revolution transformed her into a reactionary, Catherine was really inspired by liberal principles. When she wrote that "Liberty is the core of everything: without it there would be no life": when she wrote "Power, without the Nation's confidence, is nothing": I am convinced that she was absolutely sincere. Yet her prudence in not arousing opposition among the Russian nobility, her caution in not forging ahead of public opinion, may well provide instances of insincerity. She was aware that Voltaire, Diderot, and the *Encyclopédistes* exercised a dominant influence on European opinion and she strove, by all methods of flattery and expenditure, to get them on her side. She was an exuberant correspondent and she knew that Voltaire would boast about her letters and spread the news around. It is Voltaire, rather than Catherine, who comes out poorly from the correspondence.

He toadied and flattered her outrageously. He addressed her as "the star of the North," the "benefactress of Europe," as the successor of "Solon and Lycurgus," as "the first person in the universe." "Happy," he wrote, "is the author who will write the history of Catherine II." He expressed a desire to be allowed to kiss her hands and feet "which are as white as the snows of Russia." We can forgive such extravagance, since Voltaire was always apt at turning compliments. What we can less easily forgive is his defense of her two predatory wars against Turkey and of that flagrant international crime, the Partition of Poland. How could Voltaire justify that act of brigandage as being "the noble and useful task of suppressing anarchy in Poland?" How could he laud the perpetrator of that act of spoliation as "enthroned Reason?" "All this," he writes, having advocated the extermination of the Turks, "does not accord too well with my principles of toleration. But man is composed of contradictions and besides Your Majesty has turned my head." "I know," he wrote to Madame du Deffand, "that people blame her for a few trifles in regard to her husband. But that is a domestic issue with which I have no concern." Her relations with Diderot are more edifying. He came as her guest to St. Petersburg and told her exactly what he thought. He even shook her hard when she would not agree with him; her shoulders were black and blue owing to his vehemence. "You philosophers are fortunate," she wrote to him, "Your medium is paper, and paper is always patient. I, Empress that I am, have to write on the sensitive skins of human beings."

After Potemkin died, the dusk began to descend upon Catherine's glory. The Second Turkish War was not too brilliant and at one moment Catherine was exposed to Swedish invasion. Platon Zubov was by far the least respectable among her thirty odd lovers. Her ministers were distressed at the drain on the national finances, but Catherine preserved her resilience. "I am as gay and active as a chaffinch" she wrote to Grimm on February 15, 1796. Her household did not share this optimism. She had hoped to arrange a marriage between her granddaughter and the

Crown Prince of Sweden, but the negotiations were muddled by Platon Zubov and the scheme fell through. Distressed by this episode, which she regarded as damaging to her prestige, the Empress developed an acute attack of colic, to which in moments of irritation, she had always been subject. On the morning of November 9, 1796, she interrupted an audience, saying she must retire for the moment and would shortly return. They waited in the anteroom and when half an hour passed they became uneasy. The Empress was not in her bedroom or her dressing room. They then penetrated into her closet where they found her gasping on her *chaise percée* with blood on her lips. They carried her into her bedroom and laid her on a mattress on the floor. She died thirty-seven hours later without recovering consciousness.

Her enemies told the story that the stool on which she had been seated when struck by apoplexy had once been the throne of Poland which after the liquidation of that country had been brought to the Winter Palace and employed for this ignoble purpose. Her admirers contend that it was not in Catherine's character to perpetrate such an indignity; her enemies insist that such a gesture of spite was typical of the Pomeranian schoolgirl that at heart she had always remained. She wrote her own epitaph as follows:

> At the age of fourteen she made the triple resolution to please her husband, Elizabeth and the nation. She neglected nothing in trying to achieve this. Eighteen years of ennui and solitude gave her the opportunity to read many books. Enthroned in Russia, she desired nothing but the best for her country and tried to procure for her subjects' happiness, liberty, and wealth. She forgave easily and hated no one. Tolerant, undemanding, of a gay disposition, she had a republican spirit and a kind heart. She made good friends.

Not even the most bilious historian could question the accuracy of such an epitaph.

Chapter 8

Complacency
(Joseph Addison, 1672–1719)

———•◆•———

The Augustan Age in England—Causes for self-satisfaction—
Calm after storm—Stability and security—England becomes
a Great Power—Religious toleration and Deism—A balanced
Constitution—Expansion of Trade—Growth of powerful Middle Class—Economy still mainly agricultural—The aristocracy
largely rural—The cult of normality—Effect of this on contemporary literature—Lord Shaftesbury—Order, balance and lucidity—
Distrust of fancy and imagination—Attempts to establish standard English—Defects of Augustan style—Influence of scientific
research—Addison and urbanity—Pope's satire on Addison's pontifical manner—His political and social advancement—His wide
influence—*The Tatler*—*The Spectator*—The new reading public—
Addison's device for appealing to the rising Middle Class—Avoidance of controversy, party bias, gossip and invective—His didactic
purposes—The improvement of manners—His attitude towards
women—His themes—Insipidity of his ideas and characters—His
complacency has done great harm to the repute of the Augustans—
But he established a civilized sense of values.

One

THOSE OF US whose opinions regarding the first half of the
eighteenth century in England are colored by literary associations, are inclined to regard it as a period of unattractive

self-satisfaction, of unimaginative complacency. We assume, perhaps too readily, that the community was dominated by a small group of territorial magnates, intriguing against each other for the spoils of office, lavishing their fortunes on building stately ostentatious houses and on collecting works of art, lax regarding religion and morals, possessing little social conscience, seeking to imitate elaborate foreign manners, simulating an interest in literature and natural philosophy, but in fact indolent, ignorant, selfish, narrow, arrogant, unintelligent and false. In surrendering to such an assumption there are many important factors which we forget.

We forget that during the first ten years of the century, England, although possessing a population no greater than six millions, had emerged as a victorious Power on land and sea. We forget that during the fifty years from 1700 to 1750 our commerce, in spite of successive wars, expanded rapidly, creating important reserves of capital, and above all fostering the growth of a large, wealthy, expanding, energetic and self-confident middle class. Under the then prevailing mercantilist theory, the basis of our trade was the export of colonial produce to Europe. English merchants gradually began to oust their continental rivals in shipping, distributive organization, credit facilities and overseas factories and plantations. Money was plentiful and cheap. Although the National Debt, which in 1688 had scarcely exceeded a million, had by 1750 risen to eighty millions, interest on government securities was only 3 per cent. The greatest weakness in our trade balance was in timber, hemp, and tar, all of which had to be obtained from the Baltic and paid for in cash.

On the other hand we forget that England during the period was still predominantly agricultural. Four out of every five Englishmen derived their living from the land. It was not the titled landowners only who depended on agriculture, but a solid mass of country gentlemen, of squires, and below them freeholders, copyholders, tenants at will, and laborers. It was a world of merchants and traders founding their activities on a world of farmers and citizens. In spite of all that we have read about corrupt boroughs, sinecures, pensions and placemen, it was a society more broadly based and better integrated than the over-centralized systems of the Continent.

It is not therefore surprising that a community thus balanced and based should have acquired an exaggerated sense of stability. It was with horror that the Englishman of 1700 looked back upon the religious controversy and civil conflicts of the seventeenth century and recalled the misery which sectarian fanaticism had brought to the country. "Enthusiasm" in its several forms, whether puritan or royalist, had caused human unhappiness: it was natural that they should welcome "Reason" and "Good Sense," as the unguents for their wounds. The perils of the past had been surmounted; nor could they foresee the ensuing and even more intricate problems that industrialism was to create.

The atmosphere of mildness, established after a century of bitterness and hatred, came to be regarded as the natural climate of civilization. Lord Shaftesbury's *Characteristics of Men, Manners, Opinions, Times*, published in 1711 with its insistence on "moral sentiment" and its optimistic belief in the perfectibility of human nature, became the manual of the age. "The Sum of Philosophy," wrote Shaftesbury, "is to learn what is *just* in Society and *beautiful* in Nature, and the Order of the World. . . . The Taste of Beauty, and the *Relish* of what is decent, just, and amiable, perfects the *Character* of the gentleman and the Philosopher. And the study of such a Taste and *Relish* will, as we suppose, be ever the great Employment and Concern of him who covets as well to be *wise* and *good*, as *agreeable* and *polite*." "Good humor," he wrote again "is not only the best Security against *Enthusiasm*, but the best Foundation of *Piety* and *true Religion*. . . . I very much question whether anything, besides ill Humor, can be the cause of Atheism. . . . This I am persuaded of, that nothing besides ill Humor can give us dreadful or ill Thoughts of a Supreme Manager." Deism of such vagueness is both comfortable and polite; it creates no tension in the mind.

Shaftesbury accustomed men to believe, in this facile manner, in a supreme Orderer of the Universe, in the supernatural Manager, an omnipotent "Controller of Events," whom they called "God." It was assumed that He was a benevolent geometrician: when episodes occurred that might throw doubt on His benevolence, it was generally agreed that the discrepancy was due, not to any lack of benevolence on the part of Providence, but to man's inability to understand the mysterious manner in which that benevolence was accorded or withheld. If we condemn this thoughtless form of Deism, we must remember that throughout a century in which the established Church and the Universities were anything but lighthouses of progress, in which the squire was very much like the village parson and the village parson very much like the squire, an underground movement of Dissent and popular religion was seething and expanding. The Dissenters were branded by Parliament as second-class citizens under the Test and Corporation Acts, but they were an active and energetic minority and their support was often sought by the great landowners and the Whigs. Moreover, since they were denied access to the older universities, the Dissenters set up Colleges of their own at such places as Northampton, Warrington and Hackney, where a more modern and liberal education was provided than any that could be obtained at Oxford or Cambridge. Throughout the century the repute, and therefore the influence, of the Dissenters spread and grew.

Sir Lewis Namier and his school of young historians have taught us not to accept too quickly the charges of corruption and egoism that used to be leveled at eighteenth-century politicians. It is true that foreigners, such as Voltaire and Montesquieu, formed a far too rosy view of our tolerance and freedom. We must remember that Parliament was closed to Dissenters until 1828, that the two established universities would not admit them until 1871 and that until 1779 Catholics were forbidden to worship in public. Nor did the foreign interpreters of our "free Constitution" realize that a House of Commons which was so selective and exclusive was not, in the modern sense of the term, a representative assembly. But it is also true that so long as England remained a predominantly agricultural community, there was no real demand for political or franchise reform. It was this general acceptance of existing institutions that gave to foreign visitors so

JOSEPH ADDISON
Circa 1703–1712 by Godfrey Kneller.

strong an impression of stability, order, and consent. Those who criticized or refused to accept the establishment may have been exposed to unjust and highly inconvenient restrictions: they were not subjected to persecution.

The English aristocracy, in contrast to the French nobility, were not a closed corporation or a caste sharply isolated from the rest of the community. They were not, as were the courtiers of Versailles, segregated in a gilded cage, but spent most of their time on their country estates, studying the needs of their tenants, participating in their sports and amusements, and sharing the hopes and fears of a massive agricultural community. They possessed and for long retained a rural rather than an urban type of character and were thus more patient, more tolerant, less trivial, and more widely esteemed. They did not live on feudal dues, but on the rents they received from tenant farmers. They possessed, in regard to taxation law and public employment, few privileges that were denied to the common man. The local administration was largely in the hands of the smaller landowners and squires, who, as Justices of the Peace, possessed extensive powers and who were generally found in opposition to the central Government. In theory also, there was no reason why a successful businessman could not be admitted into the aristocratic circle, although in fact few of them actually entered the House of Lords. In 1704, there were 161 peers and as late as 1780 there were no more than 182. Even when in 1784 a considerable number of new peers were created, they were chosen for the most part, not from the middle class, but from the county gentry. It would thus be an exaggeration to state, as some foreign observers suggested, that the English system was liberal and democratic in the modern sense of those terms: but it certainly did manifest a more equal application of the Rule of Law, a more effective organization of checks and balances against arbitrary executive actions, greater toleration towards freedom of conscience, and a more operative respect for the rights of individuals, than could be found in any other country. The fact that the system was accepted, and even revered, by the vast majority of the population, gave to foreign, and indeed to many English, observers the impression of durable stability, which made our island appear as a rock of order and a sanctuary for the oppressed. Nor was this optimistic view based entirely on an illusion.

Two

The early years of the eighteenth century were thus welcomed by the English in the same way as a period of convalescence is welcomed after the agony, terror, and delirium of a dangerous illness. It was not so much that their minds became lulled into placidity as that they cultivated placidity as a delicious relief. What they desired above all things was to achieve calm, but, as Professor Humphreys has well remarked, the calm that they aspired to was an "imaginative normality." This aspiration was fully reflected in their literature.

English literature during the eighteenth century can roughly be divided into three periods. There was the first period, still dominated by Dryden, when writers sought to free themselves from the passion and complexity of the seventeenth-century metaphysicians, and to achieve lucidity and poise. There followed the second period, which can be defined as the true Augustan age, when writers aimed at achieving "correctness" and "good sense." And there was the third period when a reaction developed against the extreme formalism of Addison and Pope and an increasing attempt was made to liberate "Feeling" from the tyranny of "Reason."

The motto of those who founded the true Augustan mode was "follow Nature." By this they did not mean an increased sensibility to natural beauty, but an increased interest in, and awareness of, the ordinary life around them. What they wished to do was to interpret contemporary conditions mildly, stressing those virtues that were common to mankind in general and dealing with the interests or small follies of the average individual. They scrupulously refrained from arousing those turbulent passions that had so distracted the previous century. They desired to express the ideals of stability and reason in lucid and comforting terms. Inevitably our own distraught

generation is rendered impatient by their often unctuous complacency, by the placid tones of contentment that they adopted. The
expression "urbane" would by them have been regarded as an epithet
of praise: today it is used as a term of reproach, or at least of dismissal.
Inevitably their ideal of formal order has earned them much modern
criticism. Their avoidance of deep feeling, of passion and inventive-
ness has exposed them to Mr. T. S. Eliot's reproach of "a dissocia-
tion of sensibility." Even Professor Humphreys, who is in general so
sympathetic to their aims and endeavors, admits that "Art gradually
gained on vivacity." It is this superficial, and often vapid, optimism
that grates upon our nerves and tires our attention.

The issue has been admirably stated by Professor Humphreys,
whose words are well worth quoting:

> With many readers, it is true, the rational controls and
> critical cautions of Augustanism are still suspect of being
> a denial of the full life of man, but the better opinion is
> gaining ground that the Augustans' vigor and enlightened
> seriousness, achieved, within the necessary limitations, a
> constructive, and not purely restrictive, civilization such as
> only sound intelligence, healthy instinct, and a fundamen-
> tal strength of tradition could accomplish.

We are thus instructed to recognize that the Augustans did succeed
in inculcating "a thoroughly mature and responsible sense of values."
They constructed a civilization which for the first time was accessible
to the ordinary man. That assuredly was a great achievement.

The effect on literature of these ideals of placidity and order was not,
to our minds, wholly beneficial. The French genius may flourish at its
best under a system of symmetry and traditional standards. The English genius is more individual and more fanciful. It has never achieved
its fullest expression under the rule of conformity and common sense.
Perhaps the greatest contribution to English letters that was made by
the Augustans was that, by their simplification of style and language,
they rendered literature available to a far wider public. Deliberately

they adopted a colloquial manner of writing, and sought, even in conversation, to adopt what Sprat, in his *History of the Royal Society*, called "a close, naked, natural way of speaking." Their aim was to render literature, both prose and poetry, interesting, agreeable, and above all, comprehensible to an increasing circle of readers. They succeeded in providing us with a standard language which the English-speaking peoples use, write, and understand to this day. They aimed, as Gray wrote, "at extreme conciseness of expression, yet pure, perspicuous and musical." It thus is unfair to dismiss them as purely conventional: the linguistic habits which they rendered fashionable and generally accepted amounted to a creative reform. And we should be grateful.

Deliberately they departed from the excess, the freedom, the individualism, the imaginative ecstasy, as well as from the crudity and the complexity of the seventeenth century. They were anxious indeed to "fix" the new purity of style which they had perfected. Even Dryden had felt that the time had come when some official body should be created to "fix" the standards which he, as a pioneer, had evolved. "I am sorry," he wrote, "that (speaking a noble language as we do) we have not a more certain measure of it, as they have in France, where they have an Academy erected for that purpose." There are some who ask themselves whether in fact the Académie Française, constituted by Richelieu in 1634, has had a stimulating or cramping effect upon French letters. Our native genius is ill-attuned to literary dictatorship and Dryden's suggestion, although in 1711 Swift revived it and imagined that he had obtained Harley's enthusiastic support, came to nothing. Dr. Johnson, in the preface to his Dictionary, stated robustly that any such conception was "un-English." He may have been right.

The verbal habits that they rendered fashionable are not all to be commended. By their insistence that the style of poetry should differ from that of prose they introduced the custom of employing stock poetic verbiage. They delighted in elegant variation and would use such irritating expressions as "the feathered choir," "the foodful brine," or "the finny tribe." The influence of the classics, and especially of Homer, tempted them to use compound epithets, such as "rosy-bosomed Hours," and they adopted the deplorable practice (which lasted even to the days of Keats) of adding the "y" suffix to form adjectives and using such obnoxious words as "plumy," "balmy" and "downy." Moreover such "poetical" words and expressions as "verdant vales," "solemn hour" and "azure main" came to litter and deface their pages.

Their contribution to prose style, from the lovely conversational language of Dryden to the lapidary classicism of Johnson, or Gibbon, was more durable and salutary. They aimed, not at the "chaste and correct" only, but also at the "majestic and grave." By the middle of the century the cult of symmetry led to the practice of antithesis and "the balanced phrase." The most ingenious practitioner of this stylistic device was Edward Gibbon, whose reiterated antitheses, although sometimes they may suggest the monotony of a piston, often give to his phrases a stereoscopic or two-dimensional relief.

Our appreciation of the Augustan mode is checked by their own pride in it. They really believed that they had "fixed" the English language eternally and had "reached the perfection which dominates a Classical Age." To us it is horrible to imagine an eternal succession of these Augustan colonnades or to contemplate what would have happened to our prose had it not been for the vivid inventions of later generations, or for the vigor injected into it by the ever-fresh realism of the American language.

It is important also to note the effect of scientific discovery and research on the thought and literature of the period. It was Newton who, by his demonstration of the laws of gravitation and his doctrine that the planets circled around in orderly orbits, inaugurated what has been described as "the eager age for science." At the time of his death in 1727, science was generally referred to as "philosophy" or more specifically as "natural philosophy." The effect of this mania for amateur science was not encouraging to pure literature, since it threw doubts upon the value of imagination, and lowered the standards of humanism. Men came to feel that those phenomena which were incapable of being "scientifically" explained must be regarded as "fanciful." A conflict soon developed between the scientists and the humanists, comparable to that with which we are threatened today.

The Royal Society, which had been founded in 1662, rapidly became the center of intellectual enquiry and numbered among its earliest members such important figures as Dryden, Wren, Evelyn, Pepys, Waller, and Cowley. In his *History of the Royal Society*, published in 1667 Thomas Sprat, subsequently Bishop of Rochester, defined the grim ideals by which the Society was to be guided and inspired. It would be well, he contends, if "this learned and inquisitive age" were to cease meddling with supernatural mysteries, or with metaphysics, and to stick to demonstrable fact. He was thus opposed to poetry with "its abundance of phrase, its trick of metaphor, its volubility of tongue." Moreover, if the men of letters required material for their inspiration, then assuredly Science could supply it better than any "ancient lore." Reason should henceforward guide men in all their thoughts and feelings. Literature, and even conversation, should aim at bringing "all things near to Mathematical plainness as they can." Such harsh precepts were resented by the men of letters. Swift ridiculed the scientists in his *Laputa* and his *Academy of Lagado*: Pope in the Dunciad mocked them as "a tribe with weeds and shells fantastic crown'd," and Addison sought to restore the prestige of literature by his papers on *The Pleasures of the Imagination*. Even Joseph Priestley—who after all had discovered the properties, or some of the properties, of oxygen—wrote that "a taste for science, pleasing and even honorable as it is, is not one of the highest passions of our nature. The pleasures that it furnishes are but one degree above those of the sense."

Nonetheless, it seemed as if mankind were on the verge of achieving command over nature and thereby, for some odd reason, introducing a golden age of universal peace and happiness. The fact that the intricacy of the natural order had thus been demonstrated, did not diminish religious faith, since it was felt that the Great Geometrician must be even more supernaturally gifted if He could impose regularity on so highly complex and variegated a machine. As these assumptions and feelings spread in ever widening circles, a rigid distinction became established between fact and fiction, reason and imagination, thought and feeling. Such formalism if persisted in might have destroyed our art and literature. Yet man, fortunately, cannot subsist on facts alone. Newton might have dismissed poetry as "a kind of ingenious nonsense": but the poetic instinct is not easy to suppress. Before long a reaction developed against the formalism of the Augustans, and with the coming of the Romantic Movement a new and far more valuable epoch opened for English letters.

The term "complacency" which has so often been employed as a weapon of criticism against the Augustans must, in certain important respects, be reconsidered and revised. They were justifiably pleased with themselves for having discarded the fanaticism and dissensions of the seventeenth century; for having attained to a "reasonable" equilibrium in religious controversies; for having by the genius of Marlborough rendered their small island a formidable factor in the balance of power; for having acquired valuable plantations overseas; for having surpassed their former rivals as a great commercial nation; for having firmly established the Protestant faith and reduced Catholicism and Jacobitism to but incidental menaces; and for having established a political system, which, for all its faults, did certainly represent a higher standard of freedom and tolerance than any at that time attained abroad. It is not strange, and ought not to be irritating that they should have been confident that their world was becoming better and better every year and that the benefits conferred by the advance of Science and Technology offered an ever widening prospect of peace, order and prosperity. Nor is it surprising that the literature of the period should have reflected, and striven to enhance, this general sense of security, stability, and calm.

Three

As an example, even as a model, of Augustan placidity we may take the life, work, and character of Joseph Addison. It may be that his political and social advancement was too calculating, cautious, and successful to inspire elation. It may be that the dominance that he exercised over his disciples was both self-important and pompous. It may be that his avoidance of all disturbing thought savors of intellectual timidity, that his aversion from "enthusiasm" strikes us as too passionless, that the urbanity of his style becomes monotonous, and his simplicity insipid. His *Cato* and the poems which brought him fame certainly appear to us restricted, formal, and too akin to prose, but as Mr. T. S. Eliot has pointed out, it is foolish to deride Augustan poetry for being prosaic. "More prose," writes Mr. Eliot, "is bad because it is like bad poetry than poetry is bad because it is like bad prose. To have the virtues of good prose is the first and minimum requirement of good poetry." Nor is it fair to blame Addison and Pope for the fact that their successors and imitators learnt their tune by heart and continued to employ their idiom and meter long after they had ceased to be the natural vehicles for the expression of altered ways of thought and feeling. Addison was assuredly not a creative writer of the first order; he was an institution; and we incline to forget how valuable that institution proved.

Our views on Addison are inescapably colored by the damaging portrait of him which Pope, without justifiable provocation, has bequeathed to posterity. His lines, for all their familiarity, are worth quoting, not merely as an example of brilliant malice, but because they undeniably contain an element of truth:

> Peace to all such, but were there one whose fires
> True genius kindles and fair fame inspires;
> Blest with each talent and each art to please,
> And born to write, converse, and live with ease;
> Should such a man, too fond to rule alone,
> Bear, like the Turk no brother near his throne,
> View him with scornful, yet with jealous eyes,
> And hate for arts that caused himself to rise;
> Damn with faint praise, assent with civil leer,
> And without sneering, teach the rest to sneer;
> Willing to wound, and yet afraid to strike,

Just hint a fault and hesitate dislike;
Alike reserved to blame or to commend,
A timorous foe and a suspicious friend;
Dreading e'en fools, by flatterers besieged,
And so obliging that he ne'er obliged;
Like Cato, give his little senate laws,
And sit attentive to his own applause;
While wits and Templars every sentence raise,
And wonder with a foolish face or praise—
Who would not laugh, if such a man there be?
Who would not weep if Atticus were he?

As an antidote to such poison we should read Macaulay's comfortable eulogy.

Addison's career was one of almost unimpeded success. Born the son of a scholarly parson, who became Dean of Lichfield, he was educated at Charterhouse and at Queen's College, Oxford. He was elected a fellow of Magdalen, where he acquired repute by the polish and exactitude of the Latin verses which he would compose when strolling through the willow coppice (to this day known as "Addison's Walk") where the Cherwell in all modesty slides into the Thames. He possessed the gift of impressing his personality on those in power and was sent abroad at Government expense in order to study foreign languages and thus qualify for a diplomatic career. In 1705, he published his poem *The Campaign* celebrating the victory of Blenheim, and in 1713 the drama *Cato* was successfully performed. The fame that he thereby acquired placed him at the head of all contemporary writers. From 1709 to 1711 he had collaborated with Steele in editing the *Tatler*, and from 1711 to 1712 he wrote his immensely popular and influential essays for the *Spectator*. He sat in the House of Commons for eleven years, but owing to extreme bashfulness, proved incapable of making an adequate speech. In spite of this disability, he became Chief Secretary in Ireland, a Lord Commissioner of Trade and Secretary of State. He ended by marrying the Dowager Countess of Warwick and lived in splendor in historic

Holland House. He died on June 17, 1719, at the age of forty-seven and was buried in Westminster Abbey.

In spite of Pope's invective, Addison was a gentle, tolerant, benign, and diffident man, who even at the summit of his worldly success preferred to spend his nights at Button's coffee house, drinking heavily in the company of his cronies and disciples, Richard Steele, Tickell, and Ambrose ("Namby-Pamby") Philips.

He was a good classical scholar, although he cared but little for Greek letters and his passion for the Latin poets diverted his attention from the great Roman historians, philosophers, and rhetoricians. It was he who rendered an intimate acquaintance with Horace essential to any young gentleman who aspired to culture, and in truth the essential urbanity of this stout Sabine farmer, with his cult of mediocrity and an easygoing humor, was admirably attuned to the placidity of the Augustan mode. Addison was much esteemed at the time for his renderings of Latin verse, which, commendable though they be for prosody and precision, cannot compare in elegance or music with the exquisite Latin poems of Thomas Gray. Yet the fact that Addison was certainly overestimated by his contemporaries, should not lead us to underestimate today the very serious contribution that he made to taste and culture. His influence was deep, and above all wide, and on the whole it was most valuable. It was he, after all, who brought the Essay to perfection and the Essay, in its varied development, was a form of expression well suited to the gentler moods of English men of letters and the reading public.

Four

Although it was Richard Steele who invented the modern Essay in April 1709, it was Addison who gave to it a polished literary form. The *Tatler*, which first began to publish regular articles on life and manners, was issued on the Tuesdays, Thursdays, and Saturdays when the mails left London for the provinces. The idea of appealing to a public wider than the restricted London cliques in Court, Society and Coffee House, must be credited to Richard Steele, who was a born journalist. The success of the *Tatler* encouraged him to embark upon the more ambitious venture of the *Spectator*, the first series of which ran from March 1, 1711, to December 2, 1712. In the second series, which was resumed on June 18, 1714, the original characters were discarded, perhaps because Addison feared that their popularity would lead to imitation or parody. Sir Roger de Coverley, as the public were informed by a pathetic letter from his old servant, Edward Biscuit, died in October 1712. The clergyman who had figured with such piety in the first series in the end succumbed to what had always been a weak constitution. Will Honeycomb becomes a reformed character, retires to the country, and at the age of sixty marries the buxom daughter of a local farmer. Sir Andrew Freeport leaves his counting house and becomes an esteemed country squire. And Captain Sentry, Sir Roger's nephew, inherits the estate of Coverley Hall.

The Spectator himself, who during the first series had proved so modest, so inarticulate, and so sedate, changes his nature and suddenly becomes voluble and didactic. The second series, even to our sophisticated minds, lacks the charm of the first. The essays of the *Spectator* were republished and widely sold in volume form, which explains why a periodical of such comparatively short duration should have exercised so lasting an influence upon the taste of the reading public and upon the literary standards of the age. The periodical essay, which was so admirably attuned to the temper of the early decades of the century, lost its popularity about 1780, when the disasters of the American War and the subsequent tragedies of the French Revolution forced men to think of more distressing things.

As all good journalists, Steele and Addison had an alert sense of audience. During the course of the century the reading public increased rapidly until in 1758 Dr. Johnson could assert in the *Idler* that "the knowledge of the common people of England is greater than that of any other vulgar." A good index of this growth during the century of a large literate public is provided by significant statistics showing that, although in 1753 stamp duty was paid on 7,411,757 newspapers; in 1792 it was paid on 15,005,760. But it was to the middle classes, rather than to the proletariat, that the *Spectator* was addressed. Although Steele with his gift of flattery contended that his paper would appeal to the "elegant and knowing part of mankind," Addison was positive that the success of the paper would depend on its gaining the attention of the middle class. Admittedly he had but scant sympathy for "the ordinary Plebeian or Mechanic," although Steele was allowed to insert some sloppy articles on the subject of the pauper, the unemployed, and the slums. What Addison aimed at was gaining the support of the rising and expanding provincial and middle classes. "The Middle Condition," he wrote pontifically, "seems to me the most advantageously situated for the gaining of wisdom." "I shall be ambitious," he wrote again, "to have it said of me that I brought philosophy out of the closets and libraries, schools and colleges, to dwell in clubs and assemblies, at tea tables and in coffee houses." He thus decided to avoid politics, and even party politics, and to concentrate on ordinary themes which would be of common interest to the greatest number. "It is much better," he proclaimed, "to be let in to knowledge of oneself, than to hear what happens in Muscovy or Poland." The *Spectator*, therefore, would not report on foreign affairs and still less indulge in domestic controversy. Although he made it evident that he himself possessed Tory sympathies, he assured his readers that men who allowed party passions to affect their reason were "poor narrow souls" and even "despicable wretches." Party animosity, he contended, "destroyed even common sense." The aim of the *Spectator* would therefore be to discuss the art of living in terms which even ordinary people could understand. The periodical would prove itself "a Friend to no Interests but those of Truth and Virtue, nor a Foe to any but those of Vice and Folly." It would avoid social gossip and personal invective, "As, on one side," wrote Addison, "my Paper has not in it a single Word of News, a Reflection on Politics, nor a stroke of Party; so, on the other, there are no fashionable Touches of Infidelity, no obscene Ideas, no satire upon Priesthood, Marriage, and the popular Topicks of Ridicule; no private Scandal; nor anything that may tend to the Defamation of particular Persons, Families or Societies." These high ideals of journalism were preserved by the *Spectator* even in its twentieth-century form until its recent rejuvenation. They may have rendered it dull; but they preserved its reputation for undeviating respectability.

Addison, who was a lay-preacher by temperament, "a parson in a tye-wig" as Mandeville called him, could not divest himself of a didactic purpose. His aim was "to enliven morality with wit and to temper wit with morality." "As the great and only End of these my Speculations," he asserted, "is to banish Vice and Ignorance out of the territories of Great Britain, I shall endeavor as much as possible to establish among us a Taste for polite Writing." Atheism, he told his readers, was a sign of bad manners. "For my own part," he assured them, "I think the being of a God is so little to be doubted, that it is almost the only Truth we are sure of." What man needed, apart from religion, was "a clear Judgment and a good Conscience." "It is impossible," he wrote, "for any thought to be beautiful which is not just, and has not its foundation in the nature of things. The basis of all Wit is Truth; and no thought can be valuable of which good sense is not the groundwork."

He was careful not to alienate the sympathies of his middle class readers by any unpatriotic sentiments or sophisticated ideas. To him the English Government and the Anglican religion were unquestionably the pride and envy of all foreign peoples. He derided the French as "that fantastic Nation" and suggested that an Act of Parliament should be passed forbidding the importation of "French Fopperies." The *Spectator's* attitude to its women readers was correspondingly conciliatory, if somewhat patronizing. "I shall take it," wrote Steele, "for the greatest Glory of my Work if among reasonable Women this Paper may furnish Tea Table talk." Women, in Addison's opinion, should refrain from manifesting any interest in politics. "This is," he wrote, "in its nature a male Vice and made up of many angry and cruel passions that are altogether repugnant to the Softness, the Modesty, and those other endearing Qualities which are natural to the Fair Sex." He is contemptuous of such fashionable accomplishments as were beyond the reach of his provincial audiences, and condemned the teaching of French, Italian, singing and dancing. The ideal woman should cultivate the domestic sciences, such as "Pickling, Pastry, and making wines of fruits of our own growth." She should at the same time be solemn in her demeanor, taking care to prevent "Sprightliness degenerating into Levity." In matters of taste, although he seemed to be sympathetic to landscape rather than formal gardening, he defended Augustan symmetry. "I have endeavored," he writes, "to banish this Gothick Taste which has taken possession of us." He points out that on entering the Pantheon at Rome the mind is elevated and impressed, whereas no such a sense of awe is aroused by even the largest Gothic cathedral, owing to "the Greatness of Manner in the one, and the Meanness in the other."

The themes dealt with in the *Spectator* are varied if uncontroversial. They comprise old age, the street cries of London, Paradise Lost, beards, dancing, friendship, compassion, the adulteration of wine, hypocrisy, false modesty, fancy and imagination, the force of habit, the Jews, dreams, anatomy, cleanliness, manners, the theatre, punning, the English language, marriage, epic poetry, the transmigration of souls, and "that awful and tremendous subject, the Ubiquity or Omnipresence of the Divine Being." A running fight is directed against superstition, slander, the use of foreign expressions, impudence, vanity, jealousy, and party vehemence. The Spectator himself appears as a secondary character, humorously referred to as "the short faced man." Although he possesses a small country property which has been in his family since the Norman conquest, he is himself an urban rather than a rural character. When he visits Sir Roger at Coverley Hall he takes no part in shooting or hunting, owing to his "aversion to leaping Hedges." Although he pays formal tribute to the "exquisite charms" of the country, and was quite interested in watching a hen laying her eggs, he clearly prefers a coffeehouse to woods or fields. He is a taciturn man, hesitating to enter into controversy, and prefers to remain a silent observer, or "looker-on." The other characters who appear and reappear in the first series of the *Spectator* are almost equally colorless. Sir Roger de Coverly, in spite of his eccentricity, is in fact a Tory squire of conventional type. He rules his tenants and the villagers with a beneficent tyranny assisted by the parson, who has been vicar of the village for the last thirty years. He is a sound Tory, convinced that the only foreigner worth mentioning is Prince Eugene, and suffering under the perilous illusion that "one Englishman can always beat three Frenchmen." He is in fact little more than a lay figure, whose weaknesses arouse affection and whose virtues are as bland and solid as those of the averagely contented man. Even the fact that he had for long suffered from "an Attachment to a perverse Widow" scarcely ruffled his contentment and in case the reader should feel any uneasiness regarding this lady's rejection of his advances, he is assured that on his deathbed Sir Roger was comforted by a message from the widow which was of a kind tone. The minor characters of the *Spectator* are little more than faint sketches of conventional types.

Dr. Johnson's *Idler* and *Rambler* are more serious in intent and in fact contain some of his most memorable comments and criticisms. Compared to them, the tone and style of the Spectator are insipid indeed. Anne Seward, the "Swan of Lichfield," was among the first to denounce Addison's "water-gruel" style. To us the smugness of the Addison manner detracts from its once famous charm. "It is," he writes, "an unspeakable Advantage to possess our Minds with an habitual Good Intention, and to aim all our Thoughts, Words and Actions at some laudable End, whether to the Glory of our Maker, the Good of Mankind, or the Benefit of our own Souls." There runs throughout his essays a note of puritan canting that we find offensive. He disapproves of those "merry drolls" who indulge in meaningless laughter or word play. "I must confess," he writes, "that left to myself I should rather aim at Instruction than Diverting." "I have always preferred," he writes again, "Cheerfulness to Mirth. . . . The Sacred Person, who was the great Pattern of Perfection, was never seen to laugh." How dare Addison commit so pompous an irreverence?

It is true that in this unctuous and pontifical manner he succeeded in spreading to many dull and unenlightened homes the blessed habit of reading. It is a habit which once acquired is never lost and it assuredly adds both zest and comfort to life. But in the

quick and angry world in which today we live such smug complacency is all but intolerable. Addison's complacency and optimism
are as insipid as a vanilla puff. They have done much damage to the
repute of the Augustans.

Chapter 9

Savage Pessimism

(Jonathan Swift, 1667–1745)

———— •◆• ————

Whigs and Tories—The Revolution of 1688 static rather than dynamic—Individuals more significant than institutions—The Peace Party—The shiftings of power as illustrated by the frustrated ambitions of Jonathan Swift—His service under Sir William Temple—Moor Park and Hesther Johnson—Swift's early odes—He deserts Temple and goes to Ireland—His return to Moor Park—The Ancients and the Moderns—The *Battle of the Books* and the *Tale of a Tub*—Death of Temple—He returns to Dublin—Laracor—Mission to London to secure Queen's bounty for the Irish Church—He deserts the Whigs for the Tories—*The Examiner*—The patronage of Harley and Bolingbroke—The *Conduct of the Allies*—Death of Queen Anne and entry of the Whigs into power—Swift is made Dean of St. Patrick's—The disappointment of his hopes of becoming a Bishop—His embittered old age—*Gulliver's Travels*—His genius for hatred.

One

SIR LEWIS NAMIER and his pupils have taught me that to assume, as so many former historians assumed, that the eighteenth century in England is to be viewed as a struggle between two organized parties, known respectively as "Ins" and "Outs," or "Whigs" and "Tories," and retaining power by the distribution of bribes and offices, is to ignore the circumstances that "faction" in those days was largely a matter of personal or family loyalty and that the habit of corruption was less extensive than has been supposed. In this eighteenth-century portrait gallery, the aim of which is to indicate the variety of ideas and temperaments which renders so fascinating any study of the Age of Reason, it is not, as I have said, my intention, either to consider the great wars of the period, or to examine in any detail the political trans- actions which occasioned the rise or fall of successive ministries. Yet if we are properly to understand the motives that impelled so many individuals to shift their loyalties, we should realize that they were not always or wholly dictated by personal greed or ambition; their actions were often inspired by serious principles or prejudices. It is necessary to have some conception at least of what were the purposes and ideas that impelled the several groups to push for power with such acri- mony and ardor.

Although it would be incorrect to assume that anything resembling the two party system, in the modern sense of that term, existed at the outset of the eighteenth century, there was certainly operative a social and religious cleavage between those who called themselves "Whigs" and those who called themselves "Tories." The Whigs represented the low Church, the middle classes, the rapidly expanding commercial interest, and the dissenters. The Tories represented the high Church, the landowning class and the Anglican clergy. The Glorious Revolu- tion of 1688, the Bill of Rights of 1689 and the Toleration Act of the same year, established the principle that the Crown might not main- tain a standing army, or levy taxes, without the consent of Parliament and thus forever abolished the mediaeval conception of the Divine Right of Kings, and of extreme religious persecution. The freedoms founded by those Acts rendered England in the eyes of foreign observ- ers the asylum of liberty and the sanctuary of reason, tolerance, and good sense. But it would be an error to suppose that either Dutch William or his sister-in-law Queen Anne felt that it was to the Whigs alone that they owed their crowns. William III ignored party politics and desired only to be served by such ministers as he considered most resolute in prosecuting, and most efficient in conducting, his wars against Louis XIV. Queen Anne, being Anglican in her outlook, always at heart preferred the Tories to the Whigs and bitterly resented what she called "these tyrannizing lords" or the Whig junto. It was only after the succession of George I in 1714 that the Whigs became really dominant and were able to keep the Tories out of power for forty-seven years.

The Glorious Revolution was conservative rather than radical, in that it had been achieved in defense of established interests against the usurpations of the Crown. Its result was, not the encouragement of a wide progressive movement, but the confirmation and stabilization of existing civil rights and privileges. It did establish the Rule of Law, but under the teaching of Blackstone and Burke this rule became static and an actual obstacle to fundamental legislative reforms. The habit of stagnation descended upon the Church, the Civil Service, the Universities, the schools and the local authorities. Yet the Revolution of 1688 did release a fresh energy and a sense of liberation. As George Trevelyan has written; "the glory of the Eighteenth Century in Britain lay in the genius and energy of individuals acting freely in a free community." It is by examining the activity of individuals, rather than the origin and progress of institutions, that the quality of the period can best be appreciated. It was the originality, even the eccentricity, of individuals that marked the epoch, and fostered the rise of great men of action and mighty innovators and writers, such as Marlborough, Swift, Bishops Berkeley and Butler, Wesley, Clive, Warren Hastings, the two Pitts, Dr. Johnson, Captain Cook, Burke, Reynolds, Adam Smith, Hume, James Watt, Burns and William Blake.

Inevitably, after the Glorious Revolution, Britain became the leader of Europe against the threatened continental dominance of France. At the outbreak of the War of the Spanish Succession in 1701, it seemed inevitable that Louis XIV would succeed in affirming his European supremacy. Everything, except command of the seas, was in France's favor. As the ally of Spain and Bavaria, Louis XIV controlled the Spanish Netherlands, Milan, and Naples. At Blenheim in

1704 Marlborough saved Austria and knocked out Bavaria. By his victory at Ramillies in 1706, he secured mastery over the Netherlands, whereas Prince Eugene's Turin campaign gave Austria supremacy in the Italian peninsula. Marlborough himself, although an excellent diplomatist, was a poor politician. He was hated by both parties and to him the very names of "Whig" and "Tory" were detestable. But, as George Trevelyan concludes, "by the light of his unclouded genius he protected the advent of the much needed age of reason, toleration, and common sense." Some recapitulation is here necessary.

The Whig Junto, which had supported Marlborough's campaigns with tenacity, ought to have seized the opportunity of making peace in 1709. They were tied however by their own slogan of "No peace without Spain," although they were well aware that they could not turn the Bourbon monarch out of Spain by their own efforts, and were so unwise as to insist that Louis XIV must, as a condition of peace, agree to expel his grandson himself. Public opinion, which was wearied of war, began to turn against them. At this moment, they committed the blunder of impeaching for sedition Dr. Sacheverell, a high churchman, who from his pulpit in St. Saviour's, Southwark, had persistently attacked the principles of the Glorious Revolution. The Queen, who meanwhile had transferred her devotion from the Duchess of Marlborough to Abigail Hill, Mrs. Masham, was encouraged by the popular agitation in favor of Sacheverell to break with the Junto. Marlborough at this stage committed the mistake of asking to be appointed Captain General for life. He even faced the Queen with an ultimatum demanding the dismissal of Mrs. Masham under the threat of his own resignation. The Tory Robert Harley, in connivance with Abigail, advised the Queen to get rid of these Whig tyrants by stages. In June 1710, Sunderland, Marlborough's son-in-law, was deprived of his post as Secretary of State and in August Godolphin was dismissed from the Treasury. In September Parliament was dissolved and the Tories returned with a majority. In December 1711, after Robert Harley and Bolingbroke had assumed office, Marlborough himself was deprived of his command and secret negotiations for a separate peace with France were opened, through the agency of Prior, in Paris. The Duke of Ormonde, who had succeeded Marlborough as commander in chief, received secret instructions to withdraw his armies out of the line of battle. Although achieved by such disgraceful and humiliating transactions, the ensuing Treaty of Utrecht was an excellent compromise which preserved the peace of Europe for the next forty-three years. On August 1, 1714, Queen Anne died and in September the Elector of Hanover landed in England and was recognized as King George I. Harley and Bolingbroke were dismissed and the latter, fearing impeachment on account of his intrigues with the Jacobites, escaped to France.

Two

These shiftings of power are well illustrated in the fortunes of Jonathan Swift, a man who possessed one of the most powerful, if tortured, intellects of the century. He was born at No. 7 Hoey's Court, Dublin, on November 30, 1667. His father, a member of the King's Inns in Dublin, died seven months before Jonathan's birth. His grandmother was the niece of Sir Erasmus Dryden and Jonathan could thus claim cousinship with the great Restoration poet. His mother, Abigail Erick, came from a family long resident in the English midlands and shortly after Jonathan's birth she joined her relations in Leicester, leaving the infant in the charge of a devoted and intelligent nurse. The education of the orphaned boy was supervised, at least in theory, by his uncle Godwin Swift, at the time Attorney General in Tipperary. Jonathan in after life contended that all the education that Uncle Godwin had provided was "the education of a dog" and he was always tempted to attribute his own lack of balance and amiability to the fact that he had been deserted by his family when a child. At the age of six he was sent to the Kilkenny School, then regarded as "the Eton of Ireland": at the age of fifteen he matriculated at Trinity College, Dublin. He was neither industrious nor methodical and he obtained his degree only *speciali gratia*, or "on sufferance," such a concession being regarded as a disgrace.

In 1689 he had the good fortune to obtain employment in the household of Sir William Temple at Moor Park near Farnham in Surrey. His functions appear at first to have been those of a menial clerk; his salary did not exceed £20 a year and he was expected to take his meals, not with the family, but in the steward's room with the upper servants. He writhed under this humiliation. It was at this early stage also that he developed those fits of giddiness which pestered him throughout his life and which, it now seems, were occasioned by an affection of the ear, known to modern medicine as "labyrinthine vertigo."

Sir William Temple was an excellent man, scholarly and disinterested. However ineffectual or timid as a statesman he was assuredly a great diplomatist. His negotiation of the Triple Alliance and of the marriage between Princess Mary and William of Orange changed the course of history. If we are to believe Mr. Denis Johnston—and I for one am impressed by his labors of research and detection—William Temple was Swift's half-brother by blood. "His faultlessness," writes Macaulay snuffily, "is chiefly to be ascribed to his extreme dread of responsibility, to his determination rather to leave his country in a scrape than to run any chance of being in a scrape himself." "He had not," Macaulay adds with prim contempt, "sufficient warmth and elevation of sentiment to deserve the name of a virtuous man." Again and again did he refuse the offer of the post of Secretary of State and when things became difficult or dangerous he was apt to retire to Sheen or Farnham and to distract himself by cultivating wall fruit with surpassing neatness and skill. "The most exquisite," records John Evelyn, "nailed and trained, far better than I ever noted it." He might indeed have gone down to history as a solemn and unadventurous man, were it not that there hangs about him the romance of the love letters which, during the seven years of his engagement, he exchanged with Dorothy Osborne.

When on his way to France in 1648, he stopped at an inn in the Isle of Wight where he encountered Dorothy the daughter of an ardent royalist, Sir Percy Osborne. Temple, who was only twenty years old at the time, committed the indiscretion (it was probably the only, and certainly the most rewarding indiscretion, that he ever committed) of inscribing on the window of the inn the sentence "And Hamon was hanged on the gallows they had prepared for Mordecai." This inscription was reported to the Governor, whose name, it seems, was Hammond, who interpreted it as referring to Charles I and Cromwell. Temple was immediately arrested and things would have gone badly with him had not Dorothy Osborne, trusting in her innocence and beauty, come forward to assert that it was she, with her diamond ring, who had cut the inscription. Temple was then released and fell deeply in love with his rescuer. The family disapproved of their engagement, since she possessed other suitors of greater wealth and power, including Sir Justinian Isham, Lord Danby, the future Duke of Leeds, and Henry Cromwell, the fourth son of the Lord Protector. When Dorothy's looks were damaged owing to an attack of smallpox, the other suitors became less persistent, while Temple remained faithful. They were married in 1645 and lived quite happily until her death fifty years later.

Although a mild and evasive statesman, Temple was one of the first diplomatists clearly to realize that credit derived from truthfulness is more important than suspicion aroused by cunning. Such was the influence that he established with the Grand Pensionary of Holland, de Witt, that he succeeded in concluding the Triple Alliance between Great Britain, Holland and Sweden, designed to protect the Spanish Netherlands from French encroachment. After the Dutch wars of Charles I, it was Temple who was sent as Ambassador to The Hague to conclude peace and who succeeded in negotiating the marriage between William of Orange and Princess Mary, the niece of Charles II, which, ten years later, produced so beneficent a settlement. As many excellent diplomatists, he found himself ill suited to the House of Commons, and preferred his books and his gardens at Sheen and Moor Park.

It was in 1689 that Jonathan Swift, at that date aged twenty-two and still a loutish Dublin undergraduate, first entered the household of Sir William Temple. It consisted of Sir William, then aged sixty; Dorothy his wife, then aged sixty-one; Sir William's widowed sister, Lady Giffard, then aged fifty-one; a poor relation of Lady Temple, Rebecca Dingley; Mrs. Bridget Johnson, "gentlewoman to wait" on

Lady Temple; and her daughter Hesther Johnson, or "Hetty," then a child of eight. Hetty was regarded by many contemporaries as Sir William's illegitimate daughter. Much as he resented being "treated as a schoolboy" Swift derived from Temple the varnish of good manners and much knowledge of the world. Temple was a voluminous writer of political pamphlets and possessed an excellent style. According to Dr. Johnson he was "the first writer who gave cadence to English prose." Considering that he was an almost exact contemporary of Dryden, this judgment may seem to us exaggerated. But Temple assuredly conveyed to his pupil the principles of "polite" and above all concise, writing. Although Swift was never able to stifle his resentment of all patronage, he retained a feeling of rather grudging respect for Sir William. He liked Lady Temple to whom he refers as "mild Dorothea, wise and great" and as "the best companion for the best of men." He could not stand Lady Giffard with her bossy ways and after his final quarrel with her he severed all connection with Moor Park. Years afterwards, when he encountered Jack Temple in a London street, he passed him by. "I am glad," he wrote to Stella, "that I have wholly shaken off that family." Gratitude was not among his virtues.

During his early years at Moor Park he began to write pindaric odes, in the manner of Cowley. It seems strange that a man who could write admirable prose, who possessed a keen sense of the ridiculous, should in his poetry be so unaware of bathos, and have so insensitive an ear. His Ode to William III on the Battle of the Boyne is typical of his early poetic manner:

> And now I in the spirit see
> (The spirit of exalted poetry)
> I see the fatal fight begin;
> And lo! Where a Destroying Angel stands
> (By all but Heaven and me unseen)
> With lightning in his eyes and thunder in his hands;
> "In vain," said he "does utmost Thule boast
> No poysonous beast will in her breed,
> Or no infectious weed...."

"Cousin Swift," commented Dryden coldly, "you will never be a poet."

Discouraged by this criticism, and becoming increasingly restless under Temple's austere and chilly patronage, he decided that his only hope was to enter the Church. He thus ran away from Moor Park, much to Temple's indignation, and crossed to Dublin. He then discovered that he could not be ordained unless he produced a letter of recommendation from his former employer and was obliged to write a "penitential" letter to Sir William, who replied immediately giving him the reference he needed. He was ordained on January 28, 1695. He secured the post of prebend in the parish of Kilroot, east of Carrickfergus, on Belfast Lough. It was there that he acquired his lifelong antipathy to the Ulster presbyterians. It was there also that he fell in love with Miss Jane Waring, daughter of the Archdeacon of Dromore and asked her to marry him. She was a coy and sickly girl and much to Swift's fury she refused his offer. He wrote her an indignant letter and then decided that it would be wiser to make peace with Temple and to return to Moor Park.

He found things changed. Dorothy Temple had died in January 1695 and Lady Giffard ruled supreme. Hesther Johnson had grown into a vivacious dark-eyed girl of fifteen. And Temple, whose only son had drowned himself off London Bridge, was a broken and lonely old man. Swift was no longer treated as a menial amanuensis but as a trusted secretary and friend. He assisted his master in his literary labors, flirted with Hesther, whom he was already calling "Stella," and in the intervals of reading in the library would dash up the hill behind the house, hoping by such violent exercise to cure his vertigo. There was some basis for the theory, which caused him such envenomed bitterness in later life, that it was his destiny to be exploited and placed in false positions by his patrons. Temple involved him in the regrettable controversy of the Battle of the Books.

Sir William was not a profound classical scholar, but had been much interested in Fontenelle and by the controversy aroused in Paris between the Ancients and the Moderns. He therefore wrote an essay on *Ancient and Modern Learning* in which he was so imprudent as to describe the "Letters of Phalaris" as containing "more force of wit and genius" than any other letters in existence. Encouraged by this eulogy an edition of the Letters was produced by Mr. Charles Boyle, a young Oxonian. In his preface to this edition Boyle unjustly accused that mighty scholar, Richard Bentley, of having refused to let him see a manuscript of importance. Bentley, annoyed by this unjust accusation, wrote his *Dissertation on the Letters of Phalaris* in which he proved conclusively that the letters were not written by the tyrant of Acragas in the sixth century BCE but by a Greek sophist in the second century CE. Boyle, assisted by other young Oxonians, replied to Bentley, accusing him of being an old cross-grained, bourgeois, pedant, and Temple, feeling that his own scholarship had been exposed to ridicule, persuaded Swift to write *The Battle of the Books* in which he represents Bentley as having been routed by Boyle. He also introduced in to this jumbled work some sneering references to Dryden.

In the same year, it seems, he composed the *Tale of a Tub* which was intended to be a defense of the Anglican Church against the Catholics and the Dissenters. When, in his old age, Swift re-read the *Tale of a Tub* he exclaimed "Good God! What genius I had when I wrote that book!" The modern reader will not echo this eulogy. Dr. Johnson was more correct when he described it as "this wild work." It was in fact an unwise book for a young and most ambitious clergyman to write. He went so far as to suggest that authority in religion was a form of fraud and that "inspiration" and mysticism were but the results of what we should today describe as "sublimation" of the sex instinct. Whereas the outward forms of religion are rightly imposed upon the masses by the State, the favored few, while perfectly sincere in conforming to the conventional observances of their age, really only believe in rational or "natural" religion. Mr. Middleton Murry has gone so far as to describe the Tale as "a prolonged whoop of laughter over a dead self" and as "an intellectual orgy to celebrate his escape from idealism." The failure of Harley and Bolingbroke to obtain a bishopric for Swift may be ascribed to

Queen Anne's conviction that a man who, although in holy orders, could write so subversive a work as the *Tale of a Tub* must be at heart a freethinker. And in truth Swift was devoid of literary tact.

In 1699, Sir William Temple died. Swift was left some money and was appointed literary executor of his master's memoirs and manuscripts. The first two volumes were published with general approbation. Swift then decided to publish a third volume, although he must have known that Temple had not wished for the publication of all his surviving essays and papers. Lady Giffard was furious, mainly because this third volume contained some slighting references to her great friend Lady Essex. She wrote to the papers protesting that the publication of this third volume was "unauthorized and inaccurate." She enlisted the support of the Duchess of Somerset, Queen Anne's latest favorite, who replied that the publication of this third volume, against the wishes of the family and during the lifetime of Lady Essex, showed that Swift was "a man of no principle either of honor or religion." Swift thereafter savagely assailed the Duchess of Somerset in *The Windsor Prophecy*. It is not surprising that he was for the rest of his life ill regarded at Court. Once again a patron, even if posthumously, had landed him in a false position.

Three

On the death of Temple, Swift was obliged to find other protectors. He managed to secure the post of secretary to Lord Berkeley, who had been appointed one of the Lord Justices of Ireland. He had hoped that in this key position he would be able to obtain the Deanery of Deny, but he had to content himself with the Rectory of Agher and the Vicarage of Laracor. Hearing that he would now be able to support a family, Miss Jane Waring, his friend of Carrickfergus days, wrote to him suggesting that she was now in a position to accept his advances. He replied in a letter of May 4, 1700, urging her to "Show that you have chosen me by breaking free of this horrible mess of coyness on your part and worldly consideration of your family's."

She does not appear to have replied to this brutal ultimatum; that, so far as we know, was the last he ever heard of his "Varina" of Dromore. Meanwhile, he profited by his position in Lord Berkeley's household to form a lifelong friendship with Lady Betty Berkeley, subsequently Lady Betty Germaine, and to extract a D.D. from Trinity College, thus becoming "Doctor Swift" at the age of thirty-three. He was happy for a year, living in domestic bliss at Laracor with Hesther Johnson, and Mrs. Dingley, who had by then joined him in Ireland, and laying out his ponds and coppices in the manner of Moor Park.

In 1706, Swift was dispatched to London as representative of the Irish Anglicans for the purpose of extending to Ireland the benefits of Queen Anne's bounty. He found that the Whigs were only prepared to extend the bounty to the Irish clergy provided that they withdrew all opposition to the repeal of the Test Act in Ireland. Swift, who felt that the Protestant ascendancy depended upon the domination of the established Church, and who regarded all dissenters and presbyterians with loathing, was outraged by this example of Whig tolerance. His disaffection for the Party to which he was supposed to belong was increased when the Bishopric of Waterford was accorded to his enemy Dr. Milles, and when, but a few months later, Dr. Lambert was appointed Chaplain to the Lord Lieutenant, a post which Swift had ardently desired since it led by a sure and easy path to an Irish see. He had by then wisely discarded his Pindaric odes, and had adopted the gay doggerel of Hudibras as his model. His failure to establish his influence with the Whig ministers, or to obtain the ecclesiastical preferment for which he schemed, filled his proud soul with sick despair:

> I often wish'd that I had clear
> For life six hundred pounds a year,
> A handsome house to lodge a friend,
> A river at my garden's end,
> A terras walk and half a rood
> Of land set out to plant a wood . . .
> And there in sweet oblivion drown
> The cares that haunt the Court and Town.

This desire for sweet oblivion did not last for long. Having failed to obtain from the Whigs the rewards to which he felt his talents entitled him, he decided that it would prove more advantageous to change his Party and to offer his services to the Tories. Robert Harley, soon to become Earl of Oxford, was at that date organizing among the Tories a peace party aiming at the dismissal of the Duke of Marlborough and the conclusion of a separate peace with France behind the backs of our allies. In this intrigue he had the assistance of Abigail Hill, Mrs. Masham, who had replaced the Duchess of Marlborough in Queen Anne's affections, and also of the brilliant if volatile Henry St. John, later to become notorious as Viscount Bolingbroke. In 1710, Lord Sunderland (Marlborough's son-in-law) was dismissed from office and the same year the removal of Godolphin marked the end of the Whig Junto. Public opinion, however, was as yet not prepared to repudiate the debt of gratitude the country owed to Marlborough and felt that it would be dishonorable to desert the allies who had fought gallantly beside us through ten difficult and glorious years. What the peace party needed was a clever writer who could persuade the public that Marlborough was not the almost mythical hero of Whig propaganda, but a corrupt and selfish general who was deliberately prolonging the war for his own advantage and enrichment. At the same time it would be necessary to convince the rank and file of the Tory party that it would not be in the least dishonorable to make a separate peace, since from the very start our allies had failed to fulfill the conditions of the alliance and had themselves been guilty of unfaithfulness and treachery.

It was in October 1710 that Swift first met Robert Harley and was persuaded by him to offer his pen to the Tories. He was placed in charge of the party newspaper *The Examiner* and stimulated to attack the Whigs in general and the Duke of Marlborough and his Dutch friends in particular. Swift continued to write for *The Examiner* until June 1711 when he handed over the editorship to a young protégé of the name of Harrison, who proved so incompetent that he had to be given a diplomatic appointment. Swift was not absolutely convinced in his own mind that it was good tactics on the part of the Tories to insist on the dismissal and impeachment of the Duke of Marlborough. "I question," he wrote, "whether any wise State laid aside a General who had been successful nine years together, whom the enemy so much dread and his own soldiers cannot but believe must conquer." He always pretended that he himself had never descended to any "base" attack upon the Duke. This was untrue. Swift was more responsible than any other lampoonist for circulating the libel that Marlborough wished to prolong the war owing to his passion for money.

On March 8, 1711, a French agent, the Abbé de la Bourlie, who had assumed the name of the marquis de Guiscard, was being examined in the Cockpit by a committee of the Privy Council. Suddenly the prisoner drew a penknife from his pocket and stabbed Harley in the chest. The wound was not serious, but the incident increased Harley's popularity, much to the annoyance of his colleague and rival, Lord Bolingbroke, who felt that it was he who should have had the glory of being stabbed by Guiscard, since it was he who had signed the warrant for the spy's arrest. Swift was so much moved by this incident that he preserved Guiscard's penknife as an honored relic.

It was in August 1710 that Swift began the *Journal to Stella* which is among the most revealing documents in literature. Writing on September 30, 1710, he explains in frank terms the motives for his apostasy. "I am already," he writes, "represented to Harley as a discontented person that was used ill for not being Whig enough; and I hope for good usage from him. The Tories dryly tell me I can make my fortune if I please; but I do not understand them, or rather I do understand them." Of the Whigs he writes: "Rot 'em ungrateful dogs; I'll make them repent their usage before I leave this place." There were moments, however, when he was less positive that his change of party would prove as profitable as he hoped. "But I have had my revenge at least," he writes, "if I get nothing else."

His revenge, and it was indeed formidable, took the form of his pamphlet *The Conduct of the Allies* in which he sought to prepare the public for the dismissal of Marlborough and the betrayal of our friends. The first hint of this production is contained in a letter to Stella of October 26, 1711: "We have no quiet with the Whigs, they are so violent against a peace; but I'll cool them with a vengeance very soon." The pamphlet appeared on November 27, 1711, and sold a thousand copies in two days: by January 1712 eleven thousand copies had been disposed of. There came a moment when the Whigs and the war party secured a small majority in the House of Lords. Abigail feared that the Queen might be wavering and Swift in panic tried to obtain a post in some Embassy abroad, where he would be safe against Whig reprisals. But the danger passed; the Queen returned to her Masham allegiance; the Duke of Marlborough was dismissed and twelve Tory peers created from the peace party in order to secure a Tory majority. It was safe for Swift to remain in London.

Meanwhile the *Conduct of the Allies* created a wide effect. In this pamphlet Swift argued that the war had been entered upon for no real British interest; that of all the allies we were the ones who "apprehended least danger and expected least advantage." If we entered the war at all, we should have entered, not as principals but as auxiliaries. The country had been betrayed by the machinations of the Whigs and the greed of the Duke of Marlborough. "No nation," he wrote, "was ever so long and scandalously abused by the folly, the temerity, the corruption and the ambition of its domestic enemies; or treated with such insolence, injustice and ingratitude by its foreign friends." Under the treaties of alliance, the Austrian Emperor had promised to provide 90,000 men, the Dutch 60,000; and we only 40,000. As it was, we had furnished a third more than the Dutch, whereas the Emperor had refused to supply his stipulated quota on the ground that he must first deal with the Hungarian revolt. He never sent the troops he promised for the defense of Portugal and it had been owing to his diversion towards Naples that we failed to capture Toulon.

How came it that Britain should have become the "dupes and bubbles of Europe?" Because the whole power had devolved upon the Marlborough family and their supporters, "the money'd interests," "whose perpetual harvest is war and whose beneficial way of traffic must very much decline in peace." How came it that the Duke of Marlborough had allowed himself to be cheated by his friends the Dutch? "I know of no other way so probable, or indeed so charitable, to account for it, as by that immeasurable love of wealth which his best friends allow to be his predominant passion." Why should we go on fighting in order to place an Austrian Archduke upon the throne of Spain or to enable the Dutch to extend their frontier fortresses? Why, if we had to fight, did we campaign in the Low Countries and not rather use our sea power to obtain vast riches in South America and the West Indies? Was it because "the sea was not the Duke of Marlborough's element?" The continuance of the war was solely due "to mutual indulgence between our general and our allies, wherein they both so well found their accounts; to the fears of the money changers lest their tables should be overthrown."

The insidious cry of "a banker's ramp" has always had strong propaganda value and was even more effective in an age when the city merchants represented a class quite distinct from the landed gentry.

The effect of the *Conduct of the Allies* raised Swift's prestige with the peace party and its leaders. He wrote to Stella with complacency, not unmixed with skepticism:

> I did not expect to find such friends as I have done. They may indeed deceive me too. But there are important reasons why they should not. I have been used barbarously by the late ministry, I am a little piqued in honor to let people see that I am not to be despised. The assurances they give me, without any scruple or provocation, are such as are usually believed in the world: they may come to nothing, but the first opportunity that offers, and is neglected, I shall depend no more; but come away.

He was certainly impressed by Bolingbroke whom he regarded as "the greatest young man I ever knew." He frequently met Abigail Masham who, with her long red nose, reminded him of "Mrs. Malolly who was once my landlady at Trim." And with Harley he was on terms of convivial intimacy. He attended his small Saturday dinners ("much drinking, but little thinking"); he often drove in his coach with him down to Windsor. He was called "Jonathan" by the all-powerful minister in front of the Court. "I think," he wrote, "he loves me as well as a great minister can love a man in so short a time." Yet, although the Cabinet exploited him as their public relations officer, they did not accord him their whole confidence. They never, for instance, revealed to him that Prior was already in Paris negotiating a separate treaty with the French; and they never confessed to him that he had in any case no prospect of obtaining a bishopric in view of Queen Anne's suspicions of his orthodoxy. Thus when Harley and Bolingbroke quarreled and Swift tried to make peace between them, he lost much of the credit that he had possessed with each. "Tis a plaguy (*sic*)," he wrote to Stella in August 1711, "ticklish piece of work, and a man hazards losing both sides." By 1712, he realized that his influence was waning, "'tis impossible," he wrote, "to save people against their own will and I have been too much engaged in patching already. But burn politics and send me from Courts and Ministers." By March 1713 he came to see that his Tory friends were as unlikely as his former Whig friends to secure him his bishopric. He threatened to return to Ireland, "for I could not with any reputation stay longer here unless I had somethink (*sic*) honorable immediately given me." Eventually on April 16, 1717, he was offered the Deanery of St. Patrick's in Dublin. "I can feel no joy," he wrote, "of passing my days in Ireland; and I confess I thought the Ministry would not let me go; but perhaps they can't help it."

On the death of Queen Anne on August 1, 1714, and the entry of the Whigs into their prolonged period of power under the Hanoverian dynasty, Swift bade farewell to ambition. He returned to Dublin a disappointed and embittered man. He had sacrificed his honor to obtain a bishopric and his patrons had played him false. For the thirty-one years that remained to him of life his whole soul was tainted and tortured by lacerated pride.

Four

The years he spent in London were not, however, entirely filled by mortification at the failure of his cadging. He was friendly with Addison and formed with Pope, Arbuthnot, Gay, and Parnell the "Scriblerus Club" which afforded him much amusement. He lived in Chelsea, would bathe in the river, and would walk at full speed through the fields to the city, along the Mall and past Buckingham House. He had a flirtation with Miss Vanhomrig ("Vanessa") whom he treated as badly as he had treated Varina and who was slyly referred to in his letters to Stella as "a friend in the neighborhood."

On his return to Dublin he sought to persuade himself and others that he had never toadied Harley and Bolingbroke in the expectation of receiving a bishopric and that he took his disappointment with humorous resignation. "He never," he wrote in his *Verses on the Death of Dr. Swift*:

> He never courted men in station
> Nor persons had in admiration....
> Of no man's greatness was afraid
> Because he sought for no man's aid....
> Had he but spared his tongue and pen
> He might have rose like other men
> But power was never in his thought
> And wealth he valued not a groat
> Yet malice never was his aim,
> He lashed the vice, but spared the name.

This is not an accurate description of his activities in London, nor is he convincing when he tries to pass off his failure as a joke:

> 'Twas therefore cruel hard, by Jove,
> Your industry no better throve,
> Nor could achieve the promised lawn,
> Though Robin's (Harley's) honor was in pawn
> Because it chanced an old grave don
> Believed in God and you in none....

It is possible that in 1714 he married Stella secretly, although it is still not clear why he should have made a mystery of the marriage or placed the faithful Stella in so false a position. It may be, as so ingeniously suggested by Mr. Denis Johnston, that he discovered later that he was himself the illegitimate son of Sir John Temple, father of Sir William Temple, and that, owing to this misfortune, he was Stella's consanguineous uncle. At the same time, in order to justify his unwillingness to marry Vanessa (who had also followed him to Ireland) he did not deny the current rumor that a secret marriage between himself and Stella had in fact taken place.

In 1722, a patent for coining copper money in Ireland was granted to George I's mistress, the Duchess of Kendal, who sold it to the contractor William Wood. In the *Drapier's Letters* Swift attacked the scheme with vigor, contending that such corrupt and arbitrary acts of Government were "the very definition of slavery." The Government were so disturbed by this attack, and by the scandal that it aroused, that they revoked the patent and Swift found himself quite unreasonably hailed as a champion of Irish rights. He had small sympathy for any rights other than his own. In 1727, Stella died and Swift became increasingly affected by maniac depression. In 1733, a bill was introduced into the Dublin Parliament enforcing residence upon holders of ecclesiastical benefices and Swift attacked this salutary measure in the last and most ferocious of all his political satires, *The Legion Club*. By 1738 mental decay set in and he died an idiot on October 19, 1745.

Before his brain succumbed to collapse he had, however, written a book which will always remain as a monument to his genius. *Gulliver's Travels* was published in 1726. The interest of the narrative, the ingenuity with which Swift has imposed credibility by a wealth of circumstantial detail, and by the mathematical exactness of his scales and figures, have rendered the book popular with generations of schoolchildren and adults and have obscured the fact that it is intended to be a vicious satire upon mankind. Swift was devoid of any normal feelings of love or compassion: his loathing of humanity was physical in its obsession and he sought to mortify his fellow creatures by describing them in terms of scatological filth. He confessed to Pope that his aim in writing *Gulliver's Travels* had been "to vex the world rather than to divert it."

Gulliver himself is pictured as a man of education, who had studied at Cambridge and Leyden, had some knowledge of navigation, and had taken medical degrees. He was a neglectful husband and father, was always abandoning his wife to sail upon some fresh voyage, and on his return from Houyhnhnms in December 1715, he was filled with such detestation of his family that for weeks he refused to remain in the same room with them. He did not share the general optimism of the Age of Reason or believe in the perfectibility of mankind. He was in fact convinced of the "continual degeneracy of human nature," and approved of the King of Brobdingnag's description of the British nation as "the most pernicious race of little odious vermin that nature ever suffered to crawl upon the surface of the earth." To him his contemporaries were, as the Strudbruggs, "opinionative, peevish, covetous, morose, vain, talkative: incapable of friendship and dead to all natural affection." The horses, or Houyhnhnms, had alone been able to establish the rule of Reason. They had no words in their horse language for such concepts as power, government, law, war, or punishment. Being undisturbed by passion or self-interest, not knowing even the meaning of untruth, they were governed entirely by reason which was accepted by all as the sole criterion of conduct. They believed that such reason as might be possessed by the more intelligent human beings was no more than "some quality fitted to increase our natural vices." To the Houyhnhnms our lawyers would have seemed "avowed enemies of all knowledge and learning"; our doctors utterly fraudulent and capable of murdering their patients rather than admit to a false diagnosis; our statesmen completely corrupt and intent only on amassing personal fortunes; and our aristocracy a "composition of spleen, dullness, ignorance, caprice, sensuality and pride." His master, the Philosopher King of the Houyhnhnms, could scarcely believe what Gulliver told him regarding the tendency of human beings to make war upon each other and to murder thousands by discharging cannon balls by gunpowder. Their own Yahoos, commented the wise and virtuous horse, would also on occasion fight each other, and scratch and bite, "although they were seldom able to kill one another, for want of such convenient instruments of death as we had invented." "When," concludes Gulliver, "I thought of my family, my friends, my countrymen, or the human race in general, I considered them as they really were: Yahoos in shape and disposition, perhaps a little more civilized, and qualified with the gift of speech."

Seldom, in the whole of literature, has hatred assumed such ferocious forms. The tragedy of Jonathan Swift is that he was tortured not by disappointed ambition only, not alone by failure, but also by a sense of guilt.

Chapter 10
Thirteen Colonies
(1492–1783)

———— •◆• ————

The quarrel between the Colonies and the Mother Country originally due to economic rather than to political causes—The Navigation Acts—The Mercantilist doctrine—The Legends that have
arisen—The Pilgrim Fathers and the New England conscience—
The British business community take the Mercantilist Theory as
economic gospel—Their influence on Parliament is greater than
that of the Court or the landed aristocracy—Their illusions—
Convinced that the Colonists did not contribute to their own liberation from France and the Indians—Contemptuous attitude—
Only a few individuals foresaw or welcomed the manifest destiny
of America—Bacon, Chatham, Burke and Walpole—Confusion
as to the discovery of North America—The West Indies for long
thought more valuable than America—Causes of misunderstanding—Three thousand miles of Ocean—Bad communications and
information—British did not realize or welcome rapid expansion of
the Colonies in population and wealth—They were vague about the
original charters, exaggerated the differences between the several
Colonies, and underestimated their capacity for union and resistance—The contradictory conceptions of the Law of the Constitution and the Law of Nature—The rupture due to ignorance, misunderstanding and wounded pride, rather than to policy of intention.

One

IT IS DANGEROUS for an Englishman to touch even the fringe of
American history. However conscientiously he may read up the
subject, there will always remain some elements in the American

Idea that are beyond his understanding. He may even be suspected of seeking to reduce traditions to the level of tribal myths. Yet to write a study of the Age of Reason without considering the Western hurricane, by which, some would say, it was vindicated, or, as others might say, it was destroyed, would be to commit an unpardonable evasion of responsibility.

Fortunately that responsibility is today lightened by the fact that, under the inspiration of great educationalists such as Charles W. Eliot and Andréw Dixon White, American historians have themselves adopted a less gullible attitude towards their own mythology and are now generally agreed that the quarrel between the thirteen Colonies and their mother country was due not so much to political as to fiscal and economic causes. It is today widely accepted that the measures adopted by the British Government between 1763 and 1774 were not intended as arbitrary and deliberate attacks upon colonial liberties, but as financial and commercial regulations which, as Professor H. H. Bellot has written, "were in many respects reasonable and enlightened," adopted to apply in practice the then dominant economic theory of mercantilism. Under this theory it was considered a just bargain that the mother country should provide capital and military protection and that the Colonies in return should furnish raw materials. The ordinary businessman in London or in the Midlands did not regard it as in the least unfair that the Colonists should be forbidden to manufacture their own cloth and piece goods: they regarded the system, not merely as sound business, but as founded upon the generally accepted mercantilist theory of trade. It seemed to them unreasonable that the Colonists, who, although rapidly increasing in wealth and population, were still unable to pay their debts, should look upon these regulations as designed solely to benefit British industry at the expense of American industry. It appears not to have occurred to them that the Colonists would be unable to pay for their imports unless they were allowed to manufacture their own goods and to sell them in world markets. Until Adam Smith shattered the mercantilist doctrine, the business community of England held that doctrine to be the very gospel of commerce. It was the City of London, even more than King George III, who swayed the views of Parliament: as in other crises in our history, the businessmen proved themselves to be unimaginative, self-centered, and ignorant of change. The more one studies the Age of Reason, the more one realizes that the majority were utterly unreasonable and that it was but a small elite that possessed any good sense at all. By the middle of the seventeenth century, moreover, the Dutch had acquired an almost exclusive monopoly of the carrying trade, and both the British and the French were determined to break this monopoly. Hence the dynamic reforms of Colbert. Hence the early Navigation Acts of Cromwell and Charles II. These Acts achieved their objective, in that the Merchant Marine was doubled in strength within a period of eighteen years and both England and the Colonies gained thereby in wealth and power.

Unfortunately the mercantilist theory applied ill to the New England Colonies which did not produce raw materials, such as spice, sugar, and tobacco, not obtainable in the home country. Hemp and tar were not sufficient to redress the trade balance. The resultant economic muddle led inevitably to a political dichotomy. Successive British Governments being disastrously unaware of the rapidly developing conditions of the Colonies were determined, by enforced regulations, to maintain the balance of trade. The New England Colonies justifiably resented hampering restrictions imposed on them by an ignorant and unsympathetic Parliament situated three thousand miles away. "They insisted," writes James Truslow Adams, "on protection as a right, at the very time that they were flouting the Navigation Laws designed to foster the naval strength on which alone such protection could be based." British Ministers, perplexed by the inadequacy of the mercantilist theory as applied to the New England Colonies, and under constant pressure from vested interests, floundered between compromise and provocation, and committed what to us seem inexplicable errors.

But they are not inexplicable. It will be my endeavor in this chapter to indicate as objectively as possible the causes of misunderstanding and how it came that this misunderstanding led to serious confusion of thought on both sides of the Atlantic. In the several books that have been written on the subject undue emphasis has been thrown on the "policy" of the Court, the Cabinet and Parliament. The misfortune was that there existed no considered "policy," only successive attitudes of mind. These attitudes, as I have suggested, were largely influenced by the views and vested interests of the commercial community which were dominated by the then prevailing mercantilist doctrine. Even when we admit that the Navigation Acts of 1651 and 1660 did much to encourage shipbuilding, and the export of "naval stores" such as hemp, tar and timber from the Colonies, it cannot be denied that these Acts proved of disadvantage to the plantations. In an attempt, for instance, to cut down our imports of bar iron from Sweden, we encouraged the Colonies to send us pig and bar iron, but at the same time we forbade them to construct mills for rolling or slitting iron or to set up plating forges or steel furnaces. Such restrictions, although in accord with the gospel of mercantilism, were bitterly and justifiably resented by the New England industrialists.

Incidentally it is a curious historical fact that, whereas between 1700 and 1763, and again between 1789 and 1815, Great Britain produced statesmen of wide vision and generals and admirals of unconquerable ability, between 1763 and 1783 our politicians proved stubbornly unintelligent. The strange interlude of stupidity that afflicted Great Britain between the Seven Years War and the Napoleonic Wars produced results of vast and durable importance.

Two

It might be interesting to treat the quarrel between Great Britain and her Colonies as a psychological study of the stages by which ignorance produces misunderstanding, misunderstanding resentment, resentment obstinacy, and obstinacy angry pride. In England, only a minority of Whig intellectuals realized that our former plantations were expanding numerically and physically into separate nations rightly resolute to manage their own lives. The Tory majority formed by the landed aristocracy, the Court, the country gentry, the established Church, the legal profession and the London merchants and bankers, regarded the Colonists, to quote Burke's ironic phrase, "as a set of miserable outcasts, not so much sent as thrown out on the bleak and barren shore of a desolate wilderness, three thousand miles from all civilized intercourse." That such displaced persons should claim equality of rights with the subjects of the mother country appeared to them to be absurd, conceited, pretentious, and unreasonable. The Tory mind has throughout history been rendered uneasy by the unknown and has sought to restore equanimity by dismissing the incomprehensible either as ridiculous or wicked. Thus those who were unable to persuade themselves that the Colonist's claims were merely absurd, sought to find ease in the argument that they were unconstitutional and seditious. Anger and wounded dignity ensued.

Things might not have come to war had not English opinion been infected by Tory obstinacy and American opinion been inflamed by puritan dissidence. It was Old England that blinded British wisdom and New England that crystallized American resolve. Yet it is difficult, without causing offence, to analyze the mighty legends that hang like grey clouds above the story of New England.

Typical of the many legends that have arisen in the United States are those which center around the "Pilgrims" or "Saints" who, on September 6, 1620, sailed for America in the *Mayflower*, and around the later Massachusetts Bay Company established in 1628 at Salem under Winthrop, Endecott, and Dudley. "It is difficult," wrote Edward Channing in his *History of the United States*, "to treat a subject like this historically, because the matter is one of sentiment rather than fact." "The old conception of New England history," wrote James Truslow Adams in his *The Founding of New England*, "according to which that section was considered to have been settled by persecuted religious refugees, devoted to liberty of conscience, who, in the disputes with the mother country, formed a united mass of liberty-loving patriots, unanimously opposed to an unmitigated tyranny, has, happily, for many years been passing." Truslow Adams contends that their narrow theological doctrines amounted to "stripping God of every shred of what we consider moral character." He points out that of the one hundred and two passengers in the *Mayflower*, only twelve possessed even a remote connection with the original community at Scrooby. He points out that on the establishment of the Massachusetts Bay plantation in 1629, the three spiritual leaders, Winthrop, Endecott and Dudley, established a rigid theocracy under which only one in five of the Colonists was accorded any political rights at all. So far from being pioneers of democracy they proclaimed that "democracy is amongst civil nations accounted the meanest and worst of all forms of government." So far from introducing religious tolerance, they imposed a system of rigid repression. "The Lord's Lambs," comments Truslow Adams, "were anything but lamb-like." They had a special loathing for Quakers, branding the men of that sect with iron on the palms of their hands and boring holes in the tongues of women Quakers with a red-hot skewer. Those of the original immigrants who criticized this tyranny had their ears cut off and were whipped naked through the town. Charles II, on hearing of these atrocities, ordered that they must cease. Endecott was forced to obey.

The English legends are similarly distorted. We were taught at school that the Colonists refused to move a finger in their own defense against the Indians, the French, or the Spaniards and were unjustifiably incensed when Parliament insisted that they might at least contribute money for the expense of their own protection. This is an untrue and an unfair allegation. The colonial militia rendered redoubtable assistance both against the Indians and the French. And the local Assemblies might well have been prepared to contribute their share of the expenses, had they been permitted to do so voluntarily and not been ordered to do so by what they came increasingly to regard as an alien Parliament. These facts were at the time admitted even by George III himself. The average Englishman (and it is remarkable how many Britishers conform to the average) was convinced that England alone had by the expenditure of English lives and treasure conquered Canada and relieved America forever of the menace of a

French invasion from the north. They expected warm gratitude for this achievement, but found to their indignation that the Colonists, once the French danger and the consequent need for British protection were removed, became less, rather than more, amenable. It is indeed astonishing how resentful unimaginative people can become; they suspect that they have got things wrong, but refuse to admit it.

Another English legend is that during the long wars of the eighteenth century, during which the security of the mother country was often in grave danger, her overseas children remained indifferent and did nothing to help. They forfeited our sympathies by their persistent violation of the Navigation Acts, by their indulgence in unlimited smuggling, and by their readiness even to trade with the enemy. The British did not have the clear-sightedness to realize that these evasions were rendered inevitable by the harsh restrictions of the Acts themselves and that had not the Colonists engaged in some illicit form of barter they would have been unable to avoid acute inflation or to pay their debts to London. Owing to such legends and misconceptions, mutual misunderstanding developed into mutual antipathy and distrust.

It must be admitted that the English did nothing to diminish the growing tension by displaying any warm sympathy towards the Colonists. They refused to regard them as persecuted Pilgrims escaping from religious intolerance and seeking to establish in the New World an asylum for the oppressed. They failed even to recognize in them the pioneers of culture who were ready to risk the perils of an Atlantic voyage and the prospect of starving or being scalped on arrival, in order to spread the light of civilization across a savage world. They persisted in regarding the Colonists as second-rate citizens, either as felons who only escaped the gallows by being sentenced to transportation, or as shady adventurers aiming at making quick money out of less competitive conditions, or merely as wastrels who had neither the brains nor the energy to make good at home. At best the English attitude was one of patronizing benevolence; at worst it was disdain. The American people, even now that they have become the greatest Power on earth, have still not quite recovered from the superciliousness with which the English treated them two hundred and fifty years ago.

Three

It has sometimes been said that the English deserved to lose their first Empire, since, until taught a sharp and lasting lesson in 1776, they failed entirely to realize their imperial responsibilities or opportunities. It must be confessed that the average City banker, as well as the average manufacturer in Nottingham or Leicester, continued, until it was far too late, to regard the plantations as an area of speculative adventure, as a market for their manufactures, or as a dumping ground for the unwanted or the incompetent. Yet our intellectuals, as early as the sixteenth century, frequently foresaw the vast expansion to which America was destined. In England however intellectuals have always been a small and uninfluential minority.

Historians, until quite recently, have tended to place the whole responsibility on a corrupt House of Commons, dominated by the insanely obstinate King George III, and guided by his subservient ministers, such as Bute, Grenville, Townshend, and North. This has now been shown to be a disproportionate view. It is true that George III, had he been a man of any liberal imagination, might have rallied the dissenting Colonists to their personal loyalty to the Crown, a loyalty which persisted long after the English Parliament had been discredited. But to contend, as we were once taught to contend, that it was "the King's friends" who dominated the House of Commons against the wishes of the electorate is now shown, owing mainly to the researches of Sir L. Namier, to have been an exaggeration. The mass of the British people shared the view that the Colonists were in fact rebels, intent on defying the Constitution and law of the land. Today the English patriot may console himself with the thought that the only war in which we have been thoroughly defeated was one waged against men of our own race and character. He may even derive some solace from the fact that this tiny island, with a population in the sixteenth century of no more than five millions, prevented France and Spain from mastering the Continent and the Seven Seas, spread her language and her political ideas across a quarter of the globe, and produced seven independent nations who today seem destined to determine the future of mankind. It is in truth a proud miracle, comparable only to the miracle of the small city founded by Romulus and Remus among the seven hills. Yet in the eighteenth century few men could entertain such vicarious sentiments of glory. Even those who refused to regard the thirteen Colonies as either contemptible or subversive, who foresaw that within but a few generations they might out distance the mother country in population and in wealth and power, derived no exaltation from the prospect but only sensations of wounded pride, leading to jealousy. I have observed that among the less intelligent British these pangs of jealousy still subsist.

It is an error, nonetheless, to argue that understanding of, and sympathy with, the thirteen Colonies or the original pioneers were restricted to the Whig intellectuals of the eighteenth century, whose views, we should admit, may in some cases have been colored by party animosity or ambition. The eighteenth-century Liberals, such as Chatham, Burke, and Shelburne, were not alone in recognizing the strength and right of the Colonists. Older thinkers and statesmen, less eminent writers and poets, had grasped the unlimited potentialities of the newly discovered continent and had urged the necessity of constructing a creative and logical imperial policy from the start. So long ago as the sixteenth century Francis Bacon had deplored the practice of treating the plantations as dumping grounds for the unwanted. "It is," he wrote "a shameful and unblessed thing to take the scum of the people and wicked condemned men to be the people with whom you plant." He at least foresaw that before many generations had passed these plantations would develop into "New Kingdoms" and that it was a mistake to look upon them merely from the magistrate's, the jurist's, or the stock-jobber's point of view. Swift also denounced the purely commercial or economic attitude towards the plantations, denouncing those who "with the spirit of shopkeepers tried to frame rules for the administration of kingdoms." Even the poet Samuel Daniel, in his *Musophilus* of 1599, prophesied the vast expansion of the English speaking peoples, although in terms which may today strike us as all too optimistic:

> And who (in time) knows whither we may vent
> The treasure of our tongue? To what strange shores
> This gain of our best glory may be sent
> T'enrich unknowing nations with our stores?
> What worlds in the yet unformed Occident
> May come refined with th' accents that are ours?

Every British, although not perhaps every American, undergraduate, is aware of Chatham's confirmation of the American slogan of "No taxation without representation." "America," said Lord Chatham, "being neither really nor virtually represented in Westminster, cannot be held legally or constitutionally or reasonably subject to obedience to any money bill of this kingdom." It is sad indeed that this lapidary statement on the part of the greatest living Englishman failed to affect the opinions of the constitutional lawyers, the jurists, and those politicians who prided themselves on being men of reason and good sense.

Edmund Burke pleaded the cause of the American Colonists with fervor and sincerity and with an eloquence that might have been more effective at the time had it been less diffuse or delivered in a less ungainly manner. He certainly foresaw the rapid expansion of the Colonies and the absurdity of continuing to regard them as adolescents not yet of age. "Your children," he warned the House of Commons, "do not grow faster from infancy to manhood than (the American Colonists) spread from families to communities and from villages to nations." It is unfortunate that the politicians of the eighteenth century were not in a position to compare a modern atlas of the United States with the rudimentary charts which pinpointed the few landfalls and harbors that then emphasized the Atlantic seaboard and failed to indicate the vast frontier that extended beyond the

Alleghanies. Burke at least did not regard the dissentient Colonists as seditious rebels: he admired rather than deplored their resolution. "I do not choose," he said, "wholly to break American spirit, because it is the spirit that has made the country." "An Englishman," he said, "is the unfittest person on earth to argue another Englishman into slavery." "It is not," he said, "what a lawyer tells me I *may* do, but what humanity, reason, and justice tell me I *ought* to do." Here in truth spoke the true voice of the age of reason. "Magnanimity in politics," he said— and it is one of the few of his comments that have endured to posterity—"is not seldom the truest wisdom; and a great empire and little minds go ill together." It is a misfortune that Burke's vision of justice was not reinforced by a character of greater strength and integrity and that the force of his comments became involved in the clouds of his rhetoric. Yet assuredly he must have induced many ordinary people to reassess their values and their assumptions. His arguments even at the time did not fall on deaf ears.

Four

More illustrative of ordinary liberal opinion at the time are the irritable comments which Horace Walpole, scribbling in his blue room at Strawberry Hill, distributed to his several correspondents. His first attitude is one of tetchy indifference. He says he would much prefer twenty acres at Twickenham to twenty thousand on the Ohio. "American affairs," he writes in 1765, "are expected to occasion much discussion: but, as I understand them no more than Hebrew, they will throw no impediment in my way." Yet when his friend Conway became a Secretary of State he wrote urging him to "keep the Colonies in good humor." Even when the rupture had actually occurred he still strove in his epicurean way to dismiss so unpleasant a thought from his consciousness. Writing to Horace Mann on February 2, 1774, he still assumed a tone of elegant abstraction. "There is an ostrich egg laid in America, where the Bostonians have canted three hundred chests of tea into the ocean, for they will not drink tea with our Parliament. My understanding is so narrow, and was confined so long to the little meridian of England, that at this late hour of life it cannot extend itself to such huge objects as the East and West Indies." Even at the outbreak of the Revolution proper, he struggled to maintain his impassivity. "One has griefs enough of one's own," he wrote, "without fretting because Cousin America has eloped with a Presbyterian parson."

Yet Horace Walpole was something much more than an antiquarian interior decorator. He realized that the British Government were behaving with sullen obstinacy and lack of vision. He denounced them as "babies smashing an Empire to see what it is made of." He deplored "our insults to the Americans at the outset of the war." He sneered at Parliament as "a majority that has lost thirteen provinces by bullying and vaporing." He condemned George III for following "a narrow plan of royalty which has so often preferred the aggrandizement of the Crown to the dignity of presiding over a great and puissant kingdom, and threw away one predominant source of our potency by aspiring to enslave America."

Unlike so many of the intellectual aristocracy he refused to regard the Colonists as second-rate citizens. "The English in America," he wrote to Lady Ossory in 1781, "are as much my countrymen as those born in the parish of St. Martin-in-the-Fields. When my countrymen quarrel I think I am free to wish better to the sufferers than to the aggressors. . . . We have forfeited all title to respect. I appeal to the unalterable nature of justice whether this war with America is a just one. If it is not, can any honest man wish success to it?" "I am what I always was," he writes again, "a zealot for liberty in every part of the globe and consequently I most heartily wish success to the Americans. . . . We have been horribly the aggressors; and I must rejoice that the Americans are to be free, as they have the right to be, and as I am sure they have shown that they deserve to be."

He much admired the strength of American resistance. "The Americans at least," he wrote to Conway in December 1774, "have acted like men. . . . Our conduct has been that of pert children; we have thrown a pebble at a mastiff and are surprised it was not frightened." Yet although he wished the Colonists to triumph, he did not, as did Boswell, indulge in jubilation at the surrender of Yorktown. He was in fact pessimistic about the future of England, not realizing that we should be able within a few decades to create an even vaster Empire in place of the one we had lost. "I see no glimmering of hope," he wrote, "that we shall ever be a great nation again: nor do we deserve to be. . . . I have outlived the glory of my family and of my country. . . . I cannot expect to see England revive. I shall leave it at best an insignificant island. Its genius is vanished like its glories." He anticipated Macaulay, in forecasting that the New World would survive to contemplate the ruins of the old until "at last some curious travelers from Lima will visit England and give a description of the ruins of St. Paul's." "It is from beyond the Atlantic," he wrote in 1778, "that the world perhaps will see genius revive." Yet his inherent skepticism forced him to modify this reckless prophecy. "I already doubt," he confessed, "whether America will replace its predecessors. Genius does not seem to make great shoots there. Buffon says that European animals degenerate across the Atlantic."

It is easy to dismiss Horace Walpole as a mere gossipmonger, as a typical Whig who grumbled with petulance, but took no overt steps to right the wrongs of which he incessantly complained. Yet he certainly exercised a powerful influence on his cousin Henry Seymour Conway, who as Secretary of State in the Duke of Grafton's Cabinet, did in 1768 have the courage to resign in protest against the employment of coercive measures against the thirteen Colonies. We should not forget either that it was Walpole's cousin and confidant, Conway, who assailed the Government for their methods of conducting the war, who in May 1780 brought in a bill for the pacification of the Colonies, and who in March 1781 carried an address urging the King to renounce any further attempts to reduce America by force thereby causing the resignation of Lord North and the opening of negotiations for peace. Walpole might justifiably claim some influence on these transactions.

Five

We do not know, exactly, on what date North America was discovered. We are well aware that on August 3, 1492, the *Santa Maria*, the *Pinta*, and the *Nina* set sail from Palos de la Frontera and dropped down the Rio Tinto on their way, as they imagined, to the kingdom of Cathay. We know that as they passed by La Rabida they could hear the friars chanting *iam lucis orto sidere*, and that it was to the echo of that famous hymn that many of them had their last sight of Europe. We know that at 2:00 A.M. on October 12, 1492, the lookout man in the *Pinta*, Rodrigo de Triana, saw what he took to be a white cliff shining in the moonlight and shouted out with wild exultation "Tierra! Tierra!" And we know that when morning dawned Columbus in the admiral's barge displaying the royal standard of Castille was rowed ashore and fell upon his knees upon the white coral beach of what he immediately christened San Salvador, but which the English seamen later called by the less romantic name of Watling's Island. It was not the United States that Columbus had discovered; it was the Bahamas. Although in subsequent voyages he pushed farther into the Caribbean, found and created the West Indies, coasted along the shores of South America from Darien to Honduras, and realized on reaching the estuary of the Orinoco that it was not a mere island archipelago that he had discovered but a vast continent—yet these tremendous feats of navigation had little directly to do with the American Colonists who were to cause such worry and tribulation to Westminster and Whitehall and to expose England to her saddest humiliation.

It is probable, although the fact is still contested by geographers and archaeologists, that the United States was first discovered some five hundred years before Columbus when Olav Tryggvason, King of Norway, dispatched Leif Ericsson to convert the Greenlanders and when this inquisitive Viking pressed further to the west and discovered a fog-swept territory to which he gave the names of Helluland and Vinland.

More certainly the Genoese Giovanni Caboto, subsequently known as John Cabot, obtained from Henry VII on March 5, 1496, letters patent giving him "full authority, leave, and power to seek out discover and find whatsoever isles, countries, regions or provinces of the heathen and infidels which before this time have been unknown to all Christians." On May 2, 1497, John Cabot, in the ship *Mathew*, sailed from Bristol and at 5:00 A.M. on Saturday, June 24, reached Cape Breton island and took possession of it in the name of Henry VII. On his return to Bristol on August 6 he announced that he had reached the country of the Grand Khan of China. On his next voyage, he said, he would turn southward and identify the kingdom of Cipangu, which we now call Japan, and which was then considered to lie somewhere on the equator. He promised that once these lands had been discovered, investigated, and annexed, London would become the mart of Eastern commerce and an even greater center of the spice trade than Constantinople or Alexandria.

The reality of John Cabot's achievement has, however, been blurred by the later and seemingly fictitious claims of the Florentine bank clerk Amerigo Vespucci. He claimed that he had reached the mainland of America eight days before John Cabot discovered Cape Breton, namely on June 16, 1497. In 1507, his account of this voyage was printed in the *Paesi novamente ritrovati*, published in Vicenza under the title *Novo Mondo da Alb. Vesputio.* The whole story has been discredited by later scholars; but Martin Waldseemuller, professor of cosmography at the university of Saint Die in Lorraine, accepted the claims of Amerigo and even went so far as to suggest that this section of the earth should be "called America, since Americus discovered it." Strange it is that this pretentious and shady Italian should have become the eponym of two important continents.

Then in rapid succession came Balbao, Fernan Magalhaes or Magellan, and Ponce de Leon who landed in Florida in 1513. In 1524 Giovanni da Verrazano, bearing a patent from Francis I of France, reached Sandy Hook. Ten years later Jacques Cartier of Saint Malo explored the coast of Labrador. In 1604 De Monts founded Acadia and in 1608 Champlain sailed up the St. Lawrence and laid the foundations of Montreal and Quebec. Thereafter came the conquistadors to South America while our own buccaneer navigators, Drake, Frobisher, and Hawkins, were so enterprising and resolved that they prevented the Spanish navy from establishing its domination over the western seas. "To English sixteenth-century seamen," writes Professor Edward Channing, "Great Britain owes her colonial Empire and the United States its existence." But the fogs of Helluland were not the only mists to cloud Europe's early conception of America.

Six

This chapter is not intended to be provocative, nor do I seek to defend a policy which I regard as in fact indefensible. I merely wish to indicate that man is apt to become wise and censorious when analyzing in tranquility revolutionary events that have long since subsided, and I suggest that there were at the time many circumstances which explain the confusion of thought by which the British Parliament became afflicted between 1763 and 1783. One might in fact list as many as fifteen such causes of misapprehension.

The mistakes of the early discoverers, their belief that they had opened up a western passage to the Spice Islands, to Cathay and Cipangu, led men to regard the settlement of the New World as primarily a trading venture, and this commercial aspect conditioned men's minds for many generations. The fact that during the sixteenth and seventeenth centuries the scramble for America took the form of naval conflict between England, Spain and France, not only distracted attention from the Atlantic to the West Indies and the Caribbean, but led men to regard plantations as prizes of war. In the sixteenth century, moreover, there existed the strange theory that England was becoming overpopulated and that the surplus population must be shipped overseas. The Spanish Ambassador in London, during the reign of Queen Elizabeth, reported that the "principal reason for colonization is to give an outlet for so many idle and wretched people as they have in England." This led to the regrettable conception of the Colonies as dumping grounds for the unwanted and eventually produced a superior and even contemptuous attitude towards the Colonists.

The prevailing doctrine of mercantilism convinced many people that it was economically sound and just that colonial trade should so be regulated as to provide the mother country both with a source of raw materials and with a market for her manufactures. The Colonists in objecting to these discriminations and restrictions were regarded as "unreasonable" and as defying the unquestioned gospel of commerce. The three thousand miles of ocean that separated London from Boston or Philadelphia left British opinion in almost complete ignorance of the rapid development in the wealth, population, and sentiments of the thirteen Colonies. Puritanism in England had ceased to be a driving force after 1660, whereas in New England it remained for long both an inspiration and a rule. The Governors and customs officials dispatched to the Colonies were not always men of integrity or intelligence and the reports they sent home to Whitehall were not always accurate or informative.

In the seventeenth and eighteenth centuries even intelligent men were less conscious than we are today of the factors of change and development and failed to realize that the Colonies of 1763 were utterly different from the plantations of 1663. Few people were aware that a population that had been 339,000 in 1720, had by 1763 risen to two million. Even an enlightened man like Joseph Addison could in 1711 refer to the thirteen Colonies as "those parts of Her Majesty's Dominions where there is a want of inhabitants." Moreover the first generation of immigrants were succeeded by a younger generation who possessed no associations with or affection for England; and the great waves of Scottish, Irish, Huguenot and German refugees who reached America during the first half of the eighteenth century had in fact suffered in Europe from serious persecution or poverty and were determined to find in the Colonies a wholly new prospect of happiness.

The different conditions in which the thirteen Colonies had been founded obscured for the average Englishman the old principle that the Colonists had brought with them the ancient rights enjoyed by all Englishmen since Magna Carta and that, under the several patents and charters, they possessed elected Assemblies and a strong tradition of autonomous rights. Most Members of Parliament took it for granted that the Colonies differed fundamentally from each other in origins, social conditions, religion, and economics; they knew that the Colonies had found it difficult to combine to resist the Indian or the French menaces and thought it inconceivable that they would ever combine to resist their mother country. Moreover the British professional soldiers were positive that no civilian army could ever withstand the impact of trained and disciplined regiments. Even the Braddock catastrophe of July 9, 1755, when a British force was almost annihilated a few miles from the modern Pittsburg, failed to convince the professional English officer that able Colonials, such as young George Washington, might in fact know more about local conditions and perils than they did themselves. The British were inclined to identify "patriotism" with a sentimental affection for the mother country and failed to see that the rising generation had inherited a far more potent form of patriotism, namely a passion for their own rivers, plains and forests, and an ardent pride in being American. Moreover the British had no conception at all of the influence exercised on American thought and feeling by "the Frontier," and the ever renewed spirit of individualism and therefore of independence that the pioneers developed and fostered. All this unawareness may seem to us today profoundly unintelligent: yet in those days communications were still primitive and such information as reached the British public was prejudiced, fragmentary, and most unreliable.

It was this terrible ignorance, this foolish indifference, rather than any conscious desire for domination that, stage by stage, created the atmosphere of quarrel. When, on May 13, 1767, Charles Townshend introduced his Bill for taxing the Colonies, the House of Commons, as Horace Walpole wrote "too lightly adopted the plan before it had been well weighed and the fatal consequences of which did not break out until six years after." The British public felt, as I have said, that it had been by their own prowess and sacrifices that the thirteen Colonies had been preserved from invasion by the French or Spaniards. To them it seemed sensible and just that the Colonists should contribute at least something to the cost of their deliverance and preservation. Even so objective a modern historian as Dr. H. A. L. Fisher could ask, in his History of Europe, whether "it was so outrageous that the British Parliament in the exercise of its sovereign rights should impose a tax upon the Colonists to be spent in the Colonies upon an army exclusively designed for colonial defense?" The British people in the eighteenth century were convinced that there could exist only one answer to this question. Today we realize that its fallacy consists of the words "sovereign rights." King and Parliament regarded the issue in legalistic terms, and were positive that the Colonists were seeking to destroy the Law of the Constitution, as in fact they were. The Colonists based their faith and their resolution upon the new doctrine of "the Laws of Nature and Nature's God," upon the theory that all men are created equal, and upon the assertion that George III and his ministers were seeking to reduce the Colonists under "absolute Despotism" and to establish an "absolute Tyranny" over the thirteen Colonies. These extreme imputations, although justifiable in the circumstances, are not validated by historical research.

Essentially therefore the conflict arose from a dichotomy between two theories of Law, the Law of the Constitution and the Law of Nature, and once each of the contestants had taken his stand on his own particular doctrine of Right, obstinacy and therefore stubborn pride became operative. Both theories, in their way, were correct. But since the American theory triumphed and led to world-shattering results, it is assumed to have been more correct than the British theory. It certainly was ill attuned to the Age of Reason: but it was perfectly attuned to the impending age of Revolution and Romance.

It may seem otiose thus to have reexamined the elements of a distant controversy. I have sought only to indicate that there are several perfectly respectable reasons why British opinion should have been so utterly bewildered between 1763 and 1783. Such an examination,

even if it manages not to cause offence, is bound itself to become confused and to reflect the cloudy muddle of the period. It is preferable
therefore to elucidate the conflict by describing its changing effects
upon a single individual. Fortunately we have detailed knowledge of
the fluctuating emotions and thought of one most remarkable man,
who played a leading part in all these transactions. In my next chapter
I shall consider the effect of the controversy upon Benjamin Franklin.

Chapter 11

The Simple Man

(Franklin, 1706–1790)

———•◆•———

His critics—D. H. Lawrence and Bernard Fay—A typical American—His birth and boyhood—His self-education—Runs away from Boston—Reaches Philadelphia on foot—Obtains employment with the printer Keimer—His visit to London—His marriage—Starts the *Pennsylvania Gazette*—The Junto—"Poor Richard"—Becomes a leading citizen—His mechanical genius—The lightning conductor—He foresees the vast future open to the United States—Appointed Deputy Post Master General—Franklin as an Imperialist—His action against the Indians—He is dispatched to England to negotiate with the Penn Family—The Stamp Act—Its repeal—His pamphlets—His interview with Lord Hillsborough—The incident of the Hutchinson letters—The scene in the Cockpit—His friendship with Chatham—War breaks out—His mission to Paris—Negotiates the Alliance between America and France—He reaches a settlement with the British—His triumph and satisfaction—He returns to Philadelphia where he dies.

One

IT SEEMS STRANGE to Europeans that the citizens of the United States, who have so many gigantic heroes in their history, should be so addicted to hero worship that they inflate the reputes of quite minor characters who were scarcely heroes at all. Every American schoolboy is told about Patrick Henry and Paul Revere, although the former, when compared to others, was not a mighty orator any more than the latter was an outstanding horseman. Every American child, moreover, knows all about Benjamin Franklin and there is not one fact recorded in the following chapter that has not been familiar to them since they were eight or nine. To the ordinary European, however, Franklin is a vague electrician, who invented the lightning conductor and signed the Declaration of Independence. The following chapter is thus written for the enlightenment and information of European readers only. American readers can leave it out. It is regrettable that Benjamin Franklin should have had his portrait painted so frequently and that reproduction of these portraits should have been broadcast throughout the New World and the Old; Students of physiognomy can detect in these pictures evidence of the defects of character which his enemies adduced against him. In those bland features one recognizes exceptional vitality lurking behind a mask of self-esteem. The lips, in expanding into a smile of universal benevolence, appear to frame the syllables— "Holier than thou." There is a glint of craftiness about the eyes. The face suggests vanity, complacency, cunning, and caution. The portrait might be that of the philosopher of nature who appears in Johnson's *Rasselas* and who "looked round him with a placid air and enjoyed the consciousness of his own beneficence." I force myself to believe that the real Franklin was not as smarmy as his facial expression.

I am sure that it was the contemplation of one of these portraits that aroused in D. H. Lawrence such violent sensations of antipathy. In his Studies in American Classical Literature he attributes to Franklin "all the qualities of a great man" who never became anything more than "a great citizen." He picks on Franklin's incidental and uncharacteristic remark that God must have invented rum for the purpose of degrading and exterminating the Red Indians as proof of his hypocrisy and heartlessness. "Can you make a land virgin," he asks indignantly, "by killing off the aborigines?" To him Franklin's idealization of the cultivators of the soil is as sentimental as de Crèvecoeur's ecstasies over the noble savage. He is enraged that Franklin should have "set up this dummy of the perfect citizen as a pattern to America, with the result that he is responsible for millions of squirrels running in millions of cages." He becomes so vitriolic on the theme that he finally denounces Franklin as a "snuff-colored little trap," who imparted to future generations of his fellow countrymen that air of rectitude which grates harshly upon European nerves.

Monsieur Bernard Fay, again, who wrote a biography of Franklin in French, and who shares much of the expected admiration, is distracted from his eulogy by contemplating the portraits: he starts to pick at faults. He observes that Franklin's schedule of virtues to be cultivated did not at first include modesty, and that "humility" was added as an afterthought on the advice of an observant friend. He suggests that Franklin was always somewhat of a charlatan, and adduces as evidence the occasion when, staying at Bowood, he stilled the ripples of the pond by squirting upon the waters some oil that he had cunningly concealed in a tube in his walking stick. This does not seem to me a conscious act of necromancy or deception; it was merely a parlor trick indulged in for the entertainment of Lord Lansdowne's guests. Fay also refers to Franklin's promiscuous concupiscence and suggests that, under a surface enamel of benevolence, he hid a heart of stone. "He never," writes Fay, "allowed a feeling to take up too much room in his life." Nor was he in fact quite so honest as he wished his contemporaries to believe. There was the matter of the money entrusted to him by Mr. Vernon which, on his first arrival at Philadelphia, he used for his own purposes. Yet M. Fay would have known nothing of this episode had it not been for Franklin's own confession. Then there is the fact that when in Paris as Ambassador he allowed the French to imagine that he was a Quaker, because ever since Voltaire had praised the Quakers as models of integrity and reason, to be a Quaker in Paris was regarded as a most impressive thing to be. I confess that I also have been disconcerted by this pose as a Quaker, although Franklin would have excused himself by saying that it was the function of an Ambassador "to lie abroad for his country." More-over the charge of charlatanism that has so often been brought against Franklin was mainly due to his highly developed sense of histrionics. Even his gifted eulogist, Mr. Carl van Doren, admits that "Franklin was perfectly willing to bring touches of drama into his undertak-ings." This dramatic element in his character may have enraged D. H. Lawrence, irritated Bernard Fay, and distressed van Doren: but it did not amount to deliberate hypocrisy. The qualities of mind and charac-ter that rendered Franklin so dominating a figure were of granite solidity. It is they, rather than incidental moments of trickiness or hypocrisy, that rendered Franklin, and still render him, as Sir George Trevelyan has written in his monumental History of the American Revolution, "the most typical American that ever lived."

But one should avoid gazing on his portraits with too analytical an eye.

Two

Benjamin Franklin started as a typical American, in that he came of yeoman and puritan stock and was largely a self-educated and self-made man. His father, Josiah Franklin, had emigrated to Massa-chusetts in 1683, and had established himself as a tallow chandler in Boston, selling soap and candles from his shop at the corner of Union Street. He was descended from a line of Oxfordshire farmers and blacksmiths and long retained an affection for the land of his birth. By his first wife he had seven children and by his second wife, Abiah Folger of Nantucket, he had ten children. Benjamin could remember as many as thirteen of his siblings gathered round the table at fam-ily prayers. Josiah Franklin, although not very prosperous in business, was a respected member of the community. He was admitted to mem-bership of the Old South Church, a privilege enjoyed by only one in four of Boston's citizens.

Of these seventeen children, Benjamin was the youngest son. He was born on January 17, 1706, in the original Franklin home in Milk

Street, situated opposite the church. His father was aged fifty when Benjamin, at the age of seventeen, ran away from Boston. Only three times did he see his father again after his escape to Philadelphia.

His childhood was sober and thrifty; the atmosphere of his home was one of puritanism rather than of Calvinism. Benjamin was originally destined for the church, but it must have soon become apparent to his family that he was not by temperament suited to the narrow theology of New England. His uncle Benjamin, who had come to join the congested house in Union Street, had a taste for writing doggerel verse and as a child, much to his father's displeasure, Benjamin would write atrocious ballads "in the Grub Street manner." Obviously also he was not destined for a poet. He was first sent to the local grammar school and then placed with Mr. George Bromwell to learn writing and arithmetic. Although he might have proved a genius at higher mathematics he was hopeless at doing sums; it may well have been this early incapacity which explains the muddle into which in 1779 he allowed the account books of his Embassy to fall. Essentially, however, Franklin was a self-educated man. As a boy he read the *Pilgrim's Progress*, Plutarch's *Lives*, Locke on *Human Understanding*, and the *Memorabilia* of Xenophon. He sought to perfect his style by paraphrasing Addison's essays in the *Spectator*, by then rewriting them in an approach to the Augustan style and then checking his own version against the original. He attached great importance to the ability to express thoughts in lucid and persuasive language. "Prose writing," he wrote, "has been of great use to me in the course of my life, and was a principal means of my advancement." He at the same time adopted from Xenophon the Socratic habit of asking awkward questions in a humble voice. He must in truth have been an insufferable little boy.

At the age of twelve he was apprenticed to his elder brother James, who had studied the art of printing in England and was at the time publishing the *Boston Gazette*. When that journal was transferred to a rival printing establishment, James Franklin started a new paper of his own entitled *The New England Courant*. It does not appear to have been an enlightened or progressive paper, since it denounced as a "superstition of Greek old women" the practice of vaccination against smallpox, although inoculation was at that date defended and even advocated by Cotton Mather, that pillar of Congregational orthodoxy, the witch hunter of Salem, the first eminent scholar and man of letters that New England produced. At the age of sixteen Benjamin began his long career as a journalist and pamphleteer. Under the pseudonym of Mrs. Silence Dogood, who purported to have been an indentured servant who had married her master and was now a widow, he wrote regular articles for the *Courant*. Suspecting that his brother would regard him as too young and immature to become a regular contributor, he maintained his anonymity, slipping his copy in an envelope under the office door. The Dogood articles consisted of moral platitudes in imitation of the *Spectator*. "I am an enemy to vice," proclaimed Mrs. Dogood, "and a friend of virtue." She confessed to "a natural inclination to observe and reprove the faults of others," but insisted that she was "a mortal enemy to arbitrary government and unlimited power." She was a sanctimonious woman, but her articles were welcomed by the readers of the *Courant*. In after life, as I have said, Franklin claimed that this early practice in journalism, the habit he acquired of stating obvious truths in simple language, formed the foundation of his style and his career. He certainly acquired the trick of expressing platitudes in homely shape.

On June 11, 1722, his brother James was arrested by the magistrates for contempt of authority and imprisoned for a week. In the following January he was again threatened with arrest and decided to place the printing and publishing of the *Courant* in the name of his younger brother, then aged seventeen. This sudden elevation turned Benjamin's head. He admits in his *Autobiography* that he then became "saucy and provoking" to his brother James and relations became so strained that Benjamin decided to break his indenture and to escape from Boston. He sailed for New York, and on arrival applied for employment at the printing house of William Bradford. He was informed that there was no opening for an assistant or journeyman printer in New York and was advised to push on to Philadelphia where he might well obtain a job. Having by then run out of money, he decided to walk to Philadelphia and it was as an impoverished and tattered boy that he eventually reached the city with which he was to be so closely identified. Almost immediately he found employment in the printing establishment of Mr. Keimer. He obtained lodging in the house of Mr. Read, the father of Deborah Read, who eventually, after several setbacks, became his dutiful and long-suffering wife.

Three

In the early sections of Franklin's *Autobiography* we can detect a certain reticence regarding his opening years in Philadelphia. He tells us that the Governor of Pennsylvania, Sir Robert Keith, hearing of the boy who had walked to Philadelphia from New York, called at Mr. Keimer's shop to see him. Mr. Keimer's surprise at this distinguished visit was only equaled by Franklin's own astonishment. He tells us that he gazed tongue-tied at His Excellency "like a pig poisoned." The Governor was impressed by Benjamin's talents and ambition. He took him round to the inn for a glass of wine, urged him to break with Keimer and to set up a printing business of his own, and suggested that he would be well advised to return to Boston, to borrow the necessary capital from his father, and then to come back to Philadelphia and start on an independent career. In April 1724, therefore, at the age of eighteen, he returned to Boston, displaying to his father and brother the watch that he had bought in Philadelphia and his new suit of clothes. We are not told how he had managed to obtain the money for such finery: we learn only that his family, irritated by his boastfulness, refused to accord him any capital and that he returned penuriously to Philadelphia. On the way there he met a Mr. Vernon who commissioned him to collect a debt owing to him to the amount of £35. He obtained the money, but omitted to refund it to Mr. Vernon. This episode he somewhat naively refers to as an *erratum* in his life.

Sir Robert Keith was lavish in promises. He promised that he himself would finance the venture but advised Franklin to visit London where he could obtain new fonts and establish contacts with English booksellers. He also undertook to provide him with the necessary letters of introduction, but forgot to do so. This was the first of many similar occasions that taught Franklin that Government officials, although affable in their assurances, seldom carried their engagements into effect. He arrived in London with but twelve pounds in his pocket and without a single letter of introduction. He was lucky enough to find immediate employment in the printing house of Samuel Palmer in Bartholemew Close, transferring later to the even larger printing establishment of James Watts near Lincoln's Inn Fields. He lodged at the Golden Fan in Little Britain. A merchant of the name of Thomas Denham, who had been a fellow passenger on his voyage from Philadelphia to Gravesend, was intending to open a general store in America and invited Franklin to return as his assistant and clerk. They sailed back to America in July 1726 and reached Philadelphia on October 11. Mr. Denham established his store in Water Street, but died shortly after landing. Franklin was obliged to return to Mr. Keimer's printing establishment.

Before leaving on his visit to England, Franklin had become engaged to Deborah Read, but seems to have quickly extricated himself from this commitment. The jilted Miss Read accordingly married a potter of the name of Rogers, who deserted her soon afterwards and disappeared from her life. Franklin on his return proposed to a Miss Godfrey but her parents would not consent to the marriage. He then had an affair with the maid at the inn; produced an illegitimate baby who was christened William Franklin and who in later life developed political views in opposition to his father and became an ardent Tory. Deborah Read, placidly forgiving his original inconstancy and his more recent escapade, agreed to resume their engagement; they were married on September 1, 1730. Since they had no proof that her first husband Mr. Rogers was dead, the ceremony took place, not in church, but in a registry office. Fortunately for them Mr. Rogers never returned from the West Indies, where he was believed to have settled, and Deborah had never to face a charge of bigamy. But the originality of the domestic arrangements of Franklin, his son, and his grandson persisted, until the third generation.

Having by then obtained excellent new type from London, Franklin quarreled with his original patron, Keimer, and set up for himself in a house in Lower Market Street. The business prospered. He was able to start a newspaper of his own, *The Pennsylvania Gazette*, and eventually to buy out his partner Hugh Meredith, who had taken to drink and retired as a farmer to North Carolina. Keimer, who was an inefficient man, failed to survive this competition. He went bankrupt and disappeared to Barbadoes. We are left with the impression that Franklin did not behave too well either to Keimer or Meredith. He was devoured by ambition.

It was during this period that he founded the "Junto," which was something more than a debating society for the discussion of philosophy, literature, and science, but a mutual aid society which helped much to further Franklin's advancement. Unlike most clubs of this nature the Junto survived for thirty years. The other members, apart from Hugh Meredith, were Stephen Potts, George Webb, Thomas Godfrey, and Joseph Breinthel, each of whom became influential in Philadelphian civic life. The shortage of currency, which was one of the handicaps of each of the thirteen Colonies, induced Franklin to suggest the issue of paper money based on land values which he called by the attractive name of "coined land." He managed to obtain from the Assembly the contract for printing these new notes which proved a profitable undertaking. By 1732, he had paid off all his debts and was his own master. The next year he started printing an annual almanac, for which he composed his "Poor Richard" series which became immensely popular. "Poor Richard" was represented as an impecunious simple and virtuous character, cursed by a nagging wife. The confessions of "Poor Richard" were composed of moral truisms, interspersed with mottoes and trite proverbs, such as "an empty bag cannot stand upright," or "an egg today is better than a hen tomorrow."

He succeeded in selling as many as 10,000 copies of this almanac every year. It rendered the name of "Poor Richard" famous throughout the land. Its influence can still be recognized in the American predilection for short saws.

He drew up for himself the famous schedule of virtues to be cultivated and of vices to be avoided. Even as, by persistent industry, he had educated himself to write excellent English prose, so also by this regime of virtue did he hope to discipline himself into becoming the perfect citizen. Every week was set apart for the cultivation of one special virtue and at the end of the week he would give himself marks on the results. Sloth, gluttony, or thriftlessness were never among his temptations; modesty, as I have said, was added to the regime as an afterthought. It was only by constant self-discipline that he succeeded in acquiring the appearance of humility. Many of his friends regarded his overt assumption of this virtue as artificial, strained, and unconvincing.

In 1736, he was appointed Clerk to the Pennsylvania Assembly. In the following year he secured the job of Postmaster, which was of great advantage to his business and the circulation of his newspaper and almanac. In his shop, apart from his printing works, he sold such diverse articles as stationery, candles, soap, and Negro slaves. He soon became one of Philadelphia's leading citizens. He founded a subscription library and a volunteer fire brigade. He was the originator and patron of the American Philosophical Society. "The first drudgery," he wrote, "of settling new colonies is now pretty well over. There are many in every province in circumstances that set them at ease and afford leisure to cultivate the finer arts and improve the common stock of knowledge." It was thus early that he came to look beyond the confines of his own State and to conceive of intellectual union between the thirteen Colonies. Gradually he acquired the reputation of a "natural philosopher," of a scientist and inventor. It was this which rendered his name famous both in the New and the Old World.

Four

It may have been from his father that he inherited his talent for mechanical invention. Even in his boyhood days he had experimented with a raft which carried sails and increased the delight of bathing either in Boston harbor or in the creeks of the Delaware and the Schuylkill. Shortly after his arrival in Philadelphia he invented a slow combustion stove which acquired wide popularity under the name of the "Philadelphia stove." Several of these warm, economical, but unsightly objects were sold throughout the American continent and even in Europe.

It was in 1746, when he was on the verge of reaching his fortieth year, that he first manifested a passionate interest in electricity, or what he called "the electric branch of natural philosophy." In his house in Market Street he conducted experiments with a saltcellar, a pump handle, a vinegar cruet, and "some little machines I had roughly made for myself." He also experimented with the condenser invented by Pieter van Musschenbroek, which was then known to the learned societies of Europe as "the Leyden jar." When seeking in the course of these experiments to electrocute a turkey he nearly managed to electrocute himself. With the aid of a kite he succeeded in extracting electricity from the clouds and, as he subsequently told Joseph Priestley, "he collected fire very copiously from the air." It was in a "Poor Richard" article of 1753 that he first outlined, in popular form, his theory of a lightning conductor. Yet already in the previous year his experiments had attracted the attention of world scientists. A paper on what was called "the Philadelphian Experiments" was read to the Royal Society in London. In Paris in the same year Buffon drew the attention of Louis XV to these new discoveries and on May 10, 1782, a "Franklin rod" was erected by d'Abilard at Marly and was observed to catch electric sparks from thunderclouds. Recognition of the value of these inventions was not delayed. He was accorded honorary degrees at Harvard in July 1753, at Yale in September 1753, and at William and

Mary in April 1756. In November 1753 the Royal Society in London awarded him the Copley gold medal and in May 1756 elected him an honorary member of the society. "He was famous in Europe," writes van Doren, "before he knew it in America." Even in distant Königsberg, Emanuel Kant hailed him as the new Prometheus who had stolen fire from heaven. Yet Franklin never patented the "Franklin Rod" or derived any financial profit from his invention.

At first, with the aid of his Junto friends, he concentrated on his civic duties. He threw such energy into his many schemes that within a few years he had risen from the rank of a prosperous tradesman to that of foremost citizen. During the War of the Austrian Succession he published and circulated a powerful pamphlet, entitled *Plain Truth* in which he pointed out that the State of Pennsylvania, owing to the pacifism of its quaker proprietors, was undefended against possible attacks by French or Spanish privateers. He devised means whereby the Delaware River could be armed against naval attack, he borrowed cannon from New York, and in his own State he raised a militia of 10,000 volunteers. He urged that Pennsylvania should possess an Academy comparable to Massachusetts' Harvard, to Connecticut's Yale, to Virginia's William and Mary, and to New Jersey's Princeton. A board of twenty-four trustees was created with Franklin as chairman and the Philadelphia Academy was opened on January 7, 1751. He was also instrumental in organizing the city hospital. On August 13, 1751, he was elected to the Pennsylvania Assembly as representative of Philadelphia city. His illegitimate son, William, succeeded him as Clerk to the Assembly.

What renders Franklin so outstanding a figure in history is that he was the first man to envisage the future of the United States as a World Power. It had by then become evident that the policy of the French Government was to connect their forts in Canada with their possessions in Louisiana by a chain of stations running from the Great Lakes along the Ohio and Mississippi rivers, to New Orleans, thus denying to the English colonies any westward expansion and confining them to the territory between the Appalachians and the sea. Franklin was among the first to predict the future expansion of the Atlantic settlements and to realize that without union between the thirteen Colonies in a policy of common defense this glorious future might never be achieved. In May 1754 it was agreed to hold a Congress of all the Colonies at Albany and Franklin submitted to this Congress a draft scheme for federal union as against French and Indian encroachments. This scheme was adopted by the Albany Congress but was either rejected or ignored by the provincial Assemblies. The French had been able to establish with the Indians closer relations than the British, who persisted in regarding the aboriginal inhabitants as little better than wild animals, had ever managed to achieve. Franklin proposed that a Council of Indian Affairs should be created consisting of commissioners from each of the thirteen Colonies and presided over by a chairman appointed by the King. His idea was that this Council should meet in each of the provincial capitals in turn, thus avoiding State jealousies and enabling their prominent men to get to know each other. He himself, having been in August 1753 appointed by the Home Government "Deputy Postmaster General on the Continent of North America," had the opportunity to visit the postmasters in other Colonies. He thus acquired a much clearer view of the conditions in the several States and of the essential necessity of some form of federal union than was possessed by those who had rarely traveled outside the boundaries of their own provinces and whose imagination was not of continental width.

Franklin in those ways was an imaginative imperialist who envisaged a union of English-speaking peoples, independent and autonomous as regards their own affairs, but for common purposes presenting a united front against all possible enemies. In his pamphlet on *The Increase of Mankind* he predicted that within a century the population of America would exceed that of the mother country. "What an accession of power," he wrote, "to the British Empire by sea as well as by land! What increase of trade and navigation! What numbers of ships and seamen!" He foresaw the inevitable expansion beyond the frontiers and the settlement of millions in the then uncharted West. He foresaw the great tides of immigration that were bound to follow and even suggested that the Colonies should deny entry to all immigrants not of British stock. "Why," he asked, "should the Palatine boors be suffered to swarm our settlements and by herding together establish their language and manners to the exclusion of ours?" He protested strongly against the tendency of the mother country to regard the Colonies as a convenient dumping ground for the unwanted. Why should the Plantations be regarded as an ashbin for felons? He proposed that America might retaliate by collecting sacks of rattlesnakes and dumping them in England. They should be "carefully distributed in St. James' Park, in the gardens of the nobility and gentry throughout the nation, but particularly in the gardens of Prime Ministers, Lords of Trade, and Members of Parliament." "Rattlesnakes," he concluded, "seem the most suitable returns for the human serpents sent us by our mother country." From the very first, moreover, he proclaimed the principle of no taxation without representation. "It is supposed," he wrote, "to be an undoubted right of Englishmen to be taxed but by their own consent given through their representatives." This became for him a principle from which he never deviated.

Pennsylvania, it must be remembered, was at that date what was known as a "Proprietary Colony." It remained so until 1790 when the rights of the Penn family were sold in return for an annual pension of £4,000. This pension was in 1884 commuted for a lump payment of £67,000. William Penn died on July 30, 1718, and was buried in Jourdan's Meeting House at Chalfont St. Giles. His three sons, John, Thomas, and Richard, were not inspired by the high ideals of their father; they had ceased to be Quakers and instead of regarding the Colony as a sanctuary for the oppressed, they looked upon it as a vast family estate, with themselves as landlords. The Colonists, well knowing that the Penn family were making fortunes out of the rise in land values, much resented their refusal as proprietors to contribute to the local taxes. By 1756, Pennsylvania was more menaced than ever. The French were still in possession of Fort Duquesne, on the site of the modern Pittsburgh, and had captured the English fort at

BENJAMIN FRANKLIN

Engraving by H. B. Hall (1868)
after painting by J. A. Duplessis (1783)

FRANKLIN AT THE COURT OF FRANCE, 1786

(after Baron Jolly)

Oswego. The Indians became aggressive, murdering whole families in outlying farms and destroying their settlements. Thousands of refugees crowded into the capital. The Penns and the Quakers (who by then had ceased to represent the majority) refused to take any steps in defense, holding the pacifist fallacy that lambs can propitiate wolves by bleats of sweet reasonableness. Franklin by his forceful advocacy persuaded the Assembly to pass a Militia Act and was himself chosen as the Colonel of the Volunteers. He conducted an expedition into Indian Territory and constructed a fort at Gnadenhutten among the Moravian settlers which he called "Fort Allen." In November 1756 a party of Indians stormed and burnt the fort and the Moravian Colonists were exposed to massacre. The Governor in January 1757 asked the Assembly to vote a defense credit of £125,000. The Assembly agreed to a conditional grant of £100,000. The Governor vetoed their Bill and a deadlock ensued. The Assembly decided to send commissioners to England to explain their case. Franklin was chosen as commissioner and left for England on April 4, 1757. The English packet was held up for six weeks, waiting at Sandy Hook until the Governor, Lord Loudon, had found time to compose his dispatches for the London Cabinet. This was Franklin's second experience of the inconsiderate attitude of British officials and it convinced him that trouble was bound to follow unless the home Government chose as Governors and other officials sent to America men of better manners and understanding.

Accompanied by his illegitimate son William, Franklin at last reached London on July 20, 1757. He was to remain there for the next five years. This was his first diplomatic mission. He was then fifty-one years of age. Of his great contemporaries, Washington was then aged 25, John Adams 22, Jefferson 14, Madison 6 and Alexander Hamilton six months. Franklin was already regarded as a veteran. He remained a veteran until his death. He was seventy years of age when he signed the Declaration of Independence and eighty-one when he put his name to the Constitution of the United States.

Five

Although a fellow of the Royal Society and the Arts Society, he at the time possessed but few English friends. He and his son found lodgings at 36 Craven Street, Strand, in the house of Mrs. Stevenson, a motherly widow who looked after his accounts, his linen, and his health. With her and her daughter Mary he remained on terms of affectionate confidence for many years. His son William, in the true Franklin tradition, had an illegitimate son in London who was christened William Temple and whom Franklin always treated as his grandson. His friend, William Strahan, printer to Johnson, Gibbon, and Hume, gave him an introduction into literary society and after a visit to Edinburgh he formed a friendship with Lord Kames with whom he corresponded frequently. It was through Strahan that he met Dr. Johnson at a meeting of the Society known as "The Association of Dr. Bray," a society devoted to the task of educating African Negros. The meeting took place on May 1, 1760, at Dr. Bird's bookshop in Ave Maria Lane. Neither Dr. Johnson nor Benjamin Franklin makes any mention of this encounter. Johnson was always inclined to be rude to Americans.

He visited the Penn Family who received him with contemptuous chill, and referred him to their lawyer Mr. K. J. Paris. He handed to this solicitor a statement of the Assembly's wishes but it was not until November 1758 that any reply was returned to his memorial. The reply was delivered, not to Franklin, but direct to the Pennsylvania Assembly. It accused Franklin of having handled the negotiations without formality or candor. He had, it seems, omitted to address his memorial "To the True and absolute Proprietaries of the Province of Pennsylvania." The Penn family hated Franklin as much as he detested them. In the end, with the help of Lord Mansfield, Franklin was able to persuade the Committee for Plantation Affairs to rule that the Penns should be taxed for a small sum on their surveyed lands, whereas their unsurveyed lands, which then represented a large tract of territory, should remain exempt. This compromise satisfied nobody.

Meanwhile Franklin had entered into contact with members of the British Government. He had not been able to see Chatham, but he obtained an interview with the Attorney General, Charles Pratt, subsequently Lord Camden, who assured him lightheartedly that Colonies invariably when ripe dropped from the parent tree and that sooner or later the thirteen Colonies were bound to declare their independence. Franklin repudiated this horrible suggestion. "No such idea," he protested, "was ever entertained by the Americans nor will any such enter their heads unless you grossly abuse them." He still clung to his vision of a British Commonwealth of Nations. "I have long been of opinion," he wrote to Lord Kames, "that the future grandeur and stability of the British Empire lie in America; and though, like other foundations, they are low and little seen, they are nevertheless broad and strong enough to support the greatest political structure human wisdom ever yet erected." He had at that date a firm, and not wholly unjustified, confidence in the good intentions of George III, referring to him as "our Virtuous young King." Until wounded by the arrogant manners of the British aristocracy, he regarded the English as among the most charming nations of the earth. "Of all the enviable things," he wrote to his devoted landlady, Mrs. Stevenson, "that England has I envy it most its people. Why should this petty island, which compared to America is but like a stepping stone in a brook, scarce enough of it to keep one's shoes dry; why, I say, should that little island enjoy in almost every neighborhood more sensible, virtuous and elegant minds than we can collect in ranging a hundred leagues of our vast forests?"

On September 13, 1759, General Wolfe, by scaling the cliffs above the St. Lawrence, captured Quebec. By the Treaty of Paris which in 1763 put an end to the Seven Years War, France ceded to Great Britain the whole of Canada with the exception of St. Pierre and Miquelon, as well as the disputed territory between the Mississippi and the Alleghany mountains. Many Englishmen then regarded Canada as a fogbound desert of ice, valuable only for furs and fish, and would have preferred to receive the rich West Indian island of Guadaloupe. Even

Voltaire, in his *Candide*, had sneeringly referred to Canada "as a few acres of snow." The English anticipated also that, once the Colonists were freed from the menace of a French invasion on their northern and western frontiers, they would cease to rely on the protection of the mother country and become even more obstreperous. Franklin did his best to counter this opinion. If, he argued, the Colonies had failed to unite against the real menace of the French and the Indians, how could any sane person imagine that they could ever unite to defy their mother country? The British Government, feeling that England by her energies and skill had rescued America from the French danger, decided that the Colonies might well contribute to the cost of their defense against the Indians, estimated to cost £300,000 a year. George Grenville, therefore, introduced the Stamp Act which passed through both Houses of Parliament in March 1765.

Even Franklin was startled by the fury that this fiscal measure aroused in America. He urged moderation. He advised his friends in the Colonies that "a firm loyalty to the Crown and faithful adherence to the Government of this nation, which it is the safety as well as the honor of the Colonies to be connected with, will always be the wisest course for you and I to take." His attitude was not appreciated across the ocean; he was accused of being pro-English and anti-American; the Penn family and their adherents in Philadelphia, who regarded him as a "dangerous villain," exploited this anti-Franklin feeling. Realizing that the wind of popular approval was shifting, Franklin adjusted his sails. He warned his merchant friends in England that the Colonies were obstinately convinced that the principle of "no taxation without representation" was the very foundation of their liberties and that they would be prepared to boycott all British manufactures rather than accept the Stamp Act. On February 13 he was summoned to the bar of the House of Commons to give evidence. He acquitted himself excellently, warning the assembled members that if the Stamp Act were not repealed it would make "the total loss of the respect and affection of the people of America bear to this country and of all the commerce that depends on that affection." The merchants of London were impressed by these warnings and brought pressure to bear upon the Government. Grenville was obliged to resign and the Stamp Act was repealed on March 8, 1766, by Lord Rockingham's Ministry. During the year it had remained in force it had only produced £4,000 which was less than the cost of collection. Franklin's reputation in America was immediately reestablished and in his delight at the repeal he sent to his wife Deborah a "fine piece of Pompadour satin and four bottles of lavender water." The colonies of Georgia, New Jersey, and Massachusetts, in admiration of his outspokenness, appointed him their agent in London.

This interlude in the tension between England and her Colonies was not of long duration. Owing to the fall of Rockingham and the illness of Chatham the government fell into the hands of Charles Townshend, Chancellor of the Exchequer and leader of the House of Commons. Having lost his temper with the New York Assembly owing to their refusal to provide for British troops under the Quartering Act he introduced as a reprisal a small duty on glass, paper, and tea. Franklin replied to his gesture by publishing his pamphlet on *The Causes of American Discontents*. While insisting that the Colonies would never consent to be taxed by the British Parliament, he was so unwise as to assert that there existed in America no sentiments of disloyalty. "There is not," he wrote, "a single native of our country who is not firmly attached to the King by principle and by affection." He admitted however that no similar affection was extended to the House of Commons. Yet his reverence for King George III was unabated. As late as April 1769, we find him writing to Samuel Cooper "I can scarcely conceive a King of better disposition, of more exemplary virtues, or more truly desirous of promoting the welfare of all his subjects." This was an exaggerated statement. *The Causes of American Discontents* did Franklin harm both in England and America. He was regarded as a rebel by the British and as a blackleg by the Americans. Aware as he was of America's rapidly increasing wealth and population, he foresaw that within twenty years she would by her own strength be able to impose her wishes upon England. What he dreaded was some premature explosion which might force the British Government to adopt reprisals and thus destroy every hope of conciliation.

On January 16, 1771, Franklin had an interview with the Colonial Secretary, Lord Hillsborough, who refused to recognize him as agent for Massachusetts, since his appointment had not been confirmed by the Governor. Lord Hillsborough was a man whom even George III condemned as lacking in judgment: his bad manners on this occasion made Franklin despair of ever being able to instill into British ministers the knowledge, the understanding, or the sympathy essential to any amicable settlement.

It was at this stage that Franklin committed a mistake. He had obtained by indirect means letters written to England by Thomas Hutchinson, Governor of Massachusetts, and by his brother-in-law, Andréw Oliver, advising the British Government to adopt "a firm hand" in America. Franklin conceived the idea that if these letters were known in Boston it would be realized that the attitude of the English was not wholly to be ascribed to ignorance and lack of understanding, but was based on advice given them by two eminent New Englanders. The publication of these letters aroused anger both in Boston and London. It was then that the Colonists committed the act of provocation which Franklin had striven to avoid. All the Townshend duties had by then been abolished with the exception of that on tea, which was retained as a token tax of 3d a pound in order to maintain the principle that Parliament had the right to impose such duties. On December 16, 1773, a cargo of tea was seized by a band of Bostonians disguised as Red Indians and thrown into the harbor. As a reprisal for this outrage the British Government closed the port of Boston and imposed other galling penalties.

Franklin meanwhile had written two pamphlets which had aroused considerable attention. The first was entitled *Rules by which a Great Empire may be reduced to a Small One*, in which the conduct of the British Government was held up to ridicule and contempt. The second purported to be an Edict issued by the King of Prussia in September 1773 in which he claimed the right, owing to the fact that many English counties had been colonized by Hengist and Horsa, to levy duties on all English imports and exports, to prohibit the manufacture of cloth or the smelting of iron, and to dump his felons and sodomites in England "for the better peopling of the country." These pamphlets did not increase Franklin's popularity with British ministers.

As a result of the publication of the Hutchinson letters, the Massachusetts Assembly addressed a petition to the King asking for the removal of Hutchinson and Oliver. On January 29, 1774, this petition was considered by the Committee for Plantation Affairs, meeting in the Cockpit at Whitehall. The Government were represented by the Solicitor General Alexander Wedderburn. He was not a conciliatory man. Junius described him as a man "whom even treachery cannot trust" and Charles Churchill devoted to him the following scathing lines:

> Mute at the bar and in the senate loud,
> Dull 'mongst the dullest, proudest of the proud,
> A pert prim prater of the northern race
> Guilt in his heart and famine in his face.

The Cockpit on that occasion was packed with peers and privy councilors. Burke was there, and Joseph Priestley and even the young Jeremy Bentham. Wedderburn launched a violent personal attack on Franklin, accusing him of having obtained the Hutchinson letters "by fraudulent and corrupt means" and suggesting that he had intrigued to succeed Hutchinson as Governor of the Colony. Franklin, dressed in his best suit of figured Manchester velvet, stood by the fireplace "his countenance as immovable as if his features had been made of wood." The Massachusetts petition was rejected as "groundless, vexatious and scandalous and calculated only for the seditious purpose of keeping up a spirit of clamor and discontent in the said province."

The next day Franklin was notified that he had been dismissed from his post as Deputy Postmaster General. The episode of the Hutchinson letters and the Cockpit scene did not end his efforts for conciliation. He had discussions with Lord Chatham at Hayes and again at

Chevening. Lord Chatham agreed with him that the only hope was that what we now call Dominion Status should be granted to America. Franklin had meetings with two friendly Whigs, Barclay, and Dr.Fothergill. He held frequent conversations with Lord Howe. He went, arm in arm with Lord Chatham, to the House of Lords where he heard himself denounced by Lord Sandwich as "one of the bitterest and most mischievous enemies that this country has ever known." Lord Chatham defending him asserted that on the contrary Franklin "was an honor, not only to the English nation but to human nature." But he had lost confidence in the wisdom of the British Parliament. He was not certain even that he any longer desired his dream of Commonwealth Union. When he considered "the extreme corruption prevalent among all orders of men in this old rotten State and the glorious public virtue as predominant in our rising country" he feared that "to unite intimately will only be to corrupt and poison us also."

Angry and humiliated he returned to America. He reached Philadelphia on May 5, 1775, to hear that American troops had fired upon a British column at Lexington. War was now inevitable. He signed the Declaration of Independence on July 4, 1776. "Long did I endeavor," he wrote to Lord Howe on July 20, "with unfeigned and unwearied zeal, to preserve from breaking that fine and noble China vase, the British Empire. For I knew that, being once broken, the separate parts could not retain even their share of the strength or value that existed in the whole and that the perfect reunion of those parts could scarce ever be hoped for."

Whoever else was to blame for the loss of the American Colonies it was certainly not Benjamin Franklin.

Six

The moment war broke out he abandoned all sentimental affections for the English. "You and I," he wrote to William Strahan, "were long friends. You are now my enemy and I am yours." It is not soothing to any Englishman to recall the events that led to rupture:

it is intolerable for him to dwell on the conduct of the war that followed. I prefer to turn those sullied pages and to echo the words of Edmund Burke: "I shall say no more about it. Light lie the earth on the ashes of English pride."

I shall conclude with the apotheosis of Benjamin Franklin which began when he reached Paris on December 21, 1776, as Ambassador of the United States. His fame had preceded him. "There was scarcely," wrote John Adams, "a peasant, or a citizen, or a valet, coachman or footman, who did not consider him a friend of human kind." He was welcomed in the salons of Paris as the prophet of natural philosophy, as the benefactor who had brought fire from heaven, as the ideal citizen of the free world, as something between Socrates and the Vicaire Savoyard. The comte de Ségur has provided a true account of the effect produced on Paris by the arrival of the American commissioner. "Nothing," he writes, "was more astonishing than the contrast between the luxury of Paris, the elegance of our fashions, the splendor of Versailles, all those living survivals of the Autocratic pride of Louis XIV, the polite but arrogant loftiness of our great nobles—with the almost peasant clothes, the simple but proud deportment, the outspoken but honest language, the uncurled and unpowdered hair, in a word with that air of a distant age, which seemed suddenly to transport to Paris into the middle of the decadent and servile civilization of the XVIIIth century a philosopher of the time of Plato or a republican of the age of Fabius or Cato."

Franklin, who was fully aware of the value of such publicity, acted his part. He appeared at Court without powder or sword, dressed in what they believed to be Quaker uniform and carrying a rugged staff. The French Foreign Minister, the count de Vergennes, would have preferred to remain neutral and to profit by the quarrels of others. But Franklin had from the start won the support of the fashionable world and Vergennes was too expert a courtier not to know that if he defied the wishes or emotions of the *salons* he would lose his job. To Vergennes himself Franklin behaved with what Thomas Paine has excellently called "sensible gracefulness." Thus, in spite of the impoverished state of the French

Treasury, Vergennes doled out subsidies to the Americans and helped Franklin with the equipment and organization of the privateers which took such a toll of English shipping. The surrender of Burgoyne at Saratoga on October 17, 1777, convinced Vergennes that the Colonists were bound to triumph and that it would be in the interests of France to join with them before the end. Franklin pressed home this advantage and on February 6, 1778, a Treaty of Alliance was signed between France and the United States in the French Foreign Office at the Hôtel de Lautrec. For this ceremony Franklin had unearthed from his wardrobe the suit of Manchester figured velvet which four years before he had worn when facing the invectives of Wedderburn, standing upright beside the fireplace in the Cockpit of Whitehall. "The credit," writes Sir George Trevelyan, "arising from the Treaty of Alliance between France and the United States accrued to Franklin and to Franklin alone. . . . Tried by the searching test of practical performance, he takes high rank among the diplomatists of history."

Franklin was happy there in his house and garden at Passy. He flirted with his neighbors Madame Helvétius and Madame Brillon; he embraced Voltaire in public amidst the tears and cheers of a distinguished audience; he continued his researches in natural philosophy, inventing bifocal spectacles, advocating daylight saving, and studying with passion the experiments of Dr. Mesmer and the aeronautics of Montgolfier. After witnessing the first balloon ascent on August 27, 1783, he was asked whether this discovery had any future. "What good," he answered, "is a new born baby?" He foresaw that this infant discovery might give a new turn to human affairs, convincing rulers of the folly of war, since "it will be impracticable for the most potent of them to guard his dominions."

As a result of the Conway resolution and the resignation of Lord North, an informal truce was established between the British and the American armies. On the death of Rockingham, Franklin's friend Lord Shelburne became first minister. Negotiations for peace were opened immediately. Shelburne's agent Richard Oswald was sent over to Paris and after long discussion the heads of agreement were signed in Oswald's lodgings, on the morning of November 30, 1782. Franklin did not inform Vergennes of these secret negotiations or of the fact that an agreement had actually been reached implying a separate peace. He was himself overjoyed at the conclusion of hostilities. "In my opinion," he wrote to Josiah Quincy, "there never was a good war or a bad peace."

His health by then was breaking down. He left Passy in a royal litter drawn by two mules. He crossed to Southampton, and reached Philadelphia on September 14. He was accorded a rapturous welcome; the cannon thundered salutes and the church bells pealed. He lived long enough to see the country he had done so much to create settle down to the unimaginable future that he had been the first to predict. His was indeed a happy and generous life. "I have been enabled," he wrote, "so to conduct myself that there does not exist a human being who can justly say 'Benjamin Franklin has wronged me.' This, my friend, in old age, is a comfortable reflection."

He died in his home in Philadelphia on April 17, 1790 in his eighty-fifth year. He was more than a great citizen: he was a very great man.

Chapter 12
The Salons
(1660–1789)

The importance of the French salon in eighteenth-century civilization—Its value as a fusion of classes and sexes—The passion for conversation—The atmosphere of disciplined gallantry—Its influence upon correct language and pronunciation—The effect of this "Republic of Letters" upon contemporary opinion—The Marquise de Rambouillet as the founder of the salon system—Mademoiselle de Scudery—The Blue Room—The *Précieuses*—The free-thinkers—Ninon de l'Enclos—The duchesse du Maine—Madame de Lambert—The controversy between the "ancients" and the "moderns"—Madame de Tençin—Madame Geoffrin and her intellectual temple of the Saint-Honoré—Her generosity—Her bullying—Her visit to the King of Poland—Madame du Deffand—Horace Walpole—Her successors—The duchesse de Choiseul—The Holbach circle—Madame Necker.

One

IF VOLTAIRE TRANSFORMED the thoughts and Rousseau the feelings, of the eighteenth century, it was in the salons of Paris that the new conceptions of "reason" and "nature," of "free thought" and the importance of the individual, were sifted, codified, and eventually imposed. It would be an error to underestimate the influence of the salons on the culture of the civilized world. If one consults only the prints and drawings of the period, one may derive the impression that the life of the salons was nothing more than a succession of *ruelles* and *alcôves*, in which young gallants arrayed in plum-colored velvet, wearing silk waistcoats embroidered with Chinese pagodas, made love to ladies leaning negligently against the cushions, toying with lap dogs, or accepting small cups of chocolate from the hands of Negro pages with bright green turbans on their heads. Nor is it correct to assume that the color and vociferation of the macaws that figure so frequently in such illustrations mirrored the plumage or the chatter of the duchesses and marquises to whom they served as foils and pets.

We must realize in the first place that the universities of France, in contrast to those of Germany or Scotland, exerted but a remote influence on the culture either of their own country or of the continent of Europe. It would be an exaggeration also to assume that the preponderating, and in fact compulsive, influence which France extended across the civilized world during the eighteenth century, emanated solely, or even mainly, from the Court of Versailles. The last decades of the reign of Louis XIV were years of somber repentance: the reign of Louis XV, illumined though it was by the exquisite elegance of Madame de Pompadour, was too frivolous and self-indulgent to serve as an intellectual example: and, in spite of the glamour of Marie Antoinette, the court of Louis XVI was regarded as respectable but dreadfully dull. Versailles and Marly, which had so impressed foreign potentates and visitors during the seventeenth century, ceased from 1700 to exercise their hypnotic spell: dominated as the Court became by Jesuits, courtesans and courtiers, it ceased to be in any manner representative of the spirit of the age and completely lost touch with public opinion. That opinion was focused and in fact created by the salons of Paris and with a speed and an intensity which in the present age (when Society exercises no influence whatsoever upon the habits of men) are difficult to conceive.

In the second place it is necessary to dismiss from our minds any idea that the life of the salons was "social," in the sense of being confined to a single class. The astonishing efficacy of that particular melting pot is that it contained all manner of components, from the elderly courtier, to the young gallant, and above all to the self-made and self-educated writers and philosophers of the age. It was in the salons of Paris that the thinkers of the century, who were generally men of humble or at least provincial origin, acquired the polish and the self-confidence of men of the world. It was by mingling on equal terms with these intellectuals that the aristocrats of Paris acquired those philosophical convictions which they were pleased to regard as elements of "reason" or "enlightenment," but which in fact served to undermine the self-confidence and solidarity which might have preserved them from the catastrophes of the Revolution. It may well have been that all this talk of "mingling on terms of equality" was somewhat exaggerated. For all their liberalism, the French nobles retained a lively sense of their birth and breeding and continued, as Voltaire experienced in circumstances of great humiliation, to regard the middle class intellectuals as inferior animals. "It was not," writes the highly observant comte de Ségur, "so much equality as familiarity." The salons were nonetheless admirable products of a high standard of civilization; but they contained within themselves the ferment of disintegration by which that civilization was destroyed.

It was in the salons that the art of conversation, which to this day constitutes so alarming a factor in French social life, reached its fullest expression. "What is certain," writes Professor Picard, "is that disinterested conversation carried on with the sole object of exchanging ideas, of communicating or sharing sentiments, of rendering oneself liked, of showing oneself sociable and brilliant, was the true passion of the century and was transmitted by it to succeeding centuries."

This passion for talking had several valuable results. It gave a spice to social relationships; it sharpened wits; it spread ideas; and it did more than all the candles of Versailles to convince awed foreigners that France was indeed the center of the civilized world. But it also had its disadvantages. It was inclined to render social occasions competitive, exhausting and in the end artificial; many of the most spontaneous sallies had been carefully prepared by the philosophers while their hair was being powdered in anticipation of the evening's contest. The idea that a young man could achieve glory by his quickness at repartee induced many clever people to assume that brilliance was as important as wisdom and led to the injection of malice, even of cruelty, into boudoir talk. Moreover it encouraged the French in their congenital tendency to believe that an idea that is ingeniously expressed, even in the form of a bright epigram, must in some ways be true. The salon conversation was a scintillating pastime, but the shuttlecocks of brilliance that were exchanged across the supper table diverted the attention of men from the fact that what they were so brilliantly discussing were serious and dangerous things.

Another aspect of the salon to which we puritans find it difficult to assign correct proportions was the element of gallantry. It was essential, if one desired to shine in a salon and not to experience that painful "outsider" feel, to cultivate what they called *l'air galant*, by which was meant, not a flirtatious disposition exactly, but what Balzac defined as "urbanity." Mademoiselle de Scudéry described it as "a favorable natural disposition, a knowledge of the world, and a desire to please without loving anybody special." It was considered bourgeois not to pretend to be in love with these elegant women and even those who experienced no such tender emotion were obliged to simulate it, at the risk of not being derided as "no man of the world." Mademoiselle de Scudéry adds that, although it is not essential that women also should fall in love, it is to be recommended that they should gladly accept the worship of men. "All the glory of women," she writes, "consists in making splendid conquests and never losing their slaves." They should hold their lovers captive "by the power of their charm rather than by the grant of their favors." "Nobody," she comments, "can pretend to be a man of the world who has never fallen in love. The desire to please polishes the intelligence and love inspires more liberality in a quarter of an hour than ten years study of philosophy." This axiom that a man cannot hope to be welcomed socially unless he possess a talent for the deft adulation of women is one of the many reasons why we Anglo-Saxons experience so many tremors when entering Parisian boudoirs. We feel ourselves to be timid; we know ourselves to be clumsy, and we do not possess that exquisitely patient pertinacity that renders Frenchmen the most perfect lovers on earth.

The salons of Paris, incidentally, were even more influential than the Academy itself in standardizing and purifying the French language. Until they came to rule society, the current language was disfigured by many archaisms, latinisms, and phrases borrowed from the dialects of Gascony or Béarn. The French bluestockings or *Précieuses* went rather too far in their efforts to banish all common words. They thus proscribed such lovely old words as *sollicitude* and *alme*; they contended that the conjunction *car* was illiterate, even as *our précieuses* of today object to the use of "which"; but they did discover such useful expressions as *anonyme* and *s'encanailler*, which have survived. Their influence was great. They much restricted the vocabulary of Racine and they persuaded Madame de Sévigné never to employ a single common word. There were those who rebelled against their austerity, arguing that language was living organic matter which could not be sealed in bottles or pinned in desiccated form upon a board. Fénélon accused them, in his *Lettre a l'Académie*, of impoverishing the language and La Fontaine devoted to them one of his happy quips:

> *Les reines des étangs, grenouilles veux je dire,*
> *(Car que coûte-t-il d'appeler*
> *Les choses par noms honorables?)*

The Queens of the pond (by which I mean "frogs")
For what harm is it to call things
By their respectable names.

Madame d'Auchy would have much disliked that *car*.

The activities of these learned women extended also to spelling and pronunciation. They insisted that it was vulgar to pronounce *église* as *iglise*, or *ridicule* as *rédicule*. They even sought to discipline that obstreperous French diphthong "oi." In the provinces in their day *gloire* (a word in frequent use in France) was pronounced *glère*, and *croire* as *crère*, and *Roi* as *Rouet*. They altered all that.

The formality and boredom of the Court drove men and women of intelligence to seek relaxation in the salons, where there existed what they were pleased to call "a Republic of Letters." Apart from conversation, they amused themselves by composing rondeaux, madrigals and society verses, by concerts, dancing, and such parlor games as tying bows, cutting out engravings, setting each other riddles and the odd pernickety game of *parfilage*, or what we then called "drizzling," namely unpicking embroideries. The food was always excellent, but there was no central heating, and the chairs were uncomfortable. In winter they were obliged to protect themselves with screens, and the philosophers and ladies took turns to stand in front of the fire. Their literary power was enormous and, at a time when the Press was scarcely existent and there were no literary editors, the success or failure of a new book depended upon salon opinion. The leading hostesses of the day each possessed a tame literary lion; they were rightly supposed to nominate candidates for the Academy; and they could manufacture or destroy the fame of rising authors. It was thus Madame de Lambert who launched Montesquieu and Madame de Tençin who started Marivaux on his successful career. Yet above all, as I have said, the salons were important as the crucibles of public opinion. In an age when the Press was neither outspoken nor responsible, it was the salons that, in the words of Necker, formed "the invisible power which, without finances, without troops, without an army, imposes its laws upon the town, on the Court, and even on the King himself." Ségur describes them as "the brilliant schools of civilization."

Thus, in any study of the Age of Reason, we must take the salons of Paris very seriously.

Two

The salon system was inaugurated in the seventeenth century by Catherine de Vivonne, marquise de Rambouillet. She was born in Rome, her father being French Ambassador and her mother an Italian of the noble family of Savelli. At the age of thirteen she was married off to the marquis de Rambouillet by whom she had two sons and five daughters. He was, as are so often the husbands of energetic hostesses, a colorless, rather moldy little man: but their marriage was exemplary, Madame de Rambouillet never imitated the wanton habits of her friends.

Her hotel in the rue Saint Thomas du Louvre was a splendid mansion built of pink brick with stone facings in a style familiar to us from the still existing houses in the Place des Vosges. It had high windows opening upon a large garden and a much-admired oval staircase. Madame de Rambouillet's bedroom, in which, as was the fashion, she received her guests, was called "The Blue Room," being hung with azure damask edged with tassels of silver and gold. It was divided by high screens into several separate alcoves in which private conversations could be held. There were twenty chairs for the distinguished guests and the rooms were misty with the smell of hothouse flowers, the scents bubbling in the cassolettes, and the smoke of juniper logs smoldering in the fireplace. Her bedroom opened on a wide loggia in the Italian style which her guests called "La Loge de Zyrphée," from a passage in that enduring romance *Amadis de Gaule*. Among the pictures in her bedroom was the *Gioconda* of Leonardo da Vinci, who could contemplate with smirking skepticism the lavish paradoxes in which the guests indulged.

Madame de Rambouillet made three major contributions to the salon system. She was the first to mingle on a footing of absolute equality men of letters and members of the aristocracy, thus breaking with the old rigid relationship of patron and pensioner. She was the first to mix the two sexes and to encourage her women friends to take a leading part in the conversation. And she was the first to break with the coarse habits of the Courts of Henri IV and Louis XIII, to forbid lubricity of conversation and to insist that her guests spoke elegantly, correctly and soberly. Mademoiselle de Scudéry, who introduced her into *Le Grand Cyrus* under the name of Cléomire, informs us that she insisted that "every passion should be ruled by reason." It was she, wrote Segrais, who "taught good manners to a whole generation." Politics were banned. When Cardinal Richelieu suggested to her that it would be useful if she would inform him secretly of the conversations that were held in the Blue Room and of the private opinions of her visitors, she replied with sharp tact that her friends were far too well brought up to say unkind things about the Cardinal in her presence.

One of the most striking of her women friends was Angélique Paulet, who it was said had been one of the many mistresses of Henri IV, who possessed a mane of scarlet hair which tumbled over her shoulders and earned her the nickname of "the red lioness," who sang excellently to her own accompaniment on the lute, and who never married, owing, it was said, to the misfortune that all her bridegrooms were killed in duels with all her lovers. She was a remarkable girl. Another woman friend was the duchesse de Chevreuse who was supposed to have captivated even the grim Cardinal Richelieu and who certainly captivated Victor Cousin two hundred years after her death. "Never," wrote the Cardinal de Retz, "was there a woman who had less regard either for duties or scruples; the only duty she ever admitted was that of giving pleasure to her lover of the day." The younger generation were entertained by Madame de Rambouillet's daughter Julie d'Angennes, a minx of a girl, who ended by marrying the elderly and most respectable duc de Montausier. She gathered around her many bright young things, such as the duchesse de Longueville, the heroine of the Fronde, and many gallants. It was a gay and profligate circle.

> *Les demoiselles de ce temps*
> *Ont, depuis peu, beaucoup d'amants,*
> *On dit qu'il n'en manque à personne:*
> *L'année est bonne.*

"The girls of today," wrote Voltaire, "have, since a short while ago, heaps of lovers. They say that nobody is without a lover. It is a splendid year."

In the Blue Room of the Hôtel de Rambouillet gathered all the most distinguished men of the age. Richelieu and Bossuet, Malherbe,

Maynard and Louis de Balzac, were frequent visitors. The great Corneille read *Polyeucte* to the assembled company and was discouraged by the cold and even bored reception that it received. The duc de La Rochefoucauld was a frequent visitor; the Duke of Buckingham appeared glistening with diamonds, Madame de Sévigné entered the circle in 1654 and was charmed and influenced by its high distinction. The authority of Madame de Rambouillet became dominant in French cultural life. "Nothing," wrote Mademoiselle de Scudéry, "was thought beautiful unless she approved of it."

The circumstance that the Blue Room became more important than the Academy itself, that Madame de Rambouillet was so strict a disciplinarian and insisted on her guests speaking French correctly, has created the legend that her circle was predominantly a pedantic coterie and somewhat grim. Often it is incorrectly assumed that the Hotel Rambouillet suggested to Molière his *Précieuses Ridicules*, although that comedy was written in 1659 when the Hôtel Rambouillet was already on the decline, and although Molière himself expressly stated that he was not thinking of Madame de Rambouillet but of her foolish imitators, such as the vicomtesse d'Auchy.

They were in fact a gay, frivolous, and profligate lot. The poet Voiture, who played a leading part in their festivities, was a man of the people, his father being the owner of a public house, the Chapeau de Roses, at Amiens. He was exuberant, daring, and occasionally impertinent. He once took them all in by disguising himself as the newly arrived Swedish Ambassador and on another occasion he introduced two young bears into the Blue Room and hid them behind a screen.

The main purpose of Madame de Rambouillet was to perfect the art of conversation and in so doing *l'incomparable Arthénice* created a tradition that never died. Their amusements were varied and harmless. They would act comedies, compose rondeaux, indulge in complicated riddles, and took immense pleasure in writing character sketches of themselves and of their friends. With the marriage of Julie d'Angennes to an elderly duke the hotel lost something of its vivacity.

Madame de Rambouillet herself never quite recovered from the death of her favorite son at the battle of Nordlingen and died in 1665. The great days of the Blue Room were over.

Three

The successors and imitators of Madame de Rambouillet can be divided into two categories. There were those who sank into affectation and became the bluestockings, or *Précieuses*, so devastatingly ridiculed by Molière. And there were those who sought to perpetuate the intellectual distinction of the Blue Room, to discipline manners, and to purify the language according to the principles of Malherbe. There was the duchesse de Bouillon, the friend of La Fontaine, of Corneille and Turenne. There was Madame Cornuel, the first bourgeoise to create a salon, whose conversation was admired by Saint Simon and Madame de Sévigné. And there was Mademoiselle de Scudéry whose immensely popular *Le Grand Cyrus* appeared in ten volumes between 1649 and 1653. It was Madame de La Sablière, in her vast chateau at Reuilly, who first introduced into salon life a passion for "natural philosophy." It must be repeated that in the seventeenth and eighteenth century the term "philosophy" embraced, not only the problems of ethics and abstract ideas, but also the study of practical sciences, such as astronomy, physics, chemistry, and botany. It was at Reuilly that Molière gave his first reading of *Le Malade Imaginaire* and that La Fontaine composed many of his masterly fables. Boileau, who was also a visitor at Reuilly, disapproved of women studying practical sciences:

> *Que l'astrolabe en main, un autre aille chercher*
> *Si le soleil est fixe ou tourne sur son axe,*
> *Si Saturne, à nos yeux, peut faire un parallaxe.*

> Let someone else explore, astrolabe in hand,
> Whether the sun is fixed or burns on its axis,
> Whether Saturn, to our eyes, can form a parallax.

Madame de la Sablière retorted by pointing out that an astrolabe was used to determine the relative distances of the stars and that the word "parallaxe" was in any case of the feminine gender. Boileau was so hurt by this reproof on the part of a female doryphore that he never set foot in Reuilly again. Then there was Madame de Sable, who had jansenist tendencies, who was suspected by Mazarin, who loved maxims, and who often claimed to have inspired, not La Rochefoucauld only, but even the great Pascal himself. There was also Madame de La Fayette, the gifted author of *La Princesse de Clèves*, whom Boileau described as the most intelligent woman in France. It was in her salon in the rue de Vaugirard that Molière read his *Femmes Savantes* and that Madame de Sévigné met the widow Scarron, so soon to become famous as Madame de Maintenon.

The above women of taste and fashion were, at least in their outward behavior, serious, virtuous, and devout. There at the same time existed a smaller group of "libertines" or freethinkers, who attacked the tyranny of the Church and the Jesuits, who were avowed deists and believed in what they called "natural morality." The "libertines," of whom Saint-Evremond was the most notable, generally met in cabarets such as the "Pomme de Pin" or the "Croix de Lorraine" which became the cafes of the succeeding generation. Saint Evremond was a materialist who boasted that what he demanded from life were "old wood wherewith to warm myself, old friends to talk with, and old wine to cheer me." He was a constant attendant at the salon of Ninon de l'Enclos in the rue de Tournelles. This most historic of courtesans had, by the last decade of the seventeenth century, become immensely respectable. Saint Simon—a most fastidious snob—writes that it became fashionable to be received by Mademoiselle l'Enclos. "The most virtuous mothers," he writes, "intrigued to have their sons admitted into her salon, which was regarded as the focus of good company." Even Louis XIV would sometimes ask his courtiers, "what does Ninon say about it?" The future Regent was a frequent visitor; only the straightlaced Madame de Maintenon disapproved. It was to Mademoiselle de l'Enclos that Saint Evremond addressed the charming verse:

L'indulgente et sage Nature
A formé l'âme de Ninon
De la volupté d'Epicure
Et de la vertu de Caton.

Nature, benevolent and wise,
Has shaped the soul of Ninon.
She has given her the hedonism of Epicurus
And the Virtue of Cato.

In her declining years Ninon de l'Enclos became attached to the son of her solicitor, Maitre Arouet. In her will she left to the young Voltaire a sum of money wherewith to buy books. She thus constitutes a link between the seventeenth century and the Age of Reason.

Before passing from the successors of the Hôtel de Rambouillet to the great drawing room despots of the eighteenth century, there are other hostesses who must be mentioned, if only because they indicate the variety of aim and method that differentiated one salon from another. From 1700 until her death in 1753, the duchesse du Maine, wife of Louis XIV's crippled bastard by Madame de Montespan, entertained exuberantly at her château at Sceaux. In 1714, she organized fifteen tremendous festivals which became known as the "Great Nights of Sceaux." There were balls and ballets and operas and comedies and illuminations and fireworks. Although vivacious, capricious, impetuous, and very lively, the duchesse du Maine was not an intellectual. She must have been a heartless little woman, since we are told that when her old friend the duchesse d'Estrées was dying in an upstairs bedroom at Sceaux, she refused to interrupt the card game she was playing and transferred herself, her partners, and her cards to the death chamber, continuing to deal the cards upon the counterpane of her dying friend until, at 4.00 A.M., the duchess expired. It was to Sceaux that Voltaire escaped when afraid that his irritated outburst against the gamblers of Fontainebleau might result in a *lettre de cachet* and a further period of imprisonment in the Bastille. Until the scandal should have blown over, he and Madame de Châtelet were hidden behind closed shutters in one of the wings of Sceaux and it was then and there that he composed *Zadik*. On his release from internment, he took charge of further Sceaux festivities, obliging the duchess to have his own plays acted by her private company. With his usual effrontery he invited five hundred friends of his own to one of these performances. The duchess was furious and for many years a coldness ensued between them. But the duchesse du Maine was not really in the Blue Room tradition; she was a vivacious and wildly extravagant hostess who entertained.

The true tradition was carried on in the opening decades of the century by Madame de Lambert in her rooms in the Hôtel Colbert. She was a pious woman, who had published two unctuous pamphlets on the theme of a mother's advice to a daughter and of a mother's advice to a son. She took a leading part in the controversy that arose between the "ancients" and the "moderns," the former contending that any writer whose merit had been acclaimed by the judgment of generations must be above criticism, the latter arguing that literature was not a stagnant pool but a river, enriched and freshened by new tributaries. La Motte argued that we should "not hesitate to apply human reason to tradition" and asked incisively how many centuries must elapse before a man must abandon his liberty of criticizing past works of literature. Voltaire, as so often, hedged on the controversy. "Let us admire the ancients," he wrote, "but let us see to it that our admiration is not blind." The receptions of Madame de Lambert must have been formidable occasions. The intellectuals met at noon, were given a light luncheon, spent the whole afternoon reading their manuscripts to each other, and finally relaxed with a rich supper. No cards were permitted; any discussion of politics or finance was prohibited, although at the time everybody was bursting to tell everybody else of their own experiences in the great Law gamble, the South Sea Bubble of France. In this austere atmosphere Madame de Lambert received Montesquieu, Marivaux, d'Argenson, and Fontenelle. She exercised strong literary influence and President Hénault in his memoirs asserts that "a man had to pass through her salon if he wished to become an academician." A young man had to spend many hours of modest endurance in the drawing room of Madame de Lambert if he wished to gain even a Ph.D.

A more vivacious and tolerant salon was that opened by Madame de Tençin in 1726. Her youth had been very disreputable and she was known to have deposited one of her many bastard babies on the steps of a church. The screaming little waif was retrieved by kind neighbors and grew to manhood as the illustrious d'Alembert, one of the greatest and most beloved of the *Encyclopédistes*. She was not a rich woman and her receptions were on a comparatively modest scale. As New Year presents to her male admirers she would send a few yards of cloth or velvet from which breeches could be cut. Her guests included Montesquieu, Marmontel, Fontenelle, Marivaux, Lord Bolingbroke, and Lord Chesterfield. The star-turn at her receptions was Charles Duclos, a man of the people but so brilliant a conversationalist that he was elected a member of the Académie des Inscriptions before he had published a single line. He was a rough, rude man, whose spiritual home was the café de la Régence, where he could often be seen playing chess with the nephew of Rameau. He became Permanent Secretary of the Academy.

But I must now pass on to the two empresses of the Parisian salon of the eighteenth century, to Madame Geoffrin and Madame du Deffand.

Four

Thérèse Rodet, who at the age of fifteen was married to the elderly and wealthy glass manufacturer, François Geoffrin, was of bourgeois origin and as such never received at Court. Her husband, who did not appreciate her intellectual friends, and who resented the expense of her exquisite dinners, insisted on doing the shopping and housekeeping himself. He would sit silent at the end of the table, superintending the service with furious but watchful eyes. When in 1741 he died at the age of eighty, one of Madame Geoffrin's younger guests asked her what had happened to the strange old man who used so often to sit at her dinners in prolonged silence. "He was my husband," she answered coldly, "and he is now dead."

When Madame de Tençin died in 1794, the whole of her salon transferred itself in a body to that of Madame Geoffrin. Her house was situated at No. 372 rue Saint-Honoré at the corner of the present rue Cambon: relics of it still existed as late as 1939. It was well heated, the armchairs were plentiful and soft, the pictures, tapestries and mirrors excellent in design and coloring; she had one of the best chefs in Paris; and she dressed simply in lavender and grey. Although an almost uneducated and illiterate woman, she had a real taste in art. She became the patroness of painting and persuaded her friends to have their portraits done by the leading artists of the day. Every Monday she had a dinner at which artists could meet patrons and purchasers and she financed and assisted Van Loo, Boucher, Chardin, Latour, and Vernet. She also entertained musicians: Rameau was a frequent visitor and it was in her drawing room that Paris was first dazzled by the Austrian infant prodigy, Mozart. Her literary dinners, which became the nucleus of the Encyclopédiste movement, took place on Wednesdays. Foreign ambassadors and visitors crowded to her receptions; David Hume was a constant guest, being then regarded by Parisian society as the apostle of liberty and free thought: Benjamin Franklin called on her during his first journey to Paris, but proved an embarrassing visitor, since at that date he was unable even to understand the French language. Although she had never been presented at Versailles, many visiting monarchs, such as King Gustav III of Sweden and the Emperor Joseph II of Austria, paid their respects to what came to be called "Le Royaume Saint-Honoré." She corresponded with the Empress Catherine of Russia as also with the Empress Maria Theresa of Austria. Her fame was worldwide.

She was said to possess a genius for friendship and she was lavish in providing her friends with useful presents. It is said that it was Madame Geoffrin who, during the dark days, kept the *Encyclopédie* going with a gift of 100,000 crowns. One of her favorite maxims was "to give is to forgive." On one occasion, deciding that the furniture in Diderot's attic was unworthy of so great a philosopher, she had it replaced by an entirely new set. Diderot was none too pleased at being thus forcibly smartened up. "It was in this way," he wrote, "that the edifying retreat of the philosopher was transformed into the scandalous study of a fermier-général. Thus I too was made to insult the poverty of my country." Horace Walpole, who belonged to the rival camp, disapproved both of her generosity and her bullying. "In short," he wrote, "she is the epitome of empire, subsisting by rewards and punishments." She certainly possessed a genius for protection, patronage, and intimacy. "One should never," she was fond of repeating, "let the grass grow between the paving stones of friendship."

Her kindness was limited only by a compelling strain of bourgeois caution. She dropped Marmontel the moment he got into trouble with the authorities and she refused to support Voltaire in his campaign against the Abbeville persecutions. "Whenever her good offices needed courage," wrote Marmontel, "she displayed an indolent timidity."

In fact the two greatest writers of the century, Voltaire and Montesquieu, did not often figure at her Wednesday parties. She regarded Voltaire as too witty, too outspoken, to be really safe. Moreover, he was an avowed friend of her rival, Madame du Deffand. Her relations with Montesquieu were clouded by the fact that he had one day brought the manuscript of the *Esprit des Lois* for her to read and she had not manifested the enthusiasm that he expected. Her remarks upon his masterpiece were vague and cold. Her horrid daughter, Madame de Ferté-Imbault, sneaked to Montesquieu and told him that her mother had laid the manuscript aside without reading it. He ceased from then onwards to frequent the house.

This episode is not characteristic of Madame Geoffrin. In the first place, although not an intellectual, she had a wonderful eye for value. In the second place she was a strictly truthful woman, who would not pretend to have read a manuscript which in fact she had casually laid aside. Her experience with the *Esprit des Lois* was unfortunate and out of character.

MADAME DU DEFFAND

engraving by Forshel after a portrait
by Louis Carrogis Carmontelle

It was in fact by her strength of will, rather than by any brilliance of conversation, that she created and retained what remains perhaps the most famous of all salons. She was a bossy, managing, woman, and she was wont to scold her friends atrociously. Yet, although she never for one instant relaxed her discipline, she was not intimidating to the young. She possessed that most rewarding of all social gifts, namely the capacity for making her guests feel that never before had they been in such dazzling form, that never before had their remarks been so gifted or impressive. She hated gossip and would snub loud talkers, such as Diderot, who was often apt to monopolize the conversation and even to bring his great fist down with a bang upon one of her frail little side tables. She was, however, kind to Diderot, would climb up the dark stairs to visit him in his attic, and would, unlike most of his lady visitors, be polite to his grumbling wife. But she discouraged his presence at her dinner parties, since his gestures were too violent and his tone too loud. In general, if any of her guests out stepped the limits of sober decency, she would check them with the calm words, "*Voilà qui est bien.*" "I think that's enough." As Sainte-Beuve wrote, her salon was the most "perfectly administered" of all French Salons.

Yet with all her conventionality she certainly became the mother of the *Encyclopédistes* and as such a potent factor in the progress of the Age of Reason. "I remember," wrote the Abbé Delille after her death, "that all Europe clustered round her chair."

> *Il m'en souvient, j'ai vu l'Europe entière*
> *D'un triple cercle entourant son fauteuil*
> *Guétter un mot, épier un coup d'œil.*

In 1766, she startled the civilized world by embarking on a visit to Poland. Until that date she had seldom moved from her own house and, as with so many eighteenth-century Parisians, her knowledge of France or Europe was confined to her own boudoir. But in her early days she had been a close friend of Stanislas Poniatowski, Count Palatine of Cracow, and when the son of this magnate, the irresistible Stanislas Augustus, visited Paris at the age of twenty he was recommended by his father to her charge. The relations between them became that of son and mother; he would call her *maman* and she would write to him as *mon fils*. "Tell me the truth," he once wrote to her, "the stark, stark truth. Then you will indeed be my good mamma whom I shall love all my life with all my heart." Thus when Stanislas became the paramour of Catherine II and was thereafter imposed by her upon the Polish diet as King Stanislas II, Madame Geoffrin became intoxicated at standing *in loco parentis* to a monarch, puppet monarch though he might be. Madame du Deffand and her circle were contemptuous of such unreasonable enthusiasm and sneered at her as "the Queen Mother of Poland." Her journey to Warsaw, which received wide publicity, was in the nature of a triumphal progress. She refused to travel via Berlin since she had a contempt for Frederick the Great. "In fifty years from now," she predicted with startling inaccuracy, "people will have forgotten all about him." So she preferred to travel via Vienna, where the Empress Maria Theresa received her with the most flattering attentions. "People," she wrote to Paris without diffidence, "were presented to me without end. They spoke of my great reputation and my great merit."

At Schönbrunn she was presented to the little Archduchess Marie Antoinette, whom she described as an adorable child of exquisite beauty and manners. After a month's journey she reached Warsaw on June 22, 1766, and was warmly welcomed by her "son" King Stanislas II. She remained there for three months. Her bossy nature, her inability to refrain from scolding her friends, led as the weeks passed to some chill in the romantic relations between the King of Poland and his "maman." She was rude to his proud uncles, the Czartoryskis, and she told him that the Empress Catherine's representative in Warsaw, the domineering Repnin, was in fact behaving as a Viceroy and was resolved to prevent any reforms that might arrest the internal decay of Poland and interrupt Russia's policy of a third and final partition. She told him, as is the habit of strong women when talking to weak men, that he was being deceived by his advisers and his family; that he was driving straight to the abyss; that the time had come for him to "assert himself"; and that she was saddened by the discovery that her idol was so yielding. Stanislas was wounded by the truth of these remarks. Madame Geoffrin, having had her full feed of scolding, returned to Paris in November 1766 where she resumed her rule over the *Encyclopédistes*. She died in October 1777.

Madame Geoffrin and Madame du Deffand were rivals and bitter enemies. The queen of the rue Saint-Honoré would refer to the queen of the rue Saint-Dominique as "that dangerous old animal." Madame du Deffand would deride the masculine appearance and conversational dominance of Madame Geoffrin by calling her *le Geoffrin* or *la caillette*, meaning thereby "the chatterbox." Each of them regarded it as an act of black treachery if any of their regular guests accepted an invitation from the rival establishment. Madame Geoffrin was acid in her comments on Madame du Deffand's senile infatuation for Horace Walpole. Madame du Deffand uttered many epigrams regarding the Warsaw expedition. Voltaire, Diderot, and Duclos amused themselves by blowing on the flames of this animosity. Hatred sparkled and spluttered.

At the age of twenty-two Marie de Vichy had married the marquis du Deffand from whom she separated after a few months. For a fortnight she became one of the Regents' transitory mistresses, but she was shocked by the orgies of the Palais Royal, and, as her eyesight was becoming increasingly feeble, she decided to become respectable. Her intimate friend was the President Hénault, president of the Paris parliament, and she was a loyal supporter of the duc de Choiseul even after he had fallen into disgrace. She was a leading anglo-maniac, visited Bolingbroke at his castle beside the Loire, and entertained Hume, Gibbon, Gray, George Selwyn and Chesterfield. Her sad infatuation for Horace Walpole which began when she was seventy and he fifty years of age will be referred to in my next chapter.

She became totally blind and had to rely on the help of her companion Julie de Lespinasse, her major domo Wiart, and her maid Madame Devereux. She would sit motionless in her *tonneau* or barrel chair, protected from draughts. Her horrid little dog, Tonton, which Walpole inherited, would bark and snap at her guests. Her chef could not be compared in skill or extravagance to the chef of Madame Geoffrin. She enjoyed small round table suppers of some twelve people. Her neck was thin and scrannel and she spoke in a whining accent through her nose.

Madame du Deffand's constant enemy, apart from Madame Geoffrin, was boredom. "For God's sake," she once wrote to Voltaire, "rescue me from my boredom. I can interest myself in nothing. Everything bores me to death—history, ethics, novels, and plays." She was a poor sleeper and, as Duclos remarked, she dreaded nothing so much as her bed. She described herself as *noctologophile* and would combat her sleeplessness by driving round Paris at the early hours of the morning, or keeping her guests awake till dawn discussing the nature of truth, beauty, and happiness. She was a cynical woman who prided herself much on her reason and self-discipline. It must have been torture to so proud a lady to fall head over heels in love with an elderly foreigner whom she had never seen with her eyes. Although she conformed to the external formulas of religion, she was in fact a freethinker. "What is faith?" she would ask. "It is to believe firmly in what one does not understand." There were moments even when she doubted friendship.

Above her suite in the Convent of the Filles Saint-Joseph in the rue Saint-Dominique there was a little flat reserved for her poor relation and paid companion, Julie de Lespinasse, the illegitimate daughter of her brother Gaspard de Vichy by the comtesse d'Albion. Her guests formed the habit of creeping upstairs to visit Julie before descending to have supper with the blind old lady downstairs. When Madame du Deffand discovered this act of treachery, and when she realized that Julie had fallen in love with d'Alembert, she turned her niece out of the house. Julie de Lespinasse and d'Alembert then held their own salon in the rue de Bellechasse, which, much to Madame du Deffand's fury, was frequented by many of the younger generation, Condorcet, Turgot, Suard, Chastellux and Shelburne. The embarrassment of Horace Walpole, his dread that his friends might make mock of this infatuation, together with the desertion and success of Julie de Lespinasse, cast a shadow over the declining years of Madame du

Deffand. It is customary to admire her as a wonderful letter writer and an ill-used woman. I suspect that, owing to inherent skepticism, she brought most of her unhappiness on herself. She was tortured by the conflict between a longing to find truth and a conviction that all was false. But one cannot but feel compassion for a blind old woman riveted to a high armchair, and in love with a gouty Englishman of advanced middle age, who was anything but a sentimentalist and was adept at evasion.

Although Madame du Deffand had her imitators, her rivals and her successors, the true eighteenth-century salon, as a school of manners rather than as a place of entertainment, did not survive her death in 1780. There was the duchesse de Choiseul, wife of the Foreign Minister, who, even after her husband's dismissal in 1770, entertained lavishly at the Château de Chanteloup. She was much beloved. Horace Walpole called her "the sweetest, most agreeable and most sincere little creature that ever hatched from a fairy's egg." "I wish she wasn't a saint," said Madame du Deffand, "I should have preferred her to be a woman." There was the maréchale de Luxembourg who set the tone of good behavior and social etiquette, and who was kind to Rousseau when his other friends had abandoned him as a maniac. There was baron Holbach, who preached the supremacy of reason and the doctrine of "natural" morality. He was the friend of the philosopher Helvétius and formed what Rousseau in his rage would denounce as "la côterie holbachique." And finally there was plump, virtuous, Madame Necker, the Swiss pastor's daughter, the rejected bride of Gibbon, and the mother of Madame de Stael. Madame Necker did not strive to compete, either with Madame Geoffrin, or with Madame du Deffand; in fact she toadied them atrociously. Madame Geoffrin did not like being toadied by Swiss women. She scolded the former Suzanne Curchod for her "uneasy, restless and at the same time weak character." One of Madame Necker's more gushing letters elicited the following cooling reply: "My dear friend," wrote Madame Geoffrin, "I beg you to lessen your excessive admiration." In her hôtel in the rue de Cléry Madame Necker entertained some of the *Encyclopédistes* and, in the manner of Madame Verdurin, she called her salon "Le Sanctuaire." She was strictly religious and once burst into tears in the middle of dinner when some of her guests indulged in deistic talk. When asked how it came that so devout a woman should be intimate with non-believers, she replied, "Yes, I have some atheistic friends, and why not? They are my unhappy friends." She had a phobia about being buried alive; to this day her corpse, clad in full court dress, can be seen bobbing in a tank of spirits-of-wine in the vault at Coppet.

The tradition of the salon still lingers on in Paris. Men of letters still frequent the boudoirs of rich and beautiful hostesses; and they still love to talk.

Chapter 13
Dilettante
(Horace Walpole, 1717–1797)

———— • ◆ • ————

Macaulay's contempt for—Not a clubbable man—His epicureanism—Not a jingo—Modest and unpretentious—Flippant—His
writings—His views on art—And literature—His insatiable curiosity—His distrust of religious enthusiasm—His pride and integrity—His kindness—His early life—The Grand Tour-Quarrel with
Thomas Gray—His reconciliation with his father—His sinecures—
His Parliamentary career—His love of lobbying—His sincere and
consistent Liberalism—His belief in democracy—His hatred of
arbitrary rule—His pacifism—His loathing of the Slave Trade—
The limits of his Liberalism—His retirement from politics—Strawberry Hill—His visits to Paris—His views on French manners and
character—Madame du Deffand—Tonton—His correspondence
and the art of letter writing—His old age—The Misses Berry—His
death.

One

IT WAS MACAULAY, I suspect, who, by saying that he possessed
an "unhealthy and disorganized mind," rendered fashionable the
idea that Horace Walpole was not a person to be taken seriously.
I feel, on the contrary, that he should be studied and admired as one
of the most gifted, lovable, typical, prophetic outspoken and original
of eighteenth century characters.

We can understand, of course, why he should have been disliked and derided by the London clubmen of the period. He did not conform to their standards, nor did he share their tastes and vices. Dominant groups who have established their own type of behavior are always, as are colonies of rooks, intolerant of those who differ from the norm. Horace Walpole was an intellectual and thus, as an Englishman, belonged to a minority which is always suspect. He did not drink; he did not gamble; he did not keep mistresses. There was something virginal about him, which irritated the members of Brooks' as much as it irritated the members of White's: he was not a clubbable man. He did not care for women and at the age of twenty-four he indulged in the cynical observation that "it is always bad to marry, but to marry where one loves is ten times worse." Lady Townshend, whose epigrams circulated quickly round the town, asserted that Horace Walpole had never desired to kiss anything except once a tiger at the zoo. There was about him an epicene streak that grated upon male nerves. "I have," he wrote, when scarcely more than an adolescent, "the prettiest warm little apartment with all my baubles and Patapans and cats." That was not the sort of remark expected from the descendant of a long line of Norfolk squires. He had no taste for sport and took no pains to conceal his dislike for shooting and hunting or his contempt for those who engaged in such rough pastimes. "Exercise," he wrote, "is the worst thing in the world and as bad an invention as gunpowder." That was an un-English thing to say. He was a bad mixer and, not without some justification, was regarded as a snob. He himself would have defended his exclusive habits as proofs of social fastidiousness. "You know," he once wrote to a friend, "that I don't throw my liking about in the street." His epicureanism was so habitual that it was often taken to be extreme selfishness or even moral cowardice. "I am certainly," he wrote to his beloved cousin, Field Marshal Conway, "the greatest philosopher in the world without ever having thought of being so. Always employed and never busy: eager about trifles and indifferent to everything serious. Well, if that is not philosophy, then at least it is content." "There is," he wrote

HORACE WALPOLE

Horatio ('Horace') Walpole, 4th Earl of Orford.
Oil on canvas, 1754 by John Giles Eccardt

STRAWBERRY HILL

to Gray's biographer William Mason, "a serenity in having nothing to do that is delicious. I am persuaded that little Princes assume the title of Serene Highness from that sensation." He was so little of a jingo, so little of an imperialist, that his contemporaries often regarded him as unpatriotic. He did not adopt the motto of "my country, right or wrong"; he desired ardently that his country should be right. In later middle age, it is true, after he had spent several months in France, he did develop his own brand of patriotism. "Paris," he wrote in 1769, "revived in me that natural passion, the love of my country's glory. I must put it out: it is a wicked passion and breathes war." "A good patriot," he announced, "is a bad citizen." "I wish well to my country," he wrote at the time of the American War, "But I wish too that my countrymen deserved my wishes a little better."

I have already indicated how strongly he regretted the Government attitude towards the thirteen Colonies and how ardently he espoused the cause of American independence. He was in fact a cosmopolitan. "I feel myself," he once wrote, "more an universal man than an Englishman... I pray that we have done with glory. I had rather be a worm than a vulture... a single life spared were worth Peru and Mexico." Such pacifist, such anti-imperialist remarks, were repeated and much resented. Even Wordsworth could sneer at such sentiments as being those of "that cold and falsehearted Frenchified coxcomb, Horace Walpole."

He was utterly indifferent to the animosity he aroused. He made fun of everything. Field Marshal Conway, his most intimate friend, who possessed no sense of humor whatsoever, was often worried by his flippancy. "Conway," wrote Walpole, "says I laugh at all serious characters—so I do—and at myself too, who am far from being of the number. My mind is of no gloomy turn and I have a thousand ways of amusing myself. . . . It is a rule with me to avoid any disagreeable object or idea; I know I have always been a coward on points of religion and politics."

A further circumstance that sundered him from his kind was that he was bored by public life and did not hesitate to say so. "My books," he wrote, "my vertu, and my other follies and amusements take up too much of my time to leave me much leisure to think of other people's affairs; and of all affairs, those of the public are least of my concern."

He was an unpretentious man and cultivated the most un-eighteenth-century quality of modesty. Although vain and proud, he was not conceited. "I have," he wrote, "at least so little of the author in me as to be very corrigible. . . . Nothing can be more superficial than my knowledge or more trifling than my reading . . . I have no dignity." He was embarrassed when people paid him compliments. "I wonder," he once wrote to Lady Upper Ossory, "how a real genius supports the compliments he must meet with: I know that when they tumble down to my sphere they make me sweat." When one admirer spoke of his "extensive learning" he remarked that such adulation always "makes me laugh—no mortal's reading has been more superficial."

He never took any pains to disguise his own flippancy, since he regarded prudence as "a musty quality." On one occasion he appeared at a dinner party at Lord Blandford's with a garland of sweet pea on his head. He once received his guests wearing a wooden cravat carved by Grinling Gibbons and a large pair of spectacles that had once belonged to James II. He took much pleasure in what he called his "youthfullity."

It is not surprising that his contemporaries failed to take him seriously. Writing to George Montagu on August 20, 1758, he gives an excellent description of the perplexity he aroused in The Reverend Thomas Seward, Canon of Lichfield, and father of Anna Seward, when he met him staying in Conway's country house at Ragley:

> You cannot imagine how astonished a Mr. Seward, a learned clergyman, was, who came to Ragley while I was there. Strolling about the house, he saw me first sitting on the pavement of the lumber room, with Louise, all over cobwebs and dirt and mortar; then he found me in his own room on a ladder, writing on a picture, then half an hour afterwards lying on the grass in the courtyard with the dogs and the children in my slippers and without a hat. He had had some doubt whether I was a painter or a factotum of

the family; but you would have died at his surprise when
he saw me walk into dinner dressed and sit by Lady Hertford. Lord Lyttelton was there and the conversation turned
on literature—finding me not quite ignorant added to the
parson's wonder, but he could not contain himself any longer when he saw me go to romps and jumping with the two
boys—he broke out to my Lady Hertford to know who
and what sort of man I really was, for he had never met
with anything of the kind.

Two

It would be an error nonetheless to dismiss Horace Walpole as a
trivial or contemptible figure. He was anything but that. His *Cata-
logue of Royal and Noble Authors* and above all his *Anecdotes of Painting in England* are scholarly works that have retained their value. His
Castle of Otranto was immensely popular and exercised a wide influence. His voluminous letters are perhaps the most informative and
amusing of any in the language. His house at Strawberry Hill was anything but the gimcrack folly that it is sometimes represented, but was,
and still remains, an architectural experiment of great importance.
His *Essay on Modern Gardening*, in which he extolled the landscape
school of Kent and Brown, did much to spread the taste for "natural" gardening throughout England and the Continent. Although he
failed to see the beauty of the formal garden, such as that of Wrest,
and although he derided the French for their admirable artistry in
pleaching trees, he had the sense to realize that Kent sometimes went
too far in "sticking a dozen trees here and there, till a lawn looks like
the ten of spades." His historical works, although often colored by
personal prejudice, provide many vivid sidelights on the reigns of
George II and George III.

It was all very well for Macaulay to sneer at his "jackdaw" antiquari-
anism, but he really did much to revive interest in Gothic architecture
and to protect ancient buildings from vandalism. As an art critic, he

was perhaps not very reliable or original, since, while he worshipped Guido Reni and Caracci, he could not find a good word to say for the Dutch painters. He calls them "those drudging mimics of Nature's most uncomely coarseness." He never seems to have recognized the beauty of contemporary architecture, furniture, and decoration. He failed properly to appreciate either Gainsborough or Reynolds. He sneered at Adam's "gingerbread and snippets" and contended that the "filigraine and fan painting and harlequinades" of Robert Adam "never let the eye repose for a moment." He had no ear at all for music. His literary judgments were unprincipled and often perverse. He dismissed Dante as "extravagant, absurd, disgusting: in short a Methodist parson in Bedlam." He referred to Milton's "barbarous prose." He contended that the epic was unsuited to "an improved and polished state of things." He enjoyed the *Sentimental Journey* but found *Tristram Shandy* boring. To him Swift was "a wild beast who baited and worried all mankind almost, because his intolerable arrogance, pride and ambition were disappointed." He was horrified when in Paris to find that the French took Richardson so seriously. He himself considered that the novels were little more than "deplorably tedious lamentations" and that *Clarissa Harlowe* and *Sir Charles Grandison* were "pictures of high life as conceived by a bookseller and romances as they would be spiritualized by a Methodist teacher." He failed, owing perhaps to his loyalty for Gray, to recognize the genius and strength of Dr. Johnson. "With a lumber of learning and some strong parts," he wrote, "Johnson was an odious and mean character. With all the pedantry, he had all the gigantic littleness of a country school master." He accuses him of possessing "no more ear than taste," he denounced his style as "fustian," and calls him "a babbling old woman who had read the classics with no other view than to pilfer polysyllables." "How little," he wrote in 1785, "will Johnson be remembered when confounded by the mass of authors of his own caliber." "The more," he writes, "one learns of Johnson the more preposterous an assemblage he appears of strong sense, of the lowest bigotry and prejudices, of pride, of brutality, fretfulness, and vanity: and Boswell is the ape of his faults without a grain of his sense." He failed to observe the charm of Boswell, calling him "that sot Boswell" and dismissing his biography as "the story of a mountebank and his zany." He admitted Johnson's deep human charity but concluded that he was "an ill-natured bear and in opinions as senseless a bigot as an old washerwoman."

Such remarks do not fortify our confidence in Walpole's literary discrimination. But at least he was never taken in by Ossian or by Chatterton and he did realize that "the labored eloquence" of Rousseau would be "sublime if it were not affected frenzy or worse."

I have quoted sufficient to indicate the quality of Walpole's sprightliness and wit. He also possessed many solid intellectual and moral virtues. He was scholarly and industrious and had a contempt for untidy workmanship. His taste, although both uncertain and finical, was often first class, as is witnessed by the long gallery at Strawberry Hill which is in truth a beautiful as well as an ingenious cloister. He possessed that most valuable talent, an absolutely insatiable curiosity about people and things. In writing to Horace Mann on October 28, 1752, he excused himself for retailing frivolous gossip. "I don't know," he writes "whether you will not think all these very trifling histories: but for myself I love anything that marks a character strongly." This certainly is a preoccupation more significant than any love of idle gossip and illustrates Walpole's unflagging preoccupation with human personality. Unlike most of his contemporaries, he did not group his acquaintances into castes or types: what he relished were the differences between individuals and their eccentricities and quirks.

He was not a religious man and cared little for theological disputes. He hated enthusiasm and what he called "the old exploded cant of mystical devotion." He regarded with apprehension the early symptoms of revivalism. "This nonsensical *new light*," he wrote in 1748, "is extremely in fashion and I shall not be surprised if we see a revival of all the folly and cant of the last age. Whitefield preaches continually at my Lady Huntingdon's at Chelsea." In October 1766 he went to hear Wesley preach at Bath. He describes him as "a lean, elderly man, fresh-colored, his hair smoothly combed but with a soupçon of a curl at the end. Wondrous clean, but as evidently an actor as Garrick. He gabbled the early part of his sermon as though he knew it by heart, but towards the end he exalted his voice and acted very ugly enthusiasm."

He would, in the fashion of the time, have described himself a Deist. Writing to Horace Mann in 1779, he expressed his faith "in the ordinance and preservation of the great universal system, which compels us to believe in a Divine Artificer, although our intellects are too bounded to comprehend anything more." To William Mason he confesses to "the adoration and gratitude we owe to the Author of all good." These are vague statements. I doubt whether Walpole ever allowed his epicurean calm to be disturbed by thoughts of original sin, or of justification by works.

He certainly believed in virtue and hated corruption and vice. He was a man of great personal integrity, as was shown when he strove, in circumstances of difficulty and embarrassment, to administer the affairs of his nephew, Lord Orford, who was certifiably insane. Although, moreover, it never occurred to him that there was anything wrong in receiving from the State a large income out of the sinecures which his father had obtained for him, he did feel that it was his duty to see that the functions of these otiose offices should be honestly performed. He claimed that in the administration of his sinecures he had "never swerved from right, justice and the duty I owe to the public as a servant of the Government. I have held the place now above thirty years . . . but my conduct of it has been untainted." He saw to it that his deputy and the staff did not profit by their opportunities for peculation. "I will not," he wrote, "traffic for the favor of clerks by winking at their corruption." "Mankind," he proclaimed, "will not remember that honesty cannot be detected . . . I lived with a contempt for hypocrisy."

He was a proud man and would never stoop to mean practices. "I believe," he wrote in 1793, "that I have more pride than most men alive." "The possession," he wrote to Horace Mann, "of one vice—Pride—and the want of two more—Ambition and Self Interest—have preserved me from many faults." He was fundamentally a sincere man, who loved truth and hated falsehood. He urged Mason to make it clear in his biography of Gray that their famous quarrel when travel-ing in Italy together was due not to any fault on Gray's part, but to his own "presumption and folly." "I have no affectation," he wrote to Conway in 1766. "Affectation is a monster at nine and forty." Although he was a touchy man and quarreled with many of his old friends, such as George Montagu, Thomas Ashton, Mason and Bentley, he believed till the end of his life in the sanctity of friendship. "When I love any-body," he wrote, "it is for life." He held the view that all friendships should be disinterested. "It is ridiculous," he wrote, "to profit of one's friends when one does not make friendships with that view." When Conway, to whom he remained unswervingly loyal, although he was a pompous man and a bore, lost his office, Horace Walpole offered to give him £6000 of his own money. Although he and Horace Mann never met again since they had known each other in Florence in 1739, he kept up a regular correspondence with him for forty-five years, although as the century passed they had ceased to share any friends or interests. "Sir Horace and I," he wrote after forty years of almost weekly letters, "have no acquaintance in common but the Kings and Queens of Europe."

Although not a sentimental man, and although not wholly devoid of malice, Horace Walpole was essentially kind. He was deeply dis-tressed by the wholly unjustified accusation that he had allowed Chat-terton to die in his garret, knowing well that, had he known the true circumstances of this forger's penury, he would have been generous in his assistance. He described himself as "strongly tinctured with tender-ness." He was bitterly opposed to the execution of Admiral Byng and even manifested some compassion for Lord Ferrers, who in 1760 was hanged at Tyburn Tree for the murder of his steward, John Johnson. He was in fact incapable of moral indignation against the unfortunate. "I can't feel angry," he wrote, "when I see people unhappy." He detested any form of cruelty to animals. He loved dogs: "the dear, good-natured, honest, sensible creatures. Christ! How can anyone hurt them?"

Macaulay, with his abominable earnestness, entirely failed to appre-ciate Walpole's most attractive virtues.

Three

Horace Walpole was the youngest son of Sir Robert Walpole, the adroit statesman, who steered England through the difficult period of the Hanoverian succession, and who managed, by methods which have not met with the unanimous applause of historians, to remain in power for twenty-one years, to restore the finances of the country which had been shaken by the South Sea Bubble, and to preserve peace. Horace Walpole was born at No. 17 Arlington Street, London, on September 24, 1717. He was the fourth son of the Prime Minister and was eleven years younger than his father's other children. This gap in dates, coupled with the known bad relations between his parents at the time, and the fact that both physically and intellectually he was totally different from the Walpole family, arouses the suspicion that he was not in fact his father's son but the illegitimate offspring of Lord Hervey, elder brother of Pope's "sporus." As a boy, he was never able to establish easy relations with his father. "It was never," he confessed later, "my foible to think over-abundantly well of him." He resented the old man's neglect of his beloved mother and his overt flaunting of a liaison with Miss Skerret. Moreover, the Prime Minister was by temperament a deep drinking, rough riding, Norfolk squire, whereas Horace had no taste for field sports and was bored by the local gentry whom the Prime Minister loved to entertain. "I used," he wrote in later years, "to be tired to death of the conversation of the price of oats and barley." It is not to be expected that as a boy Horace was able to conceal his boredom: he was doubtless much disliked and derided by the Norfolk neighbors.

On his return, however, from the Grand Tour, he realized that Houghton was one of the most beautiful houses in England and that his father had collected a gallery of pictures second to none. Always he retained a passion for the pictures at Houghton and it was a deep sorrow to him when his lunatic nephew sold the lot to the Empress Catherine, on the walls of whose Hermitage they still resplendently hang. Sir Robert, for his part, suddenly discovered that his epicene son was in fact a most entertaining companion and in the four last years of the old man's life their relations became intimate and affectionate.

In middle age Horace developed a passionate admiration for his father and the deepest loyalty to his memory. He revered him as "a model of wisdom and imperturbability" and pronounced that he had ever been "as incapable of fear as of doing wrong." He acquired a burning animosity against all those who had plotted his father's downfall and it is this fierce prejudice which diminishes his value as a historian. Writing to his nephew in 1778 he could remind him of "that excellent man, the glory of human nature, who made us what we are." "My father," he wrote in 1779 to Horace Mann, "is ever before my eyes—not to attempt to imitate him, for I have none of his matchless wisdom, or unsullied virtues, or heroic firmness; but sixty-two years have taught me to gaze at him with ten thousand times the reverence that—I speak it with deep shame—I felt for him at twenty-two when he stood before me."

However much Horace might laud his father's integrity, the fact remained that the Prime Minister, when in power, took pains to see that all his sons were provided with lucrative sinecures. The eldest was appointed Auditor of the Exchequer with a salary of £7,000 a year; the second son became Clerk of the Pells at £3,000 a year. Horace himself was granted the sinecures of Controller of the Pipe, Clerk of the Estreats, and Usher of the Exchequer, amounting to an annual salary of £3,400 a year. It is estimated that at the date of Sir Robert's death his sons were receiving as much as £14,000 a year from public funds and that Horace in the course of his own life drew a total of some £250,000 for doing nothing at all. Such work as there was he left to a deputy who received a minimum salary. He may have been justified in claiming that he saw to it that his deputy was efficient and that no peculation was allowed. At his death, Horace Walpole, apart from his estate at Strawberry Hill, his art collections, and his house in Berkeley Square, left £91,000 in the funds.

At Eton, where he was perfectly happy, he established what he called his "triumvirate" of three friends, himself, Lyttelton and Montagu.

This was later expanded into the "Quadruple Alliance" consisting of Thomas Gray, Ashton, and Richard West. His career at King's College Cambridge was intermittent and undistinguished. Although quite a good classic, he was never able to master even the rudiments of mathematics. "I could remember," he wrote, "who was King Ethelbald's great-aunt, and not be sure whether she lived in the year 500 or 1500." On leaving the University in 1739 he embarked with Thomas Gray on the Grand Tour, being absent from England for two and a half years.

They went from Dover to Paris and thereafter spent some months at Rheims, improving their schoolboy acquaintance with the French language. Then on they journeyed to Dijon, Lyons, and Geneva, visiting the Grande Chartreuse on the way, which made such an impression on Gray that he returned there two years later and composed an ode in its honor. After a short visit to Rome and Naples, they settled in Florence early in 1740 and remained there for fifteen months. For much of their time they lived in the Villa Ambrosio on the Arno as the guests of the British Chargé d'Affaires at the court of Tuscany, Sir Horace Mann. Walpole became so intimate with this expatriate that he corresponded with him for the next forty-five years. Thomas Gray found him a bore; it may well have been this divergence of opinion that constituted the first rift in their companionship. They had already spent some twenty-six months together in the stark propinquity entailed by eighteenth-century travel. Their private possessions and habits—their sponge bags, the way they coughed or laughed, Gray's maddening trick of extending his little finger daintily when he drank a cup of coffee, Walpole's dry giggle—all these personal details had begun to grate on their nerves. Each of them was proud, sensitive, and irritable. But there were in addition to this common inability of two intelligent young men to travel uninterruptedly and equably in each other's eternal company for year after year, certain special circumstances which increased the strain between them. Walpole, being by far the richer of the two, financed the whole expedition, thus placing Gray in a position of inferiority which irked his proud soul. Walpole was the son of the still all-powerful Prime Minister and was thus lavishly flattered and entertained by the local magnates and by British representatives abroad. Gray must often have been regarded as no more than a salaried bearleader and thus frequently ignored. Moreover, whereas Gray was a thorough scholar, who insisted upon visiting every ancient monument and in copying down long Latin inscriptions, Walpole was in comparison a dilettante who was rather bored by serious archaeology, who much enjoyed Florentine society and gossip and who would always don his pink silk waistcoat embroidered with Chinese pagodas and sit up until dawn enjoying the ridottis and conversazioni of the town. It was in the course of their return journey, in May 1741, at Reggio dell' Emilia, between Parma and Modena that they each succumbed to desperation and parted in rage. Gray found his own way home, whereas Walpole, after spending a few weeks in Venice, reached Dover alone in September 1741, having been absent from England for two and a half years. It says much for the generosity of Horace Walpole's character that in later years he took the whole blame for this quarrel upon himself, admitting that he had behaved to his traveling companion with "presumption," tactlessness and conceit. In 1746, the quarrel was mended; Walpole again entered into regular correspondence with his old friend of Eton days; he developed a deep reverence for Gray's scholarship and poetry and became one of his most ardent champions. One reason, for instance, why Walpole felt such animosity against Johnson, was because the Doctor failed, in his opinion, to recognize the high merit of Gray's odes. They remained close friends until Gray's death.

During his absence abroad, Walpole had been returned to Parliament as member for Callington in Cornwall, a seat which he later exchanged, first for the family seat of Castle Rising in Norfolk, and eventually for that of King's Lynn. He only once visited his constituency and only once spoke in Parliament, when he opposed the motion to set up a Committee of Enquiry into the last twenty years of Sir Robert Walpole's administration. On this occasion, as was generally agreed, he spoke with dignity and filial piety. But he was too shy and diffident ever to become an impressive House of Commons man.

It would be a mistake nonetheless to assume that Walpole was a wholly inactive Member of the House of Commons. In order to compensate for his failure as a politician, he often pretended that he had remained aloof from the heat and dust of the struggle. He described himself as "an obscure passenger." "Ambition blushes," he wrote, "but I never had any. . . I was born at the top of the world; I have long been nobody and am charmed to be so." "Disinterestedness," he wrote to Montagu in November 1756, "is no merit to me: it happens to be my passion. . . I abhor Courts and levee rooms and flattery; I have done with all parties and only sit by and smile." He described himself as "a person who loves to write history better than to act in it."

He liked to pretend that he was bitterly opposed to party faction and to the corruption of politics. "There is so much faction," he wrote in February 1767, "and so little character and abilities in the country." Writing of the Pelham system in 1754, and ignoring the methods pursued with such cynicism by his father, or the fact that his own income was derived from sinecures, he could exclaim in righteous indignation "there never was such established bribery or so profuse." He sneers at Lord Montford, who in 1755, "asked immediately for the government of Virginia and the Foxhounds." "Parliament opens," he wrote in December 1762, "everybody is bribed, and the new establishment is perceived to be composed of adamant." He was shocked by the manner in which Members of Parliament gambled on the Stock Exchange. "From Change Alley to the House," he wrote in 1767, "it is like a path of ants."

All this sounds noble, but in fact Walpole was not as aloof as he wished his contemporaries and posterity to believe. He clung desperately to his own sinecures and was almost distraught when Ministers threatened to transfer them to some more obedient party member, or when the Treasury were unpunctual in their payments. He was hurt when Conway, on becoming Secretary of State, failed to reward him for his friendship and services. He had a natural gift for intrigue and thoroughly enjoyed lobbying. He played an active part in the transaction that led to the fall of Newcastle in 1756 and to the temporary conciliation between Pitt and Fox. So far from being aloof, he was accused by his enemies of displaying "an ardor for factious intrigues." The Duke of Grafton in his *Memoirs* records that nobody was such an expert on lobby gossip as Horace Walpole. Lord Holland, who was no amateur politician, regarded Walpole as so potent a backstairs influence that, in the hope of securing an earldom, he asked him to intercede with the Duke of Grafton on his behalf. He displayed great energy in seeking to undermine the position of those whom he believed to have secured his father's downfall. The Duke of Newcastle, although he always treated Walpole with charming courtesy, was for him "that old heathen" or "that old wretch." In any case Horace Walpole, who had an independent mind and was sincere in his convictions, was not of the material of which sound party men are made. He was so indignant when in 1767 his friend and cousin Marshal Conway was edged out of office by the intrigues of Rigby and Lord Sandwich that he resigned his seat and quitted the House of Commons forever.

He pretended of course to be delighted at having severed all connection with political life. "I was born in it: I am overjoyed to quit it and shall be indifferent to what happens to the business . . . I shall live and die in my old-fashioned Whiggism . . . Moderation, privacy and quiet sum up all my future views." In Volume II of his *Memoirs of the Reign of George II* he inserted a frank and revealing portrait of himself as a politician:

> Without the least tincture of ambition, he had a propensity to faction and looked on the mischief of civil disturbance as a lively amusement. Indignation at the persecution contracted by himself, conspired with his natural impetuosity of temper to nourish this passion. But, coming into the world when the world was growing weary of faction, and some of the objects dying or being removed against whom his warmth had been principally directed, maturity of reason and sparks of virtue extinguished this culpable ardor.

This, written in the seemingly objective form of a third-person narrative, is a revealing description of his attitude towards Parliament.

Four

The Whiggism of which he boasted was not in fact so old fashioned; in his progressive ideas he was well in advance of his class and age. He believed that the true source of power should be ultimately "in the hearts of the people." "It is amazing," he wrote to Horace Mann in April 1769, "that men do not prefer the safe, honorable, and amiable method of governing the people as they like to be governed to the invidious and restless task of governing them contrary to their inclinations." He believed ardently in the freedom of the Press and of speech. "Liberty of speech and Liberty of writing," he contended, "are the two instruments by which Englishmen call on one another to defend their common rights." "Whig principles," he wrote, "are founded on sense: a Whig may be a fool, a Tory must be so." He disliked privilege and when his friend Conway became commander in chief he begged him to "be strict in doing justice, as I think nothing so cruel as to have boys by favor put over old officers." He was hostile to Court influence, would refer to "the childish mind" of George III, and, at least until his niece married the Duke of Gloucester, the King's brother, he would sneer at the royal family as "messieurs les allemands." "My reflections led me early," he wrote in his *Memoirs of the Reign of George II*, "towards, I cannot say Republicanism, but to the most limited monarchy." "I have," he wrote to Lady Ossory in 1782, "been called a republican. I never was quite that, as no man was ever quite of any of the denominations laid down in books. But, if never republican quite, I never approached in thought, wish, inclination or reason towards a partisan of the aristocracy." As we have seen, he was strongly in favor of the thirteen Colonies in their disputes with the mother country and ardently desired that America should acquire her freedom. He was a decided anti-imperialist even in the East. "Who but Machiavel," he wrote in 1786, "can pretend that we have a shadow of a title to a foot of land in India?" He was a natural pacifist, did not believe in military glory, although very sensitive to military disgrace, and would never have approved of the hydrogen bomb. When the Montgolfier brothers made their first ascent in a balloon, Walpole foresaw immediately the menace of future aerial warfare "when balloons will be substituted for ships, our dockyards dismantled, and Salisbury Heath created into a dockyard of aerial vessels." "I hope," he wrote in 1783, "these new mechanic meteors will prove only playthings for the learned or the idle and not be converted into engines of destruction to the human race, as is so often the case of refinements or discoveries in science."

He had a horror of the Slave Trade which he regarded as a reproach to Parliament and to the Age of Reason. "We have been sitting," he wrote indignantly on February 25, 1750, "this fortnight on the African Company. We, the British Senate, that temple of liberty and bulwark of protestant Christianity, have, this fortnight, been considering methods to make more effectual that horrid selling of Negros. It has appeared to us that six and forty thousand of these wretches are sold every year to our plantations alone! It chills one's blood. I would not have to say I voted for it for the Continent of America." Such a view, expressed courageously nine years before William Wilberforce was even born, demonstrates the enlightenment of Walpole's vision and the moral courage of which he was possessed.

Yet, as with all reformers of the eighteenth century, there were limits to his Liberalism. He was opposed to any reform of our antiquated electoral system, which he feared would amount to "rashness of innovation." He spoke of Catholic emancipation as "that preposterous idea" and expressed the curious view that "Papists and Liberty are contradictions." He was horrified by the excesses of the French Revolution, much admired Edmund Burke's *Reflections on the French Revolution*, and was distressed that the doctrines of good Whigs should have been so degraded by their imitators. "I am angry," he wrote, "that the cause of liberty is profaned by such fools and rascals."

Five

On his retirement from politics, Walpole devoted his busy energy to his correspondence, his antiquarian research, the printing press which he established at Twickenham, his theories regarding the art of gardening, his historical essays, heraldry, and the planning, enlargement and decoration of Strawberry Hill.

As a young man he had been wholly urban and had had no taste at all for the delights of nature. "I am growing miserable," he wrote in April 1742, "for it is growing fine weather—that is everybody is going out of town." "At twenty," he wrote, "I loved nothing but London. I used to think no trees beautiful without lamps to them, like those at Vauxhall." But when he settled on the banks of the Thames he became "pastoral": he loved his lawns and his lilac; he even became interested in hay and cows. It was in 1747 that he bought his farm at Twickenham and by 1750 he decided that "I am going to build a little Gothic castle at Strawberry Hill." By 1755 he was becoming devoted to his home. "That sweet little spot," he called it, "little enough, but very sweet." By 1771 he was writing to Mann, "This little villa is growing into a superb castle. We have dropped all humility in our style." He laid out the garden with its sweeping lawn and the vistas down to the river and up to Richmond Hill beyond. "The deliberation," he complained, "with which trees grow is extremely inconvenient to my natural impatience." As the years passed he added with the aid of Bentley, room after room—a refectory, a library, a picture gallery, a cloister, a round tower and "lean windows fattened with rich saints." He rejoiced in "the air and enchantment of fairyism which is the tone of the place." When Madame de Boufflers remarked that Strawberry Hill was not *digne de la solidité anglaise*," he laughed for a quarter of an hour. But he had no illusions as to the eccentric quality of Strawberry Hill. "My buildings," he wrote, "are paper like my writings and both will be blown away in ten years after I am dead." "Every true Goth," he admits, "would perceive that it is more the work of fancy than of imitation." He had no liking for Tudor brickwork and described St. James's Palace as "that little tottering ruined palace in St. James's Street." He realized that the Palladian style was ill suited for small residences and that columns and statues looked absurd "when crowded into a closet or a cheesecake house." "I am almost as fond of the Sharawaggi or Chinese want of symmetry, in buildings as in grounds and gardens": Macaulay, who possessed no natural taste, denounced Strawberry Hill as a "grotesque house with piecrust battlements." It is much more interesting than that.

He paid several visits to Paris, in 1765, in 1767 and in 1771. At first he was inconvenienced by his inability to speak French fluently, and he never became absolutely at ease in the language. "Madame du Deffand has told me," he wrote during his second visit, "that I speak French worse than any Englishman she knows." So far from becoming "Frenchified" as Wordsworth grumbled, he looked upon the glory of France with a most critical eye. He was received at Versailles and found Louis XV "much handsomer than his pictures" and with "great sweetness in his countenance, instead of the farouche look that the portraits gives him." He dismissed the Dauphin, later to become the tragic Louis XVI, as "an imbecile both in mind and body." Of Marie Antoinette he wrote, "she is a statue of beauty when standing or sitting: grace itself when she moves."

His remarks upon French society and the French character are startling in their originality. He found them all "very stiff and solemn and as lacking in vivacity as the Germans." "Laughter," he wrote, "is as much out of fashion as pantins and bilboquets. Good folks, they have no time to laugh. There is God and the King to be pulled down first, and men and women, one and all, are devoutly employed in the demolition." He was shocked by the dirtiness of their houses and the bad manners that prevailed. He disliked their intellectual conventionality. "The French," he wrote, "have seldom eyes for anything that they have not been used to all their lives. . . . If something foreign arrives in Paris, they either think they have invented it or that it has always been there." He did not care for the *Encyclopédistes*, partly because they seemed intent on destruction only, and partly because "they are so overbearing and so underbred. . . . They are ten times more foolish since they took to thinking."

He first met Madame du Deffand on October 1765, when he was forty-eight years old, and when she was verging on seventy and was totally blind. He described her as "feeling in herself no difference between the spirits of twenty-three and seventy-three." He was much embarrassed by Madame du Deffand's infatuation for him. He was always begging her to be more discreet in her letters, since he knew they were opened, read and circulated both by the French and English police. "I am not at all," he wrote to Crauford, "of Madame du Deffand's opinion that one might as well be dead as not to love somebody, I think one had better be dead than love anybody." But she became for him "my dear old woman" and when she died in September 1780 she left him all her papers and her snappy little dog Tonton. When he heard she was dying, he wrote to his cousin Thomas Walpole, who was then in Paris, "I entreat you to tell her, how much I love her, and how much I feel." Walpole never obtained possession of the papers she had left him, since her executors refused to deliver them. But Tonton was shipped to England and survived, petted by Walpole, but loathed by his household and his guests, for another nine years.

After Byron he certainly can rank as the most gifted of English letter-writers. He was perfectly conscious that his letters would provide him with posthumous fame; he chose his correspondents carefully as mirrors of his varied interests; and he would insist on their returning his letters to him in batches, so as to enable him to annotate and polish them for eventual publication. He regarded himself as "collecting the follies of the age for the information of posterity." He believed that letters should be as spontaneous as conversation. "I write to you two," he informed Mary Berry, "just as I would talk—the only comfortable kind of letters." The best letters, he rightly argued, ought to resemble "extempore conversation." It is often said that his letters contain too much social gossip and one does at times come across shaming passages such as the following in a letter to Lady Upper Ossory of 1780: "I do believe there is some truth in Mons. K's story. I know no more of the haggle between Lady J. and our cousin the Duke, nor a syllable of her daughter—not even who the baronet is." Even Jane Austen seldom wrote twaddle such as that. From time to time however his correspondence flashes with epigrams such as "next to being disagreeable, there is nothing so shocking as being too agreeable." And occasionally he allows himself brilliant passages of description as his account to Mann of the illuminations, the fireworks and the bonfires, in honor of the victory of Minden: "and the poor charming moon yonder, that never looked so well in her life, is not at all minded, but seems only staring out of a garret window at the frantic doings all over the town."

Horace Walpole aged well. He suffered much from gout and pretended that his chalkstones would from time to time leap out of his fingers and fall tinkling on the tiled floor. His last years were soothed, not merely by the solicitude of his numerous nieces, but by his neighbors the Misses Berry, for whom he simulated a romantic passion. In 1791, he succeeded his lunatic nephew as Earl of Orford. "My plan is," he wrote, "to pass away calmly as cheerfully as I can." He carried out this plan, as indeed he carried out most of his plans. He died peacefully in his house in Berkeley Square on March 2, 1797, in his eighty-first year.

Chapter 14

Free Thought

(The *Encyclopédie*, 1751–1772)

—— ·◆· ——

The Law of Nature—The Noble Savage—Bayle—Quesnay—
Holbach—Contrasting opinions of Montesquieu, Voltaire and
Rousseau on such issues as Patriotism, Liberty, Authority, Prop-
erty, and the Separation of Powers—Exploitation of these ideas by
the Revolution—English political philosophy—The influence of
Locke—Bolingbroke—Hume—The *Encyclopédie*—Humanitarian-
ism—Deism—Attacks made on it by the Jesuits and the Church—
Le Breton—Pirated Editions—The Paris Salons propagate the ideas
of the *Encyclopédistes*—D'Alembert—Diderot—His industry and
persistence—His imprisonment—His quarrel with J. J. Rousseau—
His views on religion and politics—His visit to Russia—Catherine
II as the Semiramis of the North—His character and death.

One

I T IS AN exaggeration to assert that the philosophers and physiocrats of the eighteenth century were responsible for the French Revolution. That outburst was due to the circumstances that France had completely outgrown her ancient institutions and that those in power had not the vision or the authority to make the necessary adjustments. What the philosophers did do was to deprive of all self-confidence those who would naturally have defended the established system; and to inspire those who wished to destroy it with conviction, enthusiasm, phrases, and hope. They propagated the fictions that all men are born equal, that sovereignty rests with the People, that reason is infallible, and that no governmental enactment need be regarded as valid if it can be shown to violate the "Law of Nature." They would have been unable to define with any consistency or unanimity what this "Law of Nature" really was. The phrase was based upon the myth that man was born virtuous but had been degraded by false education, corrupt institutions, and bad laws.

Illustrative of the confused sentiments in which eighteenth century intellectuals indulged was the myth of the "Noble Savage." He was supposed to live a life of Arcadian happiness according to the "Law of Nature"; to cultivate the simple domestic virtues uncontaminated by the corruption of European civilization; and to pass his innocent existence without greed, cruelty, or fear. Even so balanced a man as Joseph Addison could, in 1711, when speaking of the Negro slaves in "our American plantations," represent them as examples of the "first ages of the world when men shined by a noble simplicity of behavior." "What," he exclaimed ecstatically, "what might not that savage greatness of soul which appears in these poor wretches on many occasions, be raised to were it rightly cultivated?" The science of anthropology was then in a rudimentary stage.

Already in the seventeenth century Pierre Bayle had struck the note of religious skepticism and had initiated the conceptions of the "Law of Nature" and the sovereignty of the People. The Abbé de Saint-Pierre and his group, known as the "Club de l'Entresol," were the precursors of humanitarianism and were the first to advocate an international covenant and institution to provide for the pacific settlement of disputes. Not only did the good Abbé seek to reform spelling and to invent an armchair that would be both sensible and soft, but he preached the perfectibility of man and the doctrine that, with the elimination of prejudice and ignorance, humanity could attain to utter happiness. The optimism of the age was reflected in the work of Francois Quesnay, the leader of the Physiocrats, who while rightly insisting that agriculture was the basis of French economy, and while advocating a single tax on land, contended that "twelve principles written in twelve lines" would solve every existing problem, advance the masses to higher standards of behavior and intelligence, and bring peace and satisfaction to the whole of mankind. Even so experienced a statesman as Turgot was affected by Quesnay's simplification of issues. Throughout the century the two streams of intellectual skepticism and sentimental ideology mingled their waters and caused a cataract of ideas. In the minds of three successive generations criticism of former axioms and conventions fermented rapidly. It found its extreme expression in the *System of Nature* published by Baron Paul Henri Holbach in 1770.

Holbach's views were so outspoken that they frightened Voltaire, the *Encyclopédistes*, and even Frederick the Great. He contended that the conception of God and a life after death were unscientific illusions. He denied the existence of a soul and heaped with scorn such doctrines as Original Sin and Salvation, or the theory of Free Will. Not only did he attack the Church and all forms of superstition, he also attacked the comfortable compromise of Deism; God, as conceived by the theologians, was no more than "a terrible idol." "Let us recognize," wrote Holbach, "the plain truth, that it is these supernatural ideas that have obscured morality, corrupted politics, hindered the advance of the sciences, and extinguished happiness and peace in the very heart of man." Such paradoxes had a disturbing effect.

The "enlightenment" that spread across Europe during the eighteenth century was, however, more potent than a series of negations. There were many positive and creative ideas that the three most influential men of the century, Voltaire, Montesquieu and Rousseau, inculcated into their contemporaries; ideas which spread in ever widening ripples from Paris, to England and across the seas. Voltaire has already been considered: a later chapter will be devoted to Rousseau: but it may be well at this stage to summarize and compare the divergent pronouncements of these three men on the major political problems of their time.

Their respective attitudes towards patriotism, which by most men was taken as an axiom, are in themselves illustrative of their difference of sentiment and approach. Montesquieu was intensely patriotic: Rousseau from time to time indulged in orgies of local patriotism when he recalled his boyhood at Geneva: but Voltaire was a true European in spirit and regarded patriotism as no more than one of many sentimental fallacies. Liberty again was interpreted by each of the three in different ways. To Voltaire, who believed fundamentally in established order, liberty meant little more than the abolition of injustice and the immunity of the individual from the arbitrary acts of government. Montesquieu contended that liberty had little relation to the actual form of government, since a man might be more free under a benevolent autocracy than under a democracy that denied the rights of minorities. Rousseau, on the other hand, evolved in his *Contrat Social* the pernicious view that the individual must surrender his personal rights to the community. If he opposed the "General Will," then society had the right to "force him to be free." Even if there existed such a thing as "natural rights," then it was for the community alone to define what they were; a Sovereign People could never err in making such a definition. In this way the *Contrat Social* became the "Bible of democratic despotism," and the source of much muddled thinking, injustice, and suffering.

The problem of Authority, again, was approached by these three men from utterly divergent aspects. To Voltaire authority must be centralized and accepted, except when it committed injustice to individuals. Rousseau contended that the General Will must be the sole authority and that any resistance to, or criticism of, this despotism was a heresy against the Sovereign People. The Jacobins during the Terror, who well knew that they did not represent a majority in the country, exploited one of Rousseau's trickiest exegeses and contended that, whereas they might not at the moment represent the "Will of everybody," they did represent "The General Will." Montesquieu, as we might expect, approached the problem of authority with deeper seriousness. He contended that the justification of authority was Reason, and that Reason in any civilized State was expressed in "Ancient Law." Contemporary laws might be no more than the result of impulse or transient passion: only long-established laws should possess supreme authority. Every form of government, whether monarchical, oligarchical, or democratic, contained within itself the germs of despotism. The only unassailable form of government therefore was the rule of law. If the rule of law were to dominate and preserve a community, then that community must be inspired by "virtue," that is by the wide and deep conviction that all government must operate for the good of the governed. A second method by which the rule of law could be maintained was by a system of checks and balances, or what Montesquieu called "intermediate bodies." He advocated the creation of a powerful middle class capable of resisting encroachment both from above and from below, and prepared to check the dangerous fallacy of egalitarianism, which could lead only to incompetence and eventual mob despotism.

Their different opinions on the subject of private property are also significant. Voltaire, being a very rich man, considered property to be a "natural" right and contended that any government that sought to deprive a man of his property was "acting like a thief." Rousseau, somewhat surprisingly, hedged upon the subject. He made one of his deceptive distinctions between what he called "natural inequality" and "social inequality." The latter could be remedied by State action, but was the Government justified in imposing equality by the confiscation of private incomes? He never answered this question. He merely asked whether it would be prudent "to abolish private property, destroy society, and go back to live in the forest with the bears." Montesquieu was more constructive when considering the problem. He was not fundamentally opposed to socialist doctrine and in fact expressed admiration for the communist system supposed to have been established by the Jesuits in Paraguay. Yet he hesitated to recommend collectivism, since he was aware that this could only be imposed by totalitarian methods and he detested despotism whether of the right or of the left. All he says is that the law should be vigilant in protecting the proletariat against exploitation.

The doctrine of the Separation of Powers, which is so closely associated with the name of Montesquieu, and which was so tragically misinterpreted by his disciples, was a recognition of the fact that, in a community where both the legislature and the executive were in the same hands, the judicature must enjoy complete independence if the sacred rule of law were to be maintained. Rousseau, as was to be expected, held that all judges should be elected, not realizing that elective judges might prove as subservient to their electors as nominated judges to the orders of the Government. Voltaire, who detested the contemporary parliaments (which were judicial rather than legislative bodies), believed that judges should be chosen direct by the executive. But it was Montesquieu who was the most logical of the three.

On the problem of Church and State, Rousseau, who held that "anything that disturbs social uniformity is worthless," and who preferred the theocracy of Mahomet to Christianity and the Catholic Church, evolved the idea that there should be a public religion on the model of the civil code. "Without," he wrote idiotically, "forcing any citizen to believe in this State Faith, the Sovereign People would be justified in banishing anyone who did not believe in it." In a later passage he states even that those, who having once subscribed to the religion invented by the Government, thereafter abjured it, should be put to death. Voltaire wanted the King to be supreme in religion as in everything else. Montesquieu, although himself not a freethinker, in his earlier *Lettres Persanes* advocated freedom of conscience and even held that several different religious sects would prove beneficial to the State as a whole. In the *Esprit des Lois* he modified this view, considering an established Church as a valuable "intermediary body," and suspecting that a diversity of religious sects might disturb public tranquility.

It will be seen from the above summary that the three men who inspired the thoughts and feelings of the educated classes in the eighteenth century held different views about all the more important issues of the time. The fact that they were all of them so frequently quoted by rebels and revolutionaries has led historians to exaggerate their influence. Voltaire, in his scheme for administrative reform, certainly suggested the "Cahiers" of 1789. Montesquieu certainly inspired the Declarations of the Rights of Men of 1789 and 1793, even as he suggested many of the main principles of the Constitution of the United States. The Jacobins deliberately confused the teaching of Montesquieu with the demagogy of Rousseau, and in the Declaration of 1793 were so illogical as simultaneously to proclaim the Rights of Man and the right of the People to violate these rights. This confusion of thought derived from the fundamental fallacy that "The People" could never themselves become tyrannous. It was by misquoting Montesquieu that Robespierre sought to justify the Terror. "If," he said, "in times of peace the strength of a Republican Government lies in virtue, in times of Revolution it lies both in Virtue and Fear. Fear without virtue is deadly, and virtue without fear is powerless."

It is difficult for us today to realize the immense influence exercised by Montesquieu over his contemporaries. Horace Walpole, who was not given to facile eulogies, described the *Esprit des Lois* "as the best book that ever was written." To us it seems a heavy volume, marred by ponderous and often most inaccurate digressions regarding Athens, Rome, Sparta, the Goths, and the Chinese. His conclusions, for instance, regarding the influence of climate on national character are absurd. He contends that the English climate renders the British "impatient" and that "the reason why there are so many savages in America is because the soil naturally produces the sustenance these require." His misconception of the true nature of the British Constitution led to serious results. He was a great man nonetheless; and perhaps more than any other man since Locke, advanced the true conception of Freedom.

Two

Even after the death of Louis XIV, even after the humiliation inflicted upon her by Marlborough and Eugene, France remained the dominant influence in Europe, even as Europe, in that first half of the eighteenth century, was assumed to be the center of the civilized world. Until Voltaire's visit to England in 1726, the English were regarded on the continent as a semi-barbarous people, whose philosophy, art, and literature could be of no possible interest to any educated man. Voltaire changed all that. He introduced his countrymen to the discoveries of Newton and to the political science of Hobbes, Shaftesbury, Locke, Bolingbroke, and Hume. The French, who until then had looked upon England as a hyperborean island of fogs and dull brains (an impression which many of them have retained to this day), came to invent an idealistic picture of a Utopia, where all men were free under the rule of law, where the powers of King and Parliament were perfectly balanced, where such a thing as arbitrary arrest was unheard of, and where intellectuals could write and publish anything they wished. The first of several successive waves of anglomania broke upon the shores of France.

Hitherto the cultural exchange between France and England had been almost entirely one-sided. Chaucer, the first of our major poets, had been greatly influenced by French culture, by Eustache Deschamps and by the *Roman de la Rose* of Guillaume de Lorris and Jean de Meung. It is significant that Chaucer is the first English writer to be mentioned in French literature and that he is then referred to as "an eminent translator" of French into English. A second invasion of French influence occurred when Wyatt and Surrey crossed to France in 1532 and brought back to our fog-laden shores the delicate lyrics of Clément Marot. During our civil war many poets, who were for the most part royalists, took refuge in France and returned with a deep respect for French symmetry and logic. After the Restoration the British stage was flooded with imitations of French drama, although it cannot be said that our dramatists ever really understood the perfection of Corneille, Racine, and Molière. It was not until the Augustan age of English poetry that French influence for a while became dominant. "Late, very late," wrote Pope in the first Epistle "correctness grew our care":

> Exact Racine and Corneille's noble fire
> Showed us that France had something to admire.

It was towards the middle of the century that the tide turned. *Clarissa Harlowe* created a sensation in France. It was the first important novel dealing with the private lives of ordinary people. It became, as John Morley has remarked, a "landmark of a great social, no less than a great literary, transition." Diderot attributed to Richardson his own conception of the meaning of compassion. "Oh Richardson, Richardson," he wrote on hearing in 1761 of the death of the novelist, "unique among men in my eyes." It was *Clarissa Harlowe* that spread through France, and therefore throughout Europe, the ideal of "the beautiful character," *la belle âme* or *die schöne Seele*. It was from *Clarissa Harlowe* that Rousseau derived the initial inspiration of *La Nouvelle Héloise*, which exercised so disturbing an effect upon the conscience of the eighteenth century.

At a slightly later date the Abbé Delille was deeply struck by the nature poetry of Thomson and Gray. There followed the Romantic movement and the dominance of Scott and Byron. Since then the mutual influence of the two literatures has been constant. Yet the fact remains that the French have never understood Shakespeare, in the sense that the Germans have understood him, and that only a minority of British specialists can claim to have a true appreciation of Malherbe, Boileau and Racine. In literature, British "sensibility" certainly had a lasting effect in France; but it was our political rather than our dramatic or lyrical invention that really influenced the French way of thought and thus contributed to enlightenment. If you asked a hundred educated Frenchmen today, you would find that sixty of them could give an adequate account of Newton, Locke, and Hume, whereas only four of them would ever have heard of Shelley or Keats. Thus it is with the philosophers that we shall mainly be concerned.

Among these Locke is dominant. "Never," wrote Voltaire in his *Lettres sur les Anglais*, "has there existed perhaps an intelligence so wise, so methodical, so logical. . . . Many philosophers have written romances about the soul of man. Locke appeared quite modestly and wrote its history. . . . He has been the greatest influence since Plato." Is that an exaggerated statement?

Certainly Locke, with a style incomparably more lucid and comprehensible than the tortuous epigrams of Hobbes, was the first writer on political science reasonably to expound the basis of Liberalism. To him the People were the ultimate sovereign, the depositaries of final power. The Government acts as a trustee for the purposes for which society exists. Locke laid down five principles by which this trusteeship could be justified and under which it should be operated. First, the natural right of all men to life, liberty and the pursuit of happiness. The people therefore have the right to defend themselves and their interests when these are endangered. Resistance is not rebellion. Nobody should be subjected to authority without his consent. This freedom can only be secured if the principle be accepted that minorities must obey majorities and the fiction be admitted that the acts of the majority are by Nature and Reason the acts of the whole community. Moreover, the Trustee theory of government implied the separation of powers, since to place the judiciary, the legislature, and the executive in the same hands would be to put too great a strain on human unselfishness and virtue. In seeking to prevent tyranny, the more fanatical followers of Locke tended to render difficult rapid or decisive action on the part of any central Government. Locke must not be held responsible for the several hallucinations which thereafter clustered around his central theory. To modern minds, his definition of liberty and freedom seems obvious: at the outset of the eighteenth century it came as a revelation. It would be ingratitude to forget that Locke is the true originator of our modern conceptions of Liberty— of religious liberty in his *Essay concerning Toleration;* of political liberty in his *Treatises of Government;* and of intellectual liberty in his *Essay Concerning Human Understanding.*

John Locke must also be regarded as the precursor of Bentham and Mill in placing utility as the main test of governmental action. Methods of government, he contended, were means to further the happiness of the governed. Hitherto men had judged the value of any single piece of legislation according to some deductive or a priori standard, such as the Law of God, or the Law of Nature, or the fundamental

Laws of the Kingdom. Locke argued that the only true test was the test of experience. Men should ask themselves whether a given act of government is useful and beneficial and whether it promotes general happiness. They can only decide this by experience, by seeing how the legislation works out in practice. Hence the importance of inductive evidence, of statistics, blue books and regional reports. His conception of utility appeared to him to possess a divine sanction. "God," he wrote, "has by an inseparable connection joined virtue and public happiness together; that which is for the public welfare is God's will."

Unlike Hobbes, Locke was a stout believer in the sanctity of private property, which to him was a Law of Nature. For the Government to violate this Law of Nature amounted to a breach of trust and should be resisted by the sovereign people.

Locke's successors among English political thinkers were less determinant. Bolingbroke, for instance, although sincere in his hated of corruption, argued, in his *Patriot King*, that a wise and virtuous Monarch would represent the will of a nation better than any debased Parliament. He distinguished between political parties and what he called "factions," namely groups of politicians seeking only to further their own sectional interests. What he desired was an executive composed of the best brains in every party and kept under control by a Patriot King. It was not a progressive idea. Hume was the first of these political scientists to contend that common sense is the true test of government and that such theories as Divine Right or Social Contract are no more than curious and interesting figments of the imagination. He was perhaps the most modern of all the eighteenth century theorists in that he contended that any established order was preferable to revolution; and that political theory is a dangerous speculative enterprise.

Of all these, however, Locke remains the mastermind. It was he who introduced into the language such familiar axioms as are represented by the words Individualism, Reason, Toleration, Property, Utility, and the Greatest Happiness of the Greatest Number. It was certainly not his fault if his ideas, expressed with such clarity and moderation, were misrepresented by his successors.

Three

The publication of the French *Encyclopédie* has been described by André Billy as "the greatest date in the history of intellectual civilization since the invention of printing." The essential theme of this vast publication, the first volume of which appeared in 1751, was that there were no innate ideas, but that our concepts were derived from experience through the sensations. Bacon and Locke had taught that man was by implication the center of the universe, that he was naturally good, and that he had been corrupted by false theory and evil institutions. The theme was that the universal aim was happiness, guided and controlled by reason. This prevailing optimism was, as has been said, much discouraged by the Lisbon earthquake and by the heavy casualties of the Seven Years War. "What," asks Cacambo in *Candide*, "is optimism?" "Alas," Candide replies, "it is the mania for pretending that all is right, when in fact everything is wrong." Voltaire in his later years realized that the optimistic view of mankind's destiny held by Leibnitz and the *Encyclopédistes* was a tacit admission of the inevitability of evil. It was this conviction that induced him to fight evil with such passion when it obtruded itself on his awareness. He had some vague idea that if one conquered evil in detail (as in the Calas case) one might end by defeating it in general. And in truth his triumphs in vindicating Galas and others were more than transient episodes: they were victories of principle.

The humanistic philosophy preached by the *Encyclopédistes* enhanced political and social awareness. It was they who first questioned the justice of the Slave Trade, colonialism, harsh penal systems, torture, unjust taxation, and war. They were the first to stress the importance of industry, the dignity of labor, and the value of technical knowledge. It was not Faith that they attacked, but superstition: not religion but the priesthood. They taught men, as John Morley has said, "to lose their interest, rather than their belief, in mysteries." When the actual world, with its expansion, its science, and its ever-increasing discoveries, was so exciting, why bother about myths, or even trouble to point out their mythical origins? They thus aroused a vivid interest in and an excited awareness of human potentiality. They did not preach revolution, and in fact their treatment of politics was implicit rather than direct: but they certainly created a revolutionary frame of mind.

Although in the articles on religion and dogma conventional deference was paid to orthodox opinion, in the more incidental articles on scientific subjects skepticism lurked. The *Encyclopédistes* interpreted the vague word "Nature" as "the facts of experience" and their tendency was to place physics above metaphysics and science against abstract philosophy. Enlightenment, to their minds, began as "the triumph of empirical fact" and the importance which they attached to Locke's theory of sensations led them to discard the established dualism of Descartes and to question even the existence of the soul. Animals certainly had sensations and instincts. Why should they not also have a soul? It is a question disturbing to theologians but one which many realists frequently ask. "Denied in heaven," wrote Byron of his devoted dog, "the Soul he had on earth."

The belief in sensation as the only true reality, led inevitably to the pleasure-pain conception, and by that primrose path into the shrubberies of materialism and hedonism. Voltaire, who regarded himself as a friendly cousin of the *Encyclopédistes* rather than an actual member of the movement, fully appreciated its hedonistic side:

> *J'aime le luxe et même la mollesse;*
> *Tous les plaisirs, les arts de toute espèce,*
> *La propreté, le goût, les ornements:*
> *Tout honnête homme a de tels sentiments.*

> What I like is luxury, even the soft sort,
> Every kind of pleasure, art of every description,
> Cleanliness, taste, and the amenities of life.
> All gentlemen share these feelings.

But hedonism, even utilitarianism, were but byproducts of the *Encyclopédie*. Its aim was to teach men to think.

The Church and the Jesuits were quick to recognize an enemy in the *Encyclopédie*. Their first action was to denounce the Abbé de Prades, who had contributed some perfectly harmless articles on Theology. He was deprived of his license to preach and was obliged to fly the country and take refuge in Berlin. The Bishop of Auxerre then publicly attacked the *Encyclopédie* in general and Buffon and Montesquieu in particular, on the ground that their articles were subversive. The King and the Court were in fact more frightened of the Jesuits and the Jansenists than they were of the philosophers, whose works they never read and could not understand. Thus, although the sale of the second volume was forbidden by decree of the King's Council on February 7, 1752, this order was not in practice enforced and the *Encyclopédie* continued to be published in yearly volumes until in 1757 it had reached the seventh volume and the articles on Gyromancy and Gythium. The Church by then had become thoroughly alarmed by the popularity of the encyclopedia and determined on drastic action. D'Alembert had written an article in which he had praised the religious tolerance which had impressed him during a recent visit to Geneva and Ferney. In this article he had mentioned that the theologians of Geneva did not expect their pupils to take seriously those passages in the scripture that offended against humanity or reason. The *Encyclopédistes* were denounced from the pulpits of France as atheists seeking to destroy the structure of society and the foundations of faith. The attacks became more intense when in 1758 Helvétius, a prominent *Encyclopédiste*, published his book *De L'esprit*. The public prosecutor was induced to prohibit the publication of any further volumes and the sale of those already printed. Rousseau publicly dissociated himself from the *Encyclopédistes* and even d'Alembert and Voltaire urged caution.

Diderot, in his little attic in the rue Benoit, stuck to his job. He decided to issue the ten volumes that remained in a single massive edition and handed over the job of printing to the bookseller Le Breton. The latter was so frightened by the tone of some of the articles that he had the impertinence, without consulting Diderot, to expunge any passage that might possibly cause offence. When Diderot eventually discovered this usurpation, he was enraged. He went to see Le Breton in a thunderous mood. "For years," he shouted, "you have been cheating me in a dastardly manner. You have massacred, or got some brute beast to massacre, the work of twenty good men, who have devoted to you their time, their vigils, their talents, from a love of truth and justice, with the simple hope of seeing their ideas given to the public, and reaping from them a little consideration abundantly earned. Your injustice, your ingratitude have destroyed this hope for ever. . . . You and your edition will be dragged through the mud. Henceforth you will be known as the man who committed an act of treachery and vile presumption, to which nothing that has ever happened in the world of letters can be compared."

Inevitably amid all these troubles the *Encyclopédie* was widely pirated abroad, in Geneva in 1777, at Lausanne in 1778, in Leghorn in 1770, and at Lucca in 1771. Its influence continued to spread far and wide. It permeated the salons of Paris which were the generating stations of new thought. In the drawing rooms of Madame de Lambert, Madame de Tençin, Madame du Deffand, Madame Geoffrin and Mademoiselle de l'Espinasse the intellectuals discussed little else. Nobody could claim to be a man of fashion, or even a man of the world, unless he were familiar, and even in sympathy, with the ideas of the *Encyclopédistes*. They established the mode in which Society spoke and thought.

Four

The main contributors to the *Encyclopédie* were men of learning and talent. There was d'Alembert, the assistant editor, a man of gentle character and ebullient gaiety. He was the illegitimate son of Madame de Tençin who had deposited him when born upon the steps of a Paris church. He had been rescued from this exposed position by a poor woman who took him to her house, discovered his parentage, and obliged his father to provide him with an education. He turned out a gifted mathematician and was invited by Frederick the Great to succeed Maupertuis as President of the Berlin Academy. Catherine II offered him an enormous salary to come to Russia as tutor to her son. He refused both these offers, preferring to continue living with the old woman who had saved his life as a baby when he lay there on the steps of Saint Roch, dying of exposure. He was a charming, diffident, but talkative man.

At first, the contributors to the *Encyclopédie* worked as a team. There were Turgot and Montesquieu on politics and history; Rousseau on music; Buffon on natural history: Marmontel on comedy; Quesnay on agriculture; and Holbach on chemistry. Condorcet and even Voltaire contributed occasional articles. Yet the main force of the *Encyclopédie*, the mighty power station that transmitted energy to every part of the machine, was provided by the passionate energy of Diderot. It is necessary to describe this forceful man.

Denis Diderot was born at Langres on October 5, 1713. His father was a cutler and his mother the daughter of a local tanner. His father wished him to enter the Church, or failing that to study law or medicine. He refused to work for any regular profession and escaped to Paris where he lived in a garret, supporting himself as a bookseller's hack and a Grub Street journalist. In 1743, he married Antoinette Champion, a poor, pious, uneducated, and stupid person, who in later years developed into a domestic scold. They had a daughter, Angélique, whom he dearly loved. He first had a liaison with a Madame Puisieux, who was unworthy of him, and at the age of forty-three he fell in love with Sophie Voland, who was no longer young, who suffered atrociously from indigestion, who wore spectacles, was something of a blue stocking and whose ankles swelled most mornings and most afternoons. Diderot loved her dearly, wrote to her many of his most delightful letters, and remained faithful to her until her death twenty years later. Few literary love affairs have been so respectable.

In 1749, Diderot had published his *Lettres sur les Aveugles*, which was quite innocently intended to demonstrate the derivation of ideas from the five senses. It was regarded as subversive by the Church and Diderot was imprisoned for three months in the fortress at Vincennes. Fortunately the Governor of the fortress was a relation of Voltaire's Madame du Châtelet so that Diderot after a few days was released from his dungeon cell and housed in a pavilion where he was able to receive guests and to walk in the garden. It was there that Rousseau, "choking with tenderness and joy," came to visit him.

On his release, Diderot returned to his attic rooms at the corner of the rue St. Benoit and the rue Taranne. He was not a Society man; he was a Bohemian who preferred to sit in the Café Procope with boon companions talking far into the night. Thus although Madame du Deffand would often allow him to visit her, Madame Geoffrin, her rival, regarded him as too provincial, too noisy, too unrefined for her exclusive circle. What he really liked was the society of Grimm and his friend Holbach. Rousseau hated Grimm and what he snarled at as "the Holbachians." His friendship with Diderot, who was the most convivial and patient of men, was thereby shaken. Rousseau was already suffering from the first pangs of persecution mania, and persuaded himself that Holbach and his friends were plotting against him. Diderot moreover had earned his displeasure by telling him that *Julie* was too long-winded, as indeed it is. Rousseau concluded that Diderot was "jealous" of his growing reputation; Diderot was incapable of jealousy having an ample heart: Rousseau's heart, in spite of his facility for weeping copiously, was that of a small bat. Diderot, who loved love and hated hatred, wrote to protest to Rousseau. "In the sincerest, tenderest friendships," he wrote to him, "you seek only for causes of hatred. Your heart only knows how to hate." This is a just criticism of the great sentimentalist.

Diderot, although a wonderful talker, was not an efficient writer. His plays were failures and of his many books and pamphlets the *Neveu de Rameau*, the portrait of a Paris parasite, is the only one that holds interest today. His art criticism never rose above the level of weekly journalism, his favorite picture being Greuze's "A child weeping over a dead bird." He was not a tactful man, was apt to become declamatory on the subject of virtue, especially his own virtue, and expected others to keep silent while he expounded his views. "Diderot," writes André Billy, "would have insisted on a platoon of guardemen talking philosophy." For all his defects (and they are not unattractive) Diderot's real claim to our respect and gratitude is that it was he who, by his persistence, his astonishing industry, and his enthusiasm, kept the *Encyclopédistes* together and in spite of the intrigues and obstruction of his enemies brought the massive work to its conclusion.

Diderot's ideas on religion and politics were pervasive rather than formal. He regarded himself as a pupil of Shaftesbury, basing his conception of the universe on "natural religion," which was in fact a form of optimistic skepticism. "I am a Christian," he wrote, "because it is reasonable so to be." André Billy has wittily observed that he was an atheist when in Paris and a deist when in the country. In the end his skepticism got the better of his natural religion. "I do not believe," he said when on his deathbed, "in God the Father, God the Son, or God the Holy Ghost."

According to the standards of the time, he was a good man and a moralist. He believed in energy and enthusiasm as essential to a man of talent. "The man," he wrote, "of colorless passion lives and dies a brute." His political views were eminently sensible. He argued that even bad laws must be obeyed until amended. "He who," he wrote, "on his private authority infringes a bad law, authorizes everybody else to infringe good laws." He insisted that government was always a public and never a private possession. "Authority," he wrote, "cannot be taken away from the People, to whom it belongs essentially and absolutely." In Diderot's day such sayings seemed daring paradoxes. It is not surprising that the priests should have persuaded the King to shut him up at Vincennes.

He was ill paid for his work and much cheated by the booksellers. In 1770, he had met and made friends with Prince Galitzine, a cultured emissary of Catherine II of Russia. Galitzine told the Empress, who was proud of being called the "Semiramis of the North," that Diderot was in financial trouble and knew not how to provide a dowry for his beloved daughter. The Empress thereupon purchased his library and appointed him its curator until he died. She even invited him to visit her in St. Petersburg, and in the summer of 1773, Diderot, at the age of sixty, embarked upon that then arduous journey. He remained in Russia for five months and had constant, intimate, and violent conversations with the Empress. He urged her to reform the whole system of her Empire. "Everything," she recorded later, "was to be turned upside down to make room for quite impracticable theories." He was so enraged with her refusal to agree with him that he banged his fists upon her knees. Bruised by this method of argument, she gave instructions that at all subsequent audiences a table should be set between them to defend her against further attack. He loved her dearly and admired her much. "I found her exactly," he wrote to his friend Princess Dashkov, "what you had foretold. The soul of Brutus and the charm of Cleopatra." Catherine in actual fact preferred Grimm, who was more a man of the world and did not thump her knees. She may even have resented Diderot's passionate love of preaching and teaching. She complained that, whereas Diderot could draft his schemes on paper, she had to write them on the skin of human beings, a far less tractable material. But she remained faithful and wonderfully generous to him until the day of his death.

Diderot survived long enough to read, and much to resent, the first volume of Rousseau's *Confessions*. He was present when the aged Voltaire came for his apotheosis to Paris. Voltaire reminded him of a ruined castle which was still inhabited "by some ancient sorcerer." Voltaire, who never liked being lectured, complained that Diderot "lacked one talent, and that an essential one—the gift of dialogue."

Diderot died, when eating an apricot, on July 30, 1784. Only a few weeks before he had transferred himself from his old attic in the rue St. Benoit to a fine apartment provided for him by Catherine II in the rue de Richelieu. Thus the cutler's son, with his scolding slattern of a wife, died as librarian of his own library and in conditions of grandeur.

Chapter 15
Disintegration
(Louis XV, 1715–1774)

———— •◆• ————

Accession of the infant Louis XV—The Regent d'Orléans—He induces the parliaments to declare Louis XIV's will invalid—His promises to the parliaments—They are encouraged to demand legislative powers—The King's education—The scandal of his boy companions—He is engaged to the baby Infanta of Spain—The lax morals of the Regency period—Jansenists and Jesuits—The rise of Gallicanism—Death of the Regent—The King comes of age—His character—The duc de Bourbon and Madame de Prie—The dominance of Cardinal Fleury—The King married to Marie Leczinska—Conflict with the parliaments over the bull *Unigenitus*—The King falls dangerously ill at Metz and his confession and abasement are published by the Church—Madame de Pompadour—The Renversement des Alliances—Damiens—The growth of public opinion—Hostility to the Court—Madame du Barry—The King's secret foreign policy—His death on May 10, 1774.

One

ON SEPTEMBER 1, 1715, the duc de Bouillon, Lord High Chamberlain, stepped out on to the gilded balcony that looks upon the marble court at Versailles and read an announcement to those assembled below. "The King Louis XIV is dead," he proclaimed. He then paused for a moment and replaced the black feather in his hat by a white feather. "Long live," he continued, "King Louis XV."

The new monarch was then a child of five years old, so sickly that he was not expected to live. The old King in the closing years of his reign had been deeply concerned about the problem of succession. He had lost his eldest son, the Dauphin, and his two grandsons, the duc de Bourgogne and the duc de Berry. His third grandson, the duc d'Anjou, had forfeited his claim to succession by accepting the throne of Spain. The eldest member of the Royal House was the duc d'Orléans, Louis XIV's nephew, who was then forty years of age and a man of bad reputation. His palace was the scene of drunken orgies; he was utterly cynical and selfish; he was constantly making rude jokes about the Church and even about the basic principles of the Christian religion; and he indulged in black magic. It was whispered even that he had poisoned the several first cousins and second cousins who stood between him and the succession. He was said, for all his profligacy and indolence, to be inordinately ambitious. How could the life of a frail infant be entrusted to such ogre hands?

To meet this difficulty, Louis XIV devised a plan by which, whereas the duc d'Orléans would be declared Regent with full political powers, the custody of the infant King would be entrusted to the two bastards he had had by Madame de Montespan, the duc du Maine and the comte de Toulouse, who were legitimized for that purpose. Louis XIV before his death had confessed sadly to the widow of the exiled James II that he foresaw that these testamentary dispositions were unlikely to survive his own disappearance. He was correct in this forecast. The duc d'Orléans, in his capacity of Regent, immediately informed the parliament of Paris that the late Monarch's will was not in accordance with the "fundamental laws of the kingdom." He asked them to declare the will invalid, to cancel their previous consent to the legitimization of the bastards, to deprive them of their rank, and to entrust the guardianship of the baby King to the Regent alone and to those persons whom he might himself appoint. He promised that if they agreed to do this he would govern in future "by their advice and in accordance with their wise remonstrances." This was a disastrous undertaking, since it encouraged the parliaments in their illusion that constitutionally they possessed legislative as well as legal functions, led them to form an obstinate opposition when what they considered to be their rights were not accorded to them, and induced them throughout the ensuing reign to obstruct such reforms as might have prevented the final catastrophe.

It must be repeated that it would be dangerous, owing to a similarity of title, to draw any analogy between the French parliaments and the English. There were thirteen parliaments in France and four Conseils Superiéurs. They constituted courts of appeal but also possessed the duty of registering royal decrees. They represented what Burke has well called "a corporate magistracy." They claimed that, before attesting such monarchical acts, they could criticize the proposed legislation and even "remonstrate." Yet whenever they refused to register an enactment on which the King or his ministers had really set their hearts, they were summoned to what was called a *lit de justice* and instructed by the King personally to drop all this nonsense and to register there and then. Thus their powers, so far from being analogous to those of the English Parliament, were not even as constitutional or recognized as those of the Supreme Court of the United States. Yet never did they abate their claim to exercise political authority and the constant friction that arose between them and King served to weaken the position of the monarchy and to give the illusion that in some manner the parliaments were the champions of liberty and of representative institutions. In fact, they constituted a compact hereditary corporation of some five hundred and ninety families resolved to secure, not a democratic constitution, but an oligarchy under which they should themselves be the dominant power in the State. The fact that they purchased their offices and therefore regarded them as private property which could be, and generally were, bequeathed to their sons, rendered their outlook even more feudal. Few vested interests have ever proved so consolidated, reactionary, and unenlightened. By selling himself to the parliaments in order to gain their support in invalidating the will of Louis XIV, the duc d'Orléans was committing a typically cynical, irresponsible and senseless error.

Yet the fear that he would prove a wicked uncle to the baby King turned out to be groundless. The Regent, as so many hedonists, was really fond of children and would play gaily with the little boy upon the terraces of Chantilly or Versailles. He treated the child with candid affection mingled with rather touching respect. He was nice to the old governess Mademoiselle de Vantadour, whom the orphaned King regarded as his only mother. He appointed as tutor to the child the Abbé Fleury, bishop of Fréjus, who was widely respected for his learning and integrity. And, as governor to the infant, he chose the old marechal de Villeroy, who had known the court in the best days of Louis XIV, and who with deep affection and care instructed his pupil in etiquette and deportment. The Turkish Ambassador, Mahmet Pasha, records that when the King was only eleven and a half the old marshal told the boy to show his paces to the Ambassador and beamed with pleasure when Louis XV stalked up and down the room with "the majestic walk of a partridge." I suspect that Mahmet Pasha has been mistranslated and that for "partridge" we should read "pheasant"; I have never known a partridge do more than, scuttle, but I have seen golden pheasants walking very elegantly, placing one foot after the other with deliberation.

Bishop Fleury, who in his old age became the trusted and deeply valued minister and mentor of Louis XV, was an excellent tutor. He made the boy translate into Latin long passages from *Télémaque*, in which the duties of an ideal prince are unctuously explained.

It is customary to regard Louis XV as a self-indulgent monarch, who frittered away the greatness of his country in idle frivolities, who was almost wholly uneducated, and who took small interest in the affairs of State. His mistresses, such as the exquisite Madame de Pompadour, or the jolly du Barry, might well have been forgiven. What people object to is his lower types of profligacy, especially the Pare aux Cerfs, which was not, as many have imagined, a little park where the fallow deer herded shyly under splendid trees, but an ordinary house in the town of Versailles, as it might be a house in Wimpole Street, London, or on Beacon Hill at Boston. Here he maintained a private brothel and thereby did much damage to his repute, his constitution and his powers of application. Defenders of Louis XV, such as Pierre Gaxotte and Miss Nancy Mitford, seek to give us the opposite picture of a man of great kindness, high ideals, and really superhuman sexual desires.

His development was certainly precocious. As a boy he was not accorded the delights of feminine society, with the result that he became involved with his boy friends in pastimes that culminated in a sudden scandal. The duc de Boufflers, the comte de Ligny, the marquis de Meuse and the marquis de Rambure were all arrested and sent off to their country estates. Rambure, who appears to have been the leader of the gang, was imprisoned in the Bastille. The King was not told of the reason why his companions (they were all under twenty) had so suddenly been dispersed. He was told that they had been caught pulling up the palings in the park. The expression *arracheurs des palisades* or "paling pullers" circulated as a nickname for perverts in all the Paris salons.

Villeroy and Fleury took this seriously. They realized that their pupil was no longer a child and must be quickly married. In their innocence of the world, they chose as his prospective bride an infanta of Spain who was not more than five years and a half of age.

M. Gaxotte, as is the way with loyal biographers who have a little too much to explain away, puts it all down to a split personality. One side of Louis XV's character was affectionate, considerate, gay, and lively. The other side was repressed, melancholy, timid, morose, and hesitant. He certainly, as Horace Walpole noted, was an astonishingly handsome man with sad and gentle eyes.

Two

The Regency, which lasted from 1715 to 1723, was indeed a period of laxity, but it was also a period of recovery and reconstruction. Cardinal Dubois, who desired only to live in peace and comfort, was averse from adventures, and the most active of his policies was that of restraining the Spanish Minister, Alberoni, from dragging the rest of Europe into his troublous schemes. Gradually, under the firm and cautious guidance of the Brothers Paris, the finances of France began to recover from the shock dealt to them by the Mississippi bubble and the well-meant fantasies of John Law. The industrial impulse which the Scottish financier had given to the country began to pay a dividend. Slowly confidence, and even prosperity, returned.

The grey puritanism of the last years of Louis XIV's reign was succeeded by a wild outburst of high spirits. The Regent was no puritan and Cardinal Dubois enjoyed seeing happy faces around him. In the lovely palace at Chantilly, where the Regent would live when not entertaining ballet dancers at the Palais Royal, the torches and the candles were seldom extinguished. A wave of moral laxity swept the country. "Oh the happy age of the Regency!" wrote Voltaire, in *La Pucelle*, "that fortunate age when license flourished, when frivolity, shaking its cap of bells, danced lightly across France, and when no mortal condescended to be devout":

> *Voici le temps de l'aimable Régence*
> *Temps fortuné marqué par la license,*
> *Où la folie, agitant son grelot,*
> *D'un pied léger parcourt toute la France*
> *Où nul mortel daigne être dévot.*

The last line of Voltaire's gay little verse does not in fact represent the true situation. There were several devout people who loathed each other with venomous intensity. The old controversy between the Jansenists and the Jesuits grumbled along beneath the superficial elegance and gaiety of French society. Since the days of Port Royal, the Jansenists (the Calvinists of French Catholicism) had abandoned strict theology for a more political form of controversy. Realizing perhaps that the teaching of Cornelius Jansen, the doctrines of original sin and salvation, of predestination and Grace, possessed small popular appeal, or indeed were within the comprehension of even the most expert theologians, they decided that their long fight with the Jesuits should best be concentrated against the Bull *Unigenitus* which had been issued in 1713 and which denounced the teaching of Cornelius Jansen as heretical. With the support of the parliaments, the Jansenists denounced the Bull as a flagrant attempt on the part of the Vatican to impose upon the conscience of France the Pope's personal opinion as to what was heretical and what was not. Many Frenchmen of devout faith were of the Gallican persuasion, believing that in France the Church must be Gallican or national, and that the Vatican had no right or reason to intervene. The Regent imagined that by ignoring this tiresome controversy, by pretending genially that it did not exist, he would prevent any serious division from arising within the nation. That was a cynical illusion. The French have always been seriously minded and could not be persuaded to laugh off what had begun as a sincere case of conscience and what had now developed into a conflict between a national Church and ultramontane interference. It is possible that the Regent, had he been less flippant and more resolute, might have discovered a compromise during the eight years of his dominance. He preferred to ignore the whole business, with the result that the Jansenist versus Jesuit battle bubbled along below the surface and was, especially after the parliaments had taken up the Gallican cause as a national slogan, a serious factor in widening the gulf between the nation and the throne. Cornelius Jansen, and even Pascal and La mère Angélique, would have indeed been startled had they foreseen what human unhappiness they were bequeathing to future generations. Jansenism, assuredly, is one of the most gratuitous causes that has ever distracted and inflamed the mind of man. But, whatever the Regent may have wished and felt, it was never a cause that could be flicked aside with a smile.

The years of the Regency slid away to the sound of violins. Then one evening after dinner on December 2, 1723, the Regent, seated in his arm chair beside the fire, and listening to the gay stories being told him by the duchesse de Falari, was observed to be unresponsive. The duchesse realized to her horror that he had had a stroke. One of the

curious things about court life in France was that, whereas at certain
hours the rooms and anterooms were blocked by footmen and pages
in royal livery, at certain other hours the candles were extinguished in
the long galleries and there was not a servant to be seen or heard. The
duchesse dashed along the empty corridors, and out into the courtyard screaming for help. At last a footman heard her cries and the doctors and the priests were called. But Philippe d'Orléans was not to
recover. He panted and grunted and then died.

In that year the King attained his legal majority, being thirteen
years of age.

Three

The Regent, to the unrestrained delight of Saint Simon, experimented in creating an aristocratic oligarchy, by establishing
six councils of ten members each, most of whom were dukes. Little squeaky Saint Simon himself came in the end to realize that this
form of government led to squabbles and delays: after a bit the system
was discarded. It was replaced by a plan of administration more or
less on the Louis XIV model, whereby individual ministers became
responsible, under the supervision of the King, for the more important departments—Foreign Affairs, Finance, War and Commerce.
This was a better method, being akin to the British Cabinet system,
without any one minister being nominated as Prime Minister, but it
depended for its efficiency on the application and aptitudes of the
King himself. Even when he achieved adult age, Louis XV was not
a good chairman of committee. He was bored by political problems,
disliked argument, and hated to contradict. He was abominably lazy,
hesitated to give decisions, and had no sense of urgency. By nature
he was a profligate civil servant rather than a statesman. He avoided
debate, was so shy that he was unable to smile even when he wanted
to, and preferred his own study and the perusal of official memoranda
under his own green lamp. M. Gaxotte represents him working alone
upon official documents at a splendid writing table and far into the

night. I doubt myself whether very many of Louis XV's nights were thus engaged.

In the early years of his reign the King lived mainly at the Tuileries in Paris, but in 1722 he moved to Versailles. Officially he occupied the gorgeous rooms which his great-grandfather had tenanted and slept in the monumental bed in which the Great King had died. But in fact these majestic apartments were too grand and cold for a man, who, however promiscuous may have been his love affairs, was essentially of a domestic temperament. He thus, with the help of ingenious architects, constructed a suite of private rooms communicating by a secret staircase with the state apartments. There were in the first place what were called *Les Cabinets*, namely bedroom, bathroom, dining room, library, and study looking out into an interior courtyard. Above them was an even more private suite, known as "Les Petits Appartements" situated as a penthouse under the leads and surmounted by a private roof garden containing macaws, parrots, canaries, monkeys, and pleached trees of box, or myrtle or bay in blue and white tubs. It was here that the King would play with his children, or exercise his fat angora cat.

The rigor and symbolism of Court etiquette can be assessed by the strange fact that, although it was in his private flat that the King flirted and pretended to work, the state apartments below retained their old hierophantic significance. Louis XV, like his great-grandfather, would undergo the slow, elaborate, and unbearably pompous parade of going to bed. Still would the dukes and marquises compete with each other to be accorded the resplendent honor of holding the candle or helping the King to get out of his shirt. When the last rites had been accomplished, when the carved and gilded barrier that separated the bed from the rest of the room had been ceremoniously closed, when the last courtier, bowing profoundly, had backed out of the bedroom into the adjoining Oeil de Bœuf, then Louis XV would leap out of bed again, put on his dressing gown, and accompanied by a personal page carrying a light, would skip up the secret staircase and slip into his own comfortable bed in his own comfortable room. Then in the morning the ceremony had again to be performed in reverse. It never seems to have occurred, either to Louis XV, his family, or his courtiers, that these cumbrous parades were absurdly unreal. The Monarch was King by Divine Right, and his accustomed actions must be distinguished from those of ordinary mortals, as it were liturgically.

He was selfish, self-indulgent, and heartless: but he was not a cruel man. After the victory of Fontenoy, in which he himself had acted with courage and decision, he rode over the stricken field with his eldest son. He drew the boy's attention to the dead and dying British soldiers, remarking: "This is what it means for a man of kind heart to win victories. The blood of our enemies is still the blood of fellow human beings. True glory should consist in the avoidance of such carnage."

He was, as has been said, abominably lazy; but he was not a stupid man. He possessed a wonderful memory and never forgot a face, a name, or a date. He enjoyed the society of scientists and mathematicians, but, as is the way with autocrats, he hated intellectuals. He was not so much hypocritical or treacherous as diffident; he possessed a devious mind and had an unpleasant taste for the tortuous, the clandestine, and the indirect. Essentially he was an utterly weak person who was frightened of imposing his authority. "He did not dare," writes M. Gaxotte, "to exercise his will."

He is usually represented as silent, melancholy, self-centered and morose. But when alone with his family or his mistresses he could relax into gaiety and his laughter would echo on the secret staircase or up in the roof garden among the tubs. As so often happens to kings of no great intellectual gifts and deficient sensibility, he had a passion for practical jokes, a taste which is an unvarying symptom of deficient sensibility and a second-rate mind. But he was certainly an amazing figure of glory with his handsome features and his resplendent diamonds and brocades. His glance, we are told, "beamed with a compelling, but not exaggerated, majesty." He had inherited something of the Great King's gift of inspiring awe.

Four

On the death of the Regent Orléans, the direction of affairs passed for a while to the King's cousin, the duc de Bourbon, a great-grandson of the mighty Condé. He was thirty-one years of age, remarkably dull, something of a hunchback, and blind in one eye. Even the courtiers of the ancient régime, accustomed as they were to imbecility in high places, regarded the duc de Bourbon as too incompetent to be borne. He was entirely under the influence of his mistress, the marquise de Prie, a pretty, vivacious woman, who had the misfortune to be interested in politics.

The King by then had reached the age of fifteen and it was realized that he was already capable of producing a son and heir. Would France have to wait until the little Spanish infanta attained marriageable age? The courtiers and Madame de Prie persuaded the duc de Bourbon that so long a delay would expose the dynasty to risks. The King must immediately marry some woman capable of bearing children. Thus the little infanta was bundled back to Spain, without her parents being warned what was happening; the bewildered child reappeared in Madrid, unaware either why she had been sent to Versailles or why she had been so abruptly dismissed. Her parents, not unnaturally, were incensed by this public insult. It is satisfactory to record that the discarded infanta ended up as Queen of Portugal.

Meanwhile the family, Madame de Prie and the inner circle at Versailles busied themselves with drawing up lists of other European princesses suitable to become Queen of France. A list of ninety-nine names was prepared. It included Princess Anne, the eldest daughter of the Prince of Wales, who was however crossed off the list on the ground of being a Protestant. The choice fell eventually on Marie Leczinska, the daughter of Stanislas, the dethroned King of Poland, who was then living in penurious retirement at his countryseat at Wissemburg. She was six years older than the boy King and, although renowned for her virtue and good temper, was not a woman of great social brilliance, physical attractions, or intellectual gifts. French public opinion was startled to learn that this dowdy girl, who was not even royal, should have been chosen as the bride of the greatest king on earth. They naturally invented the story that Marie Leczinska had been chosen by Madame de Prie as a person who could in no circumstances outshine her at Chantilly or Versailles. Bourbon's mistress became widely and deeply disliked.

The marriage was celebrated on September 4, 1725. Although only fifteen years of age, the King proved himself an assiduous husband. Twin daughters were born within a year after the marriage, and in 1729, to the rapturous delight of the French people, a Dauphin appeared; Louis presented Marie Leczinska with ten children in all, of whom seven survived.

Madame de Prie had probably little to do with the choice of Marie Leczinska, since her real ambition was to induce the King to marry the duc de Bourbon's sister. This was opposed by the King's old tutor and adviser, Bishop Fleury, who even went so far as to suggest that Madame de Prie should be banished from court. The duc de Bourbon alarmed by this menace, struck Fleury's name off the King's Council, and the old bishop retired in dignified resentment to his cottage at Issy. The King in a rage sent to his old tutor begging him to return. The duc de Bourbon was arrested at Rambouillet and sent under escort to Chantilly. Madame de Prie was exiled to Normandy where she eventually committed suicide. The intrigue against Fleury had failed completely. Henceforward he exercised supreme power until his death. He was aged seventy-three, when he became in substance if not in name, chief minister and he retained that post, and the affection of his master, until his death at the age of ninety in 1743. He was a virtuous and gifted statesman.

Fleury, like Robert Walpole, was a man of peace. He was austere in his personal life and he wished France to live austerely, and not to go gadding off in search of glory. Being himself an extremely mild old gentleman, he had the wisdom to choose as his two major assistants men who were rough and tough. He chose Chauvelin as his Minister of Foreign Affairs, knowing that, if need be, he would not hesitate to shout

"No!" at those who advocated a more adventurous or glamorous policy. As Minister of Finance he chose Orry, who could be fierce if need be, and who managed by 1726 to stabilize the currency and to balance the budget, an achievement which, in the days of the ancien regime, was rare indeed. Orry, as is the fate of all good Chancellors of the Exchequer, incurred great unpopularity. But Fleury was deaf to all captious intrigues. Even as Robert Walpole was driven by a burst of public hysteria into the War of Jenkins' Ear (knowing full well that Captain Jenkins had never lost his ear at all), so also was Fleury, who wished only for peace, obliged by public opinion to take part in the totally unnecessary war of the Polish Succession.

In his handling of the neverending Jansenist controversy Fleury also tried to practice patience and even appeasement. Although by then he had become a cardinal, he was not affected by any deep theological prejudices or convictions. He hated the Jansenists, not because they believed in Grace, but because they constituted a discordant minority and upset the poise of the State. With his usual patient persistence he decided to eliminate the Jansenists by isolating their leaders. When in March 1730 he proclaimed that the bull *Unigenitus* was not the law of the Church only but also the law of the land, he was not so much acting from religious zeal as from the conviction that the conflict between Free Will and Predestination divided public opinion unnecessarily and was in any case not connected with any purely French interest.

When the parliament refused to register this enactment, they were summoned to a *lit de justice* at Versailles and informed by the King in person that they were being "disobedient and rebellious." The Monarch, they were informed, had sole right to make the laws of the land. "This is my will," stated the young King. "Do not force me to make you feel that it is I who am your master." The leaders of the opposition were then exiled to some of the small provincial towns of France, where they were so atrociously bored that one by one they made humble apology and crept back to Paris. Again the Cardinal's policy of calm persistence had secured desired results. But the parliament never forgave this high-handed action.

It is presumably to the Fleury period that we should apply M. Gaxotte's fervent and eccentric eulogy of the reign of Louis XV. "Never," he writes, "has France enjoyed so wide and enlightened an administration or one so devoted to the public good and so receptive of popular wishes and ideas." "The reign of Louis XV, he writes again, "was the great century of public administration before it crystallized into bureaucracy." It is true indeed that it was under Fleury, and later under Choiseul, that was founded that excellent body of civil servants who have so often proved the saviors of France. Yet, in spite of M. Gaxotte, such high praise is scarcely merited by the post-Fleury period. It was certainly an age of intellectual effervescence and extreme social laxity and elegance. People had ceased to believe in demon dogmas and had not yet allowed sensibility to drown their eyes in causeless tears. "They knew the art of living," writes M. Gaxotte, "and they lived."

Five

In 1744, when at Metz, the King fell seriously ill. His life was despaired of and the priests gathered round his bed to extract a full confession. The King admitted his past sins and promised that, if he recovered, he would become a reformed character. The duchesse de Chateauroux, the mistress of the moment, was hurried into a carriage which drove off to the east with drawn curtains and without arms on the panels or liveried footmen on the box. In spite of these precautions it became known that this dark anonymous vehicle contained the mistress of the day and stones were thrown at it in the villages through which it passed. Meanwhile from west to east the Queen was dashing to her husband's bedside and was greeted everywhere with sympathetic acclaim. These demonstrations and counter demonstrations were reported to the King, who for the first time entertained the horrible suspicion that he might not have fully merited the name his courtiers had invented for him, the name of "Louis the well-beloved." The Metz illness is important also because the priests were so tactless as to publish the confession they had extracted from the sick King and his promises to amend his way of life. The confession was printed and read from the pulpit of every parish throughout France. Louis was enraged when he heard of the publicity given to what had been a very private occasion and complained that he had been made the victim of an ecclesiastical farce. Once he had recovered from his illness and regained his usual all too robust health, he continued to bear resentment against the Jesuits who had extracted this confession and proclaimed it far and wide. It was in the following year that he met Madame de Pompadour.

Jeanne Poisson was the daughter of a clerk in the municipality who had been accused of speculating in grain and was obliged to go into voluntary exile for eight years. Her mother, during this enforced absence, became the mistress of an amiable fermier général, Le Normant de Tournehem, who educated Jeanne and her brother and ended by allowing the girl to marry his nephew, Le Normant d'Etioles. The old fermier général had seen to it that this pretty girl should be instructed in all the social arts and graces and it has even been suggested that from the outset he had her trained to become the perfect royal mistress. She was introduced into the society of the salons, received by the formidable Madame Geoffrin, came to know Montesquieu, Marivaux, and Duclos, and corresponded with Voltaire himself. It was Binet, the Dauphin's chief valet, who introduced her to the petits appartements and on February 19, 1745, she attended the fancy dress ball which figures in the well-known print by Cochin, in which the King and Jeanne d'Etioles are depicted as flirting together, inconveniently disguised as two clipped yews. This topiary encounter produced rapid results. Within a few months Jeanne Poisson became accredited chief mistress and marquise de Pompadour. As always in Paris, the event was celebrated by street lampoons. "Need we be surprised," asked the ballad singers, "if the court feels itself degraded? After all it's from Billingsgate that the fish comes":

Si la cour se ravale
De quoi s'étonne-t-on?
N'est ce pas de la Halle
Que nous vient le poisson?

Madame de Pompadour remained the King's mistress for five years, from 1745 to 1750. When his physical passion for her began to wane, she was astute enough to provide a series of other bodies for him, retaining for herself the sole influence over his mind and heart. For a further fourteen years, until her death from tuberculosis on April 15, 1764, she remained his closest friend and adviser, the only person in whom the suspicious and guileful monarch placed any trust. She was a kind woman in her way, did much to protect the *Encyclopédistes* and the philosophers, and with her exquisite taste rendered Paris the temple of fashion, millinery, and interior decoration. She was even so tactful as to persuade the King to pay more attention, at least in public, to his consort. The Queen had become resigned to the situation and in an odd way was grateful to Madame de Pompadour. "If there has to be a mistress," she is reported to have said, "I would rather have Madame de Pompadour than anyone else." It was part of Versailles etiquette that if anyone not of royal blood died in the palace, their bodies should immediately be removed. When Madame de Pompadour died, her corpse was thus placed on a stretcher, lightly covered with a cloth, and carried out into the night by two footmen. The King, from the balcony, watched it go. It was said that he showed no sign of regret.

The foreign policy of France was traditionally governed by hostility to Austria, who was regarded as the hereditary and inevitable enemy. In the War of Austrian Succession, however, when France had gained great victories (Fontenoy in 1745, Roucoux in 1746, Lauffeldt in 1747) it became evident that the power of the Hapsburgs was on the decline and that it was England, rather than Austria, who should be regarded as the hereditary enemy of France. The French treaty with Prussia was due to expire in May 1756, but Louis and Madame de Pompadour were so dilatory that no serious or timely attempts were made to renew it. Louis did not relish being allied to a Protestant monarch, and Madame de Pompadour was hurt by the coarse gibes which Frederick the Great indulged in against her. When Frederick threw over the French alliance and signed with Great Britain the Treaty of Westminster, the French court and government accused Prussia of the darkest treachery and realized with alarm that they were now isolated in Europe. Ever since the closing years of the Great Monarch there had been some far-seeing diplomatists who predicted that the day must come when the old tradition of enmity must be reversed and an entente arranged between France and Austria. Kaunitz, the sagacious Minister of Maria Theresa, was all in favor of such a reversal of policy and Madame de Pompadour, who had the great honor of receiving a personal letter from the straitlaced Empress, induced her clever Abbé de Bernis to initiate secret negotiations. Thus when in 1756 Frederick launched the Seven Years War, France was in alliance with Austria, against the Protestant Powers. As a result, she lost her overseas Empire, but it would be exaggerated prudery only that could attribute the blame for that disaster to Madame de Pompadour.

On January 5, 1757, the King was residing at the Trianon, but had crossed the park to Versailles in order to visit his sick daughter, Madame Victoire. At 7:00 that evening he descended the staircase accompanied by the Dauphin and the duc d'Ayen to drive back to the Trianon. The carriage was waiting in the courtyard and as the King walked out into the night a man slipped between two of the guards and struck the King upon the chest. "Duc d'Ayen," remarked the King calmly, "someone has given me a blow," and then, putting his hand to his shirt, he found that it was covered with blood. "I am wounded," he said, "and there is the man who did it. Arrest him but do not kill him." The King then walked back into the palace, but as the court was at Trianon, there were no servants to be found. They had to lay the King on a mattress and cover him with a bath towel. Surgeons and priests were sent for. The news spread as far as Paris that the King had been assassinated. The wound was however found to be superficial and the King quickly recovered. He was conscious that the joy at his recovery was not as spontaneous and universal as that manifested at the time of the dauphin's birth. Again he realized the horrible fact that he was not Louis the well beloved.

Damiens, the would-be assassin, was found to be a servant of a magistrate. He had been inflamed by the invectives against the Court which he had overheard at his master's table and was angered by the alleged subservience of Louis XV to the dictates of the Pope of Rome. Damiens was certainly off his head, but he was tried nonetheless and condemned to an atrocious form of execution. The scaffold had been erected in the Place de Grève and the naked body of the footman was torn to pieces by huge pincers of red-hot iron. Casanova and his friends, from the seats that they had hired in a window overlooking the scaffold, listened to the victim's screams of agony with unperturbed glee.

Six

The monarchy meanwhile was losing prestige. The Paris salons and the intellectuals, together with the parliaments, began loudly to voice their criticisms. One of the most sagacious acts of the Government was an attempt to introduce a better regulated tax, called the *vingtième*, which should be levied on all classes of the community. The Church refused to surrender the exemptions they had for so long enjoyed and the King, yielding to the Church party in the Court, weakly surrendered. He was widely blamed for his timidity.

Since the death of Madame de Pompadour his private life had become even more undignified. Apart from the Parc aux Cerfs, he installed as his mistress in chief, Jeanne Bécu, who was little better than a woman of the streets. Her father was said to be a monk from the Picpus monastery, she had worked as a midinette and was the mistress of a notorious rake, comte Jean du Barry. The King was attracted by her high spirits and vulgar ways. Since Jean du Barry was already married, his younger brother Guillaume was brought up from Languedoc and consented, for a monetary consideration, to marry his brother's callet. A disreputable dowager was then brought up from the provinces and employed to present the comtesse du Barry at Court. Jeanne Bécu, was a kindhearted, jolly, laughing girl, and served at moments to dispel the melancholy with which Louis XV was increasingly afflicted. She managed to survive the King and died under the guillotine screaming and struggling with the executioner. She was a harmless creature who did not interfere much in politics; but she did much damage to the royal prestige.

It was known also that the King was conducting a secret foreign policy of his own, behind the backs of his Foreign Minister and his ambassadors abroad. He was strongly opposed to the partition of Poland, wishing to keep that distracted country as a barrier against Russian aggression. He regarded England as the principle enemy and had worked out a detailed scheme, under which there should be a simultaneous Franco-Spanish assault on Gibraltar, Port Mahon, Jamaica, and Ireland, together with another Jacobite rising and the landing of an invading army of 80,000 men at several points on the southeastern coast of England. Such schemes may well have been in the best interests of French policy and it is difficult to understand why, unless from a natural love of deception, he did not use his authority to impose this policy upon his ministers and his council. He preferred devious paths and his hesitations rendered his utter weakness and trickery obvious to all. One of his greatest political errors was to incur the combined enmity of the parliaments and the Church; he ill-treated them both.

On April 27, 1774, the King was taken ill on returning from hunting at the Trianon. They moved him to Versailles. His fever increased and spots appeared on his face and chest. The doctors realized that he had contracted confluent smallpox of a malignant type. All hope was abandoned. Madame du Barry, wishing to avoid the scandal of Metz left quietly without her departure being noticed. The illness increased rapidly and within a few days the splendid body of the King had been reduced to a mass of putrefaction. The stench was so horrible that all the doors and windows had to be kept wide open.

On the balcony outside the State bedroom they set a candle in a glass globe as a sign that the King was still alive. It was from that balcony, fifty-nine years before, that the duc de Bouillon had proclaimed his accession. At 3:30 on the afternoon of May 10, 1774, a footman came out onto the balcony and snuffed the candle. Louis XV was dead.

Chapter 16

Gullibility

(Cagliostro, 1743–1795)

———•◆•———

The optimism of the Century—Their conceit—They never realized how hysterical and credulous they really were—The Law
boom—The age of the charlatan—Count de Saint Germain—His
claim as a magician—Gains the support of Madame de Pompadour and is sent on a secret mission to Holland—It fails owing to
the intervention of the duc de Choiseul—Casanova—Gains support of Cardinal de Bernis—His visit to Voltaire—His "oracle"—
He obtains complete dominance over Madame d'Urfé—He per-
suades her that he can change her into a man—His impositions
in this connection—Giuseppe Balsamo, best known as "Count
Cagliostro"—His birth and early life—In England and Russia—He
acquires the protection of Prince Louis de Rohan, Cardinal of Strasbourg—Jeanne de la Motte Valois—The affair of the Queen's necklace—Cardinal de Rohan defrauded by Madame de la Motte—The
Bosquet de Venus—The purchase and theft of the necklace—Dis-
closures and confessions—Trials and verdicts—The end of Madame
de la Motte—The end of Cagliostro.

One

THE PHILOSOPHERS OF the eighteenth century were on the
whole a complacent group who felt that they were masters of
the future and that mankind was progressing rapidly towards

another golden age. They were confident that by destroying the myths handed down by theology, by teaching their contemporaries to question all previous conventions and institutions, they would establish the principles of reason and justice and liberate the earth from the fallacies and cruelties of previous centuries. In destroying the belief in the supernatural, they imagined that the peoples of the world would readily accept the ideals of the "natural" and that henceforward toleration and good sense would become the guiding stars. They did not realize that most men are foolish and that, once the sober and excellently organized disciplines of religion were removed, the resultant vacuum would be filled by frivolous ideas and cabalistic superstitions. Being under the illusion that all men are born equal and that the gift of reason was "natural" and therefore common to all mankind, they were convinced that good sense was inherent even in savages and children. "I am persuaded," wrote Lord Chesterfield—an unattractive but extremely eighteenth-century character—"that a child of a year and a half old is to be reasoned with." He himself never fully admitted that the excellent if worldly good sense that he inculcated with such persistence into his own child, Philip Stanhope, resulted in the boy becoming a clumsy, stuttering boob.

With this complacency, or perhaps we should call it "optimism," went an element of conceit which is irritating to our twentieth-century temperaments. The intellectuals of the period were forever boasting that they were completely cosmopolitan and immune to the vulgar form of enthusiasm which was known as patriotism. Yet the pride that they took in their own culture and civilization was in fact nationalistic in its exclusiveness and arrogance. Thus the Parisians, in spite of their recurrent bursts of anglomania, were as convinced in those days as they are today that no country other than France possesses any social aptitudes, any sharp intelligence, or any elegant taste. The British, at least until the surrender of Yorktown, were even more blatantly self-satisfied. Goldsmith, who was a vain but not a particularly conceited man, could devote to his compatriots the following intolerable lines:

Stern o'er each bosom Reason holds her state
With daring aims irregularly great,
Pride in their port, defiance in their eye,
I see the lords of human kind pass by.

It is not surprising that the New England Colonists failed to appreciate this pride of port, those insolent eyes. Even after we had lost the War of Independence and been humiliated in the face of Europe, we were quick to invent solaces. We would point out that the only war in which we had ever been beaten was one waged against men of our own race; and that, whereas we might, through lack of public will and private wisdom, have lost our Western Empire, we had at the same time created a new and even richer Empire in the East. Our endurance and achievement during the Napoleonic wars fully restored the pride of the British, the *superbia Britannorum*. By 1815, we were every bit as conceited as we had been before 1775. I would not say that even today, when we have ceased to be the greatest Empire in the world, all vestiges of the old *superbia* have been obliterated. It is quite a healthy resilience.

The fact remains, however, that the pride which the intellectuals of the eighteenth century took in their own intelligence, blinded them to the absurdity of the intellectual escapades and hysterical recklessness in which the century indulged. One would have supposed that the French would have been taught by their philosophers, their economists, and their *Encyclopédistes* that booms, based on credit rather than on solid assets, are bound sooner or later to collapse. The Scotsman John Law, who was born in Edinburgh in 1671, and in whom the Regent placed such unlimited confidence, was in fact an honest man; although he possessed a genius for financial manipulation, he had less understanding of the fundamental laws of economics. His Bank, his Compagnie des Indes, were not fraudulent; it was merely that the paper issued was in such excess of solid assets that, once panic set in, ruin became inevitable. The public were dazzled by the vision of legendary Mississippi riches—of mountains of gold, caves of rubies, grottoes of emeralds. They flocked to the rue Quincampoix where the exchange had been established and the shares by 1720 soared from 500 to 18,000; in the autumn of that year they slumped to the value of one louis. Law, himself a ruined man, escaped in a cab and took refuge in Holland: he died in poverty in Venice in 1729. The Regency and the central Government were deeply discredited. The men of the Age of Reason could assuredly behave most unreasonably. The old-fashioned firm of bankers, the Paris brothers then sought, and not without some success, to clear up the mess. Voltaire, who had some respect for Law, contended that he may have ruined a number of speculators; but that he did impart a powerful stimulus to French industry and commerce.

Even as they never admitted that Sensibility, when it arrived, was an unreasonable emotion, or that the gospel of Jean Jacques Rousseau was a false and debilitating gospel, so also were they seemingly unaware of how foolish to future generations would appear their astonishing credulity. It is curious to note that once creeds are abolished credulity creeps in. They thought of their century as the golden age of the Natural Philosopher. They were blind to the fact that it was also the golden age of the charlatan. It seems incredible to us that such frauds and scamps as Saint Germain, Cagliostro, and Casanova should have been able to impose themselves on men of education, intelligence, and sense. It is impossible to assess the infinite variety of the century unless some account be given of the claims and achievements of the magicians.

Two

The prototype of the century's many necromancers was the so-called count de Saint Germain, who in the course of his travels adopted such pseudonyms as Prince Racockzi, Prince Tsarogy, General Soltikov, comte de Bellayme and Lord Welldone. He contended that he could remove the flaws from precious stones and that he had invented an indelible dye. He also claimed to have discovered an elixir which could confer on those who swallowed it the benefit of eternal youth. He used convex and concave mirrors on which to project the faces of the dead, whom by his cabalistic formulas he would summon from the dark regions. He would also assert that he himself had lived a hundred years and that his memory went back to many centuries before that. He had, in fact, been on intimate terms with Alexander the Great and had on one occasion had the privilege of a very interesting conversation with Christ.

In 1745, when in London, he was arrested as a Jacobite spy but was shortly afterwards released. He attracted the attention of the Prince of Wales. Even Horace Walpole, who prided himself on his good sense and his contempt for any form of superstition or "enthusiasm," was attracted by Saint Germain. "He sings," he informed Horace Mann on December 9, 1745, "plays on the violin wonderfully, composes, is mad and not very sensible." His success in London was transitory.

In France, however, he acquired for himself a certain position of influence. He cast the horoscope of Madame de Pompadour and through her was brought to the attention of Louis XV, who was so bored with self-indulgence that he welcomed anything outside and beyond this fleshly earth. He was positive that he had with his own eyes seen Saint Germain melt three small diamonds into one enormous diamond and he had every hope that he would succeed in transmuting base metals into gold, and thus restore the sick finances of France. He had an idea also that Saint Germain by his chemical skill would invent an imperishable dye and thus give to the French dye industry the supremacy that had once been enjoyed by Tyre. He thus accorded a substantial pension to Saint Germain, fitted out a laboratory for him in the château de Chambord, and let it be generally known that he enjoyed royal favor.

He even went so far as to dispatch Saint Germain on a secret mission to Holland for the purpose of negotiating a private loan with the Dutch bankers and even, perhaps, of opening underhand peace negotiations with the British. The duc de Choiseul, at that time Foreign Minister, was rightly suspicious of the secret policy being carried out by the King and Madame de Pompadour behind the backs of his Ministry and of the French ambassadors abroad. He was determined to discredit Saint

Germain and put it about that he was not a count at all, but the illegitimate son of a low-class Portuguese Jew. He informed the States General that this emissary was without any official backing and he instructed his Ambassador at The Hague not to receive him and to see to it that his British colleague was told that the man was a fraud.

In order further to assail the prestige of this necromancer, Choiseul is said to have employed a man of the name of Gauve to impersonate Saint Germain and to render him ridiculous and suspect by boasting wildly of the intimacy he had achieved with Alexander the Great and of the many confidences made to him by Christ. His secret mission was, by such means, rendered a failure.

Disappointed by this ill success Saint Germain, under the name of Odart, traveled to Russia. The Empress Catherine was persuaded to receive him and he threw upon his concave mirror the semblance of Peter the Great who took the occasion to assure the Empress that he thoroughly approved of her having murdered his grandson and usurped the throne herself. But, apart from this curious episode, his Russian visit does not appear to have been a financial success. He returned to France and set up a dye factory at Tournai which was a perfectly authentic and, it would seem, successful enterprise.

Casanova who met Saint Germain when dining with the marquise d'Urfé found him an impressive personage. He was well educated, could speak several foreign languages with ease, and secured the support of women by giving them an ointment which, he said, would spare them the disadvantage of growing old. He would dine out frequently but refused to touch any of the food provided, saying that he must follow the special diet which had preserved him for three hundred years.

The last patron on whom Saint Germain was able to impose was the Landgraf of Hesse who afforded him hospitality and appointed him unofficial librarian. He died on February 1784 and was buried at Eckenforde.

Saint Germain was not the most notorious or sensational of the eighteenth-century magicians. He is interesting mainly because he combined in his person all the tricks, disguises, and deceptions practiced by his more famous successor Cagliostro. He also was constantly on the move, flitting to some new region when once his fraudulence had been disclosed. He also claimed to be charged with some State mission of a nature too secret to be revealed. He also boasted that he possessed the secret of eternal life, was able to turn quicksilver into silver, to enlarge and purify precious stones, and to summon the spirits of the dead. He also was a good musician and an amusing companion. He also was a trifle mad. And he also was able to gain the confidence and support of several eminent people and to live on patronage. But, whereas Saint Germain was little more than an ingenious fraud, Cagliostro and his imitator Casanova were charlatans of genius.

Three

Casanova is chiefly famous for his salacious memoirs. Even those who dislike pornography will admit that they furnish an unexampled picture of the sort of existence pursued by members of the European upper-middle classes who were outside politics, who never gained admission into the inner Court clique, and who only circled on the fringe of the philosophic or literary salons. Casanova was continually being pushed on by the police, who rightly suspected him of spying and cheating and he thus traveled backwards and forwards across Europe, enjoying amorous adventures and the delights of cardsharpers in every town. Apart from one disastrous entanglement with a London whore, Casanova was fortunate in his women and parted with them (as he invariably did part with them) on amicable terms. He was an ardent freemason and could always count on a warm welcome in masonic lodges. He gives us an astonishing panorama of brothels and palaces, of convents and taverns, of spas and casinos, of billiard saloons and gambling dens, of operas, concerts, and masked balls, of inexperienced virgins and practiced courtesans. The wild eccentricity of the eighteenth century is revealed to us in page after page of these prurient memoirs. Writing in old age in the library of Schloss Dux in Bohemia, he recalled with lascivious relish the adventures of his youth and, although he never reveals with any conviction how exactly he made his money, or why exactly he was so often being lodged in gaol or conducted across the frontier, he makes it abundantly clear that he was a gifted impostor who battened upon the gullibility of his fellow men. It was probably his masonic activities, and his connection with the Rosicrucians that were mainly responsible for his getting into such constant trouble with the authorities.

Giovanni Jacopo Casanova de Seingalt was born in Venice in 1725. He was certainly not a count, and he himself admitted that he had himself invented the name "Seingalt" by arranging capital letters drawn at random and composed in a pretty pattern. As a child he suffered from glandular deficiency and his mental development was retarded. He was sent away from school and then brought up in the household of Cardinal Acquaviva. On reaching puberty he recovered his vivacity and, according to his own account, served in some military or naval capacity in Rome, Naples, and Constantinople. On his return to Venice he was denounced as a freemason and a spy and was without trial thrown into "the prison under the leads." After fifteen months in the Piombi, he effected his escape and embarked upon his career as a forger and unremitting traveler. At different periods we find him in Paris, Madrid, Lisbon, London, Warsaw, and St. Petersburg. Eventually he obtained permission to return to Venice where he remained from 1774 to 1783, at which date he was obliged "to shake from my feet the dust of my ungrateful country." In 1783, he met graf Waldstein a relation of the Prince de Ligne, and obtained from him lodging and maintenance in Schloss Dux, where he wrote his memoirs. He died in this Bohemian castle, probably in June of 1798.

In Rome and Venice he had met the kindly Abbé de Bernis who, on becoming Foreign Minister, continued his interest in Casanova and even sent him on a mission to Holland to negotiate a loan. Unlike Saint Germain, whose negotiations were obstructed by the French Embassy at The Hague, Casanova was given full credentials and, if we are to believe what he writes, was most successful in his mission and was on his return accorded the praise of de Bernis, of the Controller

General, and of Madame de Pompadour herself, as well as a commission in solid cash.

During his wanderings in Switzerland, he was able to obtain an introduction to Voltaire and stayed for three nights at Les Délices where Voltaire was then housed. Voltaire assured him that he had devoted his whole life to exterminating "the hydra of superstition" and Casanova had the impudence to reply that this was not an achievement to boast of. "If a people," he said, "lost their superstitions, they would all become philosophers and thereby also lose the gift of obedience. You should let the people keep their hydras, since they love them." He also quarreled with Voltaire over the relative merits of Ariosto and Tasso. And, although he was one of the few visitors to speak kindly of Madame Denis, his three nights at Les Délices were anything but a success. Thereafter, from wounded vanity, he seldom missed an opportunity to refer slightingly to the philosopher of Ferney.

During his boyhood, and before he was incarcerated in the Piombi, he suffered from extreme penury and was obliged to earn his keep by playing the fiddle in taverns and on the streets. Then, one night in 1746, the Venetian Senator Bragadin had a fit on the stairs and was caught with such dexterity by the strong arms of Casanova that in gratitude he extended towards him protection, money, and love. Already Casanova had become interested in occultism. He first learnt the art from an old sorceress of Murano, and pursued his studies of the occult at Padua and later in Paris. In 1748, he endeavored by cabalistic formulas to discover the buried treasure of Cesena and he elaborated for himself what he called his "oracle" which was in fact a tabulated pyramid of numbers from which he derived oracular answers to questions put by his adherents. He had the utmost contempt for his fellow Sorcerers, deriding Saint Germain and predicting that Cagliostro would end his career as a galley slave.

The real triumph of Casanova's career as a sorcerer was the domination he achieved over the wealthy and aged Marquise d'Urfé, a mastery which he exploited with ingenious tenacity and considerable success.

Of all the stories of eighteenth-century credulity, the Madame d'Urfé episode is the most curious and revealing.

Four

When in Paris Casanova met count Nicolas de la Tour d'Auvergne a bright young spark with many aristocratic connections. They quarreled over a gambling debt, fought a duel in the Rond Point des Champs Elysées, became reconciled, and thereafter firm friends forever. Casanova had slightly wounded de la Tour d'Auvergne, who in any case was suffering from sciatica. Mixing a disgusting concoction in a bowl, Casanova painted the wound and the thigh with the "talisman of Solomon" with the result that the wound healed immediately and the sciatica disappeared. The count was so delighted by this magic medicament that he undertook to introduce Casanova to his rich aunt, the marquise d'Urfé, who had a passion for the supernatural.

Madame d'Urfé lived in a large house on what is today the Quai Voltaire. She had a small chemical laboratory and a library of occult literature, including an unknown work by Paracelsus written in a secret cipher. She confessed to Casanova that her life's ambition was to enter into communication with the elemental spirits and he undertook to assist her. He describes her as "a really educated woman and perfectly sensible, except where her ruling mania was concerned." He admits that he pretended to know more about the occult sciences than was justified by his dabblings at Padua and Murano. He persuaded her that he had a familiar spirit of the name of Paralis who provided him with answers to every question through the medium of his "oracle." "I became," he wrote, "the arbiter of her soul and I often abused the power that I exercised over her." She knew that the elementary spirits would refuse to enter into communication with a woman. Casanova, with the help of his oracle, convinced her that he could succeed in changing her sex. "I left her," he confesses, "taking with me her soul, her heart, her mind, and all the remaining vestiges of her commonsense."

GIACOMO CASANOVA

Portrait made about 1750-1755 by his brother Francesco Casanova

He first persuaded her that the only way in which she could change her sex was for her soul to pass into the body of a male child born of a mortal by an immortal spirit. The idea was that the marquise would drink the poison known as "The draught of Paracelsus" and that when in the act of expiring she would clasp the child to her bosom, hold him tightly lip to lip, and thus secure that her dying breath entered into his body. On his return from Holland he brought with him one of his own illegitimate sons by Thérèse Imer—a boy of thirteen whom he claimed fulfilled all the requirements. The marquise was delighted with the boy and called him count Aranda, although his real name was Pompeati and he came, not from Toledo, but from Vienna. Madame d'Urfé seems to have discovered that the boy Aranda had not really been born of an immortal mother and Casanova quickly devised an alternative stratagem. A new magic child was to be fathered by Casanova on a virgin of distinction and then produced as the medium for the operation.

Casanova selected as the designated virgin a discarded mistress from Bologna, called la Corticella, whom he presented to Madame d'Urfé under the Byzantine title of "Countess Lascaris." He was always postponing the operation, partly because he did not really wish the marquise to swallow the Paracelsus poison. But he was perfectly prepared to perform the preliminary stage of the operation, namely enabling Countess Lascaris to conceive a child. Unfortunately by that time the boy Aranda who was precocious by nature, had reached the age of puberty, and had made successful advances to La Corticella. Casanova was so enraged at being supplanted by this Cherubin that his oracle advised him the boy must be immediately dismissed. La Corticella was furious at being deprived of the services of her adolescent lover. She turned against Casanova and threatened to divulge the whole plot to Madame d'Urfé. Casanova was, as always, resourceful. The Oracle pronounced that the Corticella had gone off her head and that no credence should be given to anything she might say. It also urged the marquise to write to the moon to obtain confirmation of this statement. Casanova persuaded the poor old lady to write a letter to the moon and thereafter, having written out a suitable reply on green waxed paper in silver ink, he entered a bath with Madame d'Urfé and the moon's answer, which he had concealed in his hand, was discovered floating on the surface of the bath water. The moon confirmed word for word the advice given by the oracle and added that La Corticella had been taken possession of by a "black spirit" and had in fact been impregnated by a gnome. La Corticella was, as it happened, pregnant by a lover in Prague but had concealed her condition. She was so angry at being dismissed by Madame d'Urfé, who had pretended in public to be her aunt, that when taken to a respectable ball she suddenly started dancing the cancan with Folies Bergères abandon, thus shaming both her aunt the marquise and her reputed uncle the count Casanova. The latter was obliged to cast about for a successor, a task which to him was by no means uncongenial.

After the death of Madame d'Urfé Casanova pretended at least that he felt remorse at having abused her credulous nature. He admits that he knew it to be nonsense that she could change her sex by drinking a potion of salamander blood and breathing through the lips of a boy. He excuses himself by saying that nothing would ever have cured the marquise of her obsession. "I saw," he writes, "that there was nothing I could do but to encourage her mania and to profit by it." We may doubt whether in fact his remorse went very deep.

To us, who probably underestimate the secret influence of freemasonry in eighteenth-century Europe, it is inconceivable that a responsible minister such as the Cardinal de Bernis, however compelling may have been his desire to please, should have entrusted a financial mission to a foreigner who was certainly a card-sharper and suspected also of forging lottery tickets and acting as an agent for foreign governments. It is equally inconceivable that the family of Madame d'Urfé can without protest have permitted her to fall completely under the spell of a man whom they knew to be an adventurer. Yet if we find it hard to understand how a man like Casanova could ever have been trusted by anybody, it is even more incomprehensible that so patent a charlatan as Cagliostro should have acquired so sinister an influence and renown.

Five

Giuseppe Balsamo was born at Palermo on June 2, 1743. He was destined for the church but absconded from his seminary and lived a vagrant life in the streets of Palermo, being even as a child noted as a thief. He married the beautiful Lorenza Feliciani and for a while lived satisfactorily on her immoral earnings. Finding it difficult to raise journey money, they disguised themselves as pilgrims to the shrine of St. James of Compostella and begged their way. This brought them to Madrid and finally to Lisbon where they invested all they had in Brazilian topazes, hoping no doubt to dispose of them as diamonds. When in London in 1771 Guiseppe Balsamo, who at that date called himself marchese Pellegrini, arranged that his wife should be discovered in the arms of a rich Quaker and thereby obtained some useful sums in blackmail. When attending mass in Soho one morning Lorenza sobbed so pitifully that she aroused the compassion of a rich catholic landowner, Sir Edward Hales, who employed Giuseppe to paint murals for him in his home at Hayes Place near Canterbury. Giuseppe was an incompetent painter and the murals were such a fiasco that they had to be obliterated with whitewash. Thereafter he returned to his native town of Palermo where he was immediately charged with forgery and cast into jail. On his release he disappears for several months, although he pops up for odd moments at Naples and Toulon. Finally he returned to London and took rooms at No. 4 Whitcomb Street, Leicester Fields. He changed his name from marchese Pelligrini to count Cagliostro, styled himself a Colonel in the Third Regiment of Brandenburg, and made some money by dealing in jewels and predicting the winning numbers in State lotteries. At a ceremony at the King's Head tavern in Soho he was, in 1777, admitted a Freemason. He involved himself in trouble with Lord Scott and his mistress Mary Fry who claimed that he had purloined a diamond necklace and a snuff box set with jewels. For those and other reasons count Cagliostro left England and traveled first to Courland and thereafter to St. Petersburg, that Mecca of contemporary adventurers. He was welcomed by Potemkin but the Empress Catherine refused to give him an audience. She even wrote a farce called "The Impostor" which was performed at the Hermitage. During that stage of his career he claimed no more than to be a benevolent and imaginative doctor, and it certainly seems that as a faith healer he possessed exceptional powers. He contended, and not without justification, that his real mission was to minister to the poor, and he certainly devoted time and energy to treating the miserable paupers who massed outside his gates.

Eventually he found his way to Strasbourg and gained the acquaintance, the protection and the confidence of the Cardinal, Prince Louis de Rohan. Through him he met Jeanne de la Motte Valois and became innocently involved in the great scandal of the century—the affair of the Queen's necklace. He founded in Paris the "Council of Egyptian Masonry" designating himself as the master of the order under the title of Le Grand Cophte. He hoped, with Cardinal de Rohan's assistance, to persuade the Pope to accord to this order the same recognition as was accorded to the Knights of Malta or of St. John. He never succeeded in obtaining such recognition.

He was a fat and ugly man, not well washed, and unable to speak any language other than his Sicilian dialect. He was arrogant, rude, boastful and given to outbursts of frantic rage. "There is," wrote Lavater to the young Goethe, "nothing seductive about him." Yet by asserting that he possessed supernatural powers he managed to seduce several leading men and women in court and political society.

He claimed that he was under the special protection of the Seven Celestial Angels. He contended that he could cure all ills, even that of old age, by his special nostrums—his yellow pills, his Liquid for Women, his Wine of Egypt, and his Barba Jovis. He asserted that he was able to increase the size and brilliance of pearls and diamonds, that he could transmute mercury into silver, and turn hemp into silk. He would choose children as his acolytes and, after anointing them with the Oil of Wisdom, would induce them to see visions and interpret dreams. He convinced people that he had discovered two separate elixirs, one that "fixed" your age at the time you drank it, thus preserving you from the outrages of time; the other rendering you quite suddenly twenty-five years younger. These inventions were widely credited and rendered him immensely popular in French society.

When asked about his origins, he would adopt a hierophantic manner, raise a fat and dirty index on high, and reply in guttural Sicilian, "I am what I am." This retort was found impressive. He certainly convinced the Cardinal de Rohan that he had seen the alchemist manufacturing gold in the laboratory of the palace at Strasbourg and construct from tiny stones a huge diamond worth 25,000 Livres. "He will render me," proclaimed Rohan, "the richest prince in Europe." On the staircase of his great country palace at Saverne Rohan placed a bust of his tame magician inscribed with the words "The divine Cagliostro." The Prince-Cardinal may have been lightheaded, but Cagliostro was also furnished with letters of recommendation from the wise and mighty minister, Vergennes, and from the reputable and respected Minister of War, the count de Ségur.

It is interesting that the episode that earned him lasting notoriety was the Queen's Necklace affair, his part in which was comparatively innocent.

Six

Louis de Rohan, Cardinal of Strasbourg, had first met Marie Antoinette when, as a girl of fourteen, she made her solemn entry into Alsace and was greeted on the steps of the Cathedral by the beautiful young archdeacon, who bore the proud and honored name of Rohan. He was handsome, elegant, witty, well read, and a good sportsman. He was at the same time frivolous, silly, and wildly ambitious. He resolved that he would achieve such a position of power as to rival the fame and potency of Richelieu or Mazarin. At the age of twenty-six he was appointed assistant to the Bishop of Strasbourg; at the age of twenty-eight he was elected a member of the French Academy. He became

Archbishop, Cardinal, and High Almoner. Before he was forty he secured the glamorous appointment of Ambassador to Vienna.

The Empress Maria Theresa, who was straitlaced in many matters, almost refused to agree to this appointment, since she had been told that the Cardinal was lax in his conduct of life and even in his religious observances. Her prejudice against him was amply confirmed when, on January 10, 1772, he arrived in her capital. He had provided himself with a large and glittering suite, with two huge coaches of gold and mother of pearl, with armies of pages and footmen dressed in sumptuous Rohan liveries. The mules which dragged the heavy carts in which he had brought his pictures, looking glasses and tapestries from Paris, were shod with silver. Maria Theresa was shocked by such ostentation. She was even more angry when the Ambassador started to entertain the members of Austrian society and to seat his guests not at the long banqueting tables which were customary, but at small tables for six, thereby enabling the guests to chatter together and even laugh. Maria Theresa deluged her daughter Marie Antoinette, as well as her Ambassador in Paris, with letters of criticism and complaint. No archbishop, no ambassador even, should behave with such vulgar frivolity; the huge staff he had brought with him was composed of people "without merit or morals." Nor was she at all pleased when the ambassador gave banquets to the peasants and villagers at Baden, on the outskirts of Vienna, entertaining them with beer, sausages, and fireworks. The Empress became even more indignant when she learnt that Rohan had succeeded in fascinating her son, Joseph II, and that even the formidable minister Kaunitz consented to attend the Ambassador's parties, and even accepted a small miniature of the Prince-Cardinal which he mounted on a ring. Maria Theresa conceived for Rohan that passionate loathing which austere people sometimes develop for those who overtly enjoy themselves. She wrote to her Ambassador in Paris instructing him that Rohan had become *persona non grata* and must be recalled. He had, it seems, been so indiscreet as to write a dispatch in which he had described Maria Theresa as drying her tears with one hand while she carved up Poland with the other. This joke leaked and in the end it reached the ears of Marie Antoinette. How dared the Ambassador of France make mock of her sainted mother? From that moment Marie Antoinette conceived for Cardinal de Rohan a dislike which he strove passionately to eradicate and which led to most unfortunate consequences.

Seven

Jeanne de la Motte was the daughter of Jacques de Saint Remy, an army officer who had married a woman of the streets. The family were undoubtedly descended from the bastard son of Henri II and they were thus of Valois blood. She was a vivacious girl with brown hair, blue eyes under dark eyebrows, a large but amusing mouth, a fine complexion, and excellent teeth. She possessed a gentle, insinuating, and very pathetic voice. After her father's death in a military hospital, her slattern mother lived with a private soldier, who would beat the children and force them to beg in the streets. "Please," she would whine to passersby, "please give a penny to a daughter of the Valois." While once begging with this ingenious formula on the road from Paris to Passy she attracted the attention of the marquise de Boulainvilliers, who took the trouble to verify her descent from Henri II, found her employment in a dressmaking establishment and obtained for her a pension from the King of 800 livres a year. She was then placed in a fashionable convent for young ladies but, being recalcitrant under discipline, and almost insanely determined to acquire a position of fortune and eminence such as any daughter of the Valois merited and should attain, she ran away from the convent and became the mistress of a gendarmerie officer of the name of Nicolas de la Motte. Two months before twin babies were born, she married la Motte at Bar-sur-Aube on June 6, 1780. Hearing that her old protectress, the marquise de Rambouillet, was staying at Saverne with the Cardinal de Rohan, she and her husband appeared there in destitution and were taken back into favor. Jeanne de la Motte flattered the Cardinal with guile. She persuaded him that he had been shamefully ill used by the Empress Maria-Theresa and her daughter Marie Antoinette. Thus when the marquise de Boulainvilliers died it was Cardinal Rohan who became the friend and protector of Jeanne de la Motte.

The Cardinal had never recovered from the bitter feelings of disappointment occasioned by his dismissal from his embassy at Vienna and the dislike with which he knew he was regarded at Court. His one desire was to gain the favor of Marie Antoinette and thus open for himself the road that would lead to power and glory. Madame de la Motte exploited this obsession with ingenuity. She and her husband lived in two decrepit little rooms at a house (No. 10 rue Saint-Gilles) which still exists. They had no money to spend on clothes and were often short of food. She adopted the expedient of purchasing clothes on credit and then pawning them round the corner. By these means she saved enough money to take rooms at Fontainebleau where the Court was then in residence. She gave out that her aim was to recover "the family estates" and she cultivated the acquaintance of those who circled on the fringe of society. She managed to obtain admission to a reception given by Madame Elizabeth, the King's sister, and staged a fainting fit in the anteroom, thereby attracting attention to herself. She pretended to have had a miscarriage, was restored by applications of vinegar, and returned to her lodgings on a stretcher carried by two footmen in royal livery. She tried the same trick later at Versailles when the Queen was passing on her way to Mass through the Galérie des Glaces. This time the stratagem proved unsuccessful, but nonetheless she boasted that Marie Antoinette had recognized her as a cousin by blood, had promised that her "ancestral estates" should be returned to her, and had admitted her into the closest intimacy.

Among those who were so gullible as to believe these stories was the Cardinal de Rohan. Madame de la Motte not only repeated to him many confidences which, so she averred, the Queen had made to her, but also forged letters from the Queen indicating that there existed a close intimacy between them. She then told the Cardinal that the Queen had confided to her that although because of the strength of the anti-Rohan party at Court, she could not favor him openly, she would be prepared to meet him secretly and convey to him her forgiveness. Madame de la Motte therefore arranged that a streetwalker, who bore some resemblance to the Queen, should be disguised as Marie Antoinette and decked in imitation of her clothes and feathers. The Cardinal was told that the Queen would meet him after dark in the Bosquet de Venus at Versailles. Madame de la Motte propelled the poor dummy to the spot and then retired behind the hedge. The Cardinal advanced, fell on his knee, kissed the hem of what he took to be the royal skirt, and murmured words of homage and devotion. The spurious Marie Antoinette whispered "You can hope that the past will be forgotten," and the idiot Cardinal withdrew from the scene confident that his highest ambitions would now be fulfilled. His admiration for the powerful influence exercised by Madame de la Motte over Marie Antoinette was fortified by this clandestine encounter.

Meanwhile Madame de la Motte had heard that the jeweler, Karl Böhmer, had assembled what was said to be the finest diamond necklace in the world in the hope that Louis XV would buy it as a present for Madame du Barry with whom he was then infatuated. The death of Louis XV had left Böhmer with this almost unsalable jewel on his hands. He tried to dispose of it to the King of Spain, who stated that the price asked (namely one million six hundred livres) was beyond his means. Böhmer then approached Louis XVI hoping that he would purchase the necklace for Marie Antoinette. The King was prepared to do so, but the Queen rejected the suggestion with contempt. "Why, for such a sum," she protested scornfully, "we could build another battleship." It was then that Madame de la Motte conceived the idea of stealing the necklace for herself.

She managed to persuade Cardinal de Rohan that the Queen had confessed to her that she longed to possess the necklace, but that she could not purchase it directly since the King might object. What she needed was "a firm friend" who could raise the required credit and undertake the negotiations with Böhmer. The Cardinal therefore visited Böhmer, was shown the necklace, and drew up a memorandum of conditions under which the necklace would be bought. He had, it is true, been somewhat startled on seeing the necklace, since it appeared to him an ugly and vulgar object not at all in accord with Marie Antoinette's exquisite taste. Madame de la Motte, using forged letters on blue paper with the royal lily in the corner, persuaded him that the Queen was really resolved to acquire the jewel. She even returned to him the contract of sale which he had drawn up with Böhmer with each article ticked by the Queen who had written "approve" in the margin and signed the whole document "Marie Antoinette de France." Being convinced by this document, the jewelers handed over the necklace to the Cardinal and he, in his turn, gave it to Madame de la Motte who promised to pass it on to the Queen at their next meeting. Instead of taking it round to the palace, to which indeed she did not possess the entry, she hurried to her dressing room and with a clasp knife hacked the diamonds from their settings, handing some of them to her husband to dispose of in England and others to her lover, Rétaux de la Villette, to dispose of in Paris. La Motte managed to sell his share to the London Jewelers, Robert, and William Gray of Bond Street and Nathaniel Jeffreys of Piccadilly. To this day some of these diamonds figure in the tiaras of the British nobility. La Villette was less tactful. He asked so low a price for his diamonds that the Paris jewelers became suspicious and informed the police. Madame de la Motte meanwhile had retired to Bar-sur-Aube where she furnished a house luxuriously and lived with the utmost ostentation. Rumors reached the ears of the Cardinal who consulted his familiar, count Cagliostro. The latter gave sensible advice. He doubted whether the Queen would ever, in any circumstances, have agreed to a clandestine meeting; he suggested that all the letters which Madame de la Motte had produced were forgeries; and he averred that Marie Antoinette never in any document had signed herself as "Marie Antoinette de France." Cagliostro concluded therefore that the confidence of the Cardinal had been flagrantly abused, that Madame de la Motte had obtained possession of the necklace by fraud, and that the only thing for the Cardinal to do was to fling himself on his knees before the King, confess the whole story, and sue for pardon. The Cardinal did not in his foolishness adopt this advice immediately, foreseeing that any full confession would place him in a ridiculous position. But the rumors increased and spread: in the end the King asked him for the true facts. The Cardinal then confessed, the Queen was outraged that her name should in this manner have been taken in vain, and the King there and then deprived the Cardinal of his office as High Almoner and ordered his arrest. They were all bundled into the Bastille with the exception of Monsieur de la Motte who was still selling his diamonds in London and Edinburgh and whose extradition the French Government were unable to obtain.

At the ensuing trial, the Cardinal was acquitted by a majority of votes and retired to a monastery until the clouds had cleared. Villette was given a light sentence and Cagliostro was declared innocent but ordered to leave the country. La Motte, in his absence, was condemned to life service in the galleys, and Madame la Motte was sentenced to life imprisonment, to being publicly stripped and scourged, and to being branded on the shoulder with the letter "V" for *voleuse*. When taken to the steps of the Palais de Justice where the sentence was to be executed, she screamed and scratched and bit. They had to cut her clothes off her with knives and were able to inflict upon her writhing body only a few strokes of the birch. She twisted in such violent convulsions that they failed to brand her on the shoulder and were obliged to brand her on the breast. "It is thus," she screamed, "that you treat the blood of the Valois." After which she was removed by her executioners to the Salpétrière prison in a cab.

But the affair of the Queen's necklace was not merely an interesting case of fraud; it became a political controversy as embittered as the Dreyfus case of later years. The parliaments and the pamphleteers exploited it to discredit the Court; and Marie Antoinette, whose part in the whole transaction had been without reproach, found herself exposed to iniquitous calumny, and realized that the adoration with which she had been greeted by the young Rohan on the steps of Strasbourg Cathedral in 1770 had been transformed into brutal hate.

Cagliostro, who for once was innocent, was banished from France and eventually ended up as a prisoner in the castle of San Leo near Pasaro. He wrote a full confession to the Pope which he signed "Guiseppe Balsamo repentant sinner." He was not released; he would cling to the bars of his dungeon bawling to the villagers across the moat that he was an innocent man being tortured by tyrants. He died of apoplexy in August 1795 and was buried, not in consecrated ground, but in the fortress ditch.

Chapter 17
Solid Sense
(Samuel Johnson, 1709–1784)

———— •◆• ————

As a man of letters—As a poet—As a sage—His formidable personality—His austerity—His eccentricity—His uncouthness—His neurosis—His lack of aesthetic perception—Or psychological insight—His fear of death—His Tory principles—His hatred of innovation—His prejudices against America—As a conversationalist—His pedantry and pompousness—As a consolidator of the English language—His sociability—His love of younger people—His affection for Boswell—The Thrales—His benevolence and his dependents—His irrational attitude towards religion—His critical judgment—Milton—Ossian—His passion for truth and accuracy—His hatred of cant—His inflexible integrity.

One

D R. JOHNSON, WHOSE lumbering frame bestrides the eighteenth century, was venerated by his contemporaries as a sage. Today we regard him as an interesting, entertaining, and highly complex character, possessing a certain amount of common sense, but surprisingly devoid of imagination or sagacity. We have perhaps become so accustomed to identify enlightenment with "progress," sound views with Liberal principles, and Tory prejudices with narrow minds, that we have become thoughtlessly inclined to regard as "stupid" those who cling to the established order and who abominate change. The discrepancy between the eighteenth century and the modern view of Dr. Johnson is due mainly to the fact that, whereas they approached him as a scholar and a writer of poetry and prose, few of us read his published works with any concentrated attention, whereas most of us derive our impressions of this great and good man from the masterly biography of James Boswell.

As a writer, Dr. Johnson, was a most important figure. His *Dictionary* became the textbook of three successive generations. His *Rasselas* can rival *Candide* as an excellent cautionary tale, and was during his lifetime translated into several foreign languages. His *Life of Savage* was an original type of biography and his *Life of Pope* a masterpiece. His edition of *Shakespeare* was certainly a weighty work. His articles in the *Rambler* and the *Idler* are often sensible and sometimes profound. His *Lives of the Poets*, ill considered though some of his criticism may be, introduced a new reading public to the beauties of our literature, and are often most skillful biographical studies. And his poetry certainly deserves more attention than it generally receives. We are so accustomed to regard Dr. Johnson as a biographer, a critic and a writer of prose essays, that we forget that it was in poetry (and especially in his Latin poetry) that he revealed his inner feelings. He wrote verse all his life and in fact it was on his deathbed that he composed the last of his Latin poems. Nor can his poetry be dismissed with the faint praise that he himself conferred on that of Bentley: "the forcible verses of a man of strong mind, but not accustomed to write verse." Johnson from his boyhood was thoroughly accustomed to write verse.

London is certainly a potent poem. The *Elegy on Dr. Levet* has a tender charm. *The Vanity of Human Wishes* is a magnificent poem. His description of the death of Charles XII of Sweden, who was shot by a stray bullet when peeping over a trench parapet at Fredriksten, is so splendid an example of poetic condensation that I must quote it again:

His fall was destin'd to a barren strand.
A petty fortress, and a dubious hand;
He left the name at which the world grew pale
To point a moral or adorn a tale.

I agree with Mr. T. S. Eliot that "if this is not poetry then I do not know what poetry is."

It might be said that we know too much about Dr. Johnson to be awed by his dignity. Not only do we possess the Boswell biography and diaries; not only have we got the *Journal of a Tour to the Hebrides* (that most enchanting of all the books about Johnson) but we have Sir John Hawkins' biography and those of William Cook, Arthur Murphy, and Robert Anderson, Mrs. Piozzi's *Anecdotes* and *Thraliana*, and the vivid snapshots of Fanny Burney. In addition to this we have the revelations of Boswell's own diaries, discovered at Malahide Castle and purchased in 1927 by Colonel Ralph Isham who, with the assistance of American chemists, succeeded in rapidly restoring those discreditable passages which Lady Talbot de Malahide, before disposing of the documents, had carefully obliterated with Indian ink. These diaries were edited by Geoffrey Scott and, on his death, completed by Professor Pottle. We have also the researches of such excellent scholars as Groker, Dr. Birkbeck Hill, and Professors Pottle and Clifford.

The man whom Smollett acclaimed as "the Great Cham of literature" and Malone hailed as "the brightest ornament of the Eighteenth Century" has thus been more intimately revealed to us than any literary figure of a past century; it is not surprising that we should have become more fascinated by his eccentricity than impressed by the ponderous wisdom which inspired such veneration in his contemporaries. There are even some people who today regard Doctor Johnson as a comic character, and who will often enliven their after-dinner speeches by misquoting his remarks. He was certainly not a comic figure; he was a man of noble and impressive character who exercised a lasting influence on English language and letters. But I should not myself exhibit him as "the High Priest of Reason."

His attitude towards contemporary politics was as unintelligent as that of a resident of Bournemouth; some of his pronouncements and opinions startle us by their imbecility or intolerance; he was an enemy to liberal thought. Yet assuredly he was a great man of letters, a mighty Latinist, and a formidable grammarian who did much to consolidate the English language. It has often been my experience that men who concentrate their minds on Latin rather than on Greek, tend to become argumentative, pragmatic, narrow, obstinate and intolerant. Dr. Johnson was all these sad things. Even if we cannot admire his sense, his judgment, or his intolerance, we can love him for his eccentricity, respect him for his integrity of mind and character, and revere him for his wonderful benevolence.

Two

He was certainly a formidable person. It is recorded that when he entered a room the company were hushed suddenly as a form of schoolboys on the entry of the headmaster. Even Charles James Fox, who was not easily intimidated scarcely dared to enter into conversation when Johnson was there. The "inflexible dignity of his character" was as intimidating as the violent reaction aroused by any hint of contradiction. His superhuman memory, the ease with which he could refute any scholar by quoting by heart from the works of so obscure a Latinist as Giano Vitale of Palermo, provided him with machinegun batteries which nobody in the conflict of argument could oppose.

He was an eminently sociable man, mainly because he was afraid of solitude. "I am obliged," he said, "to any man who visits me." "Whoever," he said, "thinks of going to bed before twelve o'clock is a scoundrel." Yet he was also austere. He objected to the heavy drinking that was then the fashion, not so much for reasons of health or morals, but because drunkenness ruined conversation. He complained that most men were "without skill in inebriation" and that, whereas wine certainly served to stimulate talk, it increased vocabulary while dimming thoughts. He used himself to drink lemonade at the club dinners, but he never hesitated to confess that there had been a period when he also got drunk and would then "slink home in shame." It was Johnson who pronounced the salutary rule that "claret is the liquor for boys; port for men; but he who aspires to be a hero must drink brandy." His inconsistencies are part of his irresistible charm. On one occasion his young friends Beauclerk and Langton banged on his door in the Temple at three in the morning. Dr. Johnson appeared in a dressing gown with a poker in his hand, expecting burglars. "What!" the old man chuckled. "It is you, you dogs. I'll have a frisk with you." And off they frisked across the river to the South Bank. He was always sympathetic to the escapades of the young.

For all his learning, for all his dignity, for all his austerity, Dr. Johnson could not be described as a balanced character. He was in fact extremely neurotic and given to the most eccentric lapses.

There is a curious story of how Hogarth first met him when calling on Richardson the novelist, and how he at first assumed that the stout man standing in the window, rolling from side to side, making spasmodic jerks with his arms as if suffering from St. Vitus's Dance, must be some wretched epileptic whom Richardson was befriending out of charity. There he stood by the window "shaking his head and rolling himself about in a strange ridiculous manner." It was only when Johnson left the window and started to conduct conversation that Hogarth realized that he was no imbecile, but a man of remarkable mental gifts. Sir Joshua Reynolds, one of his most intimate and affectionate friends, made the acute observation that the strange physical spasms with which Dr. Johnson was so often visited, were due to a sense of guilt, "as if they were meant to repudiate some part of his past conduct." He was often afraid that he might relapse into insanity and once expressed the odd opinion that it would be good for people afflicted with nervous temperaments to live close to the lunatic asylum at Bedlam, where they could "take warning" from the conduct of the inhabitants.

Johnson, who was concerned, but not realistic, about himself, always asserted that he disapproved of any eccentricity of manner. "Singularity," he wrote in the *Adventurer*, "is, I think, in its own nature universally and invariably displeasing." Yet he took small pains to conceal or mitigate the eccentricity of his own behavior. He dressed untidily, he did not wash very much, and he hated clean linen. When not engaged in argument, he would often mumble to himself, repeating the Lord's Prayer or some passage from the scriptures. He was an extremely greedy man and would neither speak nor listen at meals until he had satisfied his appetite. He was an untidy feeder, and shocked people by his gobbling ways. Mrs. Harris, the mother of that gifted diplomatist, Lord Malmesbury, who met him in 1775, wrote to her son describing him "as beyond all description awkward, and more beastly in his dress and person than anything I ever beheld. He feeds nastily and ferociously and eats quantities most unthankfully. As for Boswell, he appears a lowbred kind of being."

It was not only in dress and table manners that Johnson was eccentric. He would pare his nails to the quick and even scrape the joints of his fingers with a penknife "till they seemed quite red and raw." When walking down a street he would insist on touching each of the posts which in those days lined the footway, if he missed one, he would return to the point where he had started and begin again. The trained psychiatrist could explain this phenomenon. He would drink as many as twelve cups of tea at a sitting. He would stuff orange peel into his pocket and then dry it as a cure for indigestion. He had a low rumbling laugh, which Davies described as "like a rhinoceros." When pleased by anything he would clap his huge hands together and exclaim "O brave we!" He loved variety and brisk movement. "If," he said, "I had no duties and reference to futurity I would spend my life in driving briskly in a post-chaise with a pretty woman." One of his many inconsistencies was that, even as he regarded himself as a most good-humored companion, so also did he believe that he possessed elegant and accomplished social manners. "Every man of any education," he said, "would rather be called a rascal than accused of deficiency in the graces." He contended that politeness was a lubricant in the social machine and was "fictitious benevolence." He never knew how horribly uncouth he really was. "I think myself," he once remarked to Boswell, "a very polite man."

Three

It is not his outward appearance only, not only his quirks and jerks, that persuade us that Dr. Johnson, so far from being the High Priest of sense and reason, was in fact a neurotic. He was addicted to extreme variations of mood. "Everything," wrote Boswell, "about his character and manners was forcible and violent; there never was any moderation; many a day did he fast, many a year did he refrain from wine but when he did eat, it was voraciously; when he did drink wine, it was copiously. He could practice abstinence, but not temperance." He had little sense of humor, nor can we readily understand (unless we plunge into his subconscious dread of death) why he should have been so amused by Bennet Langton's making a will in favor of his sisters, that he clung to the posts at Temple Bar, emitting peals of laughter so loud "that in the silence of the night his voice seemed to resound from Temple Bar to Fleet Ditch." He had almost no aesthetic sensibility, and was blind to the beauties of nature. He confessed to Mrs. Thrale that for him a blade of grass was never anything more than a blade of grass. "I have a notion," writes Boswell, "that he at no time had much taste for rural beauties. I have myself very little." It was the "wonderful immensity of London" that attracted him so forcibly and induced him to remark that no intellectual would willingly desert the town for the country: "When a man is tired of London, he is tired of life; for there is in London all that life can afford." He cared little for pictures and confesses that he "would rather see the portrait of a dog I know, than all the allegorical painting they can show me in the world." He hated music, since it suggested no new ideas to him and interrupted his own ruminations. He asserts that "he knew a drum from a trumpet and a bagpipe from a guitar, and that was about all." When Boswell assured him that when he listened to music he was inspired either by "pathetic dejection" or "daring resolution" he replied gruffly "I should never hear it, if it made me such a fool." The range of his imagination was restricted. When, on September 15, 1784, Lunardi made the first balloon ascent to be witnessed in England, Dr. Johnson predicted that aeronautics would never prove more than a pastime, since nobody would ever be able to invent balloons that could rise higher than mountains, or that could be steered in a required direction.

Even more surprising in a man of his intense curiosity about human temperament and character is that he had practically no psychological insight. His friend Baretti records, "The most unaccountable part of Johnson's character was his total ignorance of the character of his most familiar acquaintances."

He was assailed, one might almost say that he was constantly tortured, by dread. His fear of death or of insanity was pathological. He confessed to Boswell that he had never had one moment in which death was not terrible to him. He was never positive that, in spite of his virtuous life, he had acquired salvation through Grace. When an amiable clergyman tried to reassure him by speaking of divine benevolence and pardon, he replied that he was convinced that he and most human beings were "damned." "What do you mean by damned?" the clergyman mildly asked; he was met by a thunderous rejoinder. "Sent to Hell, Sir, and punished everlastingly." Coupled with his fear of death was his fear of madness. When on his deathbed, and speechless from an apoplectic stroke, he composed in Latin elegiacs a prayer that, even if his body were condemned by paralysis, his brain might at least be spared. Boswell explains this dark dread by saying that Johnson possessed "a horror of life in general" and that he was "foiled by futurity." It was more intricate than that.

Those who are obsessed by guilt and remorse often attribute their disquiet to the sense of failure, to an awareness that owing to laziness or self-indulgence they have not given full expression to the capacities with which they were endowed. Johnson assuredly felt guilty about his own laziness, about what Boswell has called "his dismal inertness of disposition." There were moments when, as so many of those who love dialectics, he regretted that he had never become a lawyer. Yet the depth and strength of Johnson's guilt feelings cannot be attributed to his regret at having followed no profession, or even to his youthful follies, when in company of Savage he roamed the town. His remorse at moments was so lacerating that he could not bear to be left alone with his own conscience and that he gave to his intimates the impression that he was laboring under the sense of having committed some horribly perverse sin. Mrs. Thrale's silly little hints do not help us to a solution of the problem. It may have been that he was afflicted with that rare perversion of wishing to be manacled and chained ("*de pedicis et manias insana cogitation*"). He was always inclined to write his more intimate confessions in Latin, and I do not agree with those Johnsonians who interpret these precise words as reference to the shackles of sloth. It may be that he reproached himself for not having been more considerate to his mother or his brother Nathaniel; or it may more probably have been, as the ingenious Professor Clifford has suggested, that his remorse centered on his treatment of his beloved but drunken wife, from whom he indeed seems to have demanded much. These bouts of melancholy self-reproach were in any case neurotic and hardly rational.

I have already warned the reader against the danger of assuming that Dr. Johnson, being a Tory and a firm supporter of the established order in Church and State, was unrepresentative of the spirit of his age. He was admittedly no prophet of Enlightenment, and if the ever-increasing tide of free thought had any effect upon him it was to drive him into paroxysms of fury. To him both Voltaire and Rousseau were unmitigated scoundrels. He was opposed to reform as he was opposed to innovation. He had no belief at all in the doctrine that men were born equal. "It is better," he said, "that some should be unhappy than that none should be happy, which would be the case in a general state of equality." He contended that differentiation and subordination were essential to happiness. If men were to achieve a state of equality, "they would soon degenerate into brutes; their tails would grow." Rousseau's theory of the noble savage aroused his resentment. "Don't cant," he bellowed at Boswell, "in defense of savages." "If a bull could speak, he might as well exclaim, 'Here I am with this cow and this grass; what being can enjoy greater felicity?'" He even approved of the Indian caste system. He confessed that were he a landed proprietor, he would dismiss any of his tenants who did not vote for the candidate he supported. "A poor man," he remarked, "has no honor. Were I in power I should turn out any man who dared to oppose me." "No member of society," he said, "has the right to teach any doctrine contrary to what that society holds to be true." "To his shame be it said," wrote Baretti, "he was always tooth and nail against toleration."

Even in small matters he adopted the reactionary point of view. He favored corporal punishment and approved of young Methodists being dismissed from Oxford. "They might be good beings," he remarked, "but they were not fit to be in the University of Oxford. A cow is a very good animal in the field; but we turn her out of the garden." He hated all foreigners and dismissed the French as "a gross, ill-bred, untaught people." "A Frenchman," he said, "must be always talking, whether he knows anything of the matter or not; an Englishman is content to say nothing, when he has nothing to say." He had a curious respect for decorum. He objected to bishops entering inns or taverns and said that they might as well play at tops with each other in Grosvenor Square. He felt that Sundays should be observed as "different from any other day. People may walk but not throw stones at birds. There may be relaxation, but there should be no levity." He hated to see clergymen laugh. He expressed regret when in November 1783 the Government abolished the old ghoulish procession of condemned criminals from Newgate to Tyburn Tree. "The age," he grumbled, "is running mad after innovation; all the business of the world is to be done in a new way; men are to be hanged in a new way; Tyburn itself is not safe from the fury of innovation." It is this old-fashioned, seventeenth-century attitude of mind which explains his violent prejudices against dissenters, methodists, actors and actresses, Scotsmen, sailors, Americans and Dr. Priestley.

Dr. Johnson's political opinions were certainly not those of a sage. It was sometimes said that his passion for tradition was so powerful that he still regarded the young Pretender as the legitimate King of England. He was often accused of nursing Jacobite principles, although he assured Boswell that, if by lifting his right hand he could have secured bonny Prince Charlie's victory at Culloden, he would not have held up his hand. Certainly he was flattered and delighted when, in the Library of Buckingham House, he had in 1767 a long conversation with George III. "They may talk of the King as they will," he remarked afterwards, "but he is the finest gentleman I have ever seen." "I find," he added naively, "it does a man good to be talked to by his sovereign."

His prejudice against America and the Americans is not easy to explain. He asserted that it would have been better for the world if Henry the Navigator, Vasco da Gama, and Christopher Columbus had never been born. His pamphlet of 1775 entitled *Taxation no Tyranny; an Answer to the Resolutions and Address of the American Congress* is a lamentable piece of invective. It shocked even Boswell, generally so unquestioning an admirer. "I could not," he writes, "perceive in it that ability of argument, or that felicity of expression, for which he was, on other occasions, so eminent. Positive assertion, sarcastical severity, and extravagant ridicule, which he himself reprobated as a test of truth, were united in this rhapsody." Boswell himself doubted whether it was just or wise to treat the Colonies "as if they were completely our subjects." He even wrote on the issue one of his absurd poems:

On a sure basis British Empire build;
Think not her youngest sons will ever yield
To unconditional, despotic sway.

He actually rejoiced when he heard of the capitulation of Yorktown. But Johnson never wavered in his view that the Americans were "a race of convicts who ought to be thankful for anything we allow them short of hanging." "I love all mankind," he would exclaim, "except the Americans." He denounced them as "Rascals, Robbers and Pirates," and said that if he had the power he would "burn and destroy them" utterly.

Miss Anne Seward, the Swan of Lichfield, who was present at one of these outbursts, looked at him with "mild but steady astonishment"; "Sir," she remarked, "this is an instance that we are always more violent against those whom we have injured."

Boswell, who regretted this fierce prejudice, seeks ingeniously to account for it by suggesting that Johnson's dislike of the Americans, and his blind unawareness of the justice of their cause, was due to the fact that he regarded it as rank hypocrisy for men whose economy was largely based on the ownership of slaves to talk of "Liberty." "How is it," Johnson said, "that we hear the loudest yelps for liberty among the drivers of Negros?" I do not myself believe that this constitutes an explanation of Johnson's mad prejudices. I think it was merely because he regarded the American cause as a damnable Whig stunt and saw in it a serious challenge to the established order. Such horrible bitterness was assuredly unworthy of a sage.

Four

As I have already said, we today judge Dr. Johnson, not as a philosopher and as an educative influence upon our language and literature, but as the most brilliant conversationalist that London has ever produced. His remarks echo for us across the ages like the boom of distant guns. He possesses, as Boswell noted, "a peculiar promptitude of mind" and could drive home an argument with some shattering image or illustration. It was in this manner that he impressed his contemporaries with his sagacity and common sense. Someone, for instance, was using the foolish argument that nobody had the right to criticize anything that he would be unable to perform himself. "Why no, Sir," replied Dr. Johnson, "that is not just reasoning. You *may* abuse a tragedy, though you cannot write one. You may scold a carpenter who has made a bad table, though you cannot make a table. It is not your trade to make tables." All his life he had "habituated himself to consider conversation as a trial of intellectual vigor and skill." He took it seriously. When Boswell asked him whether there had been good conversation the evening before, he replied, "We had talk enough, but no conversation. There was nothing *discussed.*"

The effect of his remarks was increased by the manner of his delivery. Boswell speaks of his "slow and sonorous solemnity" and Lord Pembroke brightly remarked that his sayings would not seem so remarkable were it not for his "bow-wow way." It was fascinating also to observe the variation of his moods. "Have you not observed," he himself said to Mrs. Thrale, "that my genius is always in extremes? That I am very noisy or very silent; very gloomy or very merry; very sour or very kind?" He never, even when talking to uneducated people or children varied the dignity of his discourse. "I speak uniformly," he said, "in as intelligible manner as I can." In his passion for dialectic he sometimes indulged in exaggerated or indefensible arguments and said many foolish things. He was aware of this defect. "Nobody," he confessed, "at times talks more laxly than I do." Thus he could assert that it was nonsense to talk about the migration of birds, but that swallows "conglobulate together by flying round and round, and then all in a heap throw themselves under water and lie in the bed of a river." It is only fair to Johnson to add that Gilbert White, that most observant naturalist, also believed that swallows did not migrate but hid during the winter months. "Exulting," writes Boswell, "in his intellectual strength and dexterity, he could, when he pleased, be the greatest sophist that ever contended in the lists of declamation; and, from a spirit of contradiction and a delight in showing his powers, he would often maintain the wrong side with equal warmth and ingenuity." If worsted in an argument, he would either break off the conversation, or resort to violent personal abuse.

His conversational supremacy was due to some extent to his command of language and the infinite resources of his memory. At times he could be ludicrously pompous as when he asserted that "among the anfractuosities of the human mind, I know not if it may not be one that there is a superstitious reluctance to sit for a picture." It was this heaviness of pronouncement that induced Churchill to ridicule him in *The Ghost*:

Pomposo, insolent and loud,
Vain idol of a scribbling croud (sic)
Whose very name inspires awe
Whose every word is Sense and Law.

His insistence on getting the best of every argument often led him to be brutally rude. He was himself almost unaware of this. "I look upon myself," he once remarked to Boswell, "as a good humored fellow." "No—no, Sir," Boswell protested, "that will *not* do. You are good-natured but not good-humored; you are irascible. You have no patience with folly and absurdity." There were moments indeed when Johnson became so insulting and abusive that even so humble a disciple as Boswell felt that human dignity could stand no more. When Bishop Percy ventured to suggest that, owing to his bad eyesight, Johnson had been unable to interpret a passage of writing, he burst into violent abuse. The Bishop apologized for giving offence. "Remember Sir, you told me I was short-sighted. We have done with civility. We are to be as rude as we please." At Inveraray the Reverend MacAulay, founder of a most illustrious family, came to visit him and gave to Johnson the impression that he was daring to interrupt his monologue. "Mr. MacAulay, Mr. MacAulay," shouted the Doctor, "Don't you know it is very rude to cry eh! eh! when one is talking?" There were many other people, even more humble than the Reverend MacAulay, who were woefully snubbed. When we regret and deplore this bullying on the part of Johnson, we are told that he was very kind to children and animals and that he would himself buy oysters for his cat "Hodge" lest the servants, "having the trouble, should take a dislike to the poor creature." It was quite easy to buy oysters in Fleet Street during the eighteenth century; it was never easy for Johnson, when involved in an argument, to be considerate or polite.

However much we may resent the violence of his conversational manner, we must admit that he did much to inculcate the need of precision in the use of language. To his contemporaries he was above all else "the great lexicographer" and his Dictionary of 40,000 words, with its trenchant definitions and abundant quotations, remains a monument of learning. Yet he was not a man to believe in linguistic rigidity, well knowing that language is an animal that grows and varies. He was opposed always to a literary tribunal such as the French Academy, contending that the language should have, not fetters, but wings. "The edicts," he wrote in his *Life of Roscommon*, "of an English Academy would probably be read by many, only that they might be sure to disobey them."

Yet it was precision of meaning that he invariably inculcated. He disliked the emotional use of words. When Boswell described a mountain as "immense" he was snubbed by his traveling companion who insisted that the mountain was no more than "a considerable protuberance." When somebody praised Grattan's rhetorical phrase that "we will persevere till there is not one link in the English chain left to clank upon the rags of the meanest beggar in Ireland," Johnson, without drawing attention to the lack of logic in the statement, replied by verbal accuracy. "Nay, Sir," he commented, "don't you perceive that *one* link cannot clank?" By such means he trained his society and his clubs into accuracy of expression. And that, in an age when the mists of sensibility were already gathering, was certainly a useful thing to do.

Five

In spite of his bouts of melancholy, his uncouthness, and his rough manners, Dr. Johnson was in fact a sociable person. The Literary Club, the dinners of which he regularly attended, comprised such distinguished members as Goldsmith, Gibbon, Adam Smith, Burke, Joshua Reynolds, Charles James Fox, Sheridan, and Garrick. His oldest friends, such as Dr. Bathurst, Reynolds, Garrick, and Arthur Murphy, were very dear to him. His dread of becoming old impelled him to gain the intimacy of very young people. He loved debutantes and would sit for hours patting their little hands with his great paw. He enjoyed the society of young men of the town, deriving satisfaction from vicarious debauchery. Boswell was only twenty-two when they first met, and Topham Beauclerk and Bennet Langton were scarcely of graduate age. "I love," he said, "the acquaintance of young people; because in the first place I don't like to think of myself growing old. In the next place your acquaintance must last longer, if they do last; and then young men have more virtue than old men; they have more generous sentiments in every respect. I love the young dogs of this age; they have more wit and humor and knowledge of life than we had; but then the dogs are not so good scholars." He was perfectly aware of Boswell's many faults, of his impudence, tactlessness, and debauchery, and yet he never failed to delight in his company. It was not only that Boswell was a whipping-boy who would patiently accept even the most humiliating affront; it was not even that he was well aware that Boswell was taking careful notes of his table talk; it was that Boswell's real affection and ebullient spirits were a tonic to him when his light was low. Of course there were moments when Boswell was improbous in his behavior and when he caused shame and irritation to his friends. There was the occasion when he turned up drunk at Miss Monckton's party and accosted Dr. Johnson "in a loud and boisterous manner, desiring to let the company know how I could contend with Ajax." There was the embarrassing occasion at Inveraray when he insisted on raising his glass to the Duchess of Hamilton. He would ask idiotic questions, "enough to drive a man mad," such as when did the Doctor first wear a nightcap? What would he do if shut up in a castle with a newborn baby or why was an apple round and a pear pointed? Johnson disliked Boswell's moods of self-pity and his constant boastfulness. He knew of his licentious habits and once remarked, "Had you not been here, you would now be with a wench." But he loved Boswell's reckless gaiety. "Your kindness," he wrote to him when he was approaching seventy, "is one of the pleasures of my life which I should be sorry to lose." "Come to me, my dear Bozzy," he wrote, "and let us be as happy as we can." He hoped even that the day might come when Boswell would become a reformed character, abandon the bottle and the women of the streets, and settle down as a respectable married man and the laird of Auchinleck. "I hope," he wrote, "in time to reverence you as a man of exemplary piety." This hope was not to be fulfilled.

I have often felt that the attraction exercised upon Dr. Johnson by Boswell was the exuberant curiosity of the younger man. They shared an insatiable inquisitiveness about life, and Johnson always placed curiosity high in the schedule of intellectual gifts. "A distinguished and elevated mind," he wrote in the dedication of his translation of Father Lobo, "is distinguished by nothing more certainly than an eminent degree of curiosity. Curiosity is one of the permanent and certain characteristics of a vigorous intellect."

The closest of his friendships was that with the rich brewer Thrale, who owned the brewery on the site of Shakespeare's theatre in Southwark and whose wife, Hesther Thrale, provided excellent food and comfort for Dr. Johnson, both in her villa at Streatham and down at Brighton. Garlyle called her "a bright papilionaceous creature, whom the elephant loved to play with and wave to and fro upon his trunk." Malone described her as "flippant and malicious" and even Johnson reproved her for her inability to control "that little whirligig, your tongue." Mrs. Thrale nursed and pampered him and was quick to apply the balm of flattery to his wounds. "I was head flatterer to poor Dr. Johnson," she scribbled in the margin of the *Idler*, "for many years." Johnson was not in love with Mrs. Thrale and after the death of the brewer (to whom he was deeply devoted) the ease of Streatham began to wane. Even before she created a tornado in her family and among her friends by marrying Signor Piozzi, her daughter's Catholic music master, the relations between Dr. Johnson and Hesther Thrale appear to have cooled. When she told him that she thought of selling the villa at Streatham, disposing of the brewery, and setting up her residence in Italy, he horrified her by replying that it seemed to him an excellent idea. "I fancied," she wrote, "that Dr. Johnson could not have existed without me forsooth, as we have now lived together above eighteen years and I have fondled and waited on him in sickness and in health—not a bit on't, he feels nothing in parting with me, nothing in the least; he thinks it 'a prudent scheme' and goes back to his book as usual. This is Philosophy and Truth; he always said he hated a *Feeler?*" Then came her marriage with Piozzi and Johnson announced that he did not wish to hear of her or from her again. It is pleasant to record that she lived happily thereafter with her beloved Gabriele Piozzi until his death in 1809.

Johnson always regarded loneliness and abandonment, the sense of not belonging anywhere and not being wanted, as among the most terrible afflictions that can visit mankind. His benevolence and sympathy were such that, to quote Macaulay, "he turned his house into a place of refuge for a crowd of wretched old creatures who could find no other asylum; nor could all their peevishness and ingratitude wear out his benevolence."

There was Miss Anna Williams, the blind daughter of a Welsh surgeon, who lived with him for thirty years and with whom he would drink tea every evening of his life. She was not a stupid or uneducated woman, but she was terribly self-pitying and peevish. Boswell was astonished that Johnson, with his "humane consideration of the forlorn and indigent state in which this lady was left by her father" could treat her "with the utmost tenderness." Then there was Robert Levet, who had been a waiter in a café in Paris much frequented by medical students and had from them picked up sufficient rudiments of medicine to be able on coming to London to treat some of the poor in the slums. He used to have breakfast with Dr. Johnson every morning and often at night he would shuffle back to Gough Square in a state of drunkenness. He became involved with a streetwalker who inveigled him into marriage, but fortunately she was before long arrested for picking pockets in Bow Street and disappeared from his life. Mrs. Thrale refers to Levet as "that odd old surgeon whom he kept in his house." When Levet died she noted waspishly, "Johnson indeed, always thinking neglect the worst misfortune that could befall a man, looked on a character of this description with less aversion than I do." In 1778, this strange colony was further increased by the admission of Mrs. Desmoulins, the widow of an impoverished writing master, and of Miss Carmichael, to whom Johnson referred as "Poll" or "Miss Wiggle-Waggle," and whom Boswell merely mentions as "a young woman I did not know."

These heterogeneous dependents introduced an atmosphere of turmoil into Gough Square. "Williams," wrote Johnson in despair, "hates everybody; Levet hates Desmoulins and does not love Williams; Desmoulins hates them both; Poll loves none of them. We do not much quarrel but perhaps the less we quarrel, the more we hate. There is as much malignity among us as can well subsist, without any thoughts of daggers and poisons." It is not surprising that Dr. Johnson should have been glad to escape from the tension of Gough Square and to exchange the whining acerbity of Miss Williams for the gay adulation of Boswell, the gentle cosseting of Mrs. Thrale, or the convivial conversational contests of The Club. The old bear certainly had a tender heart.

Six

I have said enough to indicate that Dr. Johnson, even in his virtue, was irrational. Adam Smith, who often attended the dinners of The Club, thought so little of his powers of judgment that he described him as "of all writers, ancient and modern, the one who kept off the greatest distance from common sense." In an age when most intellectuals were freethinkers, or at least Deists, he maintained and defended with violence the dogmas and observances of the Church of England. At the same time he was inclined to be superstitious, believed in ghosts and second sight, and did not deride the supernatural with the same violence as he derided the Americans, the Whigs, or the Scots. As always, he was himself unaware that there was anything illogical in his attitude, and would stoutly have maintained that in all his words and actions he showed himself to be a High Priest of Reason. Boswell explains this inconsistency by the ingenious contention that "he at all times made the just distinction between doctrines *contrary* to reason and doctrines *above* reason." He would, I suppose, have argued that the supernatural was *above* reason and in so doing would have aroused upon the thin lips of Voltaire the famous sardonic grin.

It could not be said either that his critical judgment was impeccable. It was foolish to dismiss Leibnitz as "a paltry fellow," to say that

Gray's Odes were greenhouse productions and reminded him of cucumbers, to reject Greek mythology as "dark and dismal regions, where neither hope nor fear, neither joy nor sorrow, can be found." After all, Johnson's own religion did not provide him with much hope or joy when he became assailed by the dread of death.

His aesthetic judgment was so enslaved by the heroic couplet, by the tom-tom tune of Dryden and Pope, that he was actually deaf to the variety and strength of blank verse. So deaf that he could actually sneer at *Lycidas* and object to the lapse from verbal dignity to which Shakespeare, to his mind, was so unfortunately addicted.

He must, however, be praised as a critic for having detected from the outset that Macpherson's Ossian could not be a translation from an original Celtic epic, and for his insistence, when Macpherson sought to justify its authenticity, that he had only to deposit the original in some library or college to remove all doubts. When Dr. Blair ventured to ask him whether he seriously believed "that any man of the modern age could have written such poems." "Yes," Johnson answered, "many men, many women and many children." Such lapidary rejoinders must have delighted the young dogs seated around the tavern table; even now, when *Ossian* has ceased to be a controversial subject, they cause us pleasure.

Yet if, as I assert, Johnson was one of the most irrational and wrongheaded scholars that has ever been, how are we to explain the veneration that he inspired in clever men and the affection and esteem that we feel for him today? His most enduring quality was what Boswell called "his inflexible integrity." In an age when intellectuals toyed much with abstract ideas, and indulged in fantasy, Johnson insisted always on the value of ascertainable fact. "He was," Boswell writes, "above little arts and tricks of deception." He would not even allow his Negro servant to tell visitors that he was "not at home," since once one encouraged servants to prevaricate with truth they fell into the habit of telling lies. To Johnson, untruthfulness was not a moral blemish only, but an intellectual defect. Even poetry, in his opinion, should combine fantasy and accuracy. "Poetry," he wrote in the *Lives*, "is the art of uniting pleasure with truth by calling imagination to the help of reason." He was profoundly bored by imaginary tales. How often, when enduring some club car story, have I not recalled the splendid denunciation of Johnson against all made up situations. "The value of every story," he said, "depends on its being true. A story is the picture either of an individual or of human nature in general; if it be false, it is a picture of nothing." He told Mrs. Thrale that he was bored by all narratives that failed to carry conviction. "When Foote has told me something," he said, "I dismiss it from my mind like a passing shadow; when Reynolds tells me something, I consider myself possessed of an idea the more." It would be excellent if the *mythomanes* of this world were to absorb this salutary lesson.

He insisted always that men of intelligence should clear their minds, and their conversation, of every form of hypocrisy or cant. "No fraud," he thundered, "is innocent." To him "the base practice of dissimulation" was both wicked and foolish. He applied these rigorous standards to himself, and never sought to defend his actions by specious arguments. When a lady asked him why he had in his dictionary defined the pastern of a horse as its "knee." "Ignorance, Madam," he replied, "pure ignorance." When told that an unknown admirer of the name of Pot had pronounced *Irene* to be the finest tragedy of modern times, "If Pot says so," he replied, "Pot lies." He once told Boswell that when at Oxford he was reproved by his tutor for cutting a lecture on logic, he had replied by saying he was sliding on the ice in Christ Church meadow. "That," remarked Boswell, "was great fortitude of mind." "No, Sir," replied Johnson, "stark insensibility." He preferred facts to theories. When somebody remarked that it was difficult to refute Bishop Berkeley's theory of the nonexistence of matter, Johnson kicked his foot hard against a stone. "I refute it *thus!*" he pronounced.

The French *Encyclopédistes*, the French philosophers, and certainly Madame Geoffrin, would have dismissed Johnson as obstinate, opinionated, and out of date. They would have regarded him as deficient in social grace, intolerable in argument, and incapable of discussing abstract ideas. I have never met a Frenchman who finds Johnson an impressive figure. But I rejoice that so dominant a character in our own eighteenth century should have taught successive generations that clear thinking depends upon accuracy of speech. That truthfulness is an intellectual, as well as a moral, virtue. And that curiosity is the mark of a vigorous mind.

Chapter 18

Sturm und Drang

(1770–1778)

The Aufklärung—German society at outset of the century—The principalities—The Universities—George Hamann—Herder—Klinger—Merck—Lenz—The moods and aspirations of the *Sturm und Drang* rebels—Excitement and frustration—Hatred of dogma—Sensuous certainty—Belief in instinct and reality—Cult of the Superman—Conception of Nature—Religion—Self-torment—Angst—The young Goethe—*Götz von Berlichingen*—His yearning for the unattainable—Herder induces him to disregard French standards and to cultivate his native language—Truth and fantasy—His good sense—Werther and the original sketch of Faust—Lessing—Goethe goes to Weimar and this is the end of *Sturm und Drang.*

One

IT IS STRANGE that a man of Frederick the Great's literary energy should have failed to notice that during his own reign, and in his own country, had arisen that remarkable revival of German language and letters which is known as the Aufklärung, or Age of Enlightenment. In the sixteenth century Martin Luther and Hans Sachs had taken the rough ores of the German dialects and pounded them into a national language of beauty and strength. During the seventeenth century, mainly owing to the impoverishment and misery caused by the Thirty Years War, there was but little occasion or zest for literature and the language declined. It was not until after 1667, when Leibnitz published his *Nova Methodus* and thereafter startled the philosophic world with his Monad theory, that German thought attracted the attention of Europe. In 1697, Leibnitz wrote his thesis *On the practice and improvement of the German language* which encouraged the university professors and students to consider whether it was really obligatory to express one's thoughts or to acquire one's learning through the alien media of Latin or French; they began to experiment in giving to their native language some norms of syntax and some literary form. Leibnitz was succeeded by such eminent writers as Lessing, Mendelssohn, and Nicolai, but it was not until Goethe, with his *Werther* of 1774, captured the younger generation, that German writers were taken at all seriously by European intellectuals. Kant's *Kritik der reinen Vernunft* appeared in 1781 and gave to German philosophy the dominating influence until then exercised by Descartes, Locke, and Hume. But it was not until 1813, when Madame de Stael published her highly intelligent work *De l'Allemagne*, that German letters became in any manner fashionable. Until then they had been an esoteric study, indulged in by the more studious philosophers or philologists.

From the very first the German Aufklärung differed from the general European enlightenment of the eighteenth century, in that it attached less importance to deductive Reason, and more importance to "instinct," sentiment, and sensual impressions. The empirical to them was as significant as the rationalistic: *Gemut* (which is but approximately equivalent to our term "Soul") became for them as sacred a word as "Reason" became for the western rationalists, Romanticism, although it originated in England, was a plant that prospered lavishly in German soil.

Twenty years before the general spread of romanticism throughout Germany there occurred a sudden explosion, interesting in its phenomena and potent in its effect. The participators in this short-lived revolution (it lasted only from 1770 to 1778) were pleased to call it "The age

JOHANN WOLFGANG VON GOETHE
Goethe at age 69, painted in 1828 by Joseph Karl Stieler.

of genius"; but it is not by that title that it is known to literary historians, who have named it the "Storm and Stress" period, the *Sturm und
Drang*. This title was taken from a play by Friederich Klinger which was
performed in 1776; it is significant that the original name of this drama
was *Wirrwarr*, reflecting the psychological confusion from which the
movement arose. It is a fascinating little revolution, not only because
it produced at least one masterpiece, but because in its motives and
ideas it reflects many of the forms of torment and anger from which our
younger generation are said to be suffering today.

Germany in those days was divided into a number of small principalities or bishoprics, each possessing its minute capital city and
an autocratic ruler, who may or may not have been enlightened. The
absence of any recognized metropolitan center rendered German
society rigid and provincial, or as they would say *kleinstädtisch*. The
several minor potentates modeled themselves on Louis XIV. Not
only did they, in their vanity, construct palaces in imitation of Versailles, which were sometimes of great beauty, but always more costly
than they could afford, but they imposed the language and manners
of France upon their courtiers and upon polite society. Even as Frederick the Great at Sans Souci ignored as barbaric all contemporary
works of German literature, so also did the smaller Electors, Dukes,
Princes and Bishops model their tastes and condition their courtiers
in imitation of French culture. The gulf which in these small principalities opened between the nobility and the middle classes was wider,
deeper, and more rigorously maintained than that which separated
even the French aristocracy from the bulk of the nation. And since
there existed in Germany no influential group of middle class intellectuals, such as spread so salutary a discipline from the Paris salons and
the London coffee houses, the young men of talent were free to frisk
and scamper like colts in an open field.

The intellectual life of the nation was further restricted by the universities, of which there existed as many as forty-one during the course
of the eighteenth century. These universities, in which the theological faculty was often dominant, were in themselves reactionary. The

curriculum was outmoded, the instruction rigid and pedantic, and the lectures which these aged theologians mumbled in Latin made little appeal to the students, who longed for intellectual novelty. "Unable," writes Professor Garland, "to be either metropolitan or aristocratic, German literature remained perforce provincial." The young men confident in their original genius despised the university dons as dull dotards. "Genius" to them meant the free expansion and expression of their personal emotions and "the enemy of genius was reason and reason was thus conceived as the weapon of pedantry." Each one of them regarded himself as a Hamlet, whose self-fulfillment was blocked by external convention. They determined to expand their *Gemüt* by giving full play to their sensibility and their imagination. "Our feelings, inclinations and passions," wrote Goethe in *Dichtung und Wahrheit*, "could, we felt, be intensified and purified with advantage." At the time the insistence on "purification" was meager and intermittent. The emotions and animosities by which they were inflamed were more subtle and indeed more interesting than those which usually inspire an adolescent revolt. It is not correct to regard them as the precursors of the Romantic Movement. The latter, when it arrived twenty years later, was a slow tide in comparison to the torrent of the *Sturm und Drang*. It is less incorrect to regard the Stürmer and Dränger as the predecessors of Sören Kierkegaard and of the spiritual restlessness which has troubled the post-war generation in the Western World.

Two

The pioneer of the *Sturm und Drang* revolt was Johann Georg Hamann. Born in Königsberg in 1730, he worked for years as clerk in the East Prussian excise office. He hated this employment and derived from it a strong antipathy to the French officials appointed by Frederick the Great and therefore to all French culture. In his *Socratic Memorabilia* he assailed the slick certainties of Reason and contended that truth was to be found only in intuitive belief. He preached the infallibility of personal experience, contended that doubts regarding

the necessity of existence, fears as to one's own strength and competence, even guilt feelings aroused by indolence and ineptitude, were
not, as the rationalists argued, symptoms of weakness, but welcome
evidence of eager, even if thwarted, energy. Unfortunately Hamann
was a confused thinker, his style stuttered and splashed, and although
he was in a sense the pioneer of the irrational revolt, his influence
would have been wholly ineffective had not many of his ideas been
adopted by Herder who possessed a tidier brain.

Johann Gottfried von Herder came of a puritan and pietistic family, had studied under Kant, and had been immensely impressed during a visit to France by the wide yet intensive philosophy of Diderot.
He admired Spinoza, yet was able, in spite of the logical power of that
agnostic, to retain his own religious faith and to seek during his whole
life to find some synthesis between feeling and action. He failed to
reconcile his ideals with his environment, and when he became court
preacher at Weimar he adopted a sardonic attitude towards his early
revolt, insisting that it was not possible for any man to achieve inner
harmony or to find any formula by which personal ideals could be
reconciled with the external world. Herder was a cantankerous man
who liked to compare himself to Swift, "that Irish dean with a whip."
His disapproval of the Frenchified culture of the German aristocracy
drove him to study and extol the native folk poetry of Germany—
the Heldenbuch, the Nibelungenlied, even the puppet show reperto-
ries—and to laud the "free" imagination of Shakespeare and Ossian.
He had a bad habit of scolding his young friends and criticizing their
efforts in harsh and unsympathetic terms. Such was the fear that his
ill-tempered objections inspired, that Goethe never dared to consult
him about either *Götz von Berlichingen* or the *Sorrows of Werther*. Yet,
from the moment when, in the winter of 1770 Goethe first met Herder
on the staircase of the *Zum Geist* inn at Strasbourg, the *Sturm und
Drang* revolt can be said to have been born. Together they directed a
review, the *Frankfürter Gelehrte Anzeigen*, which gave to their movement its first title of the "Frankfurt-Strasbourg Group" and round
which they attracted other young men of talent and enthusiasm, such

as Merck, Klinger, and Lenz. Distinct from these Rhineland rebels there existed in Göttingen another band of poets who based their lyrics on the old German folksongs. They were less important.

In that year 1770 Merck was twenty-nine years of age, Herder twenty-six, Goethe twenty-one, Lenz nineteen, and Klinger eighteen. Together they studied and praised the works of Young, Thomson, and Gray and translated passages from Ossian and Shakespeare. Their doctrine was the doctrine of "divine unrest." The extravagance of their ideas was to be matched by the wildness of their behavior. They sought to startle the bourgeois of Germany out of their provincial complacency. They made far more noise than was ever aroused by the beer mug clatter of the Auerbachskeller. Yet, apart from Goethe, the "age of genius" did not in fact produce the geniuses that they so confidently expected.

Friederich Klinger served for a while as scriptwriter to a touring theatrical company and wrote one play called *Otto* in imitation of *Götz von Berlichingen*, in which the classic unities were lavishly defied, and a better play, called *Die Zwillinge*, of which the hero Guelfo, was the type of Kraftkerl or superman who was able by force to impose his personality upon his environment. Klinger, having failed to obtain employment at the Court of Weimar, entered the Russian service and rose to be a lieutenant general. It was rare for any of the Stürmer to achieve practical success.

Merck was a gifted man, a civil servant in the State of Hesse-Darmstadt, who had considerable influence on Goethe and who sought in his sarcastic manner to restrain the wild enthusiasms of Lenz. He dissipated his small fortune and committed suicide in 1791.

Far more typical of the movement was Jacob Reinhold Lenz, who was born in West Russia in 1751, his father being the Lutheran pastor to the German community of Dorpat. After studying theology at Königsberg, where he also experienced the sharp influence of Kant, he became tutor to two young German barons with whom he traveled from garrison town to garrison town, absorbing the knowledge of barrack room life which he later incorporated into the least unsuccessful of his plays, *Die Soldaten*. Lenz was a pretty boy, with fair curls and innocent blue eyes. Goethe somewhat patronizingly, refers to him as a "Persönchen" or "little individual," and sneers at his "whimsicality." Wieland was attracted by his childishness. "He is so harmless," he wrote, "so timid, so affectionate." His behavior was not what might have been expected of the son of the vicar of Dorpat. "Remember," he wrote to a friend in 1772, "that these are our years of passion and foolishness." His love affairs may or may not have been passionate, but they were certainly foolish. He possessed the curious fantasy of falling in love with women who had been discarded by, or were connected with, men more powerful than himself. He thus flirted with Friderike Brion, daughter of the pastor of Sesenheim, whom Goethe had deserted for Lotte Buff, and he then entered into a platonic affair with Goethe's married sister, Frau Schlosser. He even, on visiting Weimar, sought to make advances to the formidable Frau von Stein. "We are heroes," he wrote to Lavater, "twirled by every puff of love."

I find it difficult to read Lenz's plays or poems or to understand how anything so disordered can have been taken seriously by clever men. Even Goethe at moments allowed himself little pangs of fleeting jealousy in regard to Lenz. It has been asserted that no German writer had displayed a greater talent in combining imagination with realism or greater skill in demonstrating the absurdity of the old classical formula. His contention was that character rather than destiny should be the theme of modern drama, and that consistency of character was the sole unity that a play required. His plays are inconsequent and it is difficult for the reader to discover whether they are meant to be tragedies or comedies. His recurrent teaching is that reason is "artificial" whereas the heart is "natural." His play the *Hofmeister*, although it depicted scenes and characters drawn from his personal experience, is fragmentary, containing as many as thirty-five scenes within four acts. The *Soldaten*, which tells of the seduction of a nice German girl, Marie Wesener, by a French garrison officer, does certainly contain some quite realistic episodes of military life, but as always is spoilt by vagaries and volubility. *Der Engländer*, written in 1776, is described as a "dramatic fantasy" and relates the love affair of Robert, the son of Lord Hot. The scene is laid in the city of Turin. Mr. Hot falls passionately in love with the Princess Armida and expresses a desire to die for love. The Princess reminds him that life is our most precious possession and presents him with her portrait in miniature as a consolation. He decides that, grasping this portrait to his heart, he will live for eternity. The Princess then becomes engaged to a rival and Mr. Hot tries to kill himself by jumping out of the window. In the hope of curing his passion for the now unattainable Armida, his family provide him with a mistress of the name of Tognina. Obedient to her instructions, this courtesan attempts to detach the miniature which hangs by a cord round Mr. Hot's neck. He snatches the scissors from her and stabs himself in the larynx. He dies with the name "Armida" on his lips. It would be wholly impossible to act a play as untidy as is *Der Engländer* and it is almost impossible to read it. Nor do I find that his poems possess either music or clarity. Their main theme is that love, even lust, is a direct gift from God and should be welcomed religiously. "How fiercely," he writes, "Burns the flame of love. It is you, oh God, who kindled it in my breast":

> *Wie die Liebesflamme brennt!*
> *Gott du hast sie angezündet.*

With all his faults, Lenz was an enthusiastic champion of the German language. He evolved the theory that German was a better medium for scientific writing since it "gave more ample freedom to the mind." He went so far as to contend that in French syntax the verb has to be fitted in to a prescribed place, whereas in German the verb can be inserted anywhere. Moreover, whereas in French the verb is usually put at the outset of a sentence or paragraph, and is therefore forgotten by the reader by the time he reaches the end of the phrase, in German the verb comes at end and there is thus no chance of it eluding the memory. More serious were his *Anmerkungen übers Theater* in which he defends original and creative genius against the pedants of the academic world.

All critics, he assures us, are heavy stuff—"*ein grosses Mass Phlegma.*" Away he shouts, with the schoolmasters, away with the three unities. "God in all his works is but one and the Poet must be one also." It was slavish subservience to the three unities that gave to French drama its "disgusting monotony." Compare *Julius Caesar* with *La Mort de César* and learn from this comparison to distinguish between genius and talent, between "nature" and the artificial.

Lenz never succeeded in achieving an integrated personality and suffered atrociously from a sense of frustration. "My heart," he wrote to Merck, "lies half sunk in mud among the nettles of my destiny; it is only by a desperate effort that it can raise itself from the slime." Goethe was always urging Lenz to devote his "meteoric talent" to something serious and well composed. He felt that Lenz's love affairs, as his passionate jealousies and hatreds, were equally "imaginative." He was irritated by his self-pity, his wildness, his exuberance, and his Angst. He refers in a curious phrase to his imagination being "somewhat of a scamp." He disapproved of his guilt feelings, his terror of reality and his self-torture, his *Selbstquälerei*. Lenz, who worshipped Goethe and was jealous of him, who contended that his whole attitude towards life had been changed by *Götz von Berlichingen*, was horrified when Goethe left for Weimar in November 1775 and shortly afterwards was appointed a Privy Councilor. The Stunner, like the Bloomsbury group, disapproved of worldly success. Accompanied by Klinger, Lenz followed his friend to Weimar and sought to ingratiate himself with the Grand Duke. With this in mind he disclosed to His Highness his plan for checking the habit of army officers to seduce middle class maidens in garrison towns by attaching to each Division a regiment of strumpets, properly uniformed, disciplined, and conditioned. His idea was ill received and it would seem indeed that in anger or despair Lenz then gave way to really atrocious behavior. Goethe was ashamed of his curly-haired Strasbourg friend and Lenz was escorted out of the Grand Duchy by the police. Shortly afterwards he developed symptoms of insanity and had to be returned to the charge of his family at Dorpat. He was partially cured of his mental ailments and earned his living by giving language lessons in St. Petersburg and Moscow. In 1792, at the age of forty-one, he was found dead and frozen in a Moscow Street.

Three

Predominantly the Stürmer were afflicted with a sense of thwarted energy and ill adjustment, being obsessed by their inability to give practical effect to the vast ambitions, ideals and emotions by which they were internally inflamed. It was the ever-enduring problem of the artist seeking to adjust himself to life. Even Goethe, who very early developed that massive sense of proportion which guided him throughout his life, felt frightened during this early stage by the fluctuations of his temperament. He compared himself to a weather vane which veered with every wind but which was bound and mortised in a fixed position and unable to take flight. He was conscious of the contradictory urge to widen his experience, to indulge in ever-renewed and expanding sensations, and at the same time to accept the solace of established conventions and to "pursue one's way, looking neither to right or left, along the grooves of habit." He, with his wonderful sense of balance, foresaw that the struggle of the individual against his environment could only end in frustration and the loss of intellectual calm. Yet he also contended that the heart was the source of "all power, all happiness, and all suffering." He was the first to recognize that frustration led to self-contempt and self-contempt produced Angst and doubts regarding one's own identity. "Often," wrote Werther, "I doubt whether I myself exist," and at such moments Nature herself ceased to be the gentle comforter and became an all-devouring source of fear and horror. "Great God," exclaims Werther, "who has given me so much, why did you not also endow me with self-confidence and self-approval?" It was Angst that deprived Werther of his vitality and power of decision and in the end drove him to suicide. Goethe always despised those who surrendered to causeless melancholy, which he considered to be the "Sin that I hate more than any other."

Inevitably the young Stürmer, convinced as they were of their own genius, felt themselves at war with the older generation and the accepted conventions. They decided that experience was the only truth, and that a man should live his life, not according to any dogma or precept, but in reliance on his own feelings. They regarded their environment as futile and based on false values, and they strove to discover a reality more fundamental than that recognized by reason or commonsense. They were not political revolutionaries and in fact accepted as inevitable the existing systems and hierarchies. It was an intellectual rebellion that they envisaged. They loathed the academic professors who did not appreciate their own fluctuations between the extremes of careless rapture and melancholy collapse. They denied that truth could ever be found, as the student Wagner believed, in the study of books or the pursuit of philosophy. They agreed with Herder in contending that truth could only be discovered in "the total, unfragmented, deep feeling of things." "Grey," wrote Goethe in the original Faust, "is all theory, but green the golden tree of life":

> *Grau, theurer Freund, its alle Theorie*
> *Und grün des Lebens goldner Baum.*

They thus developed an attitude towards life which Herder called "sensuous certainty." They resented what Goethe called "the endless boredom of day to day life." They shared with Goethe bouts of "restlessness and impatience." They agreed with Herder's remark that "Existence is its own purpose. This simple, deep, irreplaceable sense of existence is happiness." "Their ultimate touchstone of judgment," writes Professor Roy Pascal, "was personal experience, compelling experience, which intensified their consciousness of being alive. All thought which did not promote this vital element, all activity which was dissociated from it, all purely passive feelings, were condemned by them as inadequate and false." "Feeling may err," wrote Herder, "but it can only be corrected by feeling."

Contemporary society, with its limited views and established conventions, appeared abominable to them in that it obstructed instinctive activity. They refused to regard man as the instrument of external forces, be they social, political, religious, or physical. To them man only really existed if he were able to develop all his natural powers to the full. Thus they came to admire the superman, the *Kraftgenie*, or even the *Kraftkerl*, who were able to master their own environment. Herder and Lavater, the spiritual guides of the movement, were both members of the established Church and were therefore obliged to contend that self-realization must be in harmony with morality. Herder argued that subjective freedom could never arise from a rejection of law. He evolved the conception of *Humanität* and the ideal of man as "the lord and servant of Nature." By this he appears to have meant that fruitful activity depended on the recognition of some conventions, limitations, and necessities. He does not seem to have fully understood Goethe's insistence on the conflict created by man's sense of innate power and his incapacity for rendering this effective in the external world.

As always when considering the emotions and ideas of the eighteenth century we come up against the difficulty of interpreting what any given group of generation really meant by the word "Nature." To Herder Nature was never an object of aesthetic ecstasy but merely an escape from worldly distractions. To Goethe Nature was in no sense an example of order and virtue. He knew it to be incredibly wasteful and cruel. "Nature," he wrote, "is without feeling." To him Nature was an example of seething and abundant energy, providing human beings, not with any aesthetic or ethical lessons, but with renewed zest in life. It was in his moments of depression and self-criticism that Nature meant the most to him:

> *Wie herrlich leuchtet*
> *Mir die Natur!*

The Stürmer, as I have said, had no desire to destroy existing systems, although they regarded the pretensions of the aristocracy and the professors as irritating and unjustified. Their sympathy for the working classes was apathetic, but they were inclined to envy the peasants because they were so absorbed by their daily tasks that they had no time to indulge in the spiritual tensions that so distracted the intellectuals. They did not regard the proletariat as noble savages, despising most of their members as coarse and sly. Goethe, as always, took a more enlightened view and during his country excursions at Wetzlar came to have some real understanding of the charm and wisdom of rustic people, and of the simple life. The real enemies of the new movement were the pedants, and not the foolish courtiers or the menacing jacquerie. Nor did the Stürmer have any admiration for the woman of intelligence, preferring their heroines to be simple household drudges, such as Gretchen, Friderike Brion, and Lotte Buff.

Their attitude towards religion was characteristic of their many compromises with reality. They contended that God could only be revealed to us through the senses, and that the instincts, even the sexual instinct, were evidence of divine power. Many of their early teachers and pupils were either brought up in a pietistic atmosphere or had become members of the established Church. Lenz was cynical on the subject of religion, regarding it as excellent opium for the masses. "Take from the rabble their superstitions," he wrote, "and they will free their minds, as you rationalists freed your minds, and they will knock you on the head. Deprive the peasant of his Devil, and he will become a devil to his lord and prove to you that real devils exist." Goethe always regarded himself as a freethinker, or at least as a Deist. He was no mystic. "Allow me," he wrote to his friend the pastor Lavater, "to call physical wellbeing what you call an angel." He described himself as "no anti-Christian, no un-Christian, but a decided non-Christian." In middle age he defined his attitude as "resolutely pagan." He always respected conventional believers, such as Herder, Lavater, and Fräulein von Klettenburg. For him faith was love of life and trust in life. He had, as I have said, small sympathy for those who were tortured by Angst. "Faith," he wrote in his wonderful autobiography, *Dichtung und Wahrheit*, "gives a great feeling of security for the present and the future; and this security arises from our confidence in an almighty and inscrutable Being." What was important was this sense of confidence which alone abolished despair; it did not matter over much what sort of Being we figured to ourselves. "When you are wholly happy in your feelings," he wrote, "then call it what you wish, Luck, Heart, Love, or God. I have no names for it. Feeling is everything and names but noise and smoke that do but cloud the glow of heaven." Lenz, having been brought up in pietist surroundings, believed that faith gave confidence and that it was in no sense supernatural. But he also believed that "our independence, our whole existence, are based on the number, the scope, the truth, of our feelings and experiences and on the force with which we face up to them, think of them or, what is much the same, are conscious of them."

It was unavoidable that this preoccupation with the conflict between the artist and his environment, between individual genius and the conventions and limitations of the external world, should lead to moods of depression, even of suicidal despair. Goethe, in his *Die Leiden des jungen Werthers* has described better than anyone the alternation between the excitement at discovering one's own genius and the deep depression that comes from realizing that one is in fact no superman. They were all, as typified by Werther and Faust, intellectuals yearning for significant activity but succeeding only in exploiting their own emotions. The contrast between their weather vane moods of excitability and the consciousness that they were rooted in their own dull environment led them into moods of what Goethe called "self-torment," or *Selbstquälerei*. The contrast between their yearning and their inability to accomplish the marvelous, subjected them to long sessions of self-distrust and self-reproach and often induced them, as we have seen, to doubt their own identity. There were moments when the Stürmer suffered atrociously from Angst and its attendant melancholy. It is always depressing to believe passionately in "creative personality" and to be unable to create. Goethe was different. He possessed to an exceptional, even an eccentric, degree the gift of being able to sublimate his emotions, and to rid himself of his most disturbing passions by describing them on paper. Once he had written about his own *Sturm und Drang*, it ceased to worry him and he resumed the wonderful intellectual and emotional quietude that has rendered him one of the mightiest and most comforting of human influences.

Four

The *Sturm und Drang* movement, which collapsed after eight years, would not be regarded as an important literary rebellion, had not Goethe been associated with it during his Strasbourg period when he composed *Götz von Berlichingen*, *The Sorrows of Werther*, and the first draft of *Faust*, which is known as the *Urfaust*. His fellow members of the group, who were little more than boys and whose ambition, impatience, and eccentricity were more striking than their intellectual gifts, regarded the young Goethe with jealous awe. They were impressed by his energy of mind; puzzled by his seriousness and sense of responsibility; and frightened of his blazing eyes. They recognized the actual violence of his genius, what they called its "Titanic" quality, and naturally hailed him as the Prometheus of the younger generation. Yet, although Goethe was not to remain a Stürmer for long, he shared many of their hopes and anxieties as well as the emotional restlessness by which they were distracted. The difference was that, whereas Goethe possessed common sense and an astonishing capacity for escaping from emotional dilemmas, they were as frail as the almond blossom scattered by March winds.

With his solid, comfortable, cultured, and above all assured bourgeois background, Goethe never regarded himself as one of the rudderless or dispossessed. Although his background altered when he went to Weimar, became a courtier, and thereafter the most famous literary figure in Europe, he had always possessed a background and was never, as were Lenz, Merck, Klinger, and even Herder, a displaced person or an outsider. This security of background gave him a self-assurance that none of the other young men possessed. Nonetheless he was sensitive to the atmosphere of emotional and intellectual confusion that bewildered all the clever young men of 1770. There is no better description of this *Wirrwarr* than that which figures in the opening pages of *Dichtung und Wahrheit*. We must realize also that on his arrival at Strasbourg Goethe was convalescing from a serious illness and that he was in a condition of susceptibility and not in firm control of his nerves. In the company of his eccentric fellows he also suffered from adolescent fluctuations of feeling, being at one moment shaken by lusts of exhilaration and at the next plunged in melancholy uneasiness (*Unbehagen*). He also experienced the dull ache of *Sehnsucht*. "I am exhilarated," he wrote, "I am ecstatic! I feel this, yet the whole content of my joy is a violent yearning for something I do not possess, for something I do not know." There is no better definition of the divine unrest which inspired the whole *Sturm und Drang* rebellion.

Goethe shared with the other young men a belief in "creative personality" and a conviction that genius, which could break through all conventions, was more "natural" than learning: *dieses Lieblings-Genie der mütterlichen Natur*. For him also Shakespeare was the champion of instinct against form. When he first read Shakespeare he remarked that "I felt most intensely my existence enlarged by an infinity." He fully understood the internal conflict aroused in adolescents of talent by the consciousness of innate power contrasting with the incapacity to express that power in practical form. It was not love alone that drove Werther to suicide but thwarted energy, the realization that however much a man might yearn for self-fulfillment, he was always in the end "tamed by the commonplace," and inhibited by limitations and poverty of will (*in unserer Armut und Eingeschränktheit*). He also had his moments when he believed that the man of genius was perpetually doomed to be misunderstood.

Goethe when at Strasbourg came to resent the arrogant domination of polite society by French culture. He called it "aged and aristocratic." He resolved to abandon French as his second language, and "to devote himself to his mother tongue with energy and earnestness." To him the French language appeared too conventional, stilted, and monotonous to serve as a free medium for the expression of exhilarated and emancipated passions. Even Voltaire, "the wonder of his age," had become something of a back number; the *Encyclopédie* reminded him of a spinning factory in which the voice of simple emotion was drowned by the hum and rattle of machines. He agreed with Herder that the German language must be freed from the imitation of foreign models and that its very roughness constituted its strength. To the young Stürmer the German language was not so much a nationalist revival as a symbol and vehicle of youth, candor, simplicity, vigor, and sensuous emotion. "The only true art," wrote Goethe, "is characteristic art. If its influence arises from deep, harmonious, independent feeling, from feeling peculiar to itself, oblivious, yes ignorant of everything foreign, then it is whole and living, whether it be born from crude savagery or cultured sentiment." As Professor Roy Pascal has written the Stürmer "were the founders of modern German poetry, because they insisted that poetry is not an abstract, self-contained, function but a function of living individuals in a concrete situation." But Goethe was never a nationalist in the modern sense of the term. In his old age he told Eckermann that he regarded nationalism as the sign of a backward state of civilization.

In his belief that poetry should be founded on personal experience he shared the Stürmer idea that genius should be the fusion of realism and imagination, or truth and fantasy. He was of the opinion that imagination was no metaphysical abstraction but a faculty that provided a deeper insight into beauty and truth. "I had nothing," he wrote, "but it was enough. The urge for truth and the delight in fantasy":

> *Ich hatte nights und noch genug*
> *Den Drang nach Wahrheit und die Lust am Trug.*

To some extent also Goethe, in spite of his deep wisdom, believed in the *Kraftkerl* or superman. His *Götz von Berlichingen* is based on the theme of a man of force and character triumphing, at least morally, over adverse circumstances. Götz, who as a historical person was little more than a robber chief, despoiling innocent merchants on their caravan to the Leipzig fair, is represented as "a perfect Knight" resolved to die rather than to be "behoven to the caprice of any man, other than God and our faith and service to the Emperor." In the end Götz is defeated by the wiles of lesser men and exclaims when dying, "Freedom! Freedom! But now will come the age of guile."

Werther again rejected everything that did not heighten his sense of existence—routine, a profession, conventions, the diplomatic service, and class distinctions. His tensions and frustrations are brought into sharp relief against the placid domestic contentment of Lotte. Faust also striving to release himself from the ordinary and to achieve self-fulfillment fails to achieve it and by his burning egoism destroys the security of others. For Goethe, Nature herself was not a proof of the divine order nor yet a profound aesthetic experience, but the inspirer of energy. He would lie flat in the grass, ruminating upon Charlotte Buff, feeling guilty about his abandonment of Friderike Brion, and comforting himself by nature's amazing animation, as seen "even in the swarming little world between two blades of grass."

Yet although in many ways Goethe shared the exaltations and depressions of the Stürmer, he was far too sensible a genius to be carried away by their hysteria. He agreed with them that Herder's theory that art should serve a moral purpose was a "harmful inanity," but he differed from them in regarding spiritual tension, not as an excruciating inward disease, but as a useful dialectic for the development of personality. He contended that his early poems had "allowed his feelings to develop into capacities through struggle and play." He was convinced that one could relieve *Selbstquälerei* or inner torment, by putting it all down on paper. He contended that poetry should not be based solely on fantasy but should also reflect "the particular character of a given mood and circumstance." Although he fully shared their view regarding the dulling effect of the French insistence on the dramatic unities, he did not entirely reject the importance of literary form. He compared the power of a poet to the "mastery" exercised by a capable charioteer over a team of ill-disciplined horses. He described literary form as "the glass through which we focus the holy beams of dispersed nature into a fiery ray which strikes into the heart of man." He saw that the cult of personal experience might render poetry unintelligible to those who had never shared that experience; he never believed that poetic references should be so individual as to become incommunicable.

Nor did he really have much sympathy for the spiritual and intellectual torments of his fellow Stürmer. Goethe was not a morbid person and his mind enjoyed good health. He in fact regarded morbid introspection as "a great evil, a serious illness, in that it leads us to regard our life on earth as a nauseous burden." He wrote Werther in four weeks, "as if sleepwalking." His purpose was to clear his own conscience from guilt feelings regarding Friderike Brion and jealous feelings regarding Charlotte Buff. It relieved him, as he confessed afterwards, of "a stormy period." "I felt as if I had made a General Confession, happy and again and prepared for a new life." A few weeks only after leaving Wetzlar he was flirting beside the Rhine with Sophie von Laroche, and already in 1775 he had forgotten all about Friderike or Lotte and was deeply in love with Lili Schönemann. The *Leiden des jungen Werthers* is not wholly to be ascribed to his habit of "writing off" a passion. He meant it as a cautionary tale, warning his contemporaries against the evils of introspection. He intended it to "offer a comprehensible expression of an inner sickly and youthful delusion." For him Werther was "a young man who destroyed himself by too much speculation." He did not foresee that Werther would produce an entirely opposite effect, or that young men in Breslau and Brussels would before long all be dressing themselves in Werther's blue coat and buff waistcoat and contemplating suicide. "This little book," wrote Goethe in after years, "which helped me so much personally may have done great harm to others." Yet it was in fact the only unquestioned masterpiece that the *Sturm und Drang* rebellion ever produced. *Götz* is certainly not a masterpiece, and the *Ur-Faust* was surpassed by the massive compositions of his later years.

Goethe was at heart a classic. He might during his early stage have admired Strasbourg Cathedral because Herder told him he ought to do so; but he did not possess a Gothic mind. Intellectually he was more akin to Lessing than he ever was to the bully Herder. The *Laocoon*, which Lessing published in 1766, had a strong influence on the boy Goethe. "One must have been young at the time," wrote Goethe, "to realize what an impression the *Laocoon* made on us—like lightning all the consequences of his splendid thought flashed upon us; all previous criticism was discarded as an outworn garment." When, having achieved great success with his plays *Minna von Barnhelm* and *Emilia Galotti*, Lessing died in 1781, Goethe wrote to Frau von Stein, "We lost much, much by the death of Lessing; much more than we think." But Lessing, in spite of his classical learning, was essentially a precursor of the Romantics of twenty years later; he had nothing really to do with the *Sturm und Drang*. Schiller also, who was a much younger man, never came to share the boundless ambitions, desires and frustrations of the Stunner. He possessed none of the rebellious subjectivity of the Frankfurt-Strasbourg group. He believed that genius, and drama, should be carefully controlled.

And then in November 1775, Goethe left Strasbourg and Frankfurt and established himself in Weimar with the hereditary Prince, Karl August. It was in those placid surroundings that he achieved self-fulfillment and was able to render Weimar the true metropolis of German culture, the "Athens of the Ilm." Deprived of the force of his personality, the fire of his genius, the *Sturm und Drang* movement collapsed. It was not until 1789 that Goethe completed *Iphigenie auf Tauris*, which was not stürmisch in the least, but in fact a paean in honor of stability and order. But the *Sturm und Drang* rebellion, in spite of many excesses, can justly boast of achievement. It produced *Werther;* it forced many young people to think and feel differently; it gave to Germans a new pride in their own language; and it led to the construction of many theatres, at Hamburg, Mannheim, Gotha, and Vienna, which have proved the stimulus and glory of German cultural life.

Yet I am glad that my hero Goethe passed so quickly through his phase as a *Stürmer und Dränger*.

Chapter 19

Rights Of Man

(Thomas Paine, 1737–1809)

———•◆•———

Edmund Burke—How came it that he ardently defended the American Revolution and as ardently attacked the French Revolution?—His criticism of the French National Assembly—His belief in mixed and tempered government—His illogical attitude—Thomas Paine refutes Burke in his *Rights of Man*—The four stages in Paine's career—The historic effect of his *Common Sense* and *Crisis*—His indiscretion when Secretary to the Foreign Affairs Committee—He goes to France—His friendship with Lafayette—Becomes a French citizen and elected a member of the National Convention—On the committee which drafted the constitution—Votes against execution of the King—Imprisoned by the Jacobins and barely escapes the guillotine—His attack on Burke's *Reflections*—His open letter to President Washington—His return to the United States—He is shunned by American society and allowed to die in penury and squalor—Possible explanations of this ingratitude—His death—William Cobbett—The end of Thomas Paine.

One

MANY ERUDITE AND resourceful men have considered the problem of how it came that Edmund Burke, who with such generous sympathy had welcomed the aspirations of the American Colonists, or espoused the cause of the Begum of

Oudh, should have assailed with such bitter invective the aspirations of the French people to rid themselves of what is universally admitted to have been a corrupt, hollow and incompetent system. It must be remembered that his *Reflections on the French Revolution* were written in 1790 and his *Thoughts on French Affairs* in 1791—dates, that is, before the Jacobins had seized power, murdered the moderate politicians, and established under their autocracy the dictatorship of the proletariat. We can understand why Burke should have been driven to almost hysterical rage by the atrocities of the Terror, and why the *Regicide Peace* which he was writing on his deathbed, should froth with passionate vituperation. But in 1790 and 1791 most Liberals welcomed the French revolution, even as most Liberals welcomed the fall of Tsarism in 1917, and it cannot have been mere prescience of what was to follow that impelled Burke to his assault. Nor can we seriously believe that he was driven into a state of apprehension by so insignificant a propagandist as The Rev. Richard Price or the mild chatter of the Revolutionary Society in London.

It is true that there existed among the British radicals much sympathy for the cause of the French Revolution and many wild hopes that it would lead to the establishment of enlightened democracy throughout the world and the coming of eternal peace. There were many good and even educated men who held the view that the rule of the People, the supremacy of the common man, would lead to the brotherhood of nations and the end of war. Wars, in their view, had only arisen owing to the ambition of kings, the wiles of ministers, or the greed of the commercial middle classes. The ease with which the French revolutionaries had swept aside the structure of the old regime and abolished all vestiges of ancient privileges and inequalities, tempted many Englishmen to hope that even in their own slow-moving island some reforms might be introduced whereby Parliament would cease to be controlled by the nobility and gentry and something resembling a truly representative Legislature might be established.

These stirrings of hope and restlessness certainly caused anxiety to the established classes and might indeed have swollen into an irresistible popular agitation similar to that which forced the government to introduce the Reform Bills of 1832. But the excesses of the Jacobins, the propaganda of the extreme republicans, and the obvious intention of the revolutionaries to spread their doctrines by force, soon chilled all sympathy, and replaced hope by alarm. In 1791, however, those who regarded the French Revolution with horror and apprehension were far fewer than those who, like Wordsworth, believed that it was the harbinger of a new world and the presage of fraternity, goodwill, and sweet reasonableness. Burke's *Reflections*, at the date they were published, must have come as a shock and a disappointment to many of his liberal friends. How came it that a man who had devoted his whole life to supporting the cause of freedom should quite suddenly have published this illiberal work?

Was it that he had retained a chivalrous devotion for Marie Antoinette, whom in 1774, he had seen "glittering like the morning star, full of life and splendor and joy?" There had always been a chivalrous strain in Burke's nature which verged sometimes on the sentimental. "I thought," he wrote, "that ten thousand swords must have leaped from their scabbards to avenge even a look that threatened her with insult." "The age of chivalry is gone" he lamented, and indeed it remains somewhat shocking that the French aristocrats, who were so sensitive of their personal honor and who eventually trooped to the scaffold with such commendable dignity and courage, should have been so jealous of each other that they never combined in defense of a monarchy which for generations their families had adulated with servile devotion. Certainly there was a chivalrous, a sentimental, element in what to me seems apostasy on Burke's part. It was perhaps fitting that he should feel more indignant on behalf of the lovely Queen of France than he had felt for the aged betel-nut-chewing Begum of Oudh.

Historians have adduced other reasons to explain his change of front. They contend that what impressed him about the American Colonists was that, wherever possible, they respected existing forms and sought to give some legal semblance to their actions. As compared to the sober, almost cautious, deliberations of Congress, the proceedings of the French National Assembly seemed to Burke as disturbing as the shrieks of maniacs. They advocated destruction for destruction's sake, whereas the founders of America desired to rebuild on sensible, even traditional, lines. It may have been even that Burke foresaw the surpassing strength and sagacity with which the American leaders would construct their mighty nation. Although, as he admitted, the French Assembly contained many men of moderation and wisdom, he foresaw that they would be swept away by the parties of action and their voices drowned in the clamor of the mob. In the same manner, liberal-minded Britons of today would be startled were they accused of inconsistency if they approved of independence being granted to the peoples of our former Empire, and do not violently disapprove of the tyranny of the Soviet Union or the domination exercised by Moscow over the satellites. Even if we can accuse Burke of inconsistency, we cannot accuse him of insincerity.

There are those who are so disconcerted by Burke's apparent apostasy, that they denounce him as a deserter to the Tories, and even suggest that he was hypocritical in boasting so loud and long of his integrity and disinterestedness, whereas he was always using his influence to obtain benefits for his raffish family, even if not always for himself. I do not regard Burke as a profound political philosopher, but I do regard him as a writer of excellent rhetoric and as a man who believed what he said. It was not a false claim when he described himself "as one, almost the whole of whose public exertion has been the struggle for the liberty of others. . . . As one in whose breast no anger has ever been kindled but by what he considered a tyranny."

Nor should we forget that Burke in pleading with such fine fervor the rights of the American Colonists was pleading on behalf of men who were of his own race and blood, whereas the actions of the National Assembly seemed to him to arise from "the red fool fury of the Seine." Such prejudices are not worthy of a philosopher; but Burke was not a philosopher; he was a man who derived his influence from his surpassing ability to add definition and color to the unformulated feelings of many thousand less articulate human beings. He is not a man to denigrate or deride.

Two

The *Reflections on the French Revolution* were written and published in 1790 in the form of "a letter intended to have been sent to a gentleman in Paris." The gentleman in question was a young acquaintance of Burke's of the name of Dupont, and it would clearly have been embarrassing and even dangerous for him if his name had been associated with so anti-revolutionary a fulmination. Burke would have described himself as a democrat, but in fact he posed an aristocratic, even a reactionary, temperament. He disliked, and feared, the masses, whom he described as "the swinish multitude." He was suspicious of self-made men, who "being snatched from the humblest rank of subordination" had never been "taught to respect themselves" and could not therefore be trusted to exercise authority over others. He regarded the slogan of "the rights of man" as a verbal fallacy and practical nonsense. "Government," he wrote, "is not made in virtue of natural *rights*. Government is a contrivance of human wisdom to provide for human *wants*."

Confident as he was that society was not a mechanical institution, but a convention of slow organic growth, he distrusted all sudden innovation. "A spirit of innovation," he wrote, "is generally the result of a selfish temper and confined views. When ancient opinions and rules of life are taken away, the loss cannot possibly be estimated. . . . I do not like seeing anything destroyed." He was sincerely afraid of the consequences of any "leveling" reforms of the constitution and believed that the influence exercised by the court and the great landed proprietors created a useful balance within the state. "I am unalterably persuaded," he wrote, "that the attempt to oppress, degrade, impoverish, confiscate and extinguish the original gentlemen and landed property of a nation cannot be justified under any form it may assume." He would not have approved of the graduated inheritance duties and surtaxes that we now enjoy. He was not an egalitarian. "Some decent, regulated preeminence," he wrote, "some preference given to birth, is neither unnatural, nor unjust, nor impolitic. . . . Nobility is a graceful ornament to the civil order."

To Burke, Liberty should never be confused with License. It should be "manly, moral, regulated." "But what," he writes, "is liberty without wisdom and without virtue? It is the greatest of all possible evils; for it is folly, vice and madness without tuition or restraint." His belief was that society rested on a convention accepted by the vast majority. His ideal state was "a free constitution; a potent monarchy; a disciplined army; a reformed and venerated clergy; a mitigated and spirited nobility to lead your virtue, not to overlay it; a liberal order of commons to emulate and to recruit that nobility; a protected, satisfied, laborious and obedient people, taught to seek and recognize the happiness that is found by virtue in all conditions; in which consists the true moral equality of mankind, and not in the monstrous fiction which, by inspiring false ideas and vain expectations into men destined to travel in the obscure walk of laborious life, serves only to aggravate and embitter that real inequality which it never can remove." What Burke longed for was "a mixed and tempered government" and the avoidance of all extremes. "No excess," he wrote, "is good." Let us therefore keep "all the pleasing illusions that make power gentle and obedience liberal."

Such passages—and they recur again and again throughout his speeches and writings—are irritating to men of logical habits of mind. They long to seize Edmund Burke by the shoulders, to drive him into a corner, and to shout at him: "But Mr. Burke, what do you *mean* by such terms as 'manly' 'free' 'mitigated' 'spirited' 'protected' 'satisfied' 'laborious' 'virtue' 'moral equality' or 'the obscure walk of laborious life?' " He would be unable with any rational exegesis to define or defend these lax expressions and we are bound to conclude that they are just temple bells tinkling, emotive, but without meaning.

It was with such jumbled feelings disturbing his mind that Burke attacked the French National Assembly. "Who is it," he wrote, "that admires, and from the heart is attached to, national representative assemblies, but must turn with horror and disgust from such a profane burlesque and abominable perversion of that sacred institution? . . . It affects to be a pure democracy, though I think it in a direct train of becoming shortly a mischievous and ignoble oligarchy." Compared to the French National Assembly and the Constitution they were about to elaborate and impose, the British system appeared to Burke an "invaluable treasure."

His book must have brought comfort to many Tories who were alarmed by the revolution but unable to express their fears in intelligible form. But it angered many liberals, and among them it angered the radical Thomas Paine, who is also one of the most interesting psychological problems of the eighteenth century.

Three

The strange sad life of Thomas Paine divides itself into four distinct periods. There are the first thirty-seven years, from the day of his birth in 1737 to the day when he first met Benjamin Franklin in 1774, when by various shifts and subterfuges he sought to earn a living in England. There is the second period, between 1774 and 1781, which can be defined as his period of glory and when, by his great gift for propaganda, he earned for himself, and perhaps merited, the title of "Godfather of the United States." There is his French period, between 1781 and 1802, when he became a member of the National Convention and only barely escaped the guillotine. And there is the last phase, from 1802 until his death in 1809, during which he passed a penurious, disreputable, and stricken old age in America, mortified by what he regarded as the ingratitude of his adopted country.

Thomas Paine was born at Thetford in Norfolk on January 29, 1737. His father was a Quaker and a small farmer who also plied the trade of a maker of stays. His mother was a hot-tempered woman who did not spare the rod. His childhood was unhappy. He was not taught Latin at school, since the Quakers regarded Latin literature as too improper for young eyes and ears. This was a misfortune, since in the age of reason a man was not regarded as properly educated unless he could at least pretend to understand Cicero and Horace. At the age of fifteen he entered his father's business as an apprentice, but at the age of sixteen he ran away to sea and took service in the privateer the *Terrible*, under a certain Captain Death. In 1759, he returned to England and established himself as a staymaker in Sandwich, where he married a Miss Mary Lambert. The next year his wife died and, his Sandwich business having failed, he moved to Margate. In 1761, he managed to obtain employment in the Excise at Thetford with a salary of £50 a year. In 1762, he was transferred to Grantham and two years later to Alford. In 1765, he was dismissed from the Excise service having been caught out in making false entries in his books. He was forced to resume the trade of staymaker, but it appears that he was bad at fitting corsets, since in 1776 we find him working as an usher at a school in Godman's Fields and in Kensington. In 1767, he addressed a humble petition to the Excise Office begging to be reinstated in their employment. He was accorded an appointment at Grampound in Cornwall and in 1768 was promoted to a post at Lewes, where he remained for six years. He lived with a Quaker of the name of Ollive and married his daughter. He took the lead in an agitation on the part of the excise men demanding an increase of salary and was dismissed from the service on the flimsy ground of having been "absent without leave." He did not then resume his trade as staymaker, but drifted aimlessly, abandoning his second wife.

In 1774, in London, he happened to meet Benjamin Franklin, who urged him to seek a new life across the Atlantic and gave him a letter to his son-in-law, Bache, in which he described him as "an ingenious and worthy young man." Paine was certainly ingenious, but he was not young, in that he was already verging on forty years of age. Historians ever since that date have disputed whether the epithet "worthy" was correctly applied.

Armed with this introduction, Paine landed in America on November 30, 1774. He made many friends in Philadelphia and obtained employment on the *Pennsylvania Magazine*, of which, on the retirement of Robert Atkins, he became editor. At last he had discovered his true vocation: from then on he became one of the most potent journalists that there has ever been.

The Colonists at that date were united and resolved in resisting the encroachments of what they rightly regarded as a distant, ignorant, and obtuse British Parliament: but in 1776, although they had declared their independence, most of them retained a sentimental affection for the mother country and some vestigial loyalty to King George III. Many were conscious that it was mainly, although not entirely, due to the British navy and army that they had avoided being encircled or massacred by the French and the Indians and they retained a lively apprehension that, once deprived of British protection, they might again be confined within a narrow and dangerous frontier. They foresaw that the destiny of the thirteen Colonies implied a limitless expansion westwards, but they did not all foresee that they would be able to effect that expansion by their own unaided efforts. Few of them can have expected that France, owing mainly to the unsurpassed diplomacy of Benjamin Franklin, would soon cease to be an enemy and become a decisive ally.

Thus the majority of the Colonists, while determined to obtain independence, were not in favor of complete separation. As late even as November 1778 Paine himself could describe the persistent attachment of many Americans to the mother country as "obstinate." Even after Lexington, John Adams pronounced against separation and the Massachusetts Provincial Congress passed a resolution of allegiance to King George III. In September 1775 New York, New Jersey, North Carolina, Pennsylvania, and Maryland had all declared against separation. It was Thomas Paine's *Common Sense* that abolished these feelings. Had the conception of Dominion Status then existed, it is probable that most Americans, once they had been rendered entirely free to conduct their own business, would have preferred to remain within the Commonwealth. For Great Britain it was a narrow shave. Had not her Government been so proud, parental, and purblind,

Britannia might have been saddled with this boisterous daughter for the rest of her life.

Paine, although English born and bred, was the first propagandist to advocate complete separation. On January 10, 1776, he published with the Scottish bookseller, Robert Bell, his pamphlet entitled *Common Sense*. It was immediately successful, selling as many as 100,000 copies in the first six months. "It would be difficult," writes Sir George Trevelyan in his *The American Revolution*, "to name any human composition which has had an effect, at once so instant, so extended, and so lasting. *Common Sense* turned thousands to independence who before could not endure the thought. It worked nothing short of miracles and turned Tories into Whigs."

Paine's *Common Sense* was written in the simple language and with that seemingly convincing logic which make a direct appeal to unsophisticated minds. He argued that politically it was impossible that any British Government would ever understand America or meet her requirements. Economically, the London Parliament was dominated by the prevailing mercantilist doctrine, and the British merchants would always insist on keeping the Colonies in economic subjection and preventing them from developing any competitive industry of their own. He had for long, he admits, believed that wisdom would prevail and that some sort of compromise could be found under which the Colonies would be free to develop their own resources and manage their own affairs without interference. But he had now abandoned that hope and had become wholly convinced that nothing but complete separation from Great Britain would secure the future of the continent and safeguard American rights and interests. "Everything short of that," he wrote, "is mere patchwork." "The sun," he wrote, "never shone on a cause of greater worth. 'Tis not the affair of a city, a county, a province, or a kingdom; but of a continent, at least one-eighth part of the habitable globe. 'Tis not the concern of a day, a year, or an age; posterity are virtually involved in the contest and will be more or less affected even to the end of time by the proceedings now." He finally denounced those who still believed in conciliation as men ready to "shake hands with murderers" and contended that such men "must have the hearts of cowards and the spirits of sycophants."

Four

It is much to Paine's credit that he refused to take any money for *Common Sense* and that he devoted the profits from its enormous sale to the cause he had so deeply at heart. That in itself should have moved the American Government to treat him with greater consideration in later years. After all, it was Tom Paine who invented the term "The United States," an expression which since his day has obtained wide circulation.

In the autumn of 1776, he resigned his editorship of the *Pennsylvania Magazine* and joined the revolutionary army. He was appointed aide-de-camp to General Nathaniel Greene, was with him at Fort Lee on the Hudson, and thereafter, when Fort Lee was captured, made his way to Newark. It was then, during the darkest days of the war, when many contemplated surrender, that Paine published the thirteen pamphlets which he called *The Crisis*, and which to an astonishing extent succeeded in reviving an almost extinguished hope and in animating resolve. "These are the times," he wrote, "that try men's souls." It seems incredible that George Washington at least did not recognize how brilliant had been Paine's flashes of lightning at a time when the glow of hope was low.

On January 21, 1777, he was appointed to a commission sent to treat with the Indians at Easton and in the following April he was made Secretary to the Congress Committee on Foreign Affairs. He held this important post for two years, but in January 1779 he got into trouble by revealing that already the French Government were assisting the colonists with munitions and funds. Vergennes, the French Foreign Minister, was anxious to preserve at least the semblance of neutrality for fear that the British Government might declare war on France before the French fleet, which was being feverishly refitted, would be capable of resistance. That the Secretary of the American Foreign Affairs

Committee, in an article in the *Pennsylvania Packet*, should reveal the fact that the French were already almost allies and co-belligerents was most irritating to Vergennes. He instructed his agent in America, M. Gérard, to complain officially to Congress against the indiscretion of the secretary. Paine had simultaneously created some uneasiness by openly accusing Silas Deane, who was acting in Paris as "commercial agent" for the Colonies, of making money out of the contracts he concluded. Paine went so far as to call Silas Deane "a rascal," which is not a term that any careful official should employ. For these indiscretions he was obliged to resign his post as Secretary to the Foreign Affairs Committee. M. Gérard, fearing Paine might seek to avenge himself "with his characteristic impetuosity and impudence," offered him a subsidy of one thousand dollars a year if he would agree to defend the French Alliance in the Press. Paine always insisted that he had never accepted French pay. He was then given a job as clerk to the Pennsylvania Assembly. General Washington meanwhile was short of cash wherewith to pay his troops. Paine suggested that a public subscription should be raised to assist the General and said that he would himself contribute five hundred dollars to the fund. Seeing that he was badly off himself, this generous gesture was a further proof of his disinterestedness and should have been remembered to his credit.

In 1781, Thomas Paine accompanied Colonel Laurens on a mission to Paris, the object of which was to raise a substantial loan. The mission was successful and in August he returned to Philadelphia, bringing with him two million five hundred livres in silver and further military stores. He was himself so impoverished that he was obliged to borrow a dollar from a friend to pay his ferry fare across the Delaware. In 1782, he applied to Washington for some reward for his great services. He was accorded a pension of eight hundred dollars from secret service funds and he retired to a cottage at Bordentown, New Jersey, where he occupied himself with natural philosophy, designing smokeless tallow candles and an iron bridge which he hoped would make his fortune. It is still a mystery why Washington should have felt it necessary to make the grant, not openly, but from secret funds. In 1784, the

State of New York gave him a small farm at New Rochelle, which they had confiscated from a loyalist of the name of De Voe, and Congress voted him a grant of three thousand dollars.

In March 1787, he left America for France, taking with him letters of introduction from Benjamin Franklin and a model of his iron bridge. He remained in Europe for the next thirteen years. In August 1787, he crossed to London and visited his mother at Thetford. It seems strange that a British subject, the author of *Common Sense*, who had admittedly served in the army of the insurgents, should not have been arrested and tried for having adhered to the King's enemies. The eighteenth century in such matters was more lenient than the twentieth. Not only was Paine able to move about overtly and unmolested, but he was well received by Fox, Burke and the Duke of Portland. He failed to sell his iron bridge to any contractor, although in the end it was erected to span the River Wear at Sunderland. As usual, Paine himself made no money out of this transaction.

In 1790, he returned to Paris. Lafayette, imagining that he was about to sail for the United States, entrusted him with the key of the Bastille which he wished to present to General Washington. Paine at the time was detained in Europe in connection with negotiations over his iron bridge. He therefore entrusted the key to another traveler accompanied by a letter, dated May 1, 1790, in which he hailed Washington as his "great master and patron" and claimed that of all men it was he who should be the owner of this historic key. "The key," he wrote, "is the symbol of the first ripe fruits of American principles translated into Europe. . . . That the principles of America opened the Bastille is not to be doubted and therefore the Key comes to its right place." The key now hangs at Mount Vernon.

In November 1790, Burke published his *Reflections on the French Revolution* and Thomas Paine, enraged by this apostasy on the part of a man whom he had formerly so much admired, replied by writing the first part of his *Rights of Man*. It was published on March 13, 1791, and Paine shortly afterwards returned to London where he was seen in company with Home Tooke, Lord Edward Fitzgerald and other republicans. On this occasion the British Government consented to take notice of him. He was denounced as a traitor and as a dangerous agitator, and orders were given for his arrest and trial. For some odd reason it was the poet William Blake who first got wind of these impending proceedings and warned Paine in time to enable him to escape to Paris. The trial took place in his absence in December 1792; he was found guilty and condemned to outlawry.

There then began the most dramatic phase of his career. Although he could not speak a single word of French, he was declared a French Citizen by the National Assembly and in September 1792 elected as Member of the Convention for the Pas de Calais. He took his seat on September 21, 1792. In October he was appointed a member of the Committee to whom the Convention had assigned the task of drafting a constitution. There were nine members of this Committee and Brissot and Condorcet, who knew some English, were able to act as interpreters to and for Paine. The Committee met daily for several months and in the end submitted a draft Constitution which was roughly handled by the Convention. Eventually it, or what remained of it, was adopted in June 25, 1793, but almost immediately thereafter it was "suspended." Only two of the nine members of the Committee, Paine and Siéyès, survived the Revolution; Condorcet committed suicide and the corpse of Petion, who was at first supposed to have escaped abroad, was discovered in a forest half eaten by wolves. The rest went to the guillotine.

When, early in January 1793, the question of the King's execution was raised in the Convention, Paine had the tremendous courage to oppose the death penalty, suggesting that "Louis Capet" and his family should merely be banished for life to the United States. Mounting the tribune on January 19, 1793, he urged the Convention to show more clemency. "What today," he said, "seems an act of justice may in the future appear as an act of vengeance." He warned the Convention that in America Louis XVI was regarded as a liberator and that his execution would "spread universal sorrow" throughout the United States. He urged that the sentence on the King should be commuted to perpetual banishment. His speech was translated into French by the Secretary of the Convention and was greeted with shouts of anger. Marat contended that his remarks should be entirely ignored, since being a Quaker by religion, he was bound to vote against a death penalty in any case. Paine has not been given sufficient praise for his courage on that occasion: he well knew that by speaking and voting against the death penalty he was exposing his own life to immediate danger. With the fall of the Gironde his arrest seemed imminent.

In December 1793, Paine was expelled from the Conventon on the ground of being an English spy and imprisoned in the cellars of the Luxembourg. He appealed to Gouverneur Morris, then American representative in Paris, asking him to claim him as an American citizen. He even begged Washington to intervene. Gouverneur Morris, who disliked Paine, was no more than lukewarm in his support; Washington, a word from whom would have saved him, remained mute. Paine was left to languish in his dungeon for ten months, in daily expectation of being dragged to the guillotine. He contracted gaol fever and nearly died. Owing to the chance that the fatal chalk mark was put on the inside, rather than on the outside, of the door to his cell he escaped being bundled into a tumbrel and sent to the Place de la Concorde where the guillotine thudded hour after hour and the steaming blood crept inch by inch among the cobblestones. In the end Gouverneur Morris was replaced by John Monroe, who saw no reason why he should not claim Paine as an American citizen and thus secured his release.

Paine retired for a few weeks to Monroe's house, nursing his ills and his resentments. It was then that he composed two letters to President Washington accusing him of faithlessness and ingratitude. "You folded your arms," he wrote, "forgot your friend, and became silent." His first letter, owing to Monroe's prudent counsel, was not dispatched. He then wrote a second letter in which he informed Washington that "I shall continue to think you treacherous till you give me cause to think otherwise." He accused Washington of having been an incompetent leader in war and of intending, now that victory had been won, to establish an

THOMAS PAINE

autocracy. He accused him of arrogance and denounced his "cold, her-maphrodite" character. In 1796, he was so ill advised as to publish both these letters in Philadelphia to the scandal of the devout. Even the English radical, William Cobbett, then a refugee in the United States, was shocked that a man could thus assail the father of his adopted country. "Like Judas," wrote Cobbett, "he will be remembered by posterity. Men will learn to express all that is base, malignant, treacherous, unnatural, and blasphemous by one single monosyllable—Paine."

On leaving the house of kind Mr. Monroe, Paine lived with Madame Marguerite Bonneville at No 4 rue du Theatre Français. It was there, one autumn afternoon in 1797, that a thin young man, in the glittering uniform of a Directoire general, knocked at his door. Napoleon Bonaparte, fresh from his Italian victories, wished to consult the author of the *Rights of Man*. He informed Paine that his book was a constant companion and that every city in France should erect a golden statue in his honor. He also informed Paine that he was contemplating the invasion of England and would like Paine to accompany him and advise him on that expedition. For a moment Paine was dazzled by the vision of himself proclaiming the British Republic from the steps of the market hall at Thetford. But in the end he realized that the young Bonaparte did not possess a truly republican soul. Paine never took service under Napoleon. Instead he returned to America and to the last tragic stage of his life.

Five

As has been said, Burke published his *Reflections on the French Revolution* in November 1790. Paine sprang immediately to its defense. His *Rights of Man* was published by Jordan of Fleet Street on March 13, 1791. The second part followed in 1792. The first part was dedicated to Washington and the second to Lafayette. He attacks Burke and his book in no measured terms. He accuses Burke of being in receipt of a Secret Government pension and of being "in fact a pensioner in a fictitious name." In that he had personally profited by a corrupt system, his animosity towards the Revolution, which would abolish all corruption, must be interpreted as "the groans of wounded vice." He accuses Burke of having "mounted in the air like a balloon to draw the eyes of the multitude from the ground they stand on." Burke's attack was "a tribute of fear"; it was not merely a travesty on the French Revolution but "an imposition on the rest of the world." It was written with "the spouting rant of high-toned exclamation and a wild, unsystematical display of paradoxical rhapsodies."

In contrast to Burke's emotion and lack of logic, Paine proceeds to defend the Revolution logically and on the basis of the Natural Rights of Man. Man is born equal and with rights which, being natural, are of a Divine nature. Civil rights are no more than "natural rights exchanged" and therefore the Civil power has no right to invade the natural rights of man from which it is itself derived.

While admitting that Louis XVI was himself a benevolent person, he argued that the Revolution had been made, not against individuals, but against principles. This explained why, as compared with former Revolutions it had been so astonishingly moderate. In order to destroy "the monster aristocracy root and branch" the Revolution had abolished primogeniture. Not foreseeing the impending Reign of Terror, Paine refers to the "serene dignity of the present National Assembly." He believed, as so many of his fellow republicans believed, that democracies were by their nature pacifist. He predicted that within seven years every country in Europe would have adopted the French system and that an epoch of universal peace and brotherhood would thereby be inaugurated. That his admiration for the "serenity" of the National Assembly was not quite as blind as he pretended is proved by a letter he wrote at the time to Danton urging that the Assembly should be moved away from Paris in order to render it less under the influence of the howling mob.

Paine did not share Burke's sentimental veneration for the British system. He contended that a republic was the sole rational form of government, since it was based on the Social Contract, and the naturally social instincts of mankind. These instincts are so strong, so sagacious, and so obviously in the interests of all, that once the republican system had been established and fully understood, the necessity for any form of government would wither away. The British system was unrepresentative and corrupt. The monarchy itself derived from William the Conqueror, "The son of a prostitute and the plunderer of the English nation." Monarchy and aristocracies are governments of ignorance, whereas democratic republics are based on reason. Monarchy represents nothing but the usurpation of the Nation's rights and derives from "a total violation of every principle sacred and moral." All hereditary government is by its nature based on original plunder and is a "disgrace and reproach to the reason of man." In England the monarchy has always been a foreign importation. Why should the people contribute one million pounds a year for the support of a monarch, who may be an infant, or vicious, or mad? "Kings succeed each other," he wrote, "not as rationals, but as animals." How different to the absurd spectacle of England, groaning under a corrupt oligarchy and ruled by a ridiculous German creature of the name of "Guelph," was the glorious prospect of the United States, based on principles and natural rights! The wonderful example of a liberated America had "shown to the artificial world that man must go back to Nature for information." The superb example of the United States was based on the fact that first principles are more important than individuals, and that government is merely a national association acting on the principles of society. "What Athens was in miniature," he wrote, "America will be in magnitude. The one was the wonder of the ancient world: the other is becoming the admiration, the model, of the present." The two Revolutions between them would bring enlightenment to the whole world:

> The insulted German, the enslaved Spaniard, the Russian, and the Pole are beginning to think. The present age will hereafter merit to be called the Age of Reason and the present generation will appear to the future as the Adam of a new world.

Paine was a convinced Deist and in his last work *The Age of Reason*, which was published in 1798 and 1802, he made fun of the Bible, denied the miraculous birth of Christ, and referred to the founder of the Christian religion as "a virtuous and amiable man." When in Paris he set up a club for Deists which he called "The Theophilantropists." It did not survive the advent of Napoleon, but it did much harm to Paine's reputation. He was unfairly denounced as an atheist.

The Federal Press in the United States had already started a campaign against him. He was described as "that lying, drunken, brutal infidel." He had in fact attacked the Federalists as being aristocrats at heart wishing to establish an oligarchy. He went so far as to describe John Adams as "having his head as full of kings and queens and knaves as a pack of cards." The Federalists denounced him as an atheist, a drunkard, a man of low habits, and a traitor to the sacred name of George Washington. President Jefferson was quite prepared to accord him passage from Europe in a United States frigate, but was immediately assailed by the Federalist Press for offering official transport to the slanderer of Washington. Paine was obliged to cross in an ordinary passenger vessel. He landed at Baltimore on October 30, 1802. He was received quite warmly by Jefferson and spent some nights at the White House. He retired to New Rochelle with his French friend, Madame Bonneville, who had joined him with her children and was atrociously bored at New Rochelle. They moved to New York where she tried to support herself by giving lessons in French. Paine by then had completely surrendered to his drunken habits and had become an intolerable companion. He was shunned by society and on one occasion he was refused a place in a stagecoach, on the ground that he was an infidel.

It is not easy to explain why American opinion should, after his return to his adopted country, have treated him as a pariah. It may well have been that they were shocked by his drunken habits, by his freethinking on religious matters, by his cohabitation with Madame Bonneville, and by his attacks on Washington. Mr. Woodward, one of his most ardent defenders, suggests even that America in those days was in fact an aristocracy and that they were alienated by Paine's low origin and filthy ways. It may be even that they were unwilling to acclaim as their godfather a man who was English born and bred. He was certainly not an engaging companion, having acquired a blend of arrogance and self-pity, a displeasing mixture in which alcoholics frequently indulge. Yet I cannot but derive the impression that there was some other reason that explains the coldness with which Washington, and even Jefferson, regarded him. They must have suspected Paine of some act of treachery or disloyalty far worse than any that has yet been disclosed. But it is sad that the author of *Common Sense* and *The Crisis* should have been ostracized by his adopted country and allowed to die in penury and squalor. He was without any money and lived in utter destitution in lodgings in Partition Street, New York. He was able to sell his farm at New Rochelle and moved into slightly better rooms at No 59 Grove Street. He had already in 1806 had one stroke and was affectionately nursed by Madame Bonneville. He died on July 9, 1809, and was buried at New Rochelle.

William Cobbett, that worthy radical, had started, as we have seen, by bitterly attacking Thomas Paine for his slander on Washington. On studying the *Rights of Man*, however, he realized that Paine was not an apostate but a prophet. He was shocked by the fact that the godfather of the United States should be shunned by all decent Americans. He therefore exhumed Paine's body form the graveyard at New Rochelle and brought it back with him to Liverpool. For many years Cobbett preserved Paine's skeleton in his house at Botley in Hampshire and on his death he bequeathed it to his son. The son, shortly afterwards, went bankrupt and his possessions were sold by auction. Nobody has discovered who bought the bones of Paine. They have disappeared. And his works, which at the time created so prodigious an effect, are today unread.

Chapter 20

Religious Revival

(John Wesley, 1703–1791)

———— • ◆ • ————

First half of eighteenth century in England is a period of disorder and lack of confidence—Decline in the prestige of Parliament, Government and Church—European reaction against skepticism—France, Germany—The Anabaptists, the Moravians and the Pietists—The Quakers, the Baptists, the Presbyterians, the Congregationalists, Lady Huntingdon's connection—Methodists the most important—Birth and youth of John Wesley—The Holy Club—George Whitefield—Wesley's unsuccessful mission to Georgia—Miss Hopkey—His return and his conversion of May 2, 1738—Quarrels with the Moravians and with Whitefield—His unhappy marriage—His preaching—His Tory prejudices—His principles and doctrine—His great talent for organization—Expansion and achievement of Methodism.

One

IN ENGLAND THE first half of the eighteenth century was a period of moral disorder. The politicians were corrupt, the ecclesiastics lax, the middle classes intent only on making money, and the masses of the people licentious, drunken and raw. By 1742, the consumption of gin, at that date a cheap intoxicant, had risen to seven million gallons a year. The country was infested by highway robbers, and the streets and parks of the towns rendered unsafe owing to the activities of footpads and gangsters. The youths of the period, the sparks, the apprentices and the students, banded together under the name of "Mohocks" and by their escapades exposed peaceful citizens to far greater hurt and humiliation than the most active Teddy boys inflict today. William Hogarth, that stern moralist and gifted painter, was not exaggerating when he engraved his many cartoons of high and low life in the world of London. *Gin Alley*, the *March to Finchley*, and *Marriage à la Mode* were depictions of contemporary reality.

There was a general lack of confidence in law and order. Parliament was but partially representative and possessed none of the prestige that it acquired after the Reform bills of 1832. Two-thirds of the House of Commons were nominated by the great landowners. The Duke of Norfolk owned as many as eleven members and Lord Lonsdale nine. The pocket boroughs were recognized as being utterly indefensible. Old Sarum was known to send two members to Parliament although it contained not a single inhabitant. Seventy members were returned by thirty constituencies containing less than forty voters each. Three hundred of the Members of Parliament were returned by only one hundred and sixty voters, whereas the industrial cities that were already founded and expanding possessed no representation at all. Although we have been taught by modern historians that it is an error to emphasize the corruption and subservience of the House of Commons, it is evident that an assembly thus constituted could not be regarded as truly representative of the people and could thus exercise small influence outside its own restricted limits. What the British today regard as the main spring of their national life was corroded and weak.

The administration of justice was also unrepresentative of the new age. There still existed on the statute book some 253 offences, the punishment for which was death. A person could be hanged on Tyburn tree if he shot a rabbit, damaged a bridge, cut down a young tree, or stole property valued at five shillings. As late as 1816, there were fifty-eight prisoners in Newgate jail under sentence of death, among them a child of ten. Juries had become increasingly unwilling to convict prisoners guilty of comparatively minor offences, and thousands were transported overseas. More than half the children received no education at all and in the new towns there was hardly any religious instruction or opportunities for worship.

It was the decline in religion that first aroused the conscience of virtuous men. In 1728, Montesquieu could write "In England there is no religion and the subject, if mentioned in society, evokes nothing but laughter." In 1736, Bishop Butler, in his preface to his *Analogy of Religion* wrote that most men had ceased to look on Christianity even as a subject of enquiry, "its fictitious nature being so obvious." Bishop Watson considered "that there never was an age since the death of Christ, never once since the commencement of this history of the world, in which atheism and infidelity have been more generally confessed." In theory an overt atheist could be condemned to three years imprisonment and Blackstone commented "Christianity is part of the laws of England." But the freethinker was always ready to pay formal tribute to the State Church by attending Communion at Easter. Moreover the upper classes were convinced that religious practices were valuable conventions, since they provided an opium for the masses. Yet established religion had by the opening of the eighteenth century become largely a matter of form. "Our light," states the introduction to the *Proposal for a National Reformation of Manners* in 1694, "looks like the evening of the world."

The Church of England, after its practical destruction by Cromwell, had recovered with the Restoration, and Charles II was wise enough to choose good bishops. Although the establishment lost many of its best men, owing to their refusal as "Non-Jurors" to take the oath to William III, it might well, under firm guidance, have recovered its prestige at the outset of the century. There was no such guidance. The feasts of the Church were ignored; daily services were abandoned; buildings were allowed to fall into disrepair; and Holy Communion became infrequent.

Unfortunately Convocation, which alone could have imposed sound discipline and higher standards, became the scene of unseemly bickering between the Bishops and the lesser clergy and was suspended between 1717 and 1852. The practice of "pluralism," by which a clergyman could hold several livings at the same time, entrusting the care of his parishioners to the ministrations of an underpaid and often uneducated curate, increased throughout the century. In 1806, there were as many as 2,423 parishes in which the incumbent was not resident. Nor did the higher clergy set a better example. The Bishop of Winchester, for instance, only visited his diocese once in twenty-one years. There thus arose delays in ordination and confirmation, and one bishop had to deal with the accumulation caused by his own absenteeism by confirming as many as eight thousand applicants in a single day.

The bishops and the clergy had for such reasons become indolent and worldly. They neglected their spiritual duties. "Soul extinct," commented Carlyle, "stomach well alive." It was generally assumed that the bishops paid court to the Government in power and that preferment could be attained only by party loyalty. The ordinary parsons, with the exception of those university men who had obtained college livings, were often men of no education who shared the boorish sporting tastes of the local gentry. They either preached above the heads of the congregations or allowed the parish clerk to read the lessons and to drone the psalms. There was an utter absence of religious fervor or conviction and Goldsmith denounced even the better types of clergymen for their "insipid calmness." There was little in the parish church, or even in the cathedral, to arouse the interest or the emotions of the faithful.

In many country parishes the parsons were worse than uninspiring. They were dissolute and degraded. George Crabbe has left us a memorable portrait of the besotted vicar:

> The reverend wig, in sideway order placed,
> The reverend band, by rubric stains disgraced,
> The leering eye in wayward circles rolled,
> Mark him the pastor of a jovial fold,
> Whose various texts excite a loud applause,
> Favoring the bottle and the good old cause.

Two

In such circumstances it is not surprising that serious-minded people should group together in congregations and fraternities and should evolve their own tenets, sects, and ministries. Most men and women are unable to endure the terrors and pains of life without spiritual support, and if the official religion offered them is too cold to rouse their emotions, too insipid to salve their fears, or too debased to deserve their reverence, they will turn to other creeds. It was with relief that they exchanged the arid negatives of intellectualism, the dry giggles of the agnostics, for the certitudes of rigorous creeds and disciplines and for the ecstatic feelings of brotherhood and mutual support provided by some minority sect. Through the eighteenth century such searchers were offered, both in the old world and the new, a wide variety of faiths and denominations.

In France, although Paris remained the center of skepticism and anticlericalism, the Church continued to exert a powerful influence on the Court and in the Government, and the Jesuits continued to provide their unequalled methods of instruction. The Jansenists, in spite of the persecution which they suffered, remained the Calvinists of Roman Catholicism and attracted many pious souls. The nationalists (and most Frenchmen were and are fundamentally nationalist) hoped by Gallicanism to found a truly national Church, independent of Vatican interference. The quietists, taught by Fénélon and Madame de Guyon, strove to solve the problem of predestination and free will, by repressing individual will entirely and by concentrating on the passive contemplation of eternal varieties. By the end of the century the majority of the French people had become bored by rationalism and found in sensibility, in the "Gospel of Jean Jacques Rousseau," the emotional outlet for which they yearned.

In Germany, the strong thoughts and words of Luther remained dominant, although in the middle of the sixteenth century Lutherism had to some extent been discredited by the violent revolutionary

movement of the Anabaptists. This sect (which had nothing whatsoever to do with the later Baptists) claimed to represent the left or
"active" wing of Lutheranism and preached an extreme form of Christian Socialism. In 1525, under Thomas Münzer, they rose in revolt but
were quickly suppressed and their leaders executed. The movement
was however revived by an impostor of the name of John of Leyden,
who claimed to be the successor of David, captured the town of Münster, and established there his communal state. He preached polygamy
and himself possessed four wives, one of whom he beheaded with his
own hands in the market place of Münster. In the end he was taken
prisoner and executed in that same market place. The Anabaptist
movement thereafter declined.

Of far greater importance were the Moravians, a Saxon sect who
claimed to have revived the Hussite doctrine. Their leader, count
Zinzendorf, was the godson of Philipp Jacob Spener, the Pietist, who
preached that all pleasures were by their nature sinful, that, since faith
was universal, the laity should have a share in spiritual government,
and that conversion must be preceded by agonies of repentance. In
the settlement that he founded at Herrnhut, count Zinzendorf established a group of Pietists who practiced extreme austerity, believed in
the mortification of the flesh, and hoped to revive what they assumed
to be the principles of primitive Christianity. The Moravians, as we
shall see, exercised a deep influence on John Wesley and, through him,
on the whole Methodist and Evangelical movements.

Geneva throughout the century remained the Mecca of the Calvinists and its glum doctrines infiltrated into all the dissenting sects.
In America, once the intolerant theocracy of Massachusetts Bay had
been discredited, a type of Presbyterianism was evolved which, under
the influence of the Methodists and the Quakers, produced as high a
level of morality as the world has ever witnessed.

In Great Britain the reaction against the skepticism, or religious
lethargy, of the Age of Reason took many forms. Already in the seventeenth century important groups of dissenters had affirmed the
belief that religion was in its essence an affair of individual conscience

and that the State, through an established Church, was not justified in formulating and enforcing doctrines of its own. In the second half of the seventeenth century George Fox had established the Society of Friends, thereafter nicknamed "The Quakers," who insisted that religion arose from inward personal experience. They formulated no rigid creed, they possessed no liturgy or ecclesiastical hierarchy; they initiated open-air preaching and admitted the equality of women with men. Until the Toleration Act of 1689, the Quakers were persecuted, not in Massachusetts only, but also in Great Britain. In spite of this they became rich and powerful and exercised political influence out of proportion to their actual numbers. In the eighteenth century they had come, largely owing to their distinctive dress and idiom, to be regarded as a group of estimable eccentrics, constituting no menace either to Church or State. Their piety, selflessness, and philanthropy earned them ever-increasing respect. We have today learnt to appreciate the extent to which the world has benefited by their activities and example.

The Baptists also date from the seventeenth century. Originally founded in Amsterdam, they became established in Great Britain from 1612 onwards. In doctrine they did not differ fundamentally from the Church of England: the distinction was that they held that baptism should be administered to adults only, since they alone could be aware of past sins and therefore capable of repentance and conversion. Baptism, therefore, "in no wise appertaineth to infants." As the Baptist Church developed, it divided into the two sects of the General Baptists, who believed in free will and individual responsibility, and the Particular Baptists, who held the Calvinist view of predestination.

It was from Geneva also that as early as the sixteenth century came the potent and so triumphant theory of Presbyterianism. The Presbyterians rejected the conception of apostolic succession, and contended that episcopacy, whether that of Rome or of a State Church, was not in accord with original Christianity. They denied the sacerdotal character of the ministry and contended that ministers should be elected by local communicants. Their views were accepted, not only in

Scotland but throughout America, and they strongly influenced the Congregationalists, who were another powerful seventeenth-century community. The Congregationalists were first founded at a meeting held in Plummer's hall in London in June 1567, but were organized and systematized by Robert Browne in 1580. They were exposed to violent persecution, their leaders were executed, and many of them took refuge in Holland. It was a branch of the Congregationalists that established itself at Scrooby Manor in Nottinghamshire from where they emigrated to Leyden in the Netherlands. It was from this fraternity, led by John Robinson and William Brewster, that on July 22, 1620, a group of thirty men and women embarked in the *Mayflower* and became known to posterity as "The Pilgrim Fathers." The historical significance of these thirty men and women of the Scrooby fraternity has proved considerable. They also have become a legend.

Many of those who were not content with the vague encouragement of Deism became Socinians, or Molinists, or Hutchinsonians, or Unitarians. A more definite and effective group was that represented by Lady Huntingdon's connection. Lady Huntingdon, a pious if impulsive woman, founded chapels in Chelsea, Brighton, and Tunbridge Wells and appointed as her domestic chaplains such evangelists as Whitefield and Romaine. She also supported Henry Venn. The aristocracy were deeply shocked that a countess should so demean herself as to become a revivalist. "It is monstrous," wrote the Duchess of Buckingham, "to be told that you have a heart as sinful as the common wretches that crawl on the earth." How could Lady Huntingdon "relish sentiments so much at variance with high rank and good breeding?" Lady Huntingdon was not deterred by such disapproval. She founded at Trevecca a seminary for the training of preachers which was at first largely staffed by Methodists. Wesley himself came to disapprove of Trevecca and denounced "those striplings who call themselves Lady Huntingdon's preachers." Being a Calvinist by conviction, she quarreled with the Methodists and her disciples accused Wesley of being a Papist, a Jacobite agent, an antinomian, and of practicing "dirty subterfuges which degrade him to the level of an oyster woman." In the end, a compromise was reached and the breach with the Methodists was partially healed. Yet Lady Huntingdon's connection was as influential in forwarding the Evangelical revival as were the Methodists themselves.

The religious influence of these several dissenting groups, apart from the Presbyterians, was not at first nationwide. The aim of many of them was to find some sanctuary where they might practice their dissidence quietly, supported by brethren who shared their own doctrines and convictions. The real creators of the religious revival in Great Britain and overseas were John Wesley, the mighty organizer, his brother Charles Wesley, the hymnologist of the movement, and the revivalist preacher, George Whitefield.

Three

John Wesley was born at Epworth Parsonage in the Fen country on June 17, 1703. His father, Samuel Wesley, was a high church Tory, a muddle-headed, selfish, obstinate, and irritable man. His mother, Susanna Annesley, was one of the twenty-five children of a famous nonconformist, who was known as "the St. Paul of nonconformism." On her marriage to the vicar of Epworth she joined the established Church. She was a firm and pious woman who exercised a powerful influence over her nineteen children. She was highly educated, but not vivacious. The Rev. W. H. Fitchett speaks of her "unsmiling, owl-like gravity." She imposed upon John and his brothers and sisters the most rigid discipline and the severest biblical instruction.

The Rev. Samuel Wesley remained vicar of Epworth for thirty-nine years until his death in 1735. He quarreled violently with his parishioners, was miserably poor, and in fact was imprisoned for debt in Lincoln Castle when John was two years old. In 1709, the vicarage was destroyed by fire and John barely escaped with his life, regarding himself thereafter as literally "a brand snatched from the burning." There was a poltergeist who haunted the old building to whom the children gave the affectionate nickname of "old Jeffrey." To the end of his life, John Wesley believed in ghosts and witchcraft, and he and his brothers continued to engage in bibliomancy, seeking divination by opening their Bibles and immediately turning the pages if the text they first lighted on proved irrelevant to their perplexities. In spite of such superstitions, John Wesley always regarded himself as a reasonable man. "I would just as soon," he wrote, "put out my eyes to secure my faith as lay aside reason. . . . I am ready to give up any opinion which I cannot, by calm, clear reason, defend." The self-confidence which this illusion gave him enhanced his gift of persuasion.

At the age of eleven, owing to the patronage of the Duke of Buckingham, he was admitted to the foundation of the Charterhouse. The system of fagging by which the school was administered led to atrocious bullying; the elder boys would deprive the juniors of their meat ration. John Wesley does not seem to have much resented these outrages, and in fact he would assert in later years that his wonderful constitution was due to the fact that as a schoolboy he lived almost entirely on bread and water. At the age of seventeen he left the Charterhouse with a closed exhibition of £40 a year for Christ Church College, Oxford. He was an excellent classical scholar and studied with unflagging assiduity. In September 1725, he was ordained by the Bishop of Oxford and in the following year he gained a fellowship at Lincoln College. "Leisure and I," he then wrote, "have taken leave one of another. I propose to be busy as long as I live, if my health is so long indulged me." He maintained this resolution for the next sixty-five years.

In 1727, he left Oxford in order to act as curate for his father in the small parish of Wroot, some five miles from Epworth, and situated in a bog amid the fens. His parishioners were raw and hostile and his curacy proved an utter failure. He returned to Oxford in November 1729 in a mood of depression and self-distrust. He found that his younger brother Charles, who had been a leading scholar and captain of the school at Westminster, had gathered round him at Christ Church a group of four men interested in religion. They would attend Holy Communion regularly and would meet in each other's rooms to read the Bible together, and to examine the state of each other's souls. They would fast on two days a week. They would visit the condemned prisoners in Oxford Castle and pray for their redemption. They were much derided by their fellows, being called by such nicknames as "The Holy Club," "The Sacramentarians," "The Bible Moths," "The Enthusiasts" or "The Methodists." It was the last of these nicknames that survived the mirth of undergraduates.

On his return to Oxford, John Wesley, whose superiority was immediately recognized, became the admitted leader of the group. The original members of the Holy Club, on going down from Oxford, took different paths, joining the established Church or the Moravians. Charles Wesley remained loyal to his brother, whom he would always address in Latin, and they were subsequently joined by young George Whitefield, a servitor at Pembroke College.

It was George Whitefield who became the missionary of Methodism overseas. It was he also who created the art of open-air preaching and who was largely responsible for giving to Methodism its revivalist character. He was the dramatic type of orator and possessed a voice so powerful that his friend Benjamin Franklin observed that he could be heard distinctly from the Courthouse steps in Philadelphia as far as Front Street. Whitefield had been born in the Bell Inn at Gloucester and as a boy had served as tapster in the public bar. He was at one time nominated by the formidable Lady Huntingdon as one of her domestic chaplains and preached repentance at her chapels in Chelsea and Brighton. Yet it was as preacher to mass audiences in market squares and meadows that he secured his greatest triumphs. John Wesley, who always remained the scholar and the gentleman, was never sure whether he approved of Whitefield's histrionics. This effective missionary paid as many as six visits to the United States. He died at Newburyport, Massachusetts, in September 1770.

In April 1735, John Wesley's father died at the age of seventy-two. It was suggested that John should succeed him as Vicar of Epworth and thus provide a home for his widowed mother and penniless sisters. He was at the stage passing through a self-centered period. In spite

John Wesley

of what his disciples have written, there was always in John Wesley's masterfulness a strain of egoism. He refused this opportunity and obligation. "The question is," he said, "not whether I could do more good to others, there or here, but whether I could do more to myself." He insisted that he must return, for the good of his own soul, to the narrow circle of the Holy Club in Oxford. Yet within a few months, when opportunity offered, he abandoned Oxford and the Holy Club and set sail for America. "My chief motive," he admitted, "is the hope of saving my own soul."

Colonel Oglethorpe was a Member of Parliament and a fine philanthropist. He was much concerned with the harsh treatment then meted out to debtors. He had already obtained a royal charter creating the area between Florida and South Carolina a British Colony. He decided that this Colony might become a sanctuary for insolvent debtors, who until then had been confined under cruel and insanitary conditions in the jails of London and the provincial capitals. The New Colony of Georgia was entrusted to a corporation of twenty-one trustees with Colonel Oglethorpe as Chairman. Parliament voted £10,000 to the project; the Bank of England gave another £10,000; and £16,000 more was raised by private subscription. In 1733, one hundred and twenty debtors were transported to what is now Savannah and were in the next year joined by refugee Highlanders, Moravians, and Germans.

Colonel Oglethorpe, who had known the vicar of Epworth, offered Charles Wesley the post of his private secretary and John Wesley the post of pastor to the new community. Accompanied by Charles, Benjamin Ingham, and Charles Delamotte, John Wesley embarked in the *Simmonds* in October 1735 and reached Savannah on February 5, 1736. Among the passengers was a group of Moravians, whose courage during a dangerous storm left a deep impression on Wesley. The two and a half years that he spent in Georgia were for him years of mortification. He had wished to convert the Indians but discovered that they were too deeply engaged in tribal feuds to pay any attention to the doctrine of redemption. His own parishioners at Savannah and at the neighboring

Frederika were alienated by his Oxford manner and his domineering ways. They complained to Colonel Oglethorpe of both John and Charles Wesley and the brothers both felt that the Governor had not supported them with sufficient stoutness in these intrigues. There then occurred the unfortunate affair of Miss Sophia Hopkey. Wesley had certainly conveyed to her the impression that he intended to propose marriage, but the Moravians, when consulted, advised him "to proceed no further in this business." Humiliated by this rebuttal, Miss Hopkey immediately became engaged to a young colonial of the name of Williamson, whom she shortly afterwards married. John Wesley was so angered by this inconsistency that he wrote to Mrs. Williamson a letter in which personal abuse was mingled with pastoral reprobation. He even went so far as to refuse her the Sacrament when she appeared at communion. Her uncle Mr. Causton, who was the main store keeper at Savannah and a person of considerable local influence, then brought in an indictment against John Wesley on ten counts, asserting that not only had he departed from the strict liturgy prescribed by the Church of England, but that he had written to Mrs. Williamson without her husband's consent. Knowing that the jury was packed and would vote against him, John Wesley decided that it would be better to escape. He left Savannah secretly and embarked at Charleston in a vessel that landed him at Deal on February 1, 1738. His mission to Georgia had not merely been a pastoral failure but had ended in humiliation and almost in disgrace. He felt "sorrowful and very heavy" and for a while his optimism deserted him.

Four

Ever since his Oxford days John Wesley had been attracted by the idea of Christian perfection preached by Thomas à Kempis and by Jeremy Taylor in his *Holy Living* and *Holy Dying*. In 1729, he read the *Serious Call* of William Law, which affected him as deeply as it had affected Dr. Johnson. He visited Law in Putney and had long discussions with him on the theme of repentance and salvation through faith. In the end he became alienated from William Law whom he suspected, and rightly, of indulging in mysticism. One of the curious elements in Wesley's massive faith was his suspicion of all types of mysticism, which he regarded as a form of self-righteousness. "All the other enemies of Christianity," he wrote, "are triflers; the Mystics are the most dangerous; they stab it in the vitals, and the serious professors are most likely to fall by them." This breach between Law and Wesley was unfortunate, since Law's exalted intelligence and high literary capacity could only have been of advantage to the Methodist movement.

In place of Law, Wesley came under the influence of a pupil of Zinzendorff, Peter Böhler, a firm Moravian, with whom he traveled up to Oxford. Until then John Wesley felt that he had not experienced a complete conversion. "I had," he wrote, "the faith of a *servant*, though not that of a *son*." It was Peter Böhler who inspired the Wesley brothers with an urgent need for utter repentance and identification. It was but a few weeks after Border's departure for America that Charles Wesley "found peace." John Wesley had been convinced by Böhler that salvation was granted, not through works, but through Christ's atonement only. He also taught that conversion could be a sudden revelation and need not always be achieved through gradual periods of prayer, agony, and repentance. It was thus at 8:45 P.M. on Wednesday, May 24, 1738 that John Wesley received his sudden revelation. He happened on that occasion to be attending the meeting of a society in Aldersgate Street in London where a translation was read of Luther's preface to the Epistle to the Romans. Suddenly it was revealed to Wesley that he was "too learned and too wise" and that peace would never descend on him through adherence to the schools of Oxford of the formulas of the established Church. He always thereafter dated his conversion from that spring night in 1738.

He left shortly afterwards for the Moravian settlement of Herrnhut near Dresden where he remained for three months. He returned with a fervent admiration for the simple piety of the Moravians. But he was alienated by their theory that a man who did not possess perfect faith must be regarded as possessing no faith at all, and must therefore adopt the attitude of "quietism" and "be still," avoiding even the reading of the scriptures or the practice of good works, and rest in silence while awaiting the coming of Christ. Wesley was angered when the Moravian Pastor Molther came to London in October 1739 and obtained control of the little society of Methodists which he had established in Fetter Lane. Hearing that this society had gone over to the Moravians, Wesley dashed up from Bristol to London and attended a "Love Feast." He begged the brethren to follow his own teaching rather than that of Pastor Molther, and on meeting with no unanimous response, he rose in anger, announcing that he intended to sever his connection with the Fetter Lane Society and establish a new one composed of more faithful and obedient members. So saying, he called on all loyal brethren to follow him out of the hall; some eighteen responded. The drama of their exit was, however, diminished by the fact that a shrewd Moravian had hidden Wesley's hat, and the delay which followed caused an anticlimax. It was then that Wesley established his main center at the Foundry.

A divergence then arose between him and Whitefield. He had at first disapproved of Whitefield's open-air preaching and was none too delighted when he accepted the post of one of Lady Huntingdon's domestic chaplains. News reached him of Whitefield's immense successes in America (a continent in which he himself had been a failure) and even a report that Whitefield employed slave labor at the orphanage he had established overseas. He also differed from Whitefield in the controversy between predestination and free will. Whitefield, and Lady Huntingdon, inclined to the Calvinist theory that most of mankind were damned eternally and that only the "elect" could be saved. Wesley contended that so exclusive a doctrine constituted a reflection on God's benevolence. The Calvinists countered by arguing that to believe that all sinners who repented were entitled to salvation, amounted to Antinomianism, namely the belief that, since God in his mercy would pardon all mankind for their sins, one might as well enjoy the pleasures of the flesh while awaiting eventual forgiveness. Wesley accused the Calvinists of "representing God worse than the Devil." Whitefield retorted that John Wesley and his brother "preached a different gospel." Wesley also criticized what he called Whitefield's "little improprieties of manner and preaching." In the end they were reconciled, since they loved each other dearly. But among their disciples the battle between those who believed in predestination and the doctrine of election, and those who held to the theory of Free Grace, continued for years and represented a real dichotomy between the different branches of Methodism. Fortunately John Wesley, unlike Whitefield or Charles, was a born organizer; he managed to weld his own societies into a solid whole. It was under this masterly guidance that Methodism spread throughout the land.

Five

Wesley was always clumsy in his relations with women. As an undergraduate he had become attached to Miss Betty Kirkham, the sister of an Oxford friend, but owing to his habitual hesitations she decided after three years to marry a Mr. Wilson. His unhappy relations with Miss Sophia Hopkey in Savannah have already been described. On his return to England he entered into an emotional correspondence with Mrs. Pendarves, styling her "Aspasia" and signing himself "Cyrus." But in the end Mrs. Pendarves became Mrs. Delaney. He then encountered the widow of a sailor, Mrs. Grace Murray, who was an active Methodist worker at Newcastle, and in whom he believed that he found the helpmate that he sought:

> My soul a kindred spirit found
> By Heaven entrusted to my care,
> The daughter of my faith and prayer.

But Mrs. Murray married a lay preacher of the name of John Bennet and Wesley then impulsively married Mrs. Vazeille, the widow of a Fenchurch Street merchant, who rendered him miserable for thirty years. She was an insanely jealous woman, would spy on his every movement, and open his correspondence. She bullied him atrociously and one of his friends once witnessed her dragging her little husband across the floor by his hair. He complained sadly of her "common custom of saying things not true," of her coarse language, and of "not being safe in my own house." Mr. Fitchett describes her as "a human gadfly, whose business it was to sting."

It was against this miserable domestic background that Wesley conducted his campaign as itinerant preacher. He had not at first thought it right to preach outside a consecrated building, but as more and more Church of England clergymen refused him admission to their churches, he was obliged to preach out of doors. On visiting Epworth he found the church door barred against him by his father's drunken successor and was obliged to address the congregation in the churchyard standing on his father's tomb. He thereafter realized that open air preaching was the only means whereby he could convey his message to large popular audiences. He traveled through the length of England, paid repeated visits to Ireland and Scotland, and it is calculated that during the fifty years he remained an itinerant preacher he travelled a quarter of a million miles and preached some 50,000 sermons. He would walk and ride through snow and storm, frequently falling off his horse, frequently having to endure the abuse and missiles of hostile crowds. His physical endurance was phenomenal: his courage superb. At the age of eighty-three he could record in his journal, "I am a wonder to myself. I am never tired (such is the goodness of God) either by writing, preaching or traveling." In his sermons he did not adopt the dramatic style of Whitefield or even his brother's appeal to the emotions. Horace Walpole, as I have noted already, who was ill attuned to Methodism, calling it "this nonsensical new light," heard him preach in 1766 and was not unimpressed. "Wondrous clean," he called him, "but as evidently an actor as Garrick. There were parts and eloquence in his sermon; but towards the end he exalted his voice and acted very ugly enthusiasm."

It was not to intellectual aristocrats such as Horace Walpole that Wesley addressed his message: he preferred the poor. "Ye serpents," he would shout at the gentry, "ye generation of vipers, how can ye escape the damnation of hell?" Such a method of address was not in the least welcomed by the Duchess of Buckingham: the parson and the squire came to regard Wesley as a disturbing influence who attracted congregations away from the established Church and who, by his example of austerity and fervor, suggested comparisons embarrassing to themselves. John Wesley was himself at heart a Tory and an Anglican; in politics he was as reactionary as Dr. Johnson and, although he disapproved of our soldiers fighting their compatriots in America, he had scant sympathy with the cause of the Colonists. Although Methodism was the main force that awoke a social conscience in all classes in Great Britain, Wesley was not himself a very sensitive humanitarian. Although it is agreeable to record that almost the last letter that he wrote was one of encouragement to Wilberforce and the anti-slavery campaign, he had little awareness of the social problems which would be created by the industrial revolution, little criticism of the harsh penal laws then in force, or of the condition of our prisons, and so great a misconception of the purposes of education that he proclaimed that the object of schools should be to "break the will of the child." His interpretation of austerity was puritan in its strictness. He objected to drink, gambling, dancing, the theatre, clothes that were either "glistening or showy," and blood sports. He told his followers that they should avoid conversing "in a merry, gay, or diverting manner." He was not naturally a man of liberal views and remained obstinately opposed to Catholic Emancipation. Until his death at the age of eighty-eight he remained at heart an Oxford Tory, refusing to recognize that it had become inevitable that the great movement he had created would after his death separate from the Anglican Church.

Although himself a scholar he soon realized that his message was addressed, not to the sophisticated, but to the simple mind. "Let me think," he said, "as a little child! Let my religion be plain, artless, simple! Meekness, temperance, patience, faith and love—be these my highest gifts!" The system followed by Wesley and his fellow preachers was first to convince people of their utter sinfulness and then to assure them that they had been rescued from the flames of hell by the sacrifice of Jesus Christ. The first lesson to learn was the abandonment of all pride. In one of the most Blake-like of his hymns, Charles Wesley expressed the need of humbling the personality in memorable terms:

> And dare we our perfection boast
> With haughty Luciferian scorn?
> Deny our innocency, lost
> As still in God's resemblance born?
> Great Author of the second birth
> Give us our fallen souls to feel
> As godlike as the beasts on earth
> As perfect as the fiends in Hell.

The feelings of unworthiness, guilt, remorse, and repentance thus generated created a tension that was almost intolerable; then suddenly came the realization that Christ had in his person atoned for all human sins and that once we found Jesus we should be saved from the burning and live in endless felicity:

> My God I am thine;
> What a comfort divine,
> What a blessing to know that my Jesus is mine!
> In the heavenly Lamb
> Thrice happy I am,
> And my heart it doth dance at the sound of his name.

Inevitably this contrast between terror and relief produced symptoms of hysteria among the audience. People "became wounded by the sword of the spirit" and started to scream and tremble or to fall to the ground in convulsions. Wesley himself discouraged all exhibitions of hysteria or "enthusiasm." He informed his followers that they caused him "surprise and grief." He left the more emotional aspects of his revivalism to Whitefield and his brother Charles. He himself concentrated on organization, for which, according to Macaulay, he possessed a talent comparable only to that of Richelieu. The small local groups were organized into societies; there were regular love feasts and classes; and there were annual "Conferences" which grew into the Parliament or "Methodist Conference" which now disciplines the Methodist community.

The expansion of Methodism was rapid and vast. The original Holy Club at Oxford was comprised of no more than four people. By 1770, the number of Methodists had swollen to 29,406 members with 121 preachers; at the time of Wesley's death there were 71,668 Methodists in Europe, and 48,610 in America. Today the Methodists have spread across the world and constitute the largest Protestant Church in the United States. This expansion owes its origin to John Wesley's astonishing gift of organization.

Lecky goes so far as to state that it was Methodism which at the end of the eighteenth century preserved England from a revolution as terrible as that of France. Had it not been for this great movement of revival, the industrial revolution might have assumed even more dangerous shapes. Methodism, for the working classes, proved a welcome emotional sedative, while it gave to the rich a sense of responsibility and a philanthropic conscience. It passed on to the Evangelicals its high ideals of public and private duty; by its example it reformed and raised the Church of England; it purified politics, gave a fresh stimulus to popular education, and created the wave of humanitarianism that led to the abolition of slavery and penal reform. Certainly it was one of the most civilizing inspirations that have ever improved the lot of man. All this was due to the genius and virtue of the gifted and charming little scholar who was born at Epworth Parsonage on June 17, 1703.

Chapter 21
Sensibility
(Jean Jacques Rousseau, 1712–1778)

———•◆•———

The world becomes tired of reason and cultivates sensibility—the effect of Methodism on feeling and conscience—As a symbol of the reaction against symmetry and order the new theories on garden design are illuminating—John Evelyn—Pope—William Temple—Thomson—Kent—The landskip garden and the cult of the picturesque—Sharawaggi—The "return to Nature"—The Noble Savage—Johnson's contempt for the idealization of the primitive—Cowper—Jean Jacques Rousseau—His life and character—His persecution mania—His sexual abnormality—His worship of Nature—Feeling becomes more important than thinking—*La Nouvelle Héloise*—The *Discours sur l'Inégalite*—The *Contrat Social*—The irrational becomes fashionable—Effect of this upon the French Revolution—The end of the Age of Reason.

One

A NEW GENERATION ARISES every thirty years and every century contains three successive generations. In Chapter 2 I have already examined, in terms of the Ségur family, the transitions in eighteenth-century thought and feeling as experienced by a father, his son, and his grandson. The first generation, say from 1700 to 1740, were still conditioned by the formal disciplines of Church and State, took the ancien régime for granted, and believed without much questioning in revealed religion, in authority, and in the divine right of kings. The second generation, say from 1730 to 1760, reacted against the tenets of their parents, regarded revealed religion as savoring of "enthusiasm," even of superstition, became anti-clerical, valued reason above emotion, defied authority, and absorbed with delight the skeptical teaching of the *Encyclopédistes* and the ironic humanitarianism of Voltaire. The third generation, say from 1761 to the end of the century, ceased to think in logical terms, relied more on the heart than on the head, rejected the rectilinear in favor of the serpentine, favored the display of personal emotion, cultivated sensibility, wept copiously, and took pleasure in what their fathers had regarded as the "horrible" majesty of heath and mountain. For them the prophet of the new age was Jean Jacques Rousseau.

In France, the cult of sensibility, after the publication of *La Nouvelle Héloise* in 1761, assumed almost hysterical proportions. In Britain the romantic movement established itself earlier and its way was less emotional and more reserved. But in the last three decades of the eighteenth century, before Dr. Thomas Arnold had taught us to control our feelings, even the most manly Britons surrendered to sensibility. They would become what they called "broken down" at the sight of scenery, the sound of waterfalls, the contemplation of unspoilt nature, the thought of Liberty and the Noble Savage, or the recitation of "tender" lyrics. We have changed all that. Winston Churchill is perhaps the last Englishman to sob in public.

Methodism, which we are apt to regard as a dour habit of thought and feeling, was in fact one of the major influences in the triumph of emotion. The importance that it gave to personal experience as opposed to theological learning; its encouragement of self-expression even of "enthusiasm"; the stimulus it gave to "creative excitement" and to the "renascence of wonder"; the lyrical appeal of Charles Wesley's hymns: all these enhanced the importance of personality and gave to individual feeling a significance and a scope that until then had been suppressed by logic and reason. Many of the components of early romanticism can be found in the Methodist revival. William Cowper, the greatest of the early romantics, was profoundly affected by the Calvinist school of Methodism. He experienced a definitely Methodist conversion, to the accompaniment of a torturing sense of sin, followed by assurance, relief, wonder, and rapture. Had he fallen directly under the guidance of the wise John Wesley, it is probable that he would not have relapsed into melancholy mania; it was the Calvinist bully, John Newton, who, in Professor Courthope's words, "transformed him from a comparatively cheerful scholar into a shrinking and sensitive recluse and aggravated his propensity to introspection into religious mania." Methodist exaltation and Methodist vocabulary can be found in *Night Thoughts* as in the poems of Thomson and Collins. Even Christopher Smart could indulge in verses in the manner of Charles Wesley:

> Glorious, more glorious is the crown
> Of Him who brought salvation down,
> By meekness called thy Son.

Blake also was profoundly influenced by Methodism. He wrote of Wesley and Whitefield as "true witnesses," he frequently used Methodist phraseology. He was convinced that:

> The Perfect
> May live in Glory, redeemed by the sacrifice of the Lamb. . . .
> Glory! Glory! Glory! to the Holy Lamb of God!

Methodism contributed even to the revival of the macabre, which became so constant a feature in the romantic movement. James Harvey, a prominent Methodist, published his *Meditation among Tombs* in 1745. It contained many an euphuistic sentence as morbid as the following: "Instead of sumptuous tables and delicious treats, the poor voluptuary is himself a feast for fattened insects; the reptile riots in his flesh." "The great undercurrent," writes Professor Courthope, "of religious revival in the eighteenth century, equally devotional and democratic in its tendency, was a powerful factor in bringing about a revolution in English poetry as well as in English politics."

It was the coming of sensibility that prepared men's minds for the romantic movement, and sensibility was both intensified and diffused by the hymns and preaching of the Wesley brothers, who taught thousands of the illiterate to read and sing. It pleases me to reflect that the spruce little Oxford scholar, who did so much to arouse the conscience of the eighteenth century, should also have made so marked and unexpected a contribution to its culture.

Two

The change in the tide of taste and feeling which marks the later decades of the eighteenth century is well illustrated in the sudden craze for landscape gardening. Essentially the rejection of the formal garden, with its elaborate parterres of geometrical beds, its vistas of clipped yews in tubs, and its walks of pleached elms and limes, arose from a growing preference for the element of surprise over the element of expectation. The classic school of gardening, descending through Le Nôtre from the Italians and Pliny, regarded the garden as the continuation and reflection of the architecture of the house. The design must repeat the rectilinear lines of the building, prolong and balance the horizontals of the main elevation, and correct the perpendiculars. The superb designs of Le Nôtre were intended to enhance the grandeur of the facade as seen from the garden, not to reproduce the natural beauties of the garden as seen from the house. Symmetry, balance, order, were the elements of his composition; nature must be tamed to a geometrical pattern; the eye must be satisfied by the orderly and the expected, not disturbed by the wild or the surprising.

The reaction against the architectural conception of garden design began even earlier than the eighteenth century. We have already seen how Madame de Maintenon became restless under the rule of symmetry and how she came to long for something less obvious and trim. In 1679, John Evelyn, an expert in gardening, was delighted by the designs made by William Wise for the Duke of Buckingham's estate at Cliveden. There were grottoes dug in the chalk escarpments and unexpected vistas cut through the shrubberies to reveal the curve of the Thames. Evelyn described Cliveden as "a romantic object" and "admirably surprising." Pope as a young man much admired the "naturalness" of Windsor Forest, where he found that the existing features were:

Harmoniously confused
Where order in variety we see
And where, tho' all things differ, all agree.

Sir William Temple, also a keen gardener, in his 1685 essay on *The Garden of Epicurus* first mentioned the Chinese system of garden design, using the word "sharadwadgi," or "sharawaggi," which he assumed to be a Japanese word for "irregular" or "non-symmetrical." Temple was a classic by temperament and his own gardens at Sheen and Moor Park were designed symmetrically. He had the sense to see that the oriental type of garden, if it were not to appear grotesque, required for its perfection long experience and a skill such as no English gardener possessed. He warned his contemporaries not to imitate the gardens of the Far East since they would be certain to make mistakes, whereas "in regular figures it is hard to make any great or remarkable faults."

The Brompton firm of London and Wise specialized in clipped shrubs and their topiared tub trees became so suburban that the reaction against the formal garden acquired a snobbish tinge. The great landowners no longer desired to decorate their terraces with clipped box or yew, such as their visitors had observed in the front gardens of every villa on the way down through Kensington, Hammersmith, and Chiswick. Even such traditionalists as Pope and the *Spectator* started to protest against the formal school, in which architectural features were repeated without imagination, and where one could observe, "the marks of the scissors on every plant and bush." Pope in his villa at Twickenham, which he acquired in 1718, sought to introduce the element of surprise. His famous grotto was a repository for shells and minerals as well as a tunnel underneath the road. But it certainly startled expectation and aroused surprise. In 1731, in his lines on *Taste*,

Pope announced what shortly afterwards became the guiding principles of garden design. He contended that the enlightened gardener
should so plan the layout of his beds and shrubberies that his garden:

> Calls in the country, catches opening glades,
> Joins willing woods and varies shades from shades,
> Now breaks, or now directs the intending lines,
> Paints as you plant, and as you work, designs.

The use of the word "paints" in Pope's poem had an important
effect. It introduced into garden design the element of the picturesque and before long the landowners of the eighteenth century were
dreaming of transforming their straight avenues and their rectilinear
bowling greens into what James Thomson in his *Castle of Indolence*
described as:

> Whate'er Lorrain light-touched with softened hue,
> Or savage Rosa dash'd, or learned Poussin drew.

The fashion of landscape gardening spread. Fortunately William
Kent arrived to exploit it with skill and learning. Kent had studied
painting in Rome and by the time he met Lord Burlington in 1718 he
had already been so imbued with the paintings of Claude Lorraine,
Poussin, and Salvator Rosa, that he determined to "leap the fence and
see all nature as a garden." The English landscape and climate aided
his ambitions. He designed a "natural" garden for General Dormer
at Rousham near Oxford and another for the poet Shenstone at Lea-
sowes. The fashion for what was called "landskip or picturesque gardening" spread throughout the shires. Stephen Switzer in his *Icono-
graphia Rustica* advocated "as many twinings and windings as the villa
will allow"; Charles Bridgeman invented the sunk wall or "ha-ha";
and Hogarth defined the serpentine as "the line of beauty and grace."

The great garden at Stourhead in Wiltshire (which to this day,
under the care of the National Trust, remains the finest example of
English landscape gardening) was completed by Henry Hoare in
1772 and thereafter came Capability Brown and his son-in-law Henry
Holland, who "improved" most of the country seats in England

and created the English park which, as the Duke of Wellington has remarked, is the greatest contribution made by the British to the arts. The work of Capability Brown was completed by Humphry Repton, who restrained the exaggerations which the cult of the picturesque had by then occasioned and who advocated "truth to nature"; the wooded semicircle on the brow of the hills, the green sweep below munched by fallow deer, and the ponds of "natural" shape.

In France, the fashion for the English, or as they first called it "The Anglo-Chinese," garden, rapidly destroyed the tradition of Le Nôtre. The old classical schools were defeated. "We defend ourselves so badly," wrote the Prince de Ligne, "that we deserve to be beaten." He himself at Beloeil constructed a special walk of yew and cypress for the disciples of Jean Jacques Rousseau and the solace of melancholy dreamers. At Moulin-Joli there was a special, carefully worm-eaten, bench erected under a willow where men and women of the Rousseau school could sit and sob "not from sadness but from delicious sensibility." The French, who had brought to such perfection the art of formal gardening, were unable, as Horace Walpole acidly noticed, to catch the true spirit of the *jardin libre*. It may well be that the wide stretches of grass, so essential to any form of landscape gardening, are not so well adapted to the clear skies of the Ile de France, as they are to the mists of Thames and Severn. But the French in the end rejected most of their English gardens and returned to gravel, santolina, salvia, and sand.

The change of taste in garden design from the expected to the surprising, from straight to serpentine, provides a vivid illustration of the transformation of thought and feeling by which it was presaged and accompanied.

Three

The fashion for sharawaggi, the dislike of correctness, were not confined to garden design or interior decoration; they extended to religion, morals, behavior, taste. The reaction against reason, skepticism, logic, learning, self-discipline, and convention produced the special form of sensibility which we identify with the early stages of the romantic movement. Bruyère had written that no gentleman should reveal his emotions: thereafter the "man of feeling" emerged. Effusiveness became the fashion. Many British, and whole cataracts of French, tears were shed over the sad story of *Clarissa Harlowe*, the seven volumes of which appeared in 1748. Self-expression became the fashion; "correctness" was decried and there were those even who questioned the genius of Pope. "Back to Nature!" became the rallying cry, although very few were certain in their own minds what "nature" really meant. Professor Lovejoy in his *History of Ideas* has analyzed as many as eighteen different meanings of the term. It was generally assumed that the "natural" was the opposite to the "artificial" and that virtue and happiness could be achieved only by rejecting the elaborate usages of polite society, by becoming "simple," and even by reverting to what was assumed to be the golden age of primitive man.

The discoveries of science increased the growing bewilderment. The telescope had revealed the immensity of space: the microscope a teeming activity of invisible lives. The Deists comforted themselves with the thought that this vastness and complexity were but further proofs of the power of the Mighty Orderer of Nature. "All Nature's wonders," wrote Shaftesbury, "serve to excite and perfect this idea of their Author." Man came to believe in what they called "the chain of being" and the "rule of love." Even as it was mutual attraction that kept the planets in their courses, so also was it fellow feeling that linked man to his neighbor. This "chain of converse" was one of the "emanations of the Eternal Mind." Even those who could not wholly share Pope's optimistic assurance that "One truth is clear: Whatever is, is right," were comforted by the evidence of fixed rules controlling an apparently disordered Universe. "Even rude nature itself," wrote Shaftesbury, "in its primitive simplicity is a better guide to judgment than improved sophistry and pedantic learning." In spite of this advice, many men and women remained terrified by the prospect of losing the certitudes of revealed religion. "Now the distempered mind," wrote Thomson in his *Seasons*:

Now the distempered mind
Has lost that concord of harmonious powers
Which forms the soul of happiness; and all
Is off the poise within.

How comforting it would be to surrender to Shaftesbury's advice, to escape from perplexing reason, and to derive solace from the example of "rude nature itself," to:

Cut budding cowslips and with lambkins play,
Sing with a nymph or with a shepherd stray.

To Thomson again the pastoral life offered an escape from harsh reality. His "merry-hearted peasants" would recline on "downy moss" while:

Join'd to the prattle of the purling rills
Were heard the lowing herds along the vale,
And flocks loud-bleating from the distant hills.
And vacant shepherds piping in the dale;
And now and then sweet Philomel would wail. . . .

Nature, to Thomson's sensibility, was not so much an object of mystic worship as an opportunity for retirement, for escape from intellectual perplexity and the strains and rattle of a doubting world. At times this yearning for the primitive in time or space assumed exaggerated form.

One of the strangest hallucinations that marked the early phase of sensibility was the cult of the Noble Savage. In periods of over-ripeness and corruption disapproving men have always pictured to themselves a civilization based on simple virtues and unluxurious lives. Tacitus in his *Germania* had contrasted the vices of the age of Nero and Galba with the unsophisticated virtues of the Teutonic tribes, who were represented as austere, unworldly, domestic, chaste, and surpassingly brave. Columbus had defined the West Indies as the lost Garden of Eden; Montaigne had admired the uncivilized man "all naked, simply pure, in Nature's lap." Even the extreme rationalists of the first half of the eighteenth century believed in the "natural" perfectibility of mankind and held the view that in his natural state man was simple, spontaneous, and innocent. The first actual reference to the noble savage appears in Dryden's *Conquest of Granada* in 1670.

> I am as free as Nature first made man,
> E're the base laws of servitude began,
> When wild in woods the noble savage ran.

Aphra Behn in *Oroonoko* represented the civilization of Surinam as thriving "in the first state of innocence, before man knew how to sin." The Houyhnhnms of *Gulliver's Travels* also emphasized the contrast between the simplicity of horses with the self-seeking rapine of civilized man; Polly Peachum herself was married off to a noble savage; and Robinson Crusoe's good Man Friday (although he was a Carib and not, as so often represented, an African Negro) followed faithfully in this fantastic tradition.

In addition to the several diverse meanings which the eighteenth century gave to the word "Nature"—sometimes taking it to designate an ideal state of simplicity, sometimes to denote an empirical reality—their use of the word "Pride" is an indication of their growing tendency to denigrate the rational instinct which, in the first quarter of the century, was the boast and hope of the Age of Reason. In the state of nature the featherless biped called man was not so conceited as to claim to be the center of the universe, and personal ambition had not led to competition. "Pride there was not," wrote Pope:

> Pride there was not, nor arts that pride to aid;
> Man walked with beast, joint tenant of the shade.

The denunciation of "Pride" which figures as frequently in prose and verse from 1733 onwards represented an increasing distrust of intellectualism. Man was not to be assessed by the "dry light of reason" but admired as a complex of passions and instincts which combined to create our "natural constitution." Rousseau, in his paradoxical manner, could assert that "all science, even all ethics, derive from human pride." Man must abolish pride and become as simple as a pig or cow.

VAUX LE VICOMTE

LANDSCAPE GARDENING

(from a painting by Richard Wilson)

There were some men of sense, of course, who derided the whole legend. Hobbes did not for one moment agree that primitive man was more virtuous than civilized man, and more accurately described the life of the savage as being "solitary, poor, nasty, brutish, and short." Dr. Johnson, as one might expect in so urban a man, was enraged by the fantasy of the noble savage. As I have said, he snubbed Boswell sharply when he became sentimental about the islanders of the South Seas, exclaiming, "don't cant in defense of savages." He refused to believe that compassion was a "natural" instinct, arguing that children and animals were born cruel and that "pity is acquired and improved by the cultivation of reason." He was specially irritated by the suggestion that savages, having no sex inhibitions and being able to pick their yams without effort, were more blissful than men living in civilized communities, where scarcity and competition destroyed morals. A peasant might be satisfied, but he could not experience true happiness, since happiness consisted in "the multiplicity of agreeable consciousness." I have already quoted his lapidary remark about the state of man when food and sex could effortlessly be obtained: "If a bull could speak he might well exclaim, "Here I am with this cow and this grass; what being could enjoy greater felicity?" "

The noble savage legend, nonetheless, made a strong appeal to less sturdy minds. Typical of the sensibility aroused by this hallucination are the lines which Joseph Warton (who with his brother exercised a great influence on eighteenth century intellectuals) inserted in *The Enthusiast*:

> The isles of Innocence from mortal view
> Deeply retired, beneath a platan's shade,
> Where Happiness and Quiet sit enthroned . . .
> Where, fed on dates and herbs would I despise
> The farfetched cates of Luxury and hoards
> Of narrow-hearted Avarice, nor heed
> The distant din of the tumultuous world.

The Noble Savage was not invariably located in the Caribbean. James Thomson, in the *Castle of Indolence*, chose the Lapps, who "love their mountains and enjoy their storms"; Goldsmith found him in the rural population of England, a pathetic fallacy which Crabbe, with his more intimate acquaintance with the English peasantry, sturdily exposed. He described his rustics as being "a bold, artful, surly, savage race." But the legend of primitive virtue persisted until the guillotine began to crash and splash in the Place de la Concorde and men came to ask themselves whether Dryden might not have been justified in saying that "Fancy without judgment is a hot-mouthed jade without a curb."

Another symptom of sensibility was the increasing awareness of natural scenery. It is customary to regard Cowper, Thomson, Young, and Collins as the pioneers of nature poetry in England, yet if we identify nature poetry with the mystical awe experienced by Wordsworth and his disciples—the early romantics did not differ so very much from the neo-classics. Gray, it is true could write:

> The meanest floweret in the vale
> The simplest note that swells the gale,
> The common sun, the air, the skies,
> To him are opening Paradise.

But although Gray had a fine sense of the contrast between simplicity and artifice, he did not really identify his own emotions and ecstasies with nature to the extent that inspired Wordsworth to such sublime poetry. Cowper may, it is true, have believed in self-expression when, as a young man, he wrote:

> Nor think it weakness when we love to feel
> Nor think it weakness when we feel to show

But in fact he was by temperament a reserved man who wrote his best poetry when he was unmoved by emotion. His great achievement was to convince his sophisticated contemporaries of the beauty of commonplace objects and people, of the literary value of simplicity and directness. "God made the country," he wrote, "and man made the town." "For I have loved," he wrote, "the rural walk through lanes." But in fact he preferred the rectory parlor, the candles, the muffins, and the fire. James Thomson, again, who is often described by French critics as the initiator of nature poetry, was an observer rather than an enthusiast. He was an excellent observer and could write:

> auriculas enriched
> With shining meal o'er all their velvet leaves.

Yet his attitude towards nature was objective rather than emotional. Young and Collins, although so often hailed as pioneers of romanticism, were believers in "calm reason's holy law" and held that a well-disciplined mind was preferable to self-expression. To them the intellect, rather than the heart, was "the heaven-lighted lamp in man." The pioneers of the cult of sensibility and nature were not at first extravagant in their demands. Even Rousseau preferred Clarens to the Matterhorn. It was not till 1760 when *Ossian* took the world by storm that people lost their heads and identified sensibility with Hebridean mists.

It was at that later stage that melancholy became a creative component of the sensitive soul. Preoccupation with personality led to preoccupation with self and this emotional intensity led young men like Werther to feel that they had already "exhausted life," and that suicide was the only solution. "A great soul," Rene was to remark, "must contain more grief than a small soul." Those most affected by sensibility were determined to acquire a great soul, *une belle âme;* and they certainly suffered much in the process. As early as 1744, Thomas Warton, in the *Pleasures of Melancholy* had foreshadowed the whole romantic apparatus, of ruined towers, steeped in ivy, of "the abbey's moss-grown piles" and of owls hooting under the moon. An examination of the "gothick" and the "macabre" lies, however, outside the scope of this study of the urbane. The cult of Nature did not exercise any creative effect on sensibility until the very dawn of the nineteenth century.

Four

Even as Voltaire, with his sardonic smile, had introduced the age of
skepticism, so also did Jean Jacques Rousseau, with his emotional
genius, inaugurate the age of sensibility. No two authors in the history of literature have ever exercised so potent an influence upon the
thoughts and feelings of their contemporaries. It is easy to understand
how Voltaire, with his wit and eloquence, should have been able to
convince his sophisticated generation that intellect and reason were
the supreme glories of human nature and that emotion was akin to
"enthusiasm" and thus the ally of *l'infâme*. It is not so easy to explain
how Rousseau, with his lack of logic, his irrationality, and his despicable personal character, could have persuaded so intelligent a people as
the French to believe that the mind was less important than the heart,
logic less reliable than intuition, and the undisciplined expression of
emotion more valuable a guide to mankind than divine philosophy or
cultivated reflection. The fact remains that Rousseau and his doctrine
of "natural" emotion and the equality of man succeeded in destroying
the age of reason and in substituting a universe of fantasies that introduced much confusion, much unhappiness, much cruelty, and many
illusions into the civilized, and even into the uncivilized, world.

Jean Jacques Rousseau was born in Geneva on June 28, 1712. His
father was a watchmaker in such straitened circumstances that he
was unable to provide his son with a proper education. The boy was
apprenticed to a notary, and thereafter to an engraver, but absconded
from each of these engagements and thereafter led a vagabond life, of
which his *Confessions* give us but a sketchy and unreliable account.
We know that he abjured the Protestant religion, entered a Catholic
seminary, and became for a while footman to a Madame de Vercellis,
where he accused a fellow servant, Marion, of having stolen a ribbon
which he had in fact himself purloined. Eventually, at the age of sixteen, he found employment in the household of Madame de Warens
at Annecy who lavished maternal affection on him, would call him

"little one," and paid for his instruction in grammar and music. Tiring of this subservience, he bolted off to Lyons and obtained employment as secretary to a Greek archimandrite who was traveling in Europe in order to obtain subscriptions for the repair of the Holy Sepulcher. He thereafter rejoined Madame de Warens who had moved from Annecy to Chambery. Having by then reached the age of twenty, he was informed by Madame de Warens that he was no longer a boy, that he must cease to be her pupil and servant and become her lover. He was much embarrassed by this proposal, partly because he already doubted his sexual competence and partly because he felt that any physical intercourse with Madame de Warens, whom he still called "Maman," would amount to incest. They lived in the pretty little house of Les Charmettes outside Chambery where one can still see the flowerbeds he tended and the hives in which he kept the bees.

Madame de Warens was by then over thirty, was in some mysterious manner employed as secret agent by the King of Sardinia, believed in astrologers and fortune tellers, on whom she spent much of her small income, and was already becoming stout. It was with laggard footsteps that Rousseau would ascend the staircase to her bedroom, knowing that as a lover he was not destined for prowess. Madame de Warens meanwhile was also sleeping regularly with her butler, Claude Anet, and eventually imported into Les Charmettes a hairdresser's assistant of the name of Vintzenried, the son of the custodian of the Château de Chillon, and, it seems, a very virile lad. Humiliated at being thus supplanted, Rousseau ran away from Chambéry and got a job as tutor to the family of Monsieur de Mably. He always retained some affection for Madame de Warens. "My heart," he wrote, "was open to her as it was open to God." In his *Dixième Promenade*, written a few months before his own death, he describes the five years that he lived at Les Charmettes with Madame de Warens as the only perfectly happy period of his life. This may have been true, since his own mother had died when he was a baby and he had always stood in need of maternal protection. Hating the subservience to which he was exposed in the household of Monsieur de Mably, he absconded to Paris where he supported himself by giving music lessons and copying musical manuscripts. He claimed to have invented a revised method of musical notation by which the *Encyclopédistes* were much impressed. This brought him the friendship of Diderot and an entrance into intellectual society. He even contributed to the *Encyclopédie* some articles on music. But, as invariably happened, he before long became suspicious of Diderot, Marmontel, Holbach and Grimm, persuading himself that they were jealous of his genius, and were spreading throughout the Paris salons tales to his discredit.

Through the influence of Madame de Warens he obtained a post as secretary to the comte de Montagu, French Ambassador in Venice. This incursion into diplomatic life was not a success. The Ambassador suspected him of selling information to the Venetian authorities and dismissed him abruptly. The account of this episode which Rousseau inserted into his *Confessions* is so vague as to be evasive. He contends that the Ambassador "took a dislike to me, solely because I served him faithfully." The Ambassador, when questioned about it in Paris, merely replied that Rousseau had been "dismissed." It was during the Venetian period that the first symptoms of persecution mania became apparent; he became convinced that he was surrounded by enemies, informers, and spies. In his subsequent references to the episode one can detect a sense of shame.

On his return to Paris he found cheap rooms in the Hotel d'Orléans in the Luxembourg quarter. It was there that he met the chambermaid Thérèse le Vasseur, who became his mistress and eventually his wife. Their first child was said to have been born in 1746 and to have been immediately deposited on the steps of the nearest foundling hospital. The same realistic treatment was applied to its four successors. There are those who contend that the legend of the five abandoned babies was invented by Rousseau himself, in order to counter the rumor that he was sexually impotent. I also incline to think that Rousseau and Thérèse never had any children at all, and it is certainly true that, when the maréchale de Luxembourg offered to bring up one of the waifs if its identity could be established, no trace could be found of any of them in the records of the Paris foundling hospitals. Rousseau had not foreseen that he, who always proclaimed that he was devoted to children and that he enjoyed nothing so much as watching babies romping together (*"de petits bambins folâtrer et jouer ensemble"*); who, in *La Nouvelle Héloise* and above all in *Émile* had written long sermons on the solemn responsibilities of parents; would be accused of hypocrisy for abandoning his own family. Voltaire for one leapt upon the legend with malicious glee. Rousseau was then obliged to explain his supposed heartlessness in specious terms. "I believed," he wrote, "that I was acting rightly as a father and a citizen. I looked on myself as a member of Plato's Republic." This excuse did not satisfy those who contended that the apostle of the duties of parenthood and the domestic virtues should not have behaved so atrociously to Thérèse and her five legendary babies. The perplexity which the legend aroused did much damage to Rousseau's repute as a sincere humanitarian.

I incline to the theory that Rousseau was sexually impotent, or at least abnormal. As a child he had experienced exquisite delight when spanked by Mademoiselle Lambercier. "Who would have supposed," he wrote in his *Confessions*, "that this punishment inflicted on a boy of eight by a woman of thirty should have had so decisive an effect upon my tastes, my desires, and my passions for the rest of my life?" When in Venice he had visited the beautiful and accomplished courtesan, la Zulietta, and had subsided on to the sofa in floods of tears (*inondé de larmes*). "Jean," the harlot had said to him, "you had better give up trying to have women and devote yourself to mathematics." It is on such evidence that I reject the story of the five abandoned babies.

He certainly suffered from ill health, being afflicted with a scirrhous bladder, which increased his natural embarrassment in society and obliged him in middle age to wear a sort of dressing gown which he called "my Armenian robe." He was certainly a case of arrested development. "Although," he confessed, "in some respects I was born an adult, I remained a child for many years and even now I strike many people as having remained childlike." These physical disabilities go far to explain his hypersensitivity, his persecution mania, his morbid self-pity and his eventual mental derangement. He was always complaining that he had "become an example of human misery" and referring to "the long chain of my misfortunes." It is true that in 1762 the parliament of Paris ordered that *Émile* should be burnt by the public hangman and that he found it wiser to leave Paris and to take refuge in England and his native Switzerland. He certainly suffered from persecution mania, being convinced at one moment that the members of the Paris Orchestra were plotting to assassinate him, and at another moment that his destruction was being plotted by Diderot and the Holbach circle and even by the innocent and kindly David Hume. He suffered from hallucinations, when he believed that "a whole structure of shadows was being built against me" and when he was assailed by "indescribable disturbance when I was not myself."

In fact Rousseau was not to be pitied. He never lacked powerful patrons and supporters; Thérèse nursed him with devoted servitude; he experienced success and even fortune; he became a figure of world renown. But he was not, as was William Cowper, cursed with depressive mania. He had his moods of melancholy, he had his bouts of guilt, but on the whole he was accorded opportunities, if not for "happiness," then at least for "contentment." His misery arose from the very sensibility that he preached.

Five

Being himself uneducated, his motto of "back to Nature," was a means of self-protection, an assertion that instinct was preferable to reason, that the disciplined or cultured self was less true to nature than was the temperamental self. His sensations were quick and volatile, but his mental capacity was cumbrous and slow. "The fatigue of thinking," he wrote in 1761, "becomes every day more cumbrous to me." "I always feel," he wrote, "before I think. I am the most sensitive animal upon this earth. I am terrified by the buzzing of a fly." He became convinced that he "was never properly adapted to live in the society of my fellow men." When he entered a drawing room he suspected that an embarrassed hush descended on the company, since they had all been saying horrible things against himself. He thus consoled himself by withdrawing into a solitary hermitage, taking long walks alone in the forests and indulging in his passion for daydreams. "In my constant dreams of ecstasy," he wrote, "I intoxicated myself with torrents of the most delicious sentiments that have even been conceived by the heart of man." The life and mental decay of Rousseau serve as a cautionary tale for all those who seek to escape from reality.

Early in life he accepted the fact that he was bad at human relationships. "I was in despair," he wrote, "at my social clumsiness—*j'étais désolé de ma lourdise.*"

A character thus denied integration or normal development inevitably turns to nature as a painless substitute for spiritual or mental effort. Rousseau, with his yearning for solitude and his desire to be left alone with his chimeras, abandoned the turmoil of the town for "some wild spot in the forest, some deserted spot." "The country," he wrote, "is my work room." Being a man of astonishing literary genius he was able, in *La Nouvelle Héloise* and other works, to convince a whole generation that if one wanted to acquire "a perfect nature— *une belle âme*" one must renounce all desire to be clever and seek only to be good. The hero of his first novel, the Swiss schoolmaster, Saint-Preux, may strike us as a sententious and self-centered person, but to Rousseau's contemporaries he seemed the very embodiment of manly virtue. Even to our callous sensibilities his heroine, Julie, appears as a tragic and noble character. Their idealism finds vent in their love of unconfined nature. Saint-Preux was so moved when he reached the Lake of Geneva that he sat down on the bank and allowed his tears to splash into the waves. Julie was convinced that nature, in order to fulfill her true message to mankind, must be wholly untrammeled; even the birds in her aviary are not confined by wire but bribed to be sedentary by gifts of corn and berries. Even in my own youth there survived some sentimentalists (generally of German nationality) who, when visiting the woods at Clarens or Vevey, would have tears in their eyes.

Rousseau's distrust of, and incapacity for, all rational thought, induced him to preach the doctrine that man was born free and equal and that it was the depravity of civilized institutions that had induced injustice and corruption. In his *Discours sur l'Inégalité* of 1754 he advanced the theory that it is the mind that has degraded the senses and even that man's instinct for self-improvement had proved the source of competition and therefore of social misery. The Noble Savage was not debauched by any similar desire to better his condition. The great gift of compassion could achieve its full influence only in egalitarian societies; the effect of reason had been to encourage individual differentiation and the instinct of pity had thereby become blunted. The Noble Savage, moreover, being governed only by the natural instinct for reproduction was immune to the tensions and conflicts aroused by the civilized conception of Love. All progress had proved a "step towards the decrepitude of man." He did not advocate a return to complete savagery, to what he called "the gorilla state," but to a pastoral, matriarchal, and communist condition of society. "When I desire," he wrote in *Émile*, "to train the natural man, I do not want to make him a savage or to send him back to the woods: I want him to see with his own eyes and feel with his heart." In his *Contrat Social* of 1762, which exercised so atrocious an influence on the French Revolution, he drew a fantastic distinction between the "general will" and the "wishes of all." He contended that "the People" could do no wrong, and were justified even in using force to "compel their fellows to be free."

He thus in fact preached the dictatorship of the proletariat. The *Contrat Social* informed a receptive public that the perfect State was not to be created by legislation or good institutions, as the *Encyclopédistes* had taught, but by "virtue." Rousseau did not foresee that the market women of Paris, *les tricoteuses*, who screamed and chuckled as the heads of good liberals were sliced off by the guillotine, could scarcely be described as representatives of enlightened virtue. The *Contrat Social* as Dr. H. A. L. Fisher has written, "struck France with the force of a new gospel. Rivers of revolutionary sentiment were

released by the phrase 'Man is born free but is everywhere in chains.'"
Rivers of blood also.

During the last two decades of the eighteenth century men and
women in Europe, being exhausted by intellectualism and skepticism,
welcomed the gospel of Jean Jacques Rousseau with hysterical relief. It
needed the Reign of Terror to convince them that "the People" could
not be relied on to be invariably just, compassionate and righteous.
The reaction against egalitarianism and the sentimental optimism of
Jean Jacques Rousseau was voiced in the Anti-Jacobin of Canning and
Hookham Frere:

> Mark her fair votaries, prodigal of grief,
> With cureless pangs and woes that mock relief,
> Drop in soft sorrow o'er a faded flower,
> O'er a dead jackass pour the pearly shower;
> But hear, unmoved, of Loire's ensanguined flood
> Choked up with slain, or Lyons drenched in blood.

Madame de Stael was the first writer of influence to denounce the
superficial emotionalism of Rousseau's gospel. "He inflamed everything," she wrote, "but discovered nothing." A century later William
James echoed this antipathy against Rousseau. In his *Psychology* there
is a strong passage denouncing the prophet of sensibility:

> There is no more contemptible type of human character
> than that of the nerveless sentimentalist and dreamer, who
> spends his life in a weltering sea of sensibility and emo-
> tion, but who never does a manly concrete deed. Rous-
> seau, inflaming all the mothers of France by his eloquence
> to follow Nature and nurse their babies themselves, while
> he sends his own children to the Foundling Hospital, is
> the classic example of what I mean.

The full reaction against Rousseau was at the time obscured by the
advent of the Romantic movement. Yet the sensibility introduced by
that maniac of genius marks the end of the Age of Reason. The age
of science has since taught us that thought is more profitable than

instinct and brain safer than feeling. Yet Rousseau, for all his muddled ideas, did certainly teach his contemporaries to develop a social conscience and to cultivate sensibility.

Reason, we must admit, is not, after all, the most comprehensive of virtues.

Bibliography

Adams, James Truslow: *The Epic of America. The Founding of New England*. Boston, 1921.

———. *Building the British Empire*. Scribners, 1938.

Aldis, Janet: *Madame Geoffrin*. Methuen, 1905.

Angoulême, duchesse de: *Histoire Complète de la Captivité*.

Ashton, Professor T. S.: *The Industrial Revolution* (1949).

———. *Economic History of England in Eighteenth Century*.

Babbitt, I. Professor: *Rousseau and Romanticism*. 1928.

Baker, Dr. Eric: *The Herald of the Evangelical Revival*. Epworth Press, 1948.

Balderston, Catherine: *Thraliana*. 2 vols. Clarendon Press, 1942.

Beccaria, Cesare: *Dei Delitti e Delle Pene*. 1754.

———. *Opere*. 2 vols. Milan, 1821.

Bellot, H. Hale: *American History and American Historians*. Athlone Press, 1952.

Billington, Ray Allen: *Westward Expansion*. Macmillan Co., New York, 1949.

Billy, André: *Diderot*. Flammarion, 1932.

Binns, L. E. E.: *The Early Evangelicals*. Butterworth Press, 1953.

Blunt, Reginald: *Thomas Lord Lyttelton*. 1936.

Boswell, James: *Life of Johnson.* Edited by Birbeck Hill and L. F. Powell. Six vols. Oxford University Press, 1934.

———. *Journal of a Tour to the Hebrides with Samuel Johnson, LL.D.* Edited by Birbeck Hill and Powell. Oxford University Press, 1950.

———. *London Journal.* Edited by Prof. Pottle. Heinemann, 1950.

———. *Boswell in Holland.* Edited by Prof. Pottle, 1952.

———. *Boswell on the Grand Tour.* 2 vols. Edited by Prof. Pottle, 1953.

———. *Boswell in Search of a Wife.* Edited by Brady and Pottle, 1957.

Boissier, Gaston: *Saint-Simon.* (*Les Grands Ecrivains de la France*) Hachette, 1892.

Boulenger, Jacques: *L'Ameublement Francais au Grand Siècle.*

Brett-James, Anthony: *The Triple Stream.* Bowes and Bowes, 1953.

Brumfitt, J. H.: *Voltaire Historian.*

Burke, Edmund: *Speeches and Letters on American Affairs.* Everyman Edition.

———. *Reflections on the French Revolution.*

Butt, J.: *The Augustan Age.* 1950.

———. *Cambridge History of the British Empire.* Vol. I.

———. *Cambridge History of English Literature.* 15 Vols.

———. *Cambridge Modern History*: 1909 edition, Vols. VI, VII and VIII. 1957 edition, Vol. VII.

Carlyle, Thomas: *History of Frederick the Great.* 8 vols. Chapman and Hall, 1905.

Carswell, John: *The Old Cause.* 1954.

———. *Casanova Memoirs.* Pléiade edition. 2 vols.

Catherine the Great: *Memoirs.* Hamish Hamilton, 1955.

Channing, Edward: *A History of the United States.* Macmillan Co., New York, 1919.

Chase, Isabel: *Horace Walpole. Gardenist.* Princeton University Press, 1943.

Churchill, Sir Winston: *Marlborough*. 2 vols. Harrap edition, 1947.

Clark, Sir Kenneth: *The Gothic Revival*.

Clarke, W. K. L.: *Eighteenth Century Piety*. Macmillan, New York, 1944.

Clifford, Professor James: *Young Samuel Johnson*. Heinemann, 1955.

Courthope, W.J.: *A History of English Poetry*. Macmillan, 6 vols.

Cremer, R. W. Ketton: *Horace Walpole*.

Créquy, Madame de: *Mémoires*.

Crowe, Sylvia: *Garden Design*. Country Life, 1958.

Desnoireterres, Gustave: *Voltaire et Frédéric*.

———. *Iconographie Voltarienne*.

Dobson, Austin: *Horace Walpole*. Oxford University Press, 1927.

Doren, Carl Van: *Benjamin Franklin*. Putnam, 1939.

Dotten, Paul: *Life of Daniel Defoe*.

Doumic, René: *Sainte-Simon*. Hachette, 1919.

Evelyn, John: *Diary*. Edited by E. S. de Beer. 6 vols. Clarendon Press, 1955.

Faguet, Emile: *Le XVIII Siècle. La Politique Comparée de Montesquieu, Rousseau Et Voltaire*. 1902.

Fairchild, H. N.: *The Noble Savage*. Columbia University Press, 1928.

Fay, Bernard: *Franklin, the Apostle of Modern Times*. Little Brown. Boston, 1929.

———. *Federalist, The*. By Alexander Hamilton. John Jay and James Madison. Everyman edition, 1948.

Feiling, Keith: *A History of England*. Macmillan, 1948.

Fisher, H. A. L.: *A History of Europe*. 3 vols. Eyre and Spottiswoode.

Fitchett, Rev. W. H.: *Wesley and His Century*. Smith Elder, 1906.

Fitzgerald, Margaret: *First Follow Nature*. Columbia University Press, 1947.

Fontenelle B. de: *Dialogues de Morte*. 1935 edition.

———. *Histoire des Oracles*. Edited by Louis Maigron, 1908.

Ford, Boris. (Edited by): *From Dryden to Johnson*. Pelican Press.

Franklin, Benjamin: *Life and Letters*. Edited by John Bigelow. 3 vols. Lippincott Co., Philadelphia, 1893.

Frederick the Great: *Works*. Edited by G. E. Volz. 10 vols.

———. *Memoirs of the House of Brandenburg*.

———. *Antimachiavel*.

———. *Correspondence*. Edited by Foster.

———. *Briefe an Fredersdorf* 1926. Edited by Johannes Richter.

Funck-Brentano: *L'affaire du Collier*. Hachette, 1935.

Garland, H. B.: *Storm and Stress*. Harrap, 1952.

Gaxotte, Pierre: *Frédéric II*. Fayard, 1936.

———. *Le Siècle de Louis XV*. Fayard, 1933.

Gill, F. C.: *The Romantic Movement and Methodism*, 1937.

———. *Goethe's Works*. Insel Verlag, Leipzig.

Goncourt, E. and J. de: *Histoire de la Société Française Pendant la Revolution*, 1954.

Gooch, Dr. G. P.: *Frederick the Great*. Longmans, 1947.

Goodwin, Professor A. (edited by): *The European Nobility in the Eighteenth Century*. A. and C. Black, 1953.

Gosse, Edmund: *Gray*. English Men of Letters series.

Gwynn, Stephen: *The Life and Friendships of Dean Swift*. Thornton Butterworth, 1933.

———. *The Life of Horace Walpole*. 1932.

Hadfield, Miles: *Gardening in Britain*. Hutchinson, 1960.

Harrington, James: *The Commonwealth of Oceana*. Routledge, 1887.

Havens, M. A.: *Horace Walpole and the Strawberry Hill Press*. Kirgate Press, 1900.

Hilles, F. W. (edited by): *New Light on Dr. Johnson*. Yale University Press, 1959.

Hudson, Derek: *Sir Joshua Reynolds*. Bles, 1958.

Humphreys, A. R.: *The Augustan World*. 1954.

Jefferson, D. W.: *Eighteenth Century Press*. Pelican book.

Johnson, Dr. Samuel: *Poems*. Edited by Nichol Smith and Edward McAdam. Clarendon Press, 1941.

Johnston, Denis: *In Search of Swift*, 1959.

Kendrick, T. D.: *The Lisbon Earthquake*. Methuen, 1956.

Leavis, F. R.: *The Common Pursuit*. 1952.

Lecky, William: *History of England in the Eighteenth Century* (*1878–1890*).

———. *History of the Rise of Rationalism in Europe* (*1865*).

Lemaitre, Jules: *Fénélon*. Fayard, 1910.

Lenz, Jacob: *Gesammelte Schriften*. 3 vols. Cassirer, 1909.

Levi-Mirepoix, duc de: *Le Coeur Secret de Saint Simon*. Segop, 1956.

Lhermier, Pierre: *Le Mystérieux Comte de Saint-Germain*. Colbert, 1943.

Ligne, Prince de: *Memoirs and Letters*. Edited by L. Ashton. Broadway Press. Lindsay, Jack: 1764.

Loménie: *Beaumarchais et la Société de Son Temps*.

Lovejoy, Professor Arthur O.: *Essays in the History of Ideas*. Baltimore Press, 1948.

Lucas, F. L.: *The Art of Living*. Cassell, 1959.

———. *The Search For Good Sense*. Cassell, 1958.

Macaulay, T. B.: *Essays and Works*. Longmans Green edition, 18 vols.

Maclaren, Moray: *The Highland Jaunt*. Jarrolds, 1954.

MacLeish, Archibald: *Collected Poems*. Houghton Mifflin, 1952.

Maigron, Professor Louis: *Fontenelle*. Plon, 1906.

Maintenon, Madame de: *Correspondence*. Hachette edition, 1887.

Maurois, André: *Etudes Anglaises*.

Mayer, J. P.: *Political Thought. 1939*.

Mayniel, Edouard: *Cassanova et Son Temps*. Mercure de France, 1900.

Montesquieu: *De L'Esprit Des Lois*. Edited by Gonzague True. Gernier.

Morison, Samuel Eliot: *Christopher Columbus Mariner*. Faber, 1956.

Morley, John: *Voltaire*. Macmillan and Co., 1897.

———. *Diderot*. 2 vols. Macmillan and Co., 1897.

Mornet, Daniel: *Le Sentiment de la Nature*. Hachette, 1907.

Mowat, R. B.: *The Age of Reason*. Harrap, 1934.

Murry, J. Midleton: *Jonathan Swift*. Cape, 1954.

Namier, Sir Lewis: *The Structure of Politics at the Succession of George III*. Macmillan, 1929.

———. *England in the Age of the American Revolution*.

Oliver, F. S.: *The Endless Adventure*. 1935.

———. *Alexander Hamilton*. 1931.

Ollivant, J.: *Evangelical Movement in the Eighteenth Century*. 1877.

Paine, Thomas: *Complete Writings*. Edited by Foner. New York, 1945.

Pares, Richard: *King George III and the Politicians*. Clarendon Press, 1953.

Pascal, Professor Roy: *The German Sturm und Drang*. Manchester, 1953.

Passos, John Dos: *The Men Who Made the Nation*. Doubleday, New York, 1957.

Phillipson, Coleman: *Three Criminal Law Reformers*. Dent, 1923.

Photiades, Constantin: *Count Cagliostro*. 1932.

Picard, Professor Roger: *Les Salons Littéraires et la Société Française (1610–1789)*. Brentano's 1943.

Plumb, Dr. J. H.: *England in the Eighteenth Century*. Pelican edition.

Read, H.: *Reason and Romanticism*. 1926.

Realey, C. B.: *The Early Opposition to Sir Robert Walpole*. Kansas, 1931.

Robertson, Sir Charles Grant: *England Under the Hanoverians*.

Robertson, J. G.: *Genesis of Romantic Theory*. 1923.

Robinson, Howard: *Bayle the Sceptic*. Columbia Press, New York, 1931.

Rolleston, T. W.: *Life of Lessing*. 1889.

Roosevelt, Theodore: *Gouverneur Morris*. Houghton Mifflin, 1891.

Rousseau, J.J.: *Confessions and Reveries*. Pléiade edition.

———. *Contrat Social*. Fourrrat edition.

———. *La Nouvelle Héloise*.

———. *Emile*.

Rowse, Dr. A. L.: *The Later Churchills*. Macmillan, 1958.

Sainte-Beuve, C. A.: *Causeries du Lundi*. 13 Vols. 1851.

———. *Portraits Litéraires. Les Nouveaux Lundis*. 13 Vols. 1863.

———. *Portraits De Femmes*. 1856.

Saint-René Taillandier Madame: *Madame de Maintenon*. Hachette, 1923.

Saint Simon, duc de: *Memoirs*. Pléiade edition.

Sarolea, Charles: *Philosophic and Literary Essays*. Edinburgh, 1898.

Seeley, L. B.: *Horace Walpole and His World*. 1895.

Ségur, comte de: *Mémoires*. 1826.

Ségur, General de: *Mémoires*. 1873.

Sieveking, I. G.: *Memoir on Sir Horace Mann*. 1912.

Soloveytchik, George: *Potemkin*. Thornton Butterworth, 1938.

Steegman, John: *The Rule of Taste*. Macmillan, 1936.

Stendhal: *Rome, Naples et Florence*.

Stephen, Sir Leslie: *English Thought in the Eighteenth Century*. Smith-Elder. 2 Vols. 1902.

———. *Pope*. E. M. L. series. Macmillan.

———. *Swift*. E. M. L. series. Macmillan.

Swift, Jonathan: *Gulliver's Travels*. Everyman edition.

———. *Journal to Stella*. Everyman edition.

———. *Poems*. Edited by Harold Williams. 3 vols. Oxford University Press, 1937.

———. *Prose Works*. Edited by Herbert Davis. Blackwell, 1951.

Taine, Hippolyte: *L'Ancien Régime.* 1875.

Tallentyre, S. G.: *The Life of Voltaire.* 2 vols. Smith Elder, 1903.

Taylor, G. R. S.: *Robert Walpole and His Age.* Cape, 1931.

Telford, John: *Life of John Wesley.* Epworth Press, 1953.

Thackeray, W. M.: *The Four Georges.*

Tolstoi, Alexei: *Peter the Great.* English translation. Gollancz, 1936.

Trevelyan, George: *English Social History.* 1942.

———. *History of England.* Longmans, 1926.

Trevelyan, Sir George Otto: *The American Revolution.* 4 vols. Longmans, 1899.

———. *George III and Charles Fox.* 2 vols. Longmans, 1912.

Turberville, A. S.: *Johnson's England.*

Voltaire: 1770 edition, Paris. 24 vols.

———. La Pléiade edition. 1957.

———. *Lettres Sur Les Anglais.* Basle, 1734.

———. *Letters to His Niece.* Edited by Theodore Besterman.

Vulliamy, C. E.: *Mrs. Thrale of Streatham.* Cape, 1936.

Waliszewski, K.: *Le Roman d'une Impératrice, Catherine II.* Plon, 1893.

———. *Pierre le Grand.* Plon Nourrit, 1897.

———. *Autour d'un Trone Catherine II De Russie.* Plon, 1894.

Walpole, Horace: *The Letters of.* Edited by Mrs. Toynbee. 16 vols. Oxford University Press, 1903.

———. *Memoirs of the Reign of King George II.* Second edition, Henry Colburn, 1847. 3 vols.

———. *Memoirs of the Reign of King George III.* Published Richard Bentley, 1845. 4 vols.

Watson, F.: *Daniel Defoe.*

Wesley, Charles: *Short Hymns.* Farley, Bristol, 1762. 2 vols.

Wesley, John: *Journal.* Epworth Press, 1958 edition.

Whiteley, J. H.: *Wesley's England.* 1938.

Willey, Basil: *The Eighteenth Century Background*. 1940.

Wolfe-Tone: *Autobiography*.

Woodward, W. E.: *Tom Paine, America's Godfather*. 1946.

Index

D

E

Z